TEACHING AND LEARNING LANGUAGE ARTS FROM A DIVERSE PERSPECTIVE

Bassim Hamadeh, CEO and Publisher
Janny Li, Acquisitions Editor
Kaela Martin, Project Editor
Berenice Quirino, Associate Production Editor
Jackie Bignotti, Cover Designer
Alexa Lucido, Licensing Manager
Natalie Piccotti, Director of Marketing
Kassie Graves, Vice President of Editorial
Jamie Giganti, Director of Academic Publishing

Printed in the United States of America.

ISBN: 978-1-5165-3864-5 (pbk) / 978-1-5165-3865-2 (br)

FIRST EDITION

TEACHING AND LEARNING LANGUAGE ARTS FROM A DIVERSE PERSPECTIVE

AN ANTHOLOGY

STACY A. GRIFFIN, Ed.D.

CONTENTS

INTRODUCTION

Congratulations! By opening the first page of this anthology, you have chosen to read about theories, instructional strategies, and student activities that will prepare you to teach English Language Arts from a diverse perspective. For each chapter of this book, you will be given pre-reading activities that will prompt you to reflect on your current understanding of our craft. You will be given the opportunity to read carefully curated articles and book chapters that will inform your current or future teaching philosophy. After reviewing the selections, you will have access to post-reading activities that will allow you to connect theory to practice. The purpose of this anthology is to provide you with foundational knowledge that will prepare you to be an inclusive teacher.

This anthology is divided into ten chapters. Each chapter was purposely chosen to introduce you to specific populations of learners you will likely encounter in your classroom. Diversity can be a broad term that encompasses many factors. According to the National Education Association (2017), "Diversity can be defined as the sum of the ways that people are both alike and different. The dimensions of diversity include race, ethnicity, gender, sexual orientation, language, culture, religion, mental and physical ability, class, and immigration status." This book will introduce you to diverse student populations but also to diverse methods of teaching special and exceptional groups of students in diverse ways.

The first chapter includes two readings on culture. Effective educators know that students' culture must be ingrained in the classroom environment and embedded in instruction. Culture can influence every aspect of the teaching and learning experience. The two articles presented in Chapter 1 of this book focus on how to create a meaningful community of learners through mindful practice.

Chapter 2 includes two readings on working with English Language Learners (ELLs). With the national increase of ELLs, educators need meaningful strategies to meet the specific learning needs of this population. You will read about the unique characteristics of ELLs, appropriate instructional strategies, and assessment data. The articles will help you determine best practices and supports for your own ELL students.

The two selected readings for Chapter 3 will introduce you to a distinct group of learners, high-ability ELLs. These students are often referred to as gifted students who are learning a new language. You will read about effective approaches to provide challenging and appropriate instruction. In addition, you will also read about the benefits of bilingualism in American schools.

Students who come from low socioeconomic status (SES) backgrounds often encounter distinct challenges in their home and classroom environments. It is critical that preservice and new teachers understand these trials and implement strategies to minimize inequity. The two readings in Chapter 4 will provide you with the foundational knowledge you need to work with this population.

According to the Centers for Disease Control and Prevention (2016), "Autism Spectrum Disorder (ASD) is a developmental disability that can cause significant social, communication and behavioral challenges." Two readings are presented in Chapter 5 to provide you with a thorough understanding of what a spectrum disorder is, how it can affect learning, and the best practices for working with this exceptional population of students.

Chapter 6 includes two readings on Emotional Disturbance (ED). According to the Individuals with Disabilities Act (IDEA), ED is categorized as an exceptionality. The chosen articles will introduce you to academic and social attributes that may influence achievement for these learners. The studies provide meaningful and appropriate interventions and suggestions for improving the achievement of ED students.

According to the Hearing Loss Association of America (2018), almost 15 percent of students in general education classrooms experience some degree of hearing loss. For Chapter 7 of this anthology, two studies are presented to provide you with effective, research-based best practices and meaningful recommendations to facilitate the academic and social achievement of this population of diverse learners.

In Chapter 8, you will learn that speech and language impairments are the second most common disabilities, superseded only by specific learning disabilities. That means there is a high probability that you will have a language-compromised student in your own classrooms. The two readings in this section will provide you with meaningful instructional approaches to work with this group of exceptional learners.

Mild and moderate intellectual disabilities are classified as exceptionalities under IDEA. These terms replaced the now potentially offensive term *mental retardation*. These are cognitive impairments that can affect academic and social abilities, adaptive life skills, speech development, memory, and attention span. The articles in Chapter 9 were chosen to provide you with research-based methods that can be implemented in a general education classroom when working with this specific group.

In Chapter 10, you will read two articles on gifted and talented students. According to the US Office of Education, the definition for gifted or talented students is described as "children and youth with outstanding talent who perform or show the potential for performing at remarkably high levels of accomplishment when compared with others of their age, experience, or environment" (US Department of Education, 1993). The selected readings will introduce you to differentiated strategies to provide an appropriate level of challenge and support for this group. Prepare to learn how to be an effective and inclusive educator!

As you embark on your teaching journey, it is important that you are cognizant of the diverse group of students with whom you will likely work. To be the most effective educator, you need to be equipped with diverse strategies and methods for facilitating student learning. As Malcom Forbes (n.d.) has notably stated, diversity is "the art of thinking independently together." Now, prepare to make a difference …

REFERENCES

Centers for Disease Control and Prevention. 2016. *Autism Spectrum Disorder (ASD)*. Retrieved from https://www.cdc.gov/ncbddd/autism/facts.html

Hearing Loss Association of America. (2018). *Basic Facts about Hearing Loss*. Retrieved from http://hearingloss.org/content/basic-facts-about-hearing-loss

Malcolm Forbes Quotes. BrainyQuote.com, Xplore Inc. (2018). Retrieved from https://www.brainyquote.com/quotes/malcolm_forbes_151513

National Education Association. (2017). *Diversity Toolkit Introduction*. Retrieved from http://www.nea.org/tools/diversity-toolkit-introduction.html

US Department of Education. 1993. *National Excellence: A Case for Developing America's Talent*. Washington, DC: Office of Educational Research and Improvement.

CHAPTER 1

CULTURE

INTRODUCTION

Culture plays a significant role in how we create and maintain our classroom environments, as well as how we interact with our students. As educators, we must recognize that culture can influence every aspect of the teaching and learning experience. The two articles presented in Chapter 1 of this book focus on how to create a meaningful community of learners through reflective and mindful practice.

The first article, "New Teachers' Challenges: How Culturally Responsive Teaching, Classroom Management, & Assessment Literacy Are Intertwined," is focused on Culturally Responsive Teaching (CRT). According to scholar Gloria Ladson Billings, CRT is "a pedagogy that empowers students intellectually, socially, emotionally, and politically by using cultural referents to impart knowledge, skills, and attitudes" (Ladson-Billings 1994, 382). CRT can apply to how we present content, how we design our classrooms, how we create management systems, and how we fairly assess our students. According to the authors, not all educators are well-versed or comfortable with this practice, as demonstrated in the research study presented by the authors.

The second article in this section seamlessly links to the first. "Mindful Reflection as a Process for Developing Culturally Responsive Practices" prompts readers to reflect on how personal assumptions can influence interaction and communication in the classroom. The authors present six steps for mindful reflection, which can assist the teacher in identifying and overcoming any hidden bias. The process allows the educator to create a more culturally responsive classroom. The two articles are relevant to preservice and new teachers who understand the critical importance of diverse pedagogy.

REFERENCE

Ladson-Billings, Gloria. 1994. *The Dreamkeepers: Successful Teaching for African-American Students.* San Francisco, CA: Jossey-Bass.

CHAPTER 1

READING 1.1 OVERVIEW

The article "New Teachers' Challenges: How Culturally Responsive Teaching, Classroom Management, & Assessment Literacy Are Intertwined" includes an overview of Culturally Responsive Teaching (CRT) and how it relates to the classroom environment and meaningful assessment. The authors provide a synopsis of a research study aimed at identifying new teachers' conceptual understanding of CRT, their beliefs on classroom management practices, and their use of formal and informal assessments. This reading was chosen to introduce preservice and new teachers to CRT.

PRE-READING ACTIVITIES

1. What does the term *culturally responsive teaching* mean to you?
2. Develop a list of effective classroom management strategies you have observed.
3. Reflect on the term *assessment literacy*. What do you think it means to be an assessment-literate teacher?

NEW TEACHERS' CHALLENGES

HOW CULTURALLY RESPONSIVE TEACHING, CLASSROOM MANAGEMENT, & ASSESSMENT LITERACY ARE INTERTWINED

READING 1.1

BY MOI MOOI LEW AND
REGENA FAILS NELSON

Moi Mooi Lew is a faculty specialist in the Department of Teaching, Learning, and Educational Studies and Regena Fails Nelson is a professor and chair of the Department of Teaching, Learning, and Educational Studies, both in the College of Education and Human Development at Western Michigan University, Kalamazoo, Michigan.

INTRODUCTION

In the past decade, educational environments have drastically changed over time and have become more diverse and complex. The rapid influx of pluralistic populations from a variety of different societies contribute to

Moi Mooi Lew and Regena Fails Nelson, "New Teachers' Challenges: How Culturally Responsive Teaching, Classroom Management, & Assessment Literacy Are Intertwined," *Multicultural Education*, vol. 23, no. 3-4, pp. 7-13.

the diverse student population. Student diversity creates challenges to new teachers if they are not familiar with culturally responsive teaching (CRT) (Gay, 2002).

In addition, studies also show that new teachers face challenges in dealing with classroom management, curriculum planning and implementation, conducting assessments, and workload issues. The result is that many leave the profession after only a few years (Grossman & Thompson, 2008; Kyriacou & Kunc, 2007; Roehrig, Pressley, & Talotta, 2002; Scherff, 2008).

Hence, knowing that culturally responsive teaching, classroom management, and classroom assessment are some persistent issues that new teachers face in their own classroom, this project is designed to investigate the preparedness of a cohort of new teachers in dealing with those challenges, through their teacher education programs and professional development provided by their school districts.

CULTURALLY RESPONSIVE TEACHING

The influx of pluralistic populations and urbanization has rapidly increased the diversity of our nation. These pluralistic populations have retained their own unique cultures, traditions, and languages, which can impose anxieties, prejudices, and racial tensions among others. For this reason, multicultural education seeks to develop instructional curricula and practices in school communities that meet the needs of diverse student populations (Gay, 2002). The key instructional strategy suggested for use in multicultural education is culturally responsive teaching.

Gay (2002, p. 106) saw CRT as "using the cultural characteristics, experiences, and perspectives of ethnically diverse students as conduits for teaching them more effectively." Gay (2010) further defined CRT as "teaching that builds on students' personal and cultural strengths, their intellectual capabilities, and prior accomplishments" (p. 26). She noted,

> Students of color come to school having already mastered many cultural skills and ways of knowing. To the extent that teaching builds on these capabilities, academic success will result. (p. 213)

Similarly, Ladson-Billings (1994) asserted that CRT is a pedagogy that recognizes the importance of including students' cultural references in all aspects of learning. She further proposed three dimensions of culturally relevant pedagogy: holding high academic expectations and offering appropriate support such as scaffolding, acting on cultural competence by reshaping curriculum, and building on students' knowledge, and establishing relationships with students and their homes (Ladson-Billings, 1995).

In summary, cultural responsiveness implies that teachers should be responsive to their students using instructional activities that build on students' cultural strength and abilities to promote student learning. Responsive teachers do not use the same teaching methods and materials for all students. Instead, these teachers modify their knowledge and training, paying attention to classroom contexts and to individual student needs and experiences (Gay, 2002; Irvine & Armento, 2001; Ladson-Billings, 1994).

As the number of culturally diverse students increase, it becomes more important that all educators, including new teachers, become deeply attentive to ways to adapt their practice to meet all students' needs. To accomplish this task, first and foremost, CRT should not be understood in a simplistic and trivial way (Sleeter, 2012). Past research showed that oversimplified and distorted conceptions of CRT among teachers led them to reject this concept and consequently student learning did not improve (Fitchett, Starker, & Salyers, 2012; Sleeter, 2012; Young, 2010).

For example, Young (2010) studied seven teachers' conceptual understanding of culturally relevant pedagogy. The findings showed that all seven teachers valued student culture, but none of them linked it directly with improving students' academic learning.

Given this understanding of CRT, one of the critical issue that new teachers encounter is lack of familiarity with diverse students' cultures, causing the teachers to often overreact to students' nonverbal cultural manifestations by imposing rules and regulations (Irvine & Armento, 2001). For example, some students avoid making eye contact because the gesture is considered rude in their cultures. Thus teachers must be aware that if they fail to get students' attention by making eye contact, they should attempt other alternative ways to get students' attention.

Hence, in light of cultural differences, individual cultures must be considered when planning classroom management strategies. To ensure that the classroom is effectively managed, new teachers must be confident that the classroom management techniques they employ are appropriate for use with diverse student populations (Goddard 2000; McCormick & Shi, 1999).

Besides being closely related to classroom management, culturally responsive practices also play a role in determining the way teachers assess students' learning (Irvine & Armento, 2001). A culturally responsive teacher should understand the practices, purposes, usage of various assessments, and the importance of a balanced classroom assessment system to gauge diverse student learning (Stiggins, Arter, Chappuis, & Chappuis, 2006).

Additionally, culturally responsive teachers should be able to design meaningful assessments and rubrics that can accurately measure quality. It is equally important that they be able use assessment data to support individual student learning.

CLASSROOM MANAGEMENT

Classroom management issues are a leading cause of job dissatisfaction and work against retention among teachers (Liu & Meyer, 2005), particularly among new teachers (Reupert & Woodcock, 2010). These issues are also of great concern to parents, administrators, policy makers, and academics in the education field as they can impact student learning (Simonsen, Fair-banks, Briesch, Myers, & Sugai, 2008).

To promote student engagement and learning through effective classroom management, all educators should examine their beliefs and practices and review research and theories about classroom management. This examination should start long before an educator meets students on the first day of school and teachers should continue to refine their strategies throughout their professional career (Manning & Bucher, 2007).

Generally, classroom management describes teachers' efforts to oversee a multitude of activities in the classroom, including learning, social interaction, and students' behaviors (Bosch, 2006; Martin, Yin, & Baldwin, 1998). Classroom management is the combination of approaches and processes that teachers use to achieve and maintain a classroom environment in which they can teach and instruct, using tools and techniques to produce behavioral change as needed (Bosch, 2006; Goddard 2000; McCormick & Shi, 1999).

To ensure the classroom is effectively managed, teachers must be confident of their ability to set clear expectations and goals, model positive behaviors, and enforce consequences when needed. In this case, the goal of classroom management is to build a respectful learning community where children can feel safe to learn, explore, share, and express their views and feelings in positive ways.

Inevitably, classroom management is closely linked to instruction (Manning & Bucher, 2007). An educator who does not have good management skills will have a difficult time instructing students. For example, a teacher who keeps learners on task (e.g., correct developmental level, proper instructional pace, physical and psychological safety, appropriate curricular content, etc.) will be less likely to have students who misbehave. Conversely, teachers who are unprepared and disorganized will most likely encounter behavior problems (Manning & Bucher, 2007).

Along the same line, Bosch (2006) maintains that classroom management is a skill that must be learned, practiced, evaluated, and modified to fit the changing situation of contemporary classrooms. Too often, new teachers try one management strategy and become discouraged if it does not produce the desired effects immediately. Thus, Bosch (2006) suggested that new teachers must identify their own personal and professional strengths and weaknesses and examine their instructional practices. Then they should develop a management plan, implement it, and, finally, evaluate and revise that plan (Bosch, 2006).

Thus, in developing classroom management and instructional strategies, educators need to examine their personal beliefs about classroom management. For example, teachers have to decide whether they think discipline should be taught or imposed, whether teachers should be democratic or autocratic, and whether punishment works to improve or hinder student behavior. As little research has been done to understand new teachers' classroom management practices, this study is important in filling the gap with data on new teachers' beliefs and practices in the area of classroom management.

ASSESSMENT LITERACY

In professional education literature, assessment literacy has been defined as an understanding of the principles of sound assessment, including terminology and the development and the use of assessment methodologies and techniques (Popham, 2004; Stiggins, 2002). An assessment-literate teacher can identify the strengths and weaknesses of each type of assessment and is able to engage students in the assessment process (Stiggins et al., 2006).

Such teachers understand the practices, purposes of various assessments, and the importance of a balanced classroom assessment system to gauge student learning. In summary, assessment-literate teachers are able to design meaningful assessment rubrics and use assessment data to support student learning.

Nonetheless, it seems that competency in assessment has been overlooked by teachers. Black and William (1998) found that there is a "poverty of practice" among teachers, in which only a few teachers have fully understood how to implement classroom formative assessment.

After a decade, Siegel and Wissehr (2011) report almost similar findings in their research. They used a content analysis method to explore novice teachers' knowledge of assessment based on the assessment pieces that are mentioned in their reflective journals, teaching philosophies and lesson plans. Analysis of these documents indicated that novice teachers recognize the need to align assessments with learning goals and instructional strategies. It also revealed that they are using a variety of assessments. However, the assessments contained within the science units lesson plans did not fully align with the views of assessment the novice teachers presented in their teaching philosophies or journals. The findings implied that novice teachers have not applied their assessment knowledge into practice, which was reflected in their lesson plans.

More positive findings indicate that assessment literacy can be fostered through professional development activities (Stewart & Houchens, 2014). Studies have found that teachers who were involved in ongoing, sustained professional development have gained a better understanding of assessing student learning, thereby enhancing their instructional performance (Stewart & Houchens, 2014). In addition, their findings showed that teachers who have participated in professional development workshops on classroom assessment experienced a growth in their capacity to use and teach others various formative assessment strategies.

As such, assessment and its accountability should be an important component in the professional competencies for all teachers including new teachers. Accordingly, teacher education programs need to place more emphasis on developing pre-service teachers' assessment literacy so that they are better prepared to select and implement a variety of appropriate assessments to foster student learning when they become new teachers in schools (Siegel & Wissehr, 2011; Yost, 2014).

AIMS OF THE STUDY

To reiterate, the challenges that new teachers encounter in the schools are intertwined. If a new teacher is unable to perform CRT, often she will face challenges in handling students' behavior and will also be prone to inaccurately interpret students' learning too (Irvine & Armento, 2001).

For example, a student misbehaved because he was insulted by teacher's communication skills (verbal and non-verbal). A teacher who does not understand the learning difficulties of non-English speaking students can wrongly interpret their learning abilities. As such, it is imperative to investigate these three domains together in this study to better assist new teachers' in countering those critical challenges holistically.

Three research questions were developed to guide the study:

1. What is the conceptual understanding of culturally responsive teaching among new teachers and how well are they prepared to use this pedagogy?
2. What classroom management practices do new teachers adopt and how well are they prepared to manage their classroom effectively?
3. How do new teachers conceptualize classroom assessment and how well are they prepared to assess student learning?

METHODOLOGY

This study used a qualitative research design to investigate in-depth these salient issues face by new teachers.

PARTICIPANTS

There were 16 new teachers who graduated from the teacher education program in the last two years. They were referred to as 'new teachers' considering that they have started the teaching profession within the past one to two years. The recruitment procedure started in April after we obtained approval from the Institutional Review Board (IRB).

The recruitment process began by sending out invitation emails to all 16 of them. At the end of the recruitment process, we managed to collect twelve 'agree to participate' reply emails. Among the twelve new teachers, there were 10 females and two males below 30 years old, teaching in elementary schools (8 teachers), middle schools (2 teachers), and high schools (2 teachers) in the same district. A majority of them (83%) are Caucasian or White.

DATA COLLECTION

The participants were recruited through email communication and a thorough consent seeking procedure. After that, some face-to-face interviews were conducted. The interviews took place at the school buildings where the teachers were employed. During these 30-minute interviews, participants were asked to self-assess their level of effectiveness in the areas of CRT, classroom management, and classroom assessment. They were asked how well did the teacher education program prepare them in these three areas and what types of professional development did they receive from their school district in those areas.

DATA ANALYSIS

We adapted Bogdan and Biklen's (1998) approach for transcribing and analyzing the interview data for emerging themes. We reviewed the responses and generated coding categories independently based on the theoretical meaning behind each response. After that, we negotiated the coded categories in order to develop core themes from the data.

To ensure the trustworthiness of the data, we used theoretical memos throughout the data analysis process. Theoretical memos showed ideas about the coding categories, relationships between categories, and directions for further analysis. We sorted memos in order to present the emerging themes that link the categories.

ISSUES OF TRUSTWORTHINESS

To ensure validity of the data, four aspects of trustworthiness—i.e., credibility, dependability, confirmability, and transferability—were addressed through various measures in this study. For example, to ensure the credibility of the data and to minimize researcher bias, member checking and seeking participants' clarification on the derived categories were conducted throughout the data analysis process (Creswell, 2007; Marshall & Rossman, 2006).

Also, to address the matter of transferability, the research design, the context of the study, the data collection method, and the data analysis procedure were explicitly explained to ensure replication could be done in other new teacher populations (Lincoln & Guba, 1985, p. 296).

Third, to ensure the findings are consistent and could be repeated, a colleague served as an external inquiry auditor to examine the research process and the product of the research study (Lincoln & Guba, 1985). The purpose was to evaluate the accuracy and whether or not the findings, interpretations and conclusions are supported by the data.

Finally, to ensure confirmability, a reflexive journal was developed where we made regular entries during the research process. In these entries, we recorded methodological decisions and the reasons for them, the logistics of the study, and reflected on what was happening in terms of our own values and interests (Lincoln & Guba, 1985).

RESULTS AND DISCUSSION

The findings are discussed in the following three categories.

CULTURALLY RESPONSIVE TEACHING: CULTURALLY AND DEVELOPMENTALLY APPROPRIATE INSTRUCTION

It is obvious from the data that some new teachers understood CRT in a simplistic way. There was a tendency to view CRT as cultural celebrations that are disconnected from academic learning (Sleeter, 2012). It seems that participants' understanding about CRT was focused on learning about other cultural traditions instead of pedagogy that can help student learning.

For example, P6[1] stated that "… I took time outside my classroom to learn about their culture … their festival … help other kids to understand their culture too." It is hoped that learning "about" culture was not substituted for learning to teach challenging academic knowledge and skills that use cultural processes and knowledge as theoretical frameworks.

Besides, some participants mentioned that CRT is a pedagogy that incorporated cultural elements in the lessons but failed to elaborate on how learning can build on cultural strength. Thus, CRT was understood as some trivial teaching method to follow rather than understanding it as a paradigm for teaching and learning (Sleeter, 2012).

For example, P1 said that "CRT is incorporating different multicultural items throughout the classroom." Similarly, P8 mentioned that "… she used books related to different cultures."

It was encouraging to hear some participants mention that CRT is pedagogy that takes into consideration individual differences and builds on student's background in their instructional practices. For example, P5 stated that "… teacher should address a student's background to help them understand … when teaching Chemistry … I try to use something they are familiar with … using the context, relate to them, real world examples." The conception of CRT that it pays attention to classroom contexts and to individual student needs and experiences is congruent with the definitions of CRT (Gay, 2002; Ladson-Billings, 1994).

When asked to reflect on how well the teacher education program has prepared students to do CRT in the classroom, about half of the participants felt that the preparation was modest. Generally, some participants felt that the internship and field trips were helpful in learning the pedagogy (e.g., P1). There were some courses that had included content on culture or social context but not specifically focused on CRT (e.g., P2). The curriculum reviews of the current teacher education program showed that cultural diversity was mentioned in the syllabi of some courses such as ES3950 School and Society, ED4010 Teaching Elementary School Science and ED 4070 Elementary Social Studies.

In ES3950 School and Society the course is concerned with the nature and direction of American education in its changing social context and the sourse focuses on major issues affecting the advancement of education in a culturally diverse, democratic society. In one of the weekly discussion topics, "The Issue of Race," students are encouraged to discuss modern segregation, the achievement gap, and privileges of different races.

As this is not a methods or pedagogy class, it seems that the course content does not expose students to ways to integrate CRT into the classroom nor does it conceptualize what CRT is in the syllabus. Similarly, in ED4010 Teaching Elementary School Science cultural diversity is emphasized in the university and college's diversity statement. However, it is obvious that limited input is related to CRT in the course syllabus.

CRT is one of the general course outcomes in ED 4070 Elementary Social Studies in which students are expected to create cooperative learning communities within classrooms and demonstrate culturally responsive practice. One of the major topics in this course is "Culture, Cultural Diversity & Multicultural Education." Thus, this course gives more exposure on CRT to prospective teachers compared to ES3950 and ED 4010.

With respect to the professional development support that the new teachers received from the school districts, some participants mentioned that they had one professional development program on CRT in which an invited speaker talked about African American culture only (e.g., P1, P2 and P4). In another professional development program a speaker talked about cultural awareness, how to teach in diverse environment, and how to deal with LGBT issues (e.g., P11).

Some participants mentioned that a general-topic professional development workshop was organized for new teachers. The workshop, entitled "Capturing Kids' Hearts," provided information about students' background and how to handle diverse student populations (e.g., P1, P3 and P10). Nonetheless, some participants commented that there was no specific professional development workshop on CRT (e.g., P5, P6, P8 and P9) and also that this topic was not actively discussed in mentor meetings nor staff meetings (e.g., P5 and P7). Overall, it is clear that the professional development support provided to the new teachers was basically generic. The new teachers were not actually well supported to adapt CRT in the classroom.

Hence, some concerns arose. Based on the self-assessment results, almost all the new teachers rated themselves 'effective' in performing CRT. However, they commented that the teacher education program had only prepared them modestly to use CRT in their own classroom and the professional development support provided by school districts had not met their needs as well.

In sum, the teachers felt effective when they were able to develop and implement a plan for a child based on the child's individual needs rather than the child's race or culture. However, upon reflecting on the professional development they received they were able to see the benefits of how cultural knowledge and information can improve instruction for all children.

CLASSROOM MANAGEMENT: INTERNAL AND EXTERNAL LOCUS OF CONTROL

The data analysis revealed that this group of new teachers used a variety of classroom management strategies in their classrooms. The participants' beliefs and practices were somewhat congruent with classroom management principles that are proposed by scholars in the field, such as Bosch (2006), Martin, Yin and Baldwin (1998), and Manning and Bucher (2007). Their practices can be categorized into two domains in general—classroom organization and behavioral management.

For classroom organization, they emphasize daily schedules (e.g., P1, P4, P6 & P8), in which classroom settings and materials should be well organized and handled systematically (e.g., P4, P9 & P11). Specifically, P8 agreed with Manning and Bucher (2007) that classroom management is closely linked to instruction and that it is important to always keep students on task. P8 said "The more managed my classroom is, the more time I have for instruction."

In terms of behavioral management, the participants believed that it is important to adopt strategies such as redirecting (P2), relationship building (P5), setting behavioral expectations and boundaries (P3 & P10), individual conversations (P6), having a flexible management plan (P7), student engagement (P8), and using a positive behavior management system (P6, P10 & P12). Understandably, they seek help from the behavioral specialist, experienced teachers, and mentors to resolve persistent student behavior problems.

It is encouraging to see that many new teachers show positive attributes in the process of becoming an effective teacher. For instance, P1 said "I'm still learning, will be learning for a long time the best practices." Also, P4 confided "I'm still learning how to figure out the best way to function well with myself and my students."

Moreover, the participants' beliefs about classroom management practices were consistent with Bosch's (2006) assertions that classroom management is a skill that must be learned, practiced, and modified to fit the changing situation of contemporary classrooms. P3 said "I'm learning new ideas, applying different strategies and always changing throughout the year." Also, P7 reflected "Each individual student responds in a different way so I have to be flexible." Thus, new teachers were advised on how the theory can be applied to students at specific grade levels and classrooms settings (Manning & Bucher, 2007).

The majority of the participants mentioned that the preparation program taught them some classroom management knowledge and behavioral management strategies. For instance, P3 stated "They have prepared me with the knowledge before going to the real classroom. So I can try different things." P4 felt that the biggest learning issue was how to apply different kinds of classroom management plans in the classroom. Nevertheless, many participants suggested that they need more opportunities to practice the skills. According to them, "we have not been given opportunities to practice the skills during the class or the internship" (P2) and "It is very difficult to visualize it when you are not in the actual classroom" (P6).

Curriculum reviews of the current teacher education program showed that classroom management was taught in some courses such as ED3690 Classroom Organization and Management for early childhood education, and ED 3710 Classroom Organization & Management, ED 4500 Elementary Education Practicum, and ED 4085 Organizing Learning Environments for secondary education.

In ED3690, students examine and apply recent research on effective classroom management with a concentration on variables such as time on task, appropriate choice of group structures, direct instruction, and the management of time, space, and materials, as well as the analysis of classroom interactions. Pre-interns have various hands-on opportunities to prepare a classroom management plan, conduct classroom observations, micro-teach, and teach a few lessons to students.

Likewise, in ED3710 and ED 4500, the pre-interns learn how to design, teach, and evaluate nine lessons using classroom management principles to minimize "discipline problems." These hands-on learning experiences are needed to help internalize many classroom management strategies.

For secondary school option interns, classroom management is taught in ED4085. The main objective of this course is that interns will learn practical classroom management strategies that improve the learning environment. To achieve this objective, students have to participate in a field-based pre-internship (ED 4086) as a component of this course.

Parallel to ED3690, interns will be provided various hands-on opportunities to learn the skills such as developing classroom management plans and doing micro-teaching. Particularly, they are required to describe, analyze, and discuss the 17 core concepts of organizing positive learning environments and describe, analyze, and use at least 50 specific classroom management techniques that improve classroom management for effective learning environments.

These two major assignments will definitely prepare interns well in the area of classroom management. Thus, the interns should have substantial theoretical knowledge of classroom management before teaching in their own classroom. Some concern arose when many participants expressed frustration that they received less preparation in this area than they expected to have from the teacher preparation program.

In relation to professional development support by school districts, some participants mentioned that they received some training on managing classrooms through workshops such as Pre-school Program Quality Assessment (PQA), Plan-Do-Review, John Collins Writing Program, and Differential Instruction. P2 said she had a workshop on Plan-Do-Review that gave them more specific ways to run the class smoothly with some suggested classroom routines. Surprisingly, Plan-Do-Review, is a thinking routine which is supported by past research findings that state that classroom management must facilitate thinking as well (Williams, 2009).

P7 also commented that they have participated in workshops on differential instruction to help engage students in learning. Nonetheless, a few participants opined that the professional development training has not met their needs in this area. The new teachers were exposed to two different approaches to classroom management. One approach uses principles and strategies to a build a community of learners who intrinsically respect each other and the classroom environment. The second approach uses external cues and systems to manage behaviors. The new teachers are still trying to figure out how to use both approaches effectively. Therefore, more support and guidance is needed to help the new teachers implement both approaches to meet the needs of all children in their classrooms.

ASSESSMENT LITERACY: FORMAL AND INFORMAL ASSESSMENTS

The data analysis led us to three preliminary findings that need to be further verified as the study moves forward. First, the initial analysis of conceptual understanding of assessment data suggest that each participant seems to develop their own unique conceptual understanding of assessment despite the fact that they have received the same pedagogical training and professional development support from the same school district.

The majority of the beginning teachers perceived that they have competency in conducting assessment. The results demonstrated that all of the beginning teachers perceived assessment as a way to monitor and support student learning and illustrated a broader knowledge of assessment including knowledge of purposes and ways to use assessment results to monitor their students' learning progress. Based on these conceptual understandings about assessment, according to Popham (2004) and Stiggins (2002), this cohort of the new teachers is somewhat assessment-literate.

In addition, the study showed that the participants valued the formative function of assessment because they understood assessment as a tool that monitors students' learning outcomes and teachers' teaching effectiveness. They recognized both summative and formative use of assessment results to support learning and instruction. For instance, P5 noted her use of formative assessment,

> I regularly assess whether students have a problem, I also do quizzes and Q & A, and the data is informing me whether I have to reteach or move to another topic.

P6 also explained the benefits of assessment for her as,

> I will use the assessment data to make decisions about whether I need to move on or reteach, whether I should plan remedial activities or to reteach the concepts for some kids.

An 'assessment-literate' teacher should be competent in linking theory into practice, thus further study needs to be conducted to examine how well beginning teachers apply their assessment knowledge into instruction and the process of becoming assessment-literate (Popham, 2004; Siegel & Wissehr, 2011; Stiggins, 2002).

Second, more than one third (67%) of the beginning teachers commented that they had some preparation in this area from their teacher education program. It is noted that the program had incorporated assessment knowledge and skills in some courses. For instance, P2 said that all of the classes were focused on assessment pieces and they had learned to prepare different assessment pieces for different subjects and for different grade levels when they designed some lesson plans.

Likewise, P10 mentioned that they did a lot of reading assessment and also have learned some assessment terms and tools such as checklists. Nonetheless, some participants' felt that the program has some limitations (e.g., P1, P6, P9, P11 & P12). For example, P6 claimed that they were not exposed to any actual assessment pieces that were used in the schools and there were no specific classes that taught assessment.

To verify the claims, some teacher education courses' syllabi were reviewed. These curriculum reviews showed that the assessment component was incorporated in the syllabi of courses such as ED4010 Teaching Elementary School Science and ED 4070 Elementary Social Studies. In ED4010, assessment knowledge is emphasized in the course objectives which stated that, "Learn how to use a variety of strategies for assessing student knowledge, skill development, and attitudes toward science."

However, the review did not reveal what types of assessment strategies and how the assessment skills will be developed through the course. The interns are expected to develop assessment pieces to be used in the science lessons. Unfortunately, it is clear that the course syllabus did not describe any hands-on activities to help interns develop quality assessment pieces that can capture evidences of student learning.

Similarly, assessment is also one of the course outcomes in ED 4070, in which students are expected to analyze, develop and utilize various assessment methods. To achieve this learning outcome, the interns have to prepare a detailed description of the assessment process and/or document as well as a copy of any written assessment materials that they intend to use in the lesson plans.

Obviously, this assignment seems to be a very good learning platform for interns to learn how to develop assessment pieces that align with the students' learning objectives (Siegel & Wissehr, 2011). However, many beginning teachers claimed that they were not well-prepared in this area. For the sake of program improvement, these claims warrant further investigation.

Third, in terms of professional development support related to assessment, the responses were varied. Some participants felt that they were expected to be self-taught in this area (e.g., P1, P4 & P11). Some reported that they had workshops that provided training in dealing with state-wide assessment such as NWEA or M-Step (e.g., P6, P7 & P8). They have learned how to read the test scores and use the scores to inform instruction. They were also provided professional development in language arts and writing such as the John Collins Writing Program (e.g., P11).

However, it is not clear how assessment knowledge was incorporated in these professional development training. Overall, it seems that the professional development support provided for the beginning teachers is generic in nature. The new teachers felt that they were not actually well supported to develop quality assessment pieces in their own classroom.

Past research implied that teachers who have participated in professional development workshops on classroom assessment will experience a growth in their capacity to use various formative assessment strategies (Stewart & Houchens, 2014). Hence, if the claims are true enough, then the school district's professional development needs to expand to promote assessment literacy among new teachers.

In sum, the new teachers were learning how to use formal and informal assessments effectively to plan instruction and support individual needs. In this school district there was a heavy emphasis put on tracking student progress on formal assessments to use in school and teacher evaluation reports. These high stakes assessments may put pressure on teachers to teach to the test and move students through content faster than when they use informal assessments to plan and support children's learning at their level. Thus, new teachers are confused by the mixed messages and need more guidance to figure this out.

CONCLUSIONS

This study was conducted to investigate new teachers' challenges in a holistic manner. Three salient issues—culturally responsive teaching, classroom management, and assessment literacy—were investigated deeply so that the findings might advance teacher education practice to meet the contemporary needs of new teachers and their students at large.

The findings showed that some new teachers understood CRT in a simplistic way and view CRT as cultural celebrations that are disconnected from academic learning. Document reviews and participants' feedback revealed that they had not been well-prepared in this salient area.

In the area of classroom management, findings showed that participants use a variety of classroom management strategies in their classrooms. Almost all participants perceived that they are competent in managing the classroom even though they claimed that they had not been well-prepared in this area. Nonetheless, curriculum reviews revealed some disparity of the results that warrant further investigation.

Meanwhile, in the area of classroom assessment, the initial analysis suggests that each participant seems to develop their own unique conceptual understanding of assessment. Similarly, they also claim that they did not receive adequate preparation or support to develop quality assessment pieces in their own classrooms. Thus, these claims warrant further investigation, too.

Since the findings demonstrate that there is a significant gap between teacher education curriculum and the real fabric of schools in the area of culturally responsive teaching, classroom management, and assessment, some concerted measures should be planned to bridge the gap between theory and practice in those areas to assist new teachers in facing such challenges confidently. These efforts can also help to address factors contributing to new teacher turnover and retention issues.

NOTE

1 Comments and references to participants in the study are indicated by the letter P and the number assigned to each participant, thus preserving the privacy of all participants.

REFERENCES

Black, P., & William, D. (1998). Assessment and classroom learning. *Assessment in Education: Principles, Policy, & Practice, 5*, 7–74.

Bogdan, R. C., & Biklen, S. K. (1998). *Qualitative research in education: An introduction to theory and Methods* (3rd ed.). Boston, MA: Allyn & Bacon.

Bosch, K. A. (2006). *Planning classroom management: A five-step process to creating a positive learning environment* (2nd ed.). Thousand Oaks, CA: Sage.

Creswell, J. W. (2007). *Qualitative inquiry & research design: Choosing among five approaches* (2nd ed.). Thousand Oaks, CA: Sage.

Fitchett, P. G., Starker, T. V., & Salyers, B. (2012). Examining culturally responsive teaching self-efficacy in a pre-service social studies education course. *Urban Education, 47*(3), 585–611.

Gay, G. (2002). Preparing for culturally responsive teaching. *Journal of Teacher Education, 53*(2), 106–116.

Gay, G. (2010). *Culturally responsive teaching: Theory, research, and practice* (2nd ed.). New York, NY: Teachers College Press.

Irvine, J. J., & Armento, B. J. (2001). *Culturally responsive teaching: Lesson planning for elementary & middle grades.* Boston: McGraw Hill.

Goddard, J. T. (2000). Teaching in turbulent times: Teachers' perceptions of the effects of external factors on their professional lives. *Alberta Journal of Educational Research, 46*(4), 293–310.

Grossman, P., & Thompson, C. (2008). Learning from curriculum materials: Scaffolds for new teachers? *Teaching and Teacher Education, 24*, 2014–2026.

Kyriacou, C., & Kunc, R. (2007). Beginning teachers' expectations of teaching. *Teaching and Teacher Education, 23*(8), 1246–1257.

Ladson-Billings, G. (1994). *The dream keepers: Successful teachers of African-American children.* San Francisco, CA: Jossey Bass.

Ladson-Billings, G. (1995). Toward a theory of culturally relevant pedagogy. *American Educational Research Journal, 32*(3), 465–491.

Lincoln, Y. S., & Guba, E. G. (1985). *Naturalistic inquiry*. Beverly Hills, CA: Sage.

Liu, X., & Meyer, J. P. (2005). Teachers' perceptions of their jobs: A multi-level analysis of the teacher follow-up survey for 1994–5. *Teachers' College Record, 107*(5), 985–1003.

Manning, M. L., & Bucher, K. T. (2007). *Classroom management: Models, applications and cases* (2nd.ed.). Upper Saddle River, NJ: Pearson Merrill Prentice Hall.

Marshall, C., & Rossman, G. B. (2006). *Designing qualitative research* (4th ed.). Thousand Oaks, CA: Sage.

Martin, N., Yin, Z., & Baldwin, B. (1998). *Class size and teacher graduate study: Do these variables impact teachers' beliefs regarding classroom management style?* Paper presented at the Annual Meeting of the Southwest Educational Research Association. Houston, TX. (ERIC Document Reproduction Service No. ED 4189390)

McCormick, J., & Shi, G. (1999). Teachers' attributions of responsibility for their occupational stress in the People's Republic of China and Australia. *British Journal of Educational Psychology, 69*(3), 393–407.

Popham, W. J. (2004). All about accountability/why assessment illiteracy is professional suicide. *Educational Leadership, 62*(1), 82–83.

Roehrig, A. D., Pressley, M., & Talotta, D. A. (2002). *Stories of beginning teachers: First year challenges and beyond.* Notre Dame, IN: University of Notre Dame Press.

Reupert, A., & Woodcock, S. (2010). Success and near misses: Pre-service teachers' use, confidence and success in various classroom management strategies. *Teaching and Teacher Education, 26*(6), 1261–1268.

Scherff, L. (2008). Disavowed: The stories of two novice teachers. *Teaching and Teacher Education, 24*, 1317–1332.

Siegel, M. A., & Wissehr, C. (2011). Preparing for the plunge: Pre-service teachers' assessment literacy. *Journal of Science Teacher Education, 22*, 371–391.

Simonsen, B., Fairbanks, S., Briesch, A., Myers, D., & Sugai, G. (2008). Evidence-based practices in classroom management: Considerations for research to practice. *Education and Treatment of Children, 31*, 351–380.

Sleeter, C. E. (2012). Confronting the marginalization of culturally responsive pedagogy. *Urban Education, 47*(3), 562–584.

Stewart, T. A., & Houchens, G. W. (2014). Deep impact: How a job-embedded formative assessment professional development model affected teacher practice. *Qualitative Research in Education, 3*(1), 51–82.

Stiggins, R. J. (2002). Assessment crisis: The absence of assessment for learning. *Phi Delta Kappan, 83*, 758–765.

Stiggins, R. J., Arter, J., Chappuis, J., & Chappuis, S. (2006). *Classroom assessment for student learning: Doing it right, using it well.* Portland, OR: Educational Testing Service.

Young, E. (2010). Challenges to conceptualizing and actualizing culturally relevant pedagogy: How viable is the theory in classroom practice? *Journal of Teacher Education, 61*(3), 248–260.

Yost, B. L. (2014, April 6). *Novice teachers' perceptions of daily assessment and grading practices in first-year classrooms.* Paper presented at the 2014 annual meeting of the American Educational Research Association. Retrieved June 15, 2015, from the AERA Online Paper Repository.

POST-READING ACTIVITIES

1. What can you do to be an authentic culturally responsive educator?
2. What did you learn about classroom management and organization?
3. How prepared do you feel to implement formal and informal assessments?

CHAPTER 1

READING 1.2 OVERVIEW

In the article "Mindful Reflection as a Process for Developing Culturally Responsive Practices," Dray and Basler Wisneski explore how the attributions teachers assign to student behaviors may influence interaction and communication with diverse students. They provide six steps for mindful reflection that can assist educators in unpacking negative attributions. This article was selected to provide preservice and new teachers with a strategy to eliminate potential hidden bias.

PRE-READING ACTIVITIES

1. What does the word *diversity* mean to you?
2. Do you interact differently with general education students, those who are diverse, and those who present learning challenges?
3. Reflect on any hidden bias you may have toward students who do not identify with the same culture as you.

MINDFUL REFLECTION AS A PROCESS FOR DEVELOPING CULTURALLY RESPONSIVE PRACTICES

READING 1.2

BY BARBARA J. DRAY
AND DEBORA BASLER WISNESKI

Becoming a culturally responsive educator has been at the forefront of the movement to reduce inappropriate referrals to special education and disproportionate representation of students of color within special education (Fiedler, Chiang, Van Haren, Jorgensen, Halberg, & Boreson, 2008; National Center for Culturally Responsive Educational Systems, 2005). However, for many educators, working with a diverse student population can be more difficult when the student comes from a background that is unfamiliar to the teacher (Harry & Klingner, 2006). As teacher educators who prepare educators for inclusionary settings in diverse urban areas, we have noticed that issues often arise when a teacher or teacher candidate attempts to make meaning of behavior in the classroom, particularly a behavior that concerns student engagement, classroom management, or discipline of students with whom the teacher has a cultural disconnect. Teachers are not often aware of how diversity affects the way that they interpret students' actions and the ways that they interact with their students. Teachers may misinterpret a cultural difference as a potential disability.

Barbara J. Dray and Debora Basler Wisneski, "Mindful Reflection as a Process for Developing Culturally Responsive Practices," *Teaching Exceptional Children*, vol. 44, no. 1, pp. 28-36.

- How does diversity influence teachers' perceptions of behavior?
- Is there a way to use a process of mindful reflection and communication (Langer, 1989; Langer & Moldoveanu, 2000a) to help support the development of culturally responsive practices?

WHAT DOES DIVERSITY MEAN TO TEACHERS?

> Cultural diversity is a dynamic and relational reality that exists between persons rather than within any single person. For this reason, its challenge lies not so much in different behaviors as in the diverse meanings attributed to those behaviors. (Barrera & Corso, 2003, p. 3)

We agree with Barrera and Corso (2003) that diversity is never problematic in and of itself but "it is the response of individuals and institutions to diversity that can be problematic" (p. 8). A teacher can understand or misunderstand his or her diverse social world in many ways. These understandings and misunderstandings are attributable to differences in gender, race, class, geographic location, language, religion, family structures, abilities, and family and personal history. These myriad differences make diversity a way of life rather than a problem to be solved or fixed by casting the other as deficient. Instead, a teacher should view diversity as an opportunity to expand his or her understanding of himself or herself and the world.

Before a teacher can accept and embrace diversity in the classroom, he or she must reflect on the challenges that can interfere with acceptance. For example, educators overidentify students of color, particularly African Americans, in the category of emotional and behavioral disorder (EBD), although these students are underrepresented in the category of learning disabilities (LD; Harry & Klingner, 2006; Neal, McCray, & Webb-Johnson, 2003). Students of color also continue to experience higher rates of discipline referrals, as well as lower academic achievement (Drakeford, 2006; King, Harris-Murri, & Artiles, 2006). Some have argued that these outcomes occur partially because of the potential cultural, racial, and economic mismatch with the primarily White middle-class teaching force (Cartledge, Singh, & Gibson, 2008; Garcia & Ortiz, 2006). This argument suggests that without direct attention to cultural and individual differences in the classroom, some students, including those labeled LD or EBD, have limited opportunities to succeed. One recommendation that is central to the process discussed in this article is to assist teachers in developing reflective

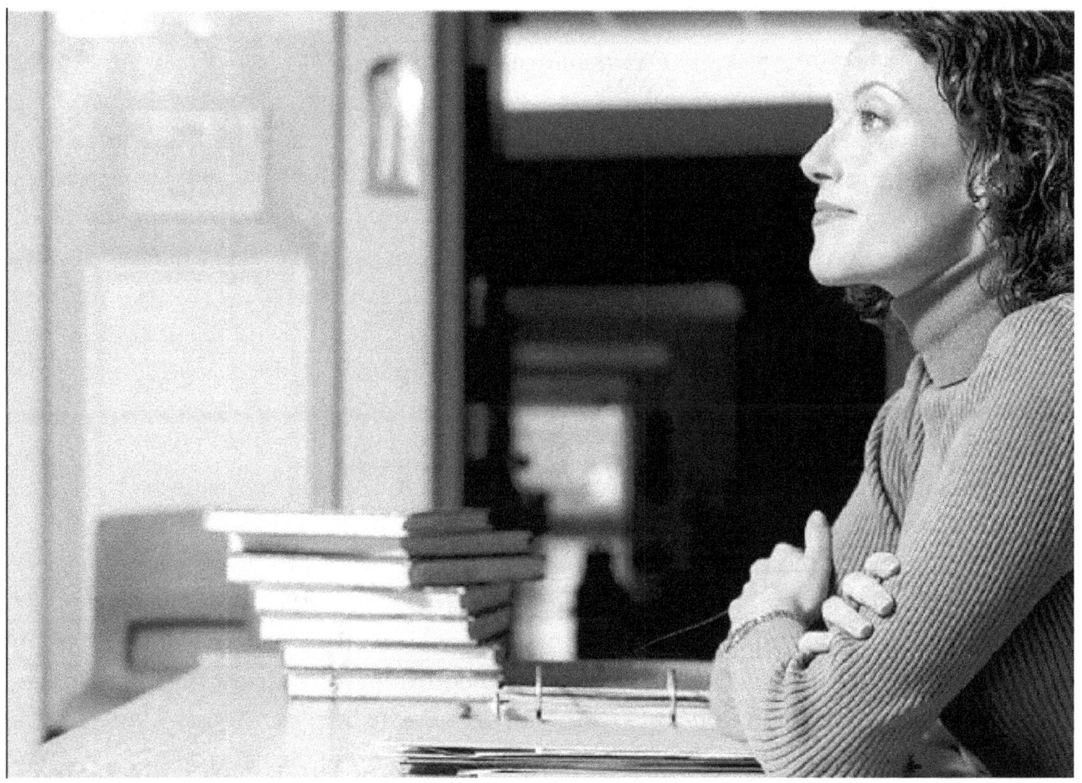

practices to gain a deeper understanding of institutions, personal assumptions, and common communication patterns that create tensions and misunderstandings between teachers and their students (e.g., Barrera & Corso, 2003; Garcia & Guerra, 2004; Kalyanpur & Harry, 1999).

> *Teachers are not often aware of how diversity affects the way that they interpret students' actions and the ways that they interact with their students on a daily basis.*

TEACHER REFLECTIONS: CONFRONTING BIAS IN CLASSROOM INTERACTIONS

In special education, scholars and educators have recognized the need for teachers to be sensitive to diversity in the classroom; this sensitivity requires that teachers look inward and reflect on their personal assumptions and biases (e.g., Fiedler et al., 2008; King et al., 2006; Wisneski & Dray, 2009). Kendall (1996) calls for teachers to take the "emotional risk" to examine their deeply held beliefs that can affect how they treat students. She suggests that this inward reflection requires being willing to listen and change to respond to the student who may be different in some way. Jacobson (2003) asks teachers to confront their discomfort through self-reflection and become aware of the prejudices and biases that everyone may have. Ramsey (2004) states, "we need to know ourselves—to honestly see our reactions to other individuals and the larger world and to analyze our underlying assumptions" (p. 20). In each case, there is the understanding that assumptions about various types of diversity in society are heavily value-laden and potentially harmful to students.

One example of negative attitudes toward some students and families is the *deficit thinking model* (Valencia, 1997; see box, "What Is the Deficit Thinking Model?"). Deficit thinking is an outcome of inaccurate and often negative attributions about students or their families. It is an unexamined prejudice often directed at students of color or from low socioeconomic backgrounds, even by teachers who may consider themselves supportive advocates of such students. Therefore, teachers need to self-reflect to unpack attributions that are potentially linked to racism, power, or privilege so that they can work more effectively and fairly with diversity in the classroom.

WHAT IS THE DEFICIT THINKING MODEL?

In the deficit thinking model, teachers believe that students fail in school because of the student's own deficiencies, not because of unfair school policies or differential treatment from teachers. A deficit perspective situates school failure within the student and suggests that deficiencies exist within the student or his or her home life and that these deficiencies are the cause of academic failure. Another common deficit perspective attributes student failure to parents and families who do not value education. As a result, teachers' attributions that are rooted in a deficit perspective guide an often ill-informed understanding that a student's failures are attributable to the student's perceived lack of ability, linguistic inferiority, or family dysfunction (Garcia & Guerra, 2004; Valencia, 1997).

RECONSIDERING COMMUNICATION IN THE CLASSROOM

In addition to reflecting on personal beliefs, teachers may need to reconsider how they communicate with students in the classroom. According to Ramsey (2004, p. 56), "effective communication requires paying close attention to what others are saying both verbally and nonverbally and genuinely trying to see and understand their perspectives, as we are making oneself understood." Effective communication requires teachers to analyze not only students' behaviors but also their own behaviors and ways of communicating.

In intercultural communication theories, mindfulness is a core concept used to help individuals reframe and reinterpret unfamiliar behavior or ways of communicating to understand rather than to judge others (Gudykunst & Kim, 2003). According to the work of Langer (1989), mindfulness is the ability to be conscious about communication with others. It is the process of purposefully responding to others by moving away from automatic-pilot or mindless responses that are based on a person's own cultural frames of reference. Automatic pilot is the process in which a person is not conscious or aware of her or his responses to others. Automatic pilot, or scripted behavior, serves well in familiar situations but not in intercultural communication. "The problem of misinterpreting strangers' behavior is compounded when we communicate with strangers because we tend to interpret strangers' behavior on the basis of our own frames of reference" (Gudykunst & Kim, 2003, p. 283).

Attributions are the explanations that people may give to a behavior (Gudykunst & Kim, 2003). They are the way that a person attributes or gives meaning to why people behave the way that they do, and attributions guide how a person responds to the behavior of others. A person who is aware of his or her attributions and takes time to reflect on them can minimize misattribution or misinterpretation of why someone behaves the way that he or she does.

Additionally, a person's cultural frame of reference or cultural background, as well as life experiences, guides how a person responds to others. When a person's cultural background and/or life experiences are vastly different from those of people with whom he or she is interacting, there is a risk for a culture clash or misunderstanding of cultures that can lead to conflict or misattribution (Gudykunst & Kim, 2003). Therefore, teachers within diverse communities should become highly aware of their personal cultural background and lens for understanding behavior, as well as cultural norms or tendencies of others, so that they can reduce attributions that lead to prejudice, deficit thinking, and overgeneralizations.

Gudykunst and Kim (2003) suggest that there are three cognitive processes, or types of attributions involved in the perception of communicating with others: description, interpretation, and evaluation.

1. *Description* is an account of what a person observed or experienced that does not attribute social significance to the behavior. It includes what the person heard and saw. People typically gather descriptions by observational data, counting, or anecdotal records. For example, "Enrique raised his hand 10 times during the story read-aloud" is a description of what occurred in the classroom.

2. *Interpretation* is the process of inferring what the behavior meant, thus attributing social significance to the behavior. Educators must remember that behaviors can have multiple interpretations. For example, at least three separate interpretative statements are possible for the descriptive example "Enrique raised his hand 10 times during story read-aloud": (a) Enrique was disruptive during story read-aloud; (b) Enrique enjoyed the story; or (c) Enrique wanted attention.

3. *Evaluation* is the process of attributing positive or negative social significance to a behavior. For example, the interpretive statement "Enrique wants attention" as an evaluative statement could vary from "I don't like that; Enrique needs to learn better turn-taking skills" to "I like that Enrique takes initiative to participate during read-alouds." It is important to recognize that attributions can be negative or positive and may lead to overgeneralizations and prejudice, which classroom teachers should minimize.

PROCESS FOR MINDFUL REFLECTION AND COMMUNICATION

Reacting to students' behavior on automatic pilot by jumping to conclusions or making assumptions about students' behaviors is very easy to do in the context of a busy school day. When teachers have difficulty interacting with students in the classroom, emotions and assumptions can cloud perceptions; likewise, teachers are more likely to give a student the benefit of the doubt when clashes occur if the student behaves in a way that the teacher desires. Therefore, just as teachers of students with disabilities often take anecdotal notes or keep running records of students' academic performance for assessment purposes, these same skills are necessary when reflecting on attributions about students in the classroom. Similar to the process of operationalizing behavior (that is, describing behavior so that it is observable and measurable) during a functional behavior analysis, we invite teachers to think about how they can understand the deeper meaning of behavior in daily classroom interactions of students who may or may not be labeled with a disability but who present behavior challenges in the classroom.

Just as teachers of students with disabilities often take anecdotal notes or keep running records of students' academic performance for assessment purposes, these same skills are necessary when reflecting on attributions about students in the classroom.

The following example of a teacher who used the process of mindful reflection and communication to unpack attributions of a student whom she perceived as having troubling behavior draws on the work of Carol Archer, who frames the prevention of culture clashes as the culture bump process (see Archer, 1990, 2003); and Ellen Langer, who has researched the importance of mindfulness as a tool for prejudice reduction (see Langer, 1989; Langer & Moldoveanu, 2000b). We developed this process and the vignette as a result of our collective experiences working with teachers to help them rethink troubling behavior in the classroom and learn to respond differently. Teachers often have deep concern for students who are easily distracted or disruptive during classroom activities, yet they often interpret students' perceived troubling behavior as a dysfunction of the student instead of examining alternative explanations for the behavior (e.g., lack of eye contact in one culture might indicate high respect; whereas in another, it might indicate lack of respect). We use this common concern to walk through the process of understanding the deeper meaning of behavior in the classroom by introducing and applying a process for mindful reflection and communication. The following case study describes and illustrates each step of the process by using a situation in which Ms. Marten (the classroom teacher) is reflecting with a mentor teacher on her attributions about a student.

STEP 1: EXPLAIN THE ATTRIBUTIONS THAT YOU HAVE ABOUT THE STUDENT

When unpacking attributions about students in the classroom, we recommend taking a moment to ask yourself the following questions:

- Have I already interpreted the behavior?
- Am I making assumptions about why the student behaves the way that he or she does?
- Have I already passed judgment on whether the behavior was good or bad? Stop and describe what you and the student said and did and in what order.
- What leads you to believe that the behavior was wrong or desirable?
- What about the behavior leads to your interpretation?

Isolated incidents rarely paint the clearest picture of the situation, so teachers should collect notes on at least three incidents of student behavior over an extended period of time (at least over a 2–4 week period) and at different times of the day (e.g., across content areas and different instructional settings). The educator must not blame or label the student or the behavior. The emphasis is on listening, observing to understand, and being willing to learn something new and different. The following description of Ms. Marten's experience demonstrates this process:

> Ms. Marten first mentioned to her mentor teacher that Antwan was disruptive during small-group guided reading. When Ms. Marten's mentor asked her to describe exactly how Antwan was disruptive, Ms. Marten restated that Antwan read along while she conducted guided reading and then began to tell a story about what he had done on the weekend.

STEP 2: WRITE OUT AND REFLECT ON YOUR FEELINGS AND THOUGHTS WHEN WORKING WITH THE STUDENT

Take into account potential issues of deficit thinking, prejudice, and overgeneralizations. After a teacher has recalled the interaction, she or he may also reflect on her or his attitudes and feelings toward the student during the interaction. As Jacobson (2003) suggests, educators must constantly engage in self-reflection about their assumptions and attitudes toward students. If they are to imagine alternative possibilities to relating to others, they must acknowledge the depths of their perspectives. Teachers can ask themselves the following questions:

- What attributes am I assigning to the student?
- Have I evaluated, interpreted, or described the behavior?
- How does this student make me feel?
- What are my worries or fears?
- What are my assumptions—why do I find the student's behavior problematic?

At this point, the teacher has acknowledged his or her prejudices or deficit thinking, despite the difficulty and uncomfortable feelings that this reflection may reveal. The teacher reflects on and rewrites interpretive or evaluative statements in descriptive terms and begins to rethink why she or he responded to the student in a particular way.

> Ms. Marten asked herself, "Have I already interpreted the student's behavior? What leads me to believe that Antwan did not follow directions?" She then realized that she was not describing the behavior but instead had already interpreted Antwan's behavior or his actions, so she started to rethink and describe:
>
> "He was mimicking—no wait, he was reading along while I read to the group, and then he began to tell a story about what he did on the weekend. Why do I perceive his behavior in a negative light? Mimic versus read-along? Why do I find his story inappropriate? Antwan is classified with a disability and he is African American: Am I making assumptions about his behavior? Do other students behave in a similar manner? How do I respond to other students in the class?"

STEP 3: CONSIDER ALTERNATIVE EXPLANATIONS BY REVIEWING YOUR DOCUMENTATION AND REFLECTIONS

This next part of the process more deeply examines the ways in which the teacher communicates and perceives the student and situation and reconsiders the initial interpretations. Review the explanations, and reflect on the reasons that the student may be doing what he or she does. Consider how this student's behavior is similar to or different from other behavior in the classroom. Teachers can ask themselves the following questions:

- What are my expectations for the situation?
- How is the student not meeting my expectations?
- In what way is the behavior interfering with learning?

> Here Ms. Marten recognized that she was on automatic pilot when she became frustrated with the guided reading lesson because Antwan was not following the expected script of communication: the question-response-evaluation or teacher-student-teacher interaction in which the teacher asks a question, the student responds, and then the teacher responds with an evaluative statement relating to the student's response. For example, the teacher asks, "What was the character doing?" The student answers, "He was eating." The teacher then responds, "Good job, he was eating an apple" or "Almost, he was preparing food."
>
> Ms. Marten could reinterpret Antwan's reading along with her while she read the story for guided reading as a clear attempt to show involvement and demonstrate his reading skills to indicate to his peers and to her that he could read too. Even though the process of guided reading includes the teacher reading alone rather than choral reading, Antwan could have been applying the rules from a previous lesson that involved choral reading. His storytelling after the read-aloud, on deeper reflection, showed connection with an incident in the story about spending time with family on the weekends. Antwan could have been making connections with the content of the story by adding how the story connected with his personal life.

Ms. Marten began to recognize that she was viewing Antwan's behavior only in negative terms at first, but she wanted to be more positive when responding to his actions. Ms. Marten remembered that when Sarah had read along during guided reading in another group, she welcomed that behavior because she saw it as an additional opportunity for Sarah to practice her reading; however, she thought that Antwan's behavior was disruptive. Why? Was it his tone, dialect, fluency, racial background, gender, or some other factor? When Ms. Marten reflected further, she realized that his classification as EBD made her more suspicious of his behavior, and the fact that he was African American had positioned him (in her mind) as more likely to misbehave.

STEP 4: CHECK YOUR ASSUMPTIONS

Ask yourself the following questions:

- Does the student's family notice the same behavior at home?
- How do family members interact with the student at home?
- Have there been any major changes or upsets in the home?

Share your reflections with a colleague, parents, and/or community members. Meet with parents to learn more about expected and observed behaviors in the home.

After you have reflected on the behavior and developed alternative explanations as well as possible biases, check your assumptions with individuals with specialized training on working with diversity, staff members who are familiar with or from the local community/culture, parents, and community members who are familiar with cultural norms of behavior. Consider talking with other professional personnel who specialize in multiculturalism, English as a second language (ESL), or bilingual education. Be wary of colleagues or informants who blame the student, community, or home life for the student's behavior; instead you want someone who understands the deeper meaning of behavior and can offer alternative explanations (e.g., cultural, linguistic, interactional) that can help you unpack attributions and reframe them in a way that leads to productive solutions and positive outcomes for students.

Ms. Marten reviewed her reflections with her mentor teacher, who had studied multicultural perspectives in education and who had

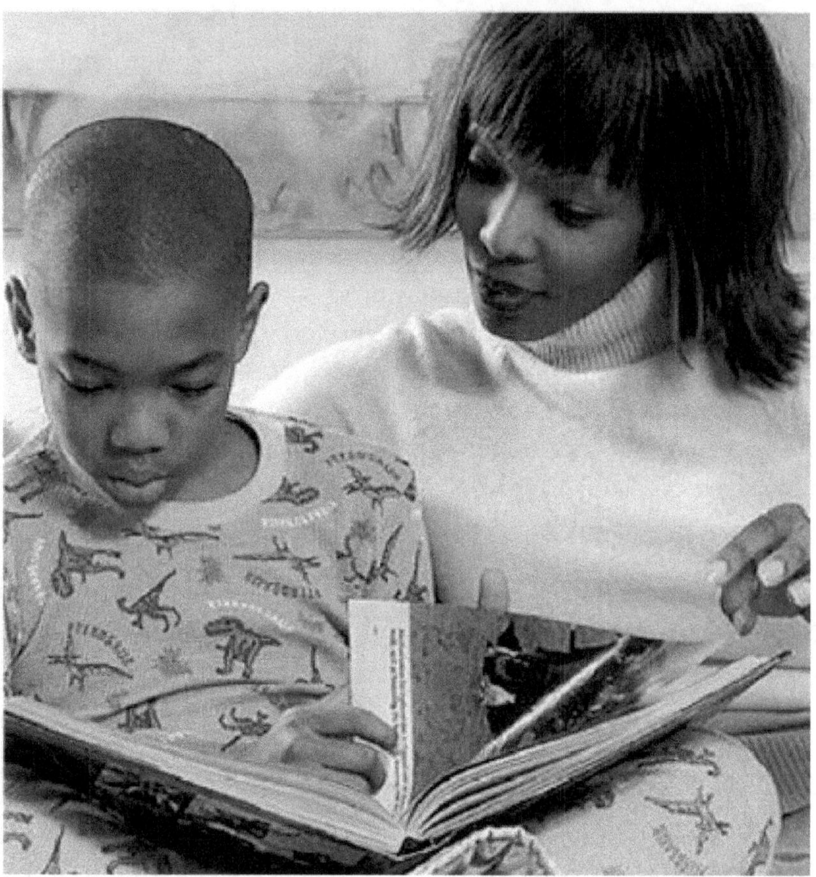

strong ties to the neighborhood community. She discussed her discomfort with some of the insights that she had uncovered related to Antwan's disability and racial background that may have clouded her understanding of his behavior in the classroom. Her mentor commended Ms. Marten for taking the risk and examining her biases and reminded Ms. Marten that she also needed to meet with Antwan's parents to ensure that she was interpreting the behavior appropriately.

Next, reach out to parents and families to learn more about their perceptions and ideas. Share your interpretations in a spirit of collaboration to learn from family members about their expectations and norms for behavior. Ask yourself the following questions:

- Am I operating from a different set of values or norms?
- How can I reach a middle ground?

- What are some alternative explanations or interpretations of the student's behavior?

> When Ms. Marten met with Antwan's parents, they shared that they have a tight-knit family and that they attend a Baptist church regularly. On the weekends, the minister encourages the congregation to participate through call-and-response sermons. Antwan's mother was a teacher's aide for students who struggle with reading, so she did many interactive literacy activities with Antwan because she found that he did better and was more motivated when he could actively participate. She had noticed that Antwan preferred to be interactive rather than remain quiet during activities. However, the mother also indicated that she was trying to teach him different routines and behavioral expectations.

STEP 5: MAKE A PLAN

Ask yourself the following questions:

- How can you change or respond differently?
- What additional resources do you need to implement the plan effectively?

After teachers have considered alternative explanations and developed a different interpretation of a situation, they are able to change their behavior. Teachers can experiment with responding differently, noting what happens and reflecting on their reactions and feelings, as well as on the student's response. The teacher should develop and implement a plan to change the classroom environment or his or her actions, and he or she should reexamine expectations for the student.

> Ms. Marten decided to be proactive by giving explicit directions about class routines to Antwan before he asked. Ms. Marten decided to listen to Antwan's statements in class for content and focus on understanding what he was trying to communicate, rather than whether his immediate expression followed the typical teacher-student-teacher response pattern. For example, instead of rejecting Antwan's comments if he did not raise his hand, Ms. Marten decided to respond to the meaning of his comment before reminding him to raise his hand, thereby recognizing and accepting his

desire and attempts to participate in class discussions and lessons. At times she would pair a statement such as "I want to hear what you have to say, Antwan," with a statement such as, "Will you please raise your hand so that I can call on you?" Ms. Marten's intent in these statements was to help Antwan begin to learn the norms of the classroom.

Ms. Marten recognized that most of the classroom interactions were formal and focused primarily on the prescribed curriculum, so she structured group time and participation to include making personal connections and sharing opinions about material. As a result of talking to Antwan's mother, Ms. Marten incorporated more movement into her lessons. For example, during think-pair-share, she asked each student to first put an index finger on his or her temple during the individual think, then face a peer with knees touching and discuss a concept during pair, and sit side-by-side next to the peer with the palms of their hands together during share.

STEP 6: CONTINUOUSLY REVISIT THIS PROCESS TO REASSESS YOUR ATTRIBUTIONS AND YOUR PROGRESS WITH THE STUDENT

Dealing with attributions in the classroom can be a complex and layered—and often uncomfortable—process, and educators should view dealing with attributions as an opportunity to learn more about others and about themselves. Therefore, educators must continuously review their relationship with the student and evaluate how their instruction and communication support the student's success in class. Educators should view this process as continuous and ongoing by revisiting each step as needed to ensure that all students are experiencing success in the classroom.

After a few weeks of reflecting on her attributions about Antwan's behaviors, mindfully exploring alternative explanations, and interacting with him in more responsive ways, Ms. Marten noticed positive changes in his performance. Antwan entered the classroom with a smile. He talked more with her about his likes and dislikes.

He participated in large-group activities, and he was more attentive and engaged when he worked with other students.

Ms. Marten also noticed a change in herself. She noticed that she was more aware when she began to overgeneralize or have prejudices about certain students, and she began to consider alternative views. She found herself often asking such questions as, "How can I understand this student better? What assumptions or values are guiding my interpretations?" instead of asking "Why won't this student behave?" or "Why can't she be more like the other students?"

FINAL THOUGHTS

Although we have described this process of mindful communication and reflection within a special education context, we believe that the process can be applied across settings to help teachers develop a deeper understanding of students' behavior by reflecting on the environment, cultural underpinnings, and biases that may be interacting to create a mismatch in the classroom. The intention is to support teachers in a process of deep reflection that transforms historically deficit views and responses to students with disabilities or from culturally and linguistically diverse backgrounds, in addition to developing practices that are culturally responsive and ensure that all students are well supported and successful in the classroom.

In particular, the process of mindful reflection and communication can help teachers do the following:

- Evaluate their own assumptions, prejudices, and biases about race, culture, and disability and consider how they affect the teacher's interactions with and expectations for their students.
- Objectively describe behaviors without interpretation to consider appropriate and consistent ways of responding.
- Interpret behaviors to support rather than inhibit learning.
- Consider the many different ways that children demonstrate engagement and attentiveness, how these ways closely tie with culture, and how culture influences students' many ways of responding and interacting with others in the classroom.

- Recognize that children are children first and foremost and that their behaviors do not define them, and consider whether or why you have different behavioral expectations for different children.

The end goal of this process is to accomplish the following:

- Develop mindful relationships with children and their families to support learning through building on the students' strengths and assets instead of focusing on their delays or need.
- Recognize and teach in developmentally, contextually, and culturally appropriate ways of responding to the behavior of all children.
- Create a culturally and linguistically responsive and supportive learning community that recognizes and celebrates differences.

We hope that this process enables teachers to become aware of and recognize their own biases when interpreting behavior in the classroom so that they may use culturally and linguistically responsive practices. The concern is that when teachers act on automatic pilot or do not take the time to reflect, they may risk misinterpreting culture and language ability as disability. Figure 1.1 furnishes a summary of the steps for mindful reflection and communication. We hope that this process assists teachers in understanding the role of their own cultural lens in examining student behavior to reduce the potential for them to interpret culture and language ability as disability.

Figure 1.1 Steps for mindful reflection and communication.

Step 1: Explain the attributions that you have about the student.

a. Describe what you and the student said and did.
b. How did the student react to your actions or comments?
c. Collect notes on multiple days and at different times of the day.

Step 2: Write out or reflect on your feelings and thoughts when working with the student. Take into account the potential for misinterpretations resulting from deficit thinking, prejudice, and overgeneralizations.

a. How does this student make you feel? What are your worries or fears?
b. What are your assumptions? Why do you find the student problematic?
c. Have you evaluated, interpreted, or described the behavior?
d. Try to rewrite the examples in descriptive terms.

Step 3: Consider alternative explanations by reviewing your documentation and reflections.

a. Review the explanations and reflect on why the student may be doing what he or she does. Look for patterns in your behavior and the student's behavior.

b. What are your expectations for the situation? How is the student not meeting your expectations? In what way is the behavior interfering with learning?
c. List alternative explanations or interpretations of the student's behavior.
d. What external factors and/or personal factors could be influencing the student's behavior? What recent changes have occurred in the student's life, disability, acculturation, and so forth?

Step 4: Check your assumptions. Share your reflections with a colleague, parents, and/or community members. Meet with parents to learn more about expected and observed behaviors in the home.

a. Share your list of alternative explanations or interpretations of the student's behavior with a colleague, parents, and/or community members.
b. Meet with the family to learn more about their perspective in understanding the behavior. Do they notice the same behavior at home? Do they find it problematic? How do they interact with the student at home? Have there been any major changes or upsets in the home?
c. Be open and responsive to the family's ideas and perspectives. Seek to understand rather than to judge.

Step 5: Make a plan.

a. How will you change or respond differently?
b. Brainstorm ideas on how to change the environment, your actions, and/or expectations for this student.
c. Experiment with responding differently. Note what happens. Reflect on your feelings as well as the student's response.
d. Frequently communicate with the family. Ask whether family members have noticed a difference. What have they been trying that works?
e. Consult with colleagues, parents, and/or community members while you experiment to check your assumptions and interpretations.

Step 6: Continuously revisit this process to reassess your attributions and your progress with the student.

a. Notice when you are overgeneralizing, attributing behavior within a deficit perspective, or behaving in prejudiced ways toward certain students.
b. Remember that this process is a continuous one, so revisit the steps periodically to continue your growth and understanding of students.

REFERENCES

Archer, C. (1990). *Living with strangers in the U.S.A.: Communicating beyond culture.* Thousand Oaks, CA: Prentice Hall.

Archer, C. M. (2003). *The toolkit for culture and communication.* Houston, TX: University of Houston, Department of Intellectual Property.

Barrera, I., & Corso, R. M. (2003). *Skilled dialogue: Strategies for responding to cultural diversity in early studenthood.* Baltimore, MD: Paul H. Brookes.

Cartledge, G., Singh, A., & Gibson, L. (2008). Practical behavior-management techniques to close the accessibility gap for students who are culturally and linguistically diverse. *Preventing School Failure,* 52(3), 29–38.

Drakeford, W. (2006). *Racial disproportionality in school disciplinary practices.* National Center for Culturally Responsive Educational Systems. Retrieved from http://www.nccrest.org/publications/briefs.html

Fiedler, C. R., Chiang, B., Van Haren, B., Jorgensen, J., Halberg, S., & Boreson, L. (2008). Culturally responsive practices in schools: A checklist to address disproportionality in special education. *TEACHING Exceptional Children,* 40(5), 52–59.

Garcia, S. B., & Guerra, P. L. (2004). Deconstructing deficit thinking: Working with educators to create more equitable learning environments. *Education and Urban Society, 36,* 150–167.

Garcia, S. B., & Ortiz, A. A. (2006). *Preventing disproportionate representation: Culturally and linguistically responsive pre-referral interventions.* National Center for Culturally Responsive Educational Systems (NCCREST). Retrieved from http://www.nccrest.org/

Gudykunst, W. B., & Kim, Y. Y. (2003). *Communicating with strangers: An approach to intercultural communication* (4th ed.). New York, NY: McGraw-Hill.

Harry, B., & Klingner, J. (2006). *Why are so many minority students in special education? Understanding race and disability in schools.* New York, NY: Teachers College Press.

Jacobson, T. (2003). *Confronting our discomfort: Clearing the way for anti-bias in early studenthood.* Portsmouth, NH: Heinemann.

Kalyanpur, M., & Harry, B. (1999). Cultural underpinnings of special education. In *Culture in special education: Building reciprocal family-professional relationships* (pp. 1–14). Baltimore, MD: Paul H. Brookes.

Kendall, F. E. (1996). *Diversity in the classroom: New approaches to the education of young children.* New York, NY: Teachers College Press.

King, K. A., Harris-Murri, N. J., & Artiles, A. J. (2006). *Proactive culturally responsive discipline.* National Center for Culturally Responsive Educational Systems (NCCREST). Retrieved from http://nccrest.org/Exemplars/exemplar_culturally_responsive_discipline.pdf?v_document_name=culturally%20responsive%20discipline

Langer, E. J. (1989). *Mindfulness.* Cambridge, MA: Da Capo Press.

Langer, E. J., & Moldoveanu, M. (2000a). The construct of mindfulness. *Journal of Social Issues, 56*(1), 1–9.

Langer, E. J., & Moldoveanu, M. (2000b). Mindfulness research and the future. *Journal of Social Issues, 56*(1), 129–139.

National Center for Culturally Responsive Educational Systems. (NCCREST). (2005). *Cultural considerations and challenges to response to intervention models: An NCCREST position statement.* Author. Retrieved from http://www.nccrest.org/publications/position_statements.html

Neal, L. I., McCray, A. D., & Webb-Johnson, G. (2003). The effects of African American movement styles on teachers' perceptions and reactions. *Journal of Special Education, 37*(1), 49–57.

Ramsey, P. G. (2004). *Teaching and learning in a diverse world.* New York, NY: Teachers College Press.

Valencia, R. (1997). Conceptualizing the notion of deficit thinking. In R. Valencia (Ed.), *The evolution of deficit thinking* (pp. 1–12). London, England: Palmer Press.

Wisneski, D. B., & Dray, B. J. (2009). Examining diversity through mindful reflection and communication. *Focus on Teacher Education, 9*(3), 2–4, 8.

Barbara J. Dray (Colorado CEC), Assistant Professor, Special Education and Linguistically Diverse Education, University of Colorado-Denver. **Debora Basler Wisneski**, Associate Professor, Early Childhood Education, School of Education, University of Wisconsin-Milwaukee.

Correspondence concerning this article should be addressed to Barbara J. Dray, School of Education and Human Development, University of Colorado, 1201 5th St., Campus Box 106, Denver, CO 80204 (e-mail: barbara.dray@ucdenver.edu).

TEACHING Exceptional Children, *Vol. 44,* No. 1, pp. 28–36.

POST-READING ACTIVITIES

1. Reflect on any personal assumptions and hidden bias you may have. How can you overcome these?
2. What is the deficit thinking model?
3. What steps are included in mindful reflection and communication?

CHAPTER 2

ENGLISH LANGUAGE LEARNERS

INTRODUCTION

According to the National Center for Education Statistics (2017), the population of English Language Learners (ELLs) who attend public schools has significantly increased over the past decade. The percentage of ELLs is generally higher in urban communities. During 2014–2015, of all states, California reported the highest percentage of ELLs in public schools. Teacher candidates must understand the unique characteristics of ELLs, identify appropriate instructional strategies, and use assessment data to determine best practices and supports. Two readings are presented in this chapter to help future educators prepare for working with the growing population of ELLs.

The first reading is a book chapter titled "Teaching Language Arts to ELLs." The reader will learn about the challenges and issues facing ELLs in the classroom regarding reading, writing, listening, and speaking. The authors explain how to meet the diverse challenges by presenting strategies for four of the language arts domains. There are clear and detailed examples on how to use each specific strategy in an appropriate and meaningful way. In addition, the authors accentuate the importance of integrating English Language Arts into all curricular areas.

The second reading provides an overview of some instrumental work by Jim Cummins, a notable researcher in the literacy development of students who are acquiring English as an additional language. Readers will learn about Basic Interpersonal Communication Skills (BICS), which refers to basic communicative fluency, and Cognitive Academic Language Proficiency (CALP), which concerns using more complex language. Cummins' Quadrants are also clearly outlined and explained. The quadrants represent a series of instructional choices that teachers can use based on the ELLs' need for contextual support and the degree of cognitive demand.

Both readings in this section are inextricably linked by the content presented on student activities, teacher strategies, and levels of scaffolding. As the population of ELLs increases, so does the need to prepare teachers who are skilled in working with students who are being exposed to a new language in social and academic contexts. The readings presented will serve as a foundation for this learning.

REFERENCE

National Center for Education Statistics. 2017. *The Condition of Education 2017 (2017–144).* US Department of Education.

CHAPTER 2

READING 2.1 OVERVIEW

The focus of this reading is on teaching language arts to English Language Learners (ELLs). The chapter begins with the case study of a sixteen-year-old student who is illiterate in both her native language and English. The authors describe the measures taken to facilitate the student's understanding of the English language and her progress in content areas. The text includes the characteristics associated with reading, writing, listening, and speaking and explains how there is reciprocity between the domains. In addition, the authors include the specific challenges that ELLs encounter when acquiring each of the skills. Practical and purposeful strategies are provided, with examples for helping language learners become proficient in each domain.

PRE-READING ACTIVITIES

1. What challenges do you think ELLs encounter when learning academic content?
2. List, describe, and explain strategies you already know for teaching ELLs reading, writing, listening, and speaking.
3. Which comprehension strategies do you know about that can support an ELL's understanding of text?

READING 2.1

TEACHING LANGUAGE ARTS TO ELLS

BY LYNN A. SMOLEN AND WEI ZHANG

CASE SCENARIO

Racine was a young adolescent from Congo whose first experience in a classroom was when she stepped into Sam Román's 6th grade science class at Thomas Jefferson International Newcomer's Academy. At age 16, she towered over the other students in the class, but her smile and warmth won everyone's hearts. She spoke no English and had not had any formal schooling in any language. As a result, she was illiterate. She understood some basic French, but her native language was Swahili. The first month of school was rather traumatic for her as she struggled to understand English with very little success. Mr. Román was able to help her navigate daily activities using conversational French, but she was unable to understand academic content in French. The Swahili instructional aide was only available to come to the class for one period a day to assist Racine and when he did, Racine bombarded him with questions on every subject area. As she began to utter basic words in

Lynn A. Smolen and Wei Zhang, "Teaching Language Arts to ELLs," *Teaching ELLs Across Content Areas: Issues and Strategies*, ed. Nan Li, pp. 49-82.

English, she asked Mr. Román for a math book to practice. When he gave her a workbook with basic arithmetic, she returned it fully completed in less than two weeks. Her determination and dedication propelled her to improve by leaps and bounds. From a pre-primer reading level in August, she progressed to a mid-first grade level by December. She was so determined to learn that by the end of the school year she was reading at a mid-third grade level. Due to her age and her progress, she was placed in the ninth grade for the next school year. Today she is on track to graduate from high school in two years.

Racine's case illustrates that English Language Learners (ELLs) can be academically successful despite tremendous obstacles that they face. She had no prior education when she stepped into Sam Román's sixth grade class, yet with the support of dedicated caring teachers and staff and her own determination, Racine was able to accelerate her progress in acquiring English and learning academic content to catch up with her peers. Teachers' knowledge and understanding of how to support ELLs are the keys to the success of these students. This is particularly true in the English language arts, as literacy is the basis for all subject areas. Regardless of the grade level or subject matter, teachers must understand the challenges that ELLs face and the ways to help them acquire English language and literacy in the subject areas they teach.

ISSUES FOR TEACHING ELLS LANGUAGE ARTS

In this chapter, we focus on teaching language arts to ELLs. This is an important topic to begin with discussing teaching ELLs across the content areas because the development of the language arts, specifically teaching listening, speaking, reading, and writing, is critical for the academic success of the English learners. The acquisition of knowledge and skills in math, science, social studies, and the visual and performing arts is dependent on proficiency in oral language, reading, and writing, and particularly on the ability to use academic language in these areas. In order for ELLs to succeed academically, they need to learn content (math, science, and social studies) and the English language skills needed to learn that content at the same time. In essence they have to do double the work that native speaking students have to do at the same grade level. This is very challenging given the fact that they also have to learn academic content through a different cultural lens from the mainstream culture and with a language that they are still in the process of acquiring. ELLs at various grade levels perform at a range of the English proficiency levels. It is important that teachers can provide differentiated instruction for the ELLs at their appropriate proficiency levels. For example, the teacher must have a differentiated method for a middle-school ELL with the minimal proficiency vs. another middle-school ELL at a more proficient level in English (Goldenberg, 2008).

In the age of high stakes testing and new state standards, ELLs are especially challenged with language arts. The Common Core State Standards (CCSS) call for rigorous teaching and learning, yet ELLs often come to U.S. schools with limited proficiency in English. Furthermore, many of these students come to school with limited schooling experiences and from homes in which parents know little about the structure of American schools and the requirements of the curricula. Parents often lack an understanding of how they can help their children and are frequently told that they should not speak their home language to their children. To further exacerbate this situation, ELLs often are in classrooms in which teachers have had limited training in how to adapt instruction to meet their needs. This chapter provides teachers with guidelines on how to effectively teach English language arts to ELLs.

To begin with this discussion, it is important for teachers to know that many of the strategies they use to teach language arts to native speakers of English are appropriate for ELLs. For example, it is quite appropriate for them to use literature circles and reader's theatre to promote collaborative literacy development while providing opportunities for peer interaction. It is also valuable for the teachers to teach strategies such as visualizing, predicting, inferring, synthesizing, and summarizing to teach reading comprehension. However, they need to understand that these strategies may have to be modified for ELLs since the ELL students are likely to require more scaffolding and explicit, direct instruction with background knowledge, cultural nuances, vocabulary, and complex grammatical structures.

Teachers also need to understand that ELLs are in the process of learning English, therefore, they are operating with an interlanguage (a language that is somewhere between their first language and their second language) and as a result, their oral and written production will not sound like the English language produced by a native speaker. Furthermore, it is important to realize that it takes time to acquire

English oral and written skills, especially academic English language skills (Short & Echevarría, 2016).

CHALLENGES FOR ELLS IN CLASSROOMS

Although ELLs often bring strengths to learning English, such as the knowledge of how language works and the ability to listen and read for meaning in their first language, they also face many challenges which can be greater if they are expected to learn in classrooms where instruction is directed towards native speakers of English and insufficient attention is devoted to differentiation of instruction. These challenges and ways to meet them for the four language domains (i.e., listening, speaking, reading, and writing) are discussed in the sections below.

LISTENING CHALLENGES FOR ELLS

Listening is receiving language through the ears. In the listening process, we identify the sounds of speech and process them into words and sentences (Li, 2015). When we listen, we use our ears to receive individual sounds (letters, stress, rhythm, and pauses) and use our brain to convert these into messages that mean something to us. Listening requires focus and attention. It is a skill that some people need to work at harder than others related to focus and attention.

Listening in a second language requires even greater focus. Although listening is an active and integrative process, listening in a second language environment can be difficult for ELLs because they hear English through the filter of their native language that has different sound patterns and may use stress in a different way from their native language. The ELLs are also challenged by sounds in English that may not exist in their native language or are articulated differently from English. For example, the sounds of th, dh, r, h, and l are difficult for many non-native speakers of English from different language backgrounds.

Also, ELLs may not be used to the stress, rhythm, and intonation patterns in English because stress may be conveyed in a very different manner from their native language. English is a stress-timed language and a listener needs to pay careful attention to the stressed words in a sentence in order to understand what the speaker considers to be important. For example, in the sentence: "There are *five main* causes of the Civil

War," the words that have a tonic syllable (the stressed syllable in a word in a sentence that carries the most important meaning) are *five* and *main*. A native English speaker is likely to know that he/she should pay attention to the words in the sentence that are stressed by the speaker and will expect the statement to be followed by a discussion of the five main causes of the Civil War. On the other hand, an ELL is less likely to pay attention to the words in the sentence that are stressed by the speaker and may miss the intended meaning.

ELL's listening is also challenged by reduced forms, disfluent speech, fast-paced speech with few pauses, and speech interlaced with colloquial language (Brown, 2015). English speakers use reduced forms in a variety of ways, such as phonologically (e.g., "Gimme it" for "Give me it."); morphologically (e.g., "he'd" and "she'll"); and pragmatically (e.g., "Books away" for "Put your books away."). Disfluent speech contains a lot of false starts, fillers (e.g., "um," "well," "OK"), and awkward pauses. Some speakers speak very fast and have few pauses, which make it challenging for ELLs to listen with comprehension. Colloquial language also makes speech difficult to comprehend. It includes idioms (e.g., "Hit the lights."), slang (e.g., "She's hot!"), and cultural references such sports terms (e.g., "down to the wire" and "Monday morning quarterback"). Additionally, by its very nature listening is evanescent; once something is said, the speaker moves on. There is no opportunity for the listener to go back to listen again to what was just said, so if there is no written or audio recorded version of what was said by the teacher the ELL has no way to recapture it.

SPEAKING CHALLENGES FOR ELLS

Speaking can be defined as to deliver language through our mouth. To speak, we create sounds using many parts of our body, including the lungs, vocal tract, vocal chords, tongue, teeth, and lips to utter and express (Li, 2015). Speaking usually requires at least a listener. When two or more people speak or talk to each other, the conversation is formed and called a dialogue. Speaking is one of the four language skills and it requires practice.

Like listening, speaking is challenging for ELLs as it is far more complex than learning vocabulary and grammar rules. In order for ELLs to be understood, they need to have acceptable pronunciation, fluency, vocabulary, and grammar. They also need to have some understanding of how to say things in a socially and culturally appropriate way. Speech acts involve knowing how to speak for different purposes such as in conversations (two-way communication); formal presentations (one-way communication); and participation in whole class discussions by asking and answering questions, sharing ideas, and offering opinions. Additionally, they need to understand how to use nonverbal communication so that there is no cross-cultural misunderstanding (Wright, 2015).

In its review of research on oral language development, the Center for Research on Education, Diversity, and Excellence (CREDE), found that ELLs take a number of years to develop oral English proficiency and tend to make more rapid advances in proficiency in Levels 1 through 3 and slower progress beyond Level 3. They suspect that the slowdown at higher levels may be due to a lack of instructional attention to oral language development once ELLs reach an intermediate level of oral proficiency (Genesee, Lindholm-Leary, Saunders, & Christian, 2006). This finding emphasizes the importance of building ELLs' oral language at all five levels of second language development.

READING CHALLENGES FOR ELLS

Reading can be explained as the process of looking at a series of written symbols and getting meaning from them (Li, 2015). When we read, we use our eyes to receive written symbols (letters, punctuation marks, and spaces) and we use our brain to convert them into words, sentences, and paragraphs that communicate something to us. Reading is a receptive skill and it is through that we receive information.

Reading presents a challenge to ELLs, just as do listening, speaking, and writing. It shares some important characteristics with listening. Like listening, reading is a receptive skill that is active and integrative. Its successful performance draws on a language learner's world knowledge, knowledge of the English language, and alphabetic system. It is also affected by the learner's short-term and long-term memory (Arrington, Kulesz, Francis, Fletcher, & Barnes, 2014; Hall, Jarrold, Towse, & Zarandi, 2015). As with listening, both bottom-up processing and top-down processing are involved. In bottom-up processing, the reader decodes and encodes words and reads and interprets phrases and sentences, that is, she reads from parts to the whole; in top down processing the reader activates her schema to determine what prior knowledge she has on the topic and genre she will read, that is, she previews the text and develops an overview of what she is about to read. Both top down and bottom up processing are necessary and an effective reader uses an interactive process, going back and forth between top down and bottom up processing. Second language readers tend to use either bottom up or top down processing when reading which makes their reading less effective (Brown, 2015).

According to Kenneth Goodman (1967), reading is a psycholinguistic guessing game in which the reader uses his prior knowledge and knowledge of the phonological, syntactic, and semantic structure of the language to predict what the author will say, then samples enough text to confirm or disconfirm his predictions. The reading process is much the same in the first and second language (Carrell, Devine, & Eskey,

1988; Goodman & Goodman, 1978; Grabe, 1991). However, there are some significant differences.

First and second language readers bring different resources to the reading task. First language readers are familiar with the English language and usually have background knowledge that they can connect to the text. On the other hand, second language readers have limited English proficiency and often lack relevant background knowledge and cultural knowledge to connect to a text that has been written in English on a topic that is culturally bound by the English-speaking environment. Lacking relevant background knowledge that is pertinent to the text often results in limited comprehension of what they read. Another limitation is their vocabulary knowledge in English. Inadequate knowledge of the meanings of words in a text can negatively impact comprehension (Anderson, 2014; Graves, August, & Mancilla-Martinez, 2013; Peregoy & Boyle, 2013).

WRITING CHALLENGES FOR ELLS

Writing is the process of using symbols (letters of the alphabet, punctuation, and spaces) to communicate thoughts and ideas in a readable form (Li, 2015). We usually write with a pen or pencil (handwriting) or a keyboard (typing). With a pen or pencil we usually write on a surface such as paper or whiteboard. A keyboard is normally attached to a typewriter, computer, or mobile device. To write correctly, we must understand the basic system of a language. For example, we must have the knowledge of grammar, punctuation, and sentence structure. Vocabulary is also necessary for correct spelling and formatting.

Second language writers spend less time planning writing than native speakers do, and are less fluent and accurate in vocabulary and grammar. Also, they are slower and more laborious in all stages of composing in the target language than first language writers. Most use their native language at some point in the composing process, which makes the process less automatic. They pay more attention to language issues as they write, focusing mostly on the sentence level. As a result, they have difficulty paying enough attention to the composing process and consideration of the overall organization of what they are writing (Williams, 2005).

MEETING THE CHALLENGES AND PLANNING TO TEACH

MEETING THE CHALLENGES OF LISTENING IN A SECOND LANGUAGE

It is helpful when teachers become aware of the challenges of listening in a second language and make modifications in their speech by slowing down; using pauses after making key points; reducing the number of colloquialisms, slang words, and idioms; and providing contextual support for listening with PowerPoint slides, pictures of key ideas, realia (real objects), word walls, concrete demonstrations, and outlines of lectures. They can also demonstrate how stress is used to emphasize important ideas in lectures and discussions, and point out how the mouth forms to pronounce different sounds.

An important way to promote listening comprehension is to provide opportunities for students to listen to authentic language from network television websites and video-sharing systems such as YouTube. For example, the "Friends" (2016) series on YouTube provides students with short, entertaining skits that relate to their everyday lives. For older students who are more proficient in English, short TED Talks (www.ted.com/talks) are excellent for developing listening comprehension. There is also a variety of listening comprehension tasks offered by Randall's ESL Cyber Listening Lab (www.esl-lab.com). When creating listening activities it is advisable to have students listen to a video or podcast at least twice. The first time they should listen to get the gist of what is said and the second time they should listen for specific details. Additionally, it is beneficial for teachers to guide ELLs' listening before, during, and after listening. For pre-listening the teacher could provide students with the topic of the listening text and ask them to activate their knowledge about it through brainstorming. They can then write down predictions about what they think they will learn. During listening, students can monitor their listening to see if their predictions are correct and after listening they can discuss the main ideas and supporting details of the text. More information about how to help ELLs with pronunciation of English is discussed in the section in this chapter under teaching strategies.

MEETING THE CHALLENGES OF SPEAKING IN A SECOND LANGUAGE

An important way to promote speaking skills of ELLs is to pay attention to the amount of teacher talk versus student talk. If teachers do most of the talking in class, students will not have an opportunity to practice speaking. Teachers should cut back on the time they spend lecturing and provide opportunities for students to engage in guided class discussions. They can ask open-ended and higher-order questions such as:

"Why do you think _______ happened?"
"How does the author create a sense of suspense in the novel?"
"Do you agree with what _______ said about _______?" "Why or why not?"

Teachers should also encourage ELLs to develop their speaking skills with cooperative learning, think-pair-share, role play, readers' theater, and information gap activities. Heterogeneous groups should be the norm so that ELLs have the opportunity to talk with students who are more proficient in English than they are. It is best if teachers plan lessons so that students have many opportunities to engage in meaningful conversations with peers about important concepts they are learning in each content area across the curriculum so that they can develop academic language in English (Zwiers, O'Hara, & Pritchard, 2014).

MEETING THE CHALLENGES OF READING IN A SECOND LANGUAGE

Having well-developed oral language in English is vital for ELLs' development of reading and writing. Therefore, it is important that teachers support ELL's in developing oral language as they are taught literacy skills. Additionally, it is beneficial for teachers to emphasize making meaning in all reading instruction, use scaffolding techniques, and promote extensive reading (Peregoy & Boyle, 2013; Ediger, 2014). To promote understanding, language should be presented in context rather than in isolation. Context can be developed by teaching vocabulary using examples of words in sentences or with pictures. Providing background knowledge on a topic, helping students relate new concepts to their own life experiences, and providing concrete examples to illustrate key ideas are other ways in which context can be provided.

Due to ELL's limited English proficiency, some teachers tend to emphasize bottom-up strategies, such as learning sight words, phonics, and syllabication, and de-emphasize or ignore the development of top down strategies such as activating background knowledge and making predictions. It is essential for teachers to teach reading comprehension regularly and consistently to all ELLs throughout the curriculum, even to beginning level ELLs and emergent readers. With pictures, stress and intonation, and gestures, meaning can be emphasized using shared reading, guided reading, and interactive read aloud activities.

In shared reading, an approach that is commonly used with emergent and early readers, the teacher focuses on a picture book, usually in a large format such as a big book, reads the book to a group of children several times, engaging them in a book walk and a variety of activities such as predicting events in a story, learning letter-sound associations, finding rhyming words, and reading repetitive phrases. One example of shared reading is when a teacher reads the big book, *Have You Seen My Cat?* by Eric Carle (2012). In this book, a little boy loses his cat and travels around the world asking, "Have you seen my cat?" For the first reading, the teacher could engage the children in a book walk, pointing to the pictures and asking them questions about what is happening in the story. During the second reading, the teacher could ask the students to listen to her read the story aloud. For the third reading the teacher could ask the students to notice the repetitive question, "Have you seen my cat?" As she reads, the teacher could emphasize this repetitive question, model how to read it, and ask students to join her in reading this part chorally. After reading, the teacher could ask the students to discuss their favorite part of the story.

Interactive read alouds are an excellent way for teachers to model good reading strategies and emphasize comprehension. In an interactive read aloud, teachers read a book aloud to a small group or whole class and engage students in discussion of the story. For example, with the book *Pink and Say* by Patricia Polacco (1994), the teacher could read the book aloud and stop at key points to ask questions about the concepts and events in the story. In this story, a young White boy and a young African American boy fight in the Civil War side by side. At one point in the story, the young African American boy's mother is killed. In this section, the teacher could ask students questions about how African American people were treated during this time period and whether or not they think this was fair and just.

Guided reading is a reading approach in which a teacher guides a small group of readers to read the same book using before reading, during reading, and after reading activities. Before reading activities include previewing the book, having students discuss their background knowledge and personal connections with the topic of the book, reviewing key vocabulary, and practicing pre-reading strategies such as predicting and questioning. During reading activities include discussion of key events and ideas, summarizing important ideas in the book, and practicing fluent reading. After reading activities include discussion of key points in the book, answering questions about characters or events in the story, summarizing the key ideas of the story, and making personal responses by writing about their favorite part of the story or dramatizing an event in the story. Guidance and prompting provided by the teacher support the readers and help them build their comprehension of the text.

Extensive reading is to provide opportunities for students to read as much as possible over an extended period of time for enjoyment and to use texts at an easy, comfortable level. Students should have choice in what they read and should be encouraged to select books that they can read smoothly and at a reasonable rate without having to look up words or needing to translate them from English to their own language. Extensive reading of books written at a comfortable level provides ELLs with lots of practice and fosters more proficient reading. To promote extensive reading, teachers should introduce students to a variety of books on different topics and in different genres by doing book talks, read alouds, and encouraging visits to the library. It is also effective to immerse the classroom in a variety of different kinds of print: nonfiction, poetry, children's and adolescent magazines, big books, word walls, and bulletin boards with displays of interesting words.

MEETING THE CHALLENGES OF WRITING IN A SECOND LANGUAGE

Since ELLs have more difficulty in composing than native speakers, it is very important that teachers provide direct instruction in all aspects of the writing process and support ELLs with scaffolding techniques. Modeled writing, shared writing, and guided writing are examples of instructional strategies that are very helpful for beginning and younger ELL writers. Modeled writing is a way for teachers to provide direct demonstration of how writers think as they write a message. With this technique, teachers write a message on the Smartboard or chalkboard and think aloud as they compose, making sure to be clear and accurate. For example, the teacher could write a summary of a field trip that the students took. Below is a short example.

> I am going to write a summary of our field trip to Hale Farm and Village last week. In the first paragraph I should make it clear where and when the field trip took place and who participated in the trip. Let's see ... On October 10th the class took a field trip to Hale Farm and Village. The class had a wonderful time. Hmmm. I think I need

> to include in the first sentence which class it was and where the village was located ...

Modeled writing is particularly beneficial for ELLs because they may not have models of English writing at home (Wright, 2015). The writing sample can be posted on the classroom wall as an example for students to follow. Supporting information could be added to the text by highlighting punctuation in yellow and labeling sections in a contrasting color with reminders such as, "The first paragraph introduces the topic;" "This paragraph tells who, when, and where."

Shared writing is similar to modeled writing except that it invites students to participate in the composing process. The teacher writes on the board and asks the students to suggest words and content to include. Throughout the process, the teacher scaffolds the students' attempts by making suggestions for vocabulary and grammar. For example, when writing a group response to Strega Nona by Tomie dePaola (1979), a student might suggest that the teacher writes, "Strega Nona was an awesome story!" The teacher could then have the students brainstorm what they thought was awesome about the story and guide them to generate more specific descriptive adjectives such as hilarious, amusing, engaging, and so forth.

Guided writing is similar to shared writing except that it usually focuses on an area of need. For example, teachers can begin by examining students' writing to determine an area of weakness that needs to be addressed, such as sentence clarity, organization of ideas, or descriptive details. They can then provide direct instruction in that area to an individual or group of students with a 10- to 15-minute mini lesson and encourage them to practice the skill or strategy in their own writing. Providing students with feedback and opportunities to share their writing is also important in guided writing.

For ELLs who are at the intermediate or advanced stages of writing, teaching the writing process through an approach such as writer's workshop can be helpful. In writer's workshop teachers provide direct instruction and scaffolding as they guide students through prewriting, drafting, revising, editing, and publishing. This approach is particularly appropriate for ELLs because it allows them to focus on the expression of ideas first and work on corrections later (Peregoy & Boyle, 2013). Additionally, it provides a collaborative support system for students as they engage frequently with their writing group to discuss and share their writing.

Teachers who use the writing process approach may want to use corrective feedback judiciously so that students do not feel overwhelmed by the challenges of writing in a language they do not yet command. They may want to focus on errors students are ready to self-correct and those that interfere with meaning. In students' compositions, they could underline errors students are ready to self-correct and directly correct those errors that students are not yet competent to correct themselves. Recurring grammatical and mechanical issues that are found in students' writing can be taught with direct instruction in mini-lessons (Wright, 2015).

TEACHING STRATEGIES

The four skills of listening, speaking, reading, and writing are the domains of language teaching and learning. Listening and reading are receptive skills; speaking and writing are productive skills. Similar to the developmental trajectory in first language acquisition, the productive skills seem to develop at a slower pace than the receptive skills for second language learners. In spite of this distinction, the four skills are interdependent rather than discrete. For instance, research has shown that oral English fluency has a strong impact on language learners' text-level literacy skills (Wright, 2015). In an education system driven by standardized testing, the importance of reading and writing overshadows that of listening and speaking, but language instruction should provide opportunities for language learners to develop all four skills simultaneously as they attain proficiency in English.

Driven by current research in second language teaching and learning, the teaching strategies presented in this section take into consideration both the language arts teacher and the language learner. First, effective instruction of the four skills is grounded in the language instructor's understanding of how language works (Echevarría & Graves, 2011). This is the explicit knowledge of which sounds are used in English, how these sounds are combined into words, how words are formed, how they are combined into sentences, and how meanings are conveyed in speaking and writing as well as what words should be taught and learned. Key concepts about language related to the development of each of the four skills thus are integrated into the discussion of teaching strategies. Second, effective instruction of the four skills should target how ELLs learn a second language. Unlike learning a first language in which learning takes place intuitively and implicitly, second language learners tend to approach the task of learning a second language analytically (Lightbown & Spada, 2013; Pinter, 2013). They are consciously or unconsciously seeking patterns as they constantly compare and contrast the language they know and the language they are learning. Explicit instruction of the four skills thus is considered important to ELLs.

LISTENING STRATEGIES

Even though listening is a receptive skill, it is nevertheless an active and integrative activity. Its successful performance draws on a language learner's world knowledge and knowledge of the English language and its appropriate use (pragmatics); it is also affected by the learner's short-term and long-term memory (Richards, 1985). When listening to a second language, the language learner is engaged constantly in constructing and reconstructing the message through developing, testing, accepting, rejecting, or revising what is being said and what it means. Both bottom-up processing and top-down processing are involved. In bottom-up processing, the learner assembles the message piece by piece from the speech stream, going from the parts to the whole, beginning with sounds to words to sentences in an effort to comprehend the message; in top-down processing, the learner starts from prior knowledge of the topic to gain comprehension of the parts that construct the message by means of predicting and inferring (Scrivener, 2011). Strategies for teaching listening therefore should include the following three components:

- A component allowing the learner to develop the necessary background knowledge for a topic, including the more general world knowledge and the more specific knowledge of a particular academic topic;
- A component allowing the learner to develop the schema of a genre; and
- A component allowing the learner to focus attention on the key words that carry the most essential meaning for the comprehension of a text.

The listening strategies explained below are examples of ways to teach listening based on these three components. They provide practical examples that teachers can apply directly in their classrooms.

CONTEXTUALIZING FOR KEY WORDS

Context is important for us to convey and understand a message, but academic texts typically are context reduced (Cummings, 2008; Schleppegrell, 2004). For instance, when the sentence *"The President wants more icebreakers"* is said out of context, it could mean a number of things: that the president wants more Ice Breaker mints, he wants more warm-up games for social gatherings, or he wants more ships designed for clearing a passage through ice. Only when the context is made clear that the president made comments about "keeping up" in the Arctic against Russia's fleet of icebreakers during his recent trip to Alaska is given, does the meaning of the key word *icebreaker* become clear. Language learners, with the pressure of trying to make meaning in a second language or limited by their lack of experience with a topic, could easily misinterpret the context and fail to focus on the key words that are important for understanding a message. So the often-used key words approach to listening comprehension needs to be modified so it is contextualized for ELLs.

Key words in academic texts tend to be content words, such as nouns, verbs, adjectives, and adverbs. They are the meaning-making units of a sentence (Fromkin, Rodman, & Hyams, 2011). To prepare ELLs for a listening task, such as understanding an academic text read to them, teachers should first carry out a two-step text analysis of the academic text to identify the world knowledge and topic-specific knowledge needed for comprehending the text as well as the words in the text that expand on the topic and relate to the knowledge demand. Second, teachers should prepare students for the new vocabulary with focused instruction. Third, teachers should match students' age and proficiency level with the listening task for the key words in the text.

Below is an illustration of the strategy of contextualizing for key words with, "A Day at the Beach," a poem for first graders (Froese, 2013). The italicized words in the poem are the key words that need explicit instruction.

A Day at the Beach
by Charon Froese

A day at the beach
What could be
More fun
Than playing in
The sand
The surf
The sun
Building castles
And rivers
And splashing
In the waves
There's no better
Way to spend
Hot summer days.

First, the two-step text analysis shows that the title of the poem speaks clearly about the topic: A day at the beach. In particular, the poem is structured in a question–answer format: It starts with the question, "What could be more fun than … " and ends with the answer, "There's no better way to spend hot summer days." Based on this analysis, the italicized key words expand on the topic and relate to the question–answer structure of this poem.

Second, to prepare ELLs to listen to the poem, the teacher can show students pictures or video clips of beach scenes to activate their experiences or imagination about playing on a beach on a hot summer day. Next, the teacher can introduce beach-related vocabulary in focused instruction, including objects on a beach and activities that people engage in at the beach such as playing in the sand and splashing in the waves. While the focused instruction on vocabulary does not have to be limited to the key words in the poem, the teacher should at least make sure that students know the key words. After that, the teacher conducts a series of listening activities:

1. The teacher reads the poem to students for the first time and students listen.
2. The teacher shows the poem with the key words missing to students.
3. The teacher reads the poem for the second time and students complete a cloze activity to fill in the missing words with pictures.
4. The teacher initiates a discussion on the parts of speech of the key words to draw students' attention to the meaning-making function of these words.
5. The teacher reads the poem with the students followed by students reading the poem on their own.

Third, to match the listening task to students' age and proficiency level, the above-mentioned cloze activity can take a number of different forms. For instance, intermediate students can choose words from a word bank to complete the cloze activity, and more proficient learners can fill in the missing key words directly. In addition, a discussion on what the author thinks is the best way to spend a hot summer day can be used to assess students' comprehension. For less proficient students, the discussion can be initiated and guided by the teacher. For more proficient students, the discussion can be extended to what students themselves think are the most enjoyable things to do on a beach and how they can justify their opinions. Such a discussion can also lead to a writing assignment for students to write or draw about their own "perfect summer day" to elicit more language production from them.

CONSTRUCTING FOR TEXT FRAME

When listening to a text in English, ELLs may wrestle with each word and lose track of what is being said. It is thus important that they are explicitly taught how to tolerate ambiguity and focus on the overall meaning of a text rather than individual words and sentences (Richards, 1985). Furthermore, teachers should bring their attention to the overall organization and linguistic features of a text to facilitate and deepen understanding. Genre-based studies on text structure have yielded a rich literature on the organization and linguistic features of different types of texts. If students know the typical pattern of a text, they are able to activate their prior knowledge and knowledge of lexical sets associated with a topic in an effort to understand the text. Therefore, teaching the text structure of the most commonly taught genres can be an effective strategy to prepare ELLs to grasp the main idea and important details.

For example, narratives and arguments are two commonly taught genres in English language classrooms. As summarized in Figure 2.1, the two genres have their unique text organizational patterns. It is effective to pre-teach the text organization patterns using annotated sample texts before asking ELLs to listen to a target text. Then in the actual listening session, the teacher can divide the listening text into sections based on its text organization. This offers the teacher opportunities to scaffold the content of the text and allows ELLs time to process what has been taught and heard. To accompany the listening activity, worksheets derived from the text structures can be used for note taking, which could be reviewed one section at a time.

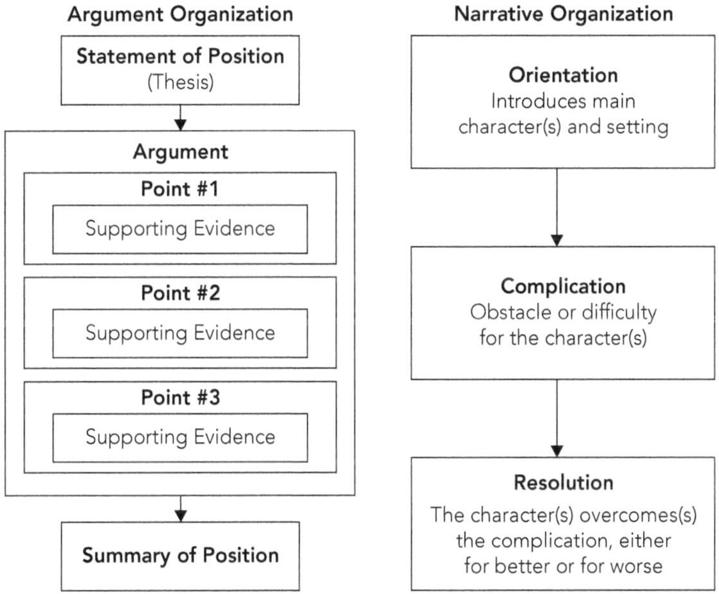

Figure 2.1 This figure is the text organization of narratives and arguments.

Source: Based on Derewianka (1990, pp. 40–42; p. 75–76).

FOCUSING ON COHESION DEVICES

Texts are often connected by linking words or special classes of words. They are the cohesion devices of a text that connect ideas together (Eggins, 2004; Lukin, 2008). The cohesion devices employed by academic texts often are the following types: (a) nouns and pronouns; (b) transitional words (e.g., *for example* and *in other words* for elaboration; *on the other hand* and *however* for extension; and *then, still, because,* and *similarly* for enhancement); and (c) purposeful choice of words that are typically related nouns and verbs (e.g., *professor/teach*) or words of certain semantic relations such as synonyms and antonyms (Eggins, 2004). Directing ELLs' attention to words and phrases that carry the ideas of a text forward helps to emphasize the key points of a text. For instance, the conjunction *however* is used in between two parts of a sentence with the actual or more important meaning resting on the second part, the part that immediately follows this word. In argumentative writing, apart from the thesis statement, the message immediately following transitional words and phrases that advances the argument calls for special attention because it expresses the main points supporting the thesis statement.

To implement the Focusing on Cohesion Devices strategy for listening, teachers need to first identify words and phrases that are used as the cohesion device in a text. Then a tiered listening task can be used in which students listen to a text multiple times to complete a series of tasks that are increasingly more demanding. For instance, in the first listening session of an argument, students are asked to write down only the transitional words or phrases that they have heard. In the second listening session, students are asked to write down three to five key words in the sentence immediately following each transitional word or phrase. In the third listening session, students fill in other information in the sentence immediately following each transitional word or phrase. Finally, students construct a thesis statement based on what has been written down and compare the thesis statement with the actual thesis statement found in the text.

SPEAKING STRATEGIES

Speech is fundamental to human communication. Learning to talk seems effortless with guaranteed success in first language acquisition, but learning to speak fluently in a second language is considerably more difficult. Unlike other language skills, speaking is not just a brain function; it is also a neuromuscular skill. Its processing involves both the motor control of the speech organs and a speaker's phonological knowledge (Moyer, 2013). Successful performance in speaking involves the speaker's phonological, grammatical, sociolinguistic, and world knowledge as well as the processing capacities of the individual at the time of speaking. To be a competent speaker in a second language, a learner needs to demonstrate four interactive competences proposed by Hymes (1972) as communicative competence: (a) grammatical competence (the correctness and accuracy of utterances); (b) sociolinguistic competence (the appropriateness of utterances); (c) discourse competence (the coherence and cohesiveness of utterances); and (d) strategic competence (the use of communicative strategies, such as paraphrasing). Hymes's theory of communicative competence defines what a speaker needs to know in order to be communicatively competent in a speech community. According to Hymes, a person who acquires communicative competence acquires both knowledge and ability for language use.

Speaking becomes even more challenging in the case of learning to discuss academic content in a second language. It not only requires general speaking skills, it also demands knowledge of academic vocabulary and content as well as discourse organization and planning, specific to a content area. At the minimum, in order to teach pronunciation and speaking effectively, teachers should know the vowels and consonants in English, how the pronunciation of vowels can vary according to context, and how these sounds co-articulate in a sentence (Derwing & Munro, 2015). In the English language arts classroom, explicit instruction in speaking can be integrated into read-aloud activities and reading fluency practices. The following strategies are designed with integrated teaching of speaking in the content areas.

ARTICULATING FOR VOCABULARY BUILDING

Academic vocabulary in English language arts, similar to academic vocabulary in other content areas, typically comprises the key words used in academic texts and in discussions of academic content. These words are often content words with more than one syllable. Being able to say these words facilitates the mental retention of these words and enables academic conversation as learners build up a repertoire of words at their disposal.

In English, if a word has more than one syllable, one of the syllables receives more prominence. This is the primary stress of the word. The stressed syllable is pronounced relatively longer and louder than other syllables. In particular, stress can also carry lexical meaning in English, or differentiate one word from another. For instance, stress on bi-syllabic words can differentiate the part of speech as in ***pro**duce* (noun) and *pro'**duce*** (verb), ***im**port* (noun) and *im'**port*** (verb). What's more, ELLs often find words with three or more syllables difficult to pronounce, especially when they occur in a sentence with other words, such as *characteri'**za**tion* and ***an**notated bibli'**o**graphy*.

Given ELLs' potential difficulty with multi-syllabic words, these words should be highlighted and practiced so that ELLs can use them to access content knowledge and engage in academic conversations. When first introduced, the teacher should enunciate these words more than once with appropriate hand gestures and emphatic pronunciation, such as in a louder and clearer voice, to draw students' attention to them. Students should also repeat these words orally after the teacher while clapping for the stressed syllable. In focused instruction on multi-syllabic content words such as in a review class, lists of multi-syllabic words can be grouped together based on parts of speech (e.g., adjectives) or stress patterns (e.g., four syllable words with the primary stress on the second syllable, x X x x). Then a chant can be created for students to clap for the primary stress as listed in Table 2.1. More advanced students can mark the primary stress on the words before reading them in a chant with accompanying musical beats.

ANNOTATING FOR COMPREHENSIBILITY

As a stress-timed language, the rhythm of English speech is created by the alternation between stressed and unstressed words. Stressed words in a sentence are mostly content words, such as nouns, verbs, adjectives, and adverbs. Other words in a sentence, such as articles, pronouns, prepositions, conjunctions, and auxiliary verbs are typically not stressed and are grouped together with a stressed word to form phonological phrases, each of which receives about an equal amount of time in an utterance. The intonation of speech, or the pitch movement gliding through the stressed and unstressed words in a sentence, together with rhythm, function as the "road signs" of English. They direct listeners' attention to the emphasis in a sentence and make the relationship between ideas clear "so that listeners can readily identify these relationships and understand the speaker's meaning" (Gilbert, 2008, p. 2).

Table 2.1 **Adverbs with stress pattern X x x x and x X x x.**

X x x x	x **X** x x
'**con**sequently	e'**nor**mously
'**per**sonally	a'**ppa**rently
'**per**manently	a'**ccor**dingly
'**prac**tically	in'**crea**singly

In focused pronunciation instruction, teachers often emphasize accurate pronunciation of individual sounds, but rhythm and intonation are actually more important for the comprehensibility of a message, that is, how easy a message is to understand from the listener's perspective (Derwing & Munro, 2015; Gilbert, 2008). ELLs whose native languages are not stress timed, or ELLs with relatively lower oral proficiency, might lack the intuition to tune into the stress pattern marked by stressed words that would facilitate a listener's comprehension of an utterance.

An emphasis on teaching the rhythm and intonation of English thus enables students to actively engage in predicting and catching up with the meaning of what they are reading. It has also been shown to have a positive effect on their listening comprehension, even when explicit instruction is not given (Bradlow, Pisoni, Akahane-Yamada, & Tohkura, 1997). So to raise students' awareness of the essentials of English speech, the following should be demonstrated explicitly with concrete examples:

- English sentences should be parsed phrase by phrase with the marker on the stressed words;
- Unstressed words should be pronounced with relatively lower volume of the voice and relatively fast; and
- The pitch movement of intonation should fall on the stressed words to give emphasis.

In focused instruction on the rhythm and intonation of English sentences, the teacher can first choose materials with relatively low vocabulary and knowledge demand so that attention can be concentrated on the pronunciation itself. Second, the teacher can underline the stressed words and stressed syllables in each sentence. Third, the teacher can parse each sentence into phrases around the stressed syllables. Fourth, the teacher can read the annotated text with students. Fifth, students can read the annotated text on their own. Finally, when students have had enough experience in annotating texts, they can annotate the reading text on their own.

Poems are often taught in English language arts classes. With their built-in rhythmic patterns, poems offer many opportunities for pronunciation instruction. Actions can also be added to the reading of poems to differentiate the stressed and unstressed words. Younger students would enjoy tapping the desk for stressed words and tapping their shoulders for unstressed words; older students can take one shoe off and then stomp the foot with a shoe for stressed words and the foot without a shoe for unstressed words. Once students have a better grasp of how stressed and unstressed words alternate in a sentence, the teacher can challenge them with texts with less regular rhythmical patterns. Below, the poem, "Little Things" (Carney, 2010) and the excerpt from "A Courtroom in the Classroom" (Stahl, 2014) illustrate one way to mark the stress patterns of texts (bolded, underlined words are the stressed words and equal length should be assigned to words between slashes. Also note that the marking is for pronunciation practice and therefore follows the rules of syllabification of English speech, which is not the same for syllabication for reading instruction. For example, the word *wanted* can be divided as ***want**-ed* in reading instruction).

Li**ttle **Things
by Julia A. Carney

Little /**drops** of /**wa**ter,
Little /**grain**s of /**sand**,
Make the /**might**y /**o**cean
And the /**beau**teous /**land**.

And the /**li**ttle /**mo**ments,
Humble /**though** they /**be**,
Make the /**might**y /**a**ges
Of e/**ter**nity.

So our /**li**ttle /**e**rrors
Lead the **soul** a/**way**,
From the /**paths** of /**vir**tue
Into/**sin** to /**stray**
Little /**deeds** of /**kind**ness,
Little /**words** of /**love**,
Make our /**ear**th an /**E**den
Like the /**hea**ven a/**bove**.

*A **Court**room /in the **Class**room*
by Michael Stahl

Miss **Blake** /**want**ed /to **show** /her **third** grade /**class** /**what** it's **like** /inside a **court**room/ of the U**ni**ted /**States**/, so she de**ci**ded /to **stage** /a **role** play/. There are **ma**ny /**di**fferent/ **peo**ple /in the **court**room/ during a **tri**al/. **All** of them /have **di**fferent /but im**por**tant /**jobs**/ or **roles**

FAST READING FOR FLUENCY

Languages differ from one another in their sound inventories and the specific ways to put those sounds together. Speakers of different languages accordingly form a habitual way to bring together the speech organs to suit the sound inventory and its combinations. When speaking a second language, learners need to re-configure their speech organs for the second language. Fast reading forces very active movement of the speech organs. It can be an effective way to help students gain better motor control of the flow of speech. To begin this practice, the teacher should choose a short text that has been previously annotated and read. The teacher can then ask students to read the text multiple times, each time at a faster speed. To make this practice more interesting, a fast reading competition can be held at regular times to encourage practice outside of class. Students can also form fast reading pairs and enter the competition in pairs.

READING COMPREHENSION STRATEGIES

ELLs learning to read in English, just like their native English-speaking peers, benefit from a balanced approach to reading instruction, and specifically, with explicit teaching of the components of literacy such as phonemic awareness, phonics, vocabulary, fluency, reading comprehension, and writing (Goldenberg, 2008; Peregoy & Boyle, 2013; Wright 2015). It is important that teachers teach ELLs how to become good readers by focusing on meaningful contexts using interesting literature and nonfiction texts at students' instructional level. When possible, it is helpful for students to be taught how to read in their native language and supported in transferring literacy skills from their first language to their second language. Additionally, it has been found that materials that are culturally relevant to ELLs facilitate reading comprehension (Wright, 2015).

ELLs benefit from being taught reading strategies that will facilitate their comprehension of texts. Good readers typically use many strategies to comprehend texts (Pressley, 2002), as listed in Table 2.2.

Table 2.2 **Strategies used by good readers to comprehend text.**

- Planning and forming goals before reading
- Forming predictions before reading
- Reading selectively according to goals
- Rereading as appropriate
- Monitoring reading continuously
- Identifying important information
- Filling in gaps in the text through inferences and prior knowledge
- Making guesses about unknown words to be able to continue reading without major disruptions
- Using discourse-structure information to guide understanding
- Integrating ideas from different parts of the text
- Building interpretations of the text while reading
- Building main idea summaries
- Evaluating the text and the author, and forming feelings about the text
- Attempting to resolve difficulties
- Reflecting on information in the text

Source: Pressley, 2002, pp. 294–296.

When good readers read challenging texts they use a variety of strategies with an increased metacognitive awareness (Grabe & Stoller, 2014). Metacognitive strategies help them to become aware of their own thinking as they read, monitor their reading as they encounter words and ideas that are challenging, and employ fix-up strategies such as rereading and reading ahead to help themselves understand when meaning breaks down.

An instructional model that has been found to improve student engagement and achievement for ELLs is the Gradual Release of Responsibility (GRR) model (Fisher & Frey, 2008; Frey & Fisher, 2009). This model has four components: focus lessons, teacher guided instruction, collaborative learning, and independent application (Frey & Fisher, 2008). During focus lessons teachers model thinking, ask students questions to scaffold their learning, and build metacognitive awareness of how they are to use a particular skill or strategy. In the guided instruction phase, teachers and students engage in dialogue so students become aware of how they should apply the skill or strategy. During the collaborative learning phase, students work in small groups and interact with group members to complete a task. They are held individually accountable for their contributions to the goals of the group. Finally, during independent learning, students engage in independent tasks that extend their learning (Frey & Fisher, 2008). Teachers often call this model I do it, we do it, you do it together, you do it alone. When introducing a new reading strategy to ELLs it is valuable for teachers to use the GRR model so they have the necessary support to comprehend text. Some examples of activities that help students learn good reader strategies are described below. Each of these activities should be used with modeling and explanations from the teacher and meaningful collaboration and discussion amongst students before and after reading.

KWHL: WHAT DO I KNOW? WHAT DO I WANT TO KNOW? HOW WILL I MEET MY GOALS? WHAT HAVE I LEARNED?

KWHL is a widely applicable activity that is designed to promote strategic reading and motivate students to engage with text. K stands for "What do I know?" W stands for "What do I want to know?" H stands for "How will I meet my goals while reading?" and L stands for "What have I learned?" This strategy encourages students to activate their background knowledge, set goals for reading, monitor their reading to focus on important ideas, evaluate the information they have learned, connect back to their goals, and list what they have learned. It is particularly useful with nonfiction. Table 2.3 provides an illustration of a KWHL chart on the topic of immigrants.

Table 2.3 **Example of KWHL chart used with passage on immigrants in the United States. Sample shows possible student responses before and after reading.**

K	W	H	L
• People who have come from a different place to our country • People who have to learn our laws • People who have to adjust to our way of life	• Why do they come here? • What problems do they cause? • Do they bring some good things to our country? • How do they become U.S. citizens?	• Preview text to find main ideas. • Write questions to answer when reading the text. • Read to find answers to my questions. • Evaluate whether or not I have answered the questions by rereading sections.	• Immigrants come to the United States to find a better way of life or to flee war, oppression, or poverty. • Sometimes they cause problems because the people who already live in the United States are afraid they will take their jobs. • They bring good things such as skills, knowledge, and willingness to work hard. • They have to pass a citizenship test.

Source: Based on Grabe and Stoller (2014, p. 199).

ANTICIPATION–REACTION GUIDE

Anticipation–Reaction Guide is a comprehension activity that encourages students to use cognitive and metacognitive strategies as they actively engage with reading a text before, during, and after reading. Table 2.2 provides an example of this activity on the topic of Leonardo da Vinci. With this activity students make predictions about what they will read, read to verify their predictions, and then find evidence in the text to support their answers. To prepare for this activity, the teacher reads the text to determine the main ideas and supporting details and then develops an anticipation guide with statements to be used to predict information in the text. Before reading, the teacher asks students to read the statements on the guide and mark whether or not they agree (A) or disagree (D) with them. Then the students share their responses with a partner and read the text to determine if their predictions are correct. After reading, they return to the statements to mark whether or not the author agreed or disagreed with the statements. The final step is for the students to provide evidence from the text to support their after-reading answers and to discuss what they learned with the whole class.

Before Reading		After Reading
D	A Renaissance man is someone who excels in many different areas.	A
	p. 95 "A person who excels in many areas—a "Renaissance man."	
D	Scholars during the Renaissance believed that human ability to learn was limitless.	A
	p. 95 "... many Renaissance scholars and artists believed that the human ability to learn was unlimited."	
D	It is easier today to be a Renaissance man than in the past.	D
	p. 96 "... knowledge has grown tremendously ... it is difficult for anyone today to master many fields of knowledge and become a Renaissance man or woman."	
A	da Vinci's interest in art and his interest in science were directly linked.	A
	p. 96 "Some of his scientific studies were tied to his work as an artist."	
D	da Vinci's drawing techniques for human anatomy revolutionized medical studies.	A
	p. 96 "In science, Leonardo's techniques for drawing human anatomy (body structure) revolutionized medical studies and are still used today."	

Figure 2.2 Sample anticipation guide used with *Leonardo da Vinci, Renaissance Man.* The sample shows possible student responses before and after reading.

Source: Based on Baltas and Nessel (1999, p. 93–96).

SURVEY, QUESTION, PREDICT, READ, RESPOND, AND SUMMARIZE (SQP2RS)

SQP2RS is an activity described by Echevarría, Vogt, & Short (2013) which engages students in before, during, and after reading to build their comprehension. It is usually used with expository text and can often be used as a study guide. This before reading, during reading, and after reading strategy helps students use metacognitive thinking skills as they set goals for their reading, approach the text with an inquiring mind, and summarize what they have learned.

The steps of the SQP2RS strategy are as follows:

1. *Survey:* Students survey the text by looking at the title, headings, subheadings, and other graphic features to get an overview of what it is about.
2. *Question:* In groups, students come up with questions they think will be answered in the text and write them on a template or post them on a large classroom chart.
3. *Predict:* Based on their questions, the students as a small group or whole class generate key ideas they think will be discussed in the text.
4. *Read:* Students read the text with a partner or in a small group, searching for answers to their questions and attempting to verify or disconfirm their predictions.
5. *Respond:* Students answer their questions in small groups and discuss the key concepts in the text.
6. *Summarize:* Students work with a partner or a small group to summarize the main ideas in the text. This summary can be written on their template or on a large classroom chart.

TIERED TEXTS

Another way for teachers to provide students with scaffolding for their reading comprehension is to have them read texts of gradually increasing difficulty or tiered texts. Tiered texts are texts related to the same topic or story that gradually build readers' background knowledge and understanding of the events in a story to provide access to a more challenging text. This activity is an excellent way to scaffold reading comprehension because it builds students' background knowledge and exposes them to similar vocabulary and academic language across texts to prepare them to comprehend a target text. An example is a tiered text set for Shakespeare's *Romeo and Juliet* as described by Moss, Lapp, and O'Shea (2011). Their model uses a three-tiered system. In tier one, the teacher builds background knowledge about Shakespeare and the Elizabethan period with a read aloud of the picture book, *William Shakespeare and the Globe* by Aliki (2000). After discussing this book, the teacher follows up by having students view Franco Zeffirelli's (1995) film version of *Romeo and Juliet* to learn about the plot and the characters in the play by viewing. In tier two, students practice and prepare to read a challenging text by reading the graphic novel, *Picture this! Shakespeare: Romeo and Juliet* (Page & Petit, 2005). This is followed up by having students create a sociogram of the characters in the play so that they have the opportunity to explore the characters at a deeper level. After this scaffolding, the students are ready to read and discuss the target text, *Romeo and Juliet* by William Shakespeare (2004). After reading the original play, they respond to it by either creating a PowerPoint that retells the story or by developing an iMovie that illustrates the point of view of a particular character in the play (Moss, Lapp, & O'Shea, 2011). This three-tiered approach is an excellent example of literacy instruction based on the GRR model (Fisher & Frey, 2008; Pearson & Gallagher, 1983).

WRITING INSTRUCTION STRATEGIES

Writing is a complex literacy skill. Just as in speaking, writing is a productive process, so fluency (flow of ideas) and accuracy (correct sentences) share the same importance. It requires competence in four different areas:

- Linguistic knowledge (grammar and vocabulary);
- Functional discourse knowledge (differences between written and spoken English);
- Rhetorical knowledge (conventions of writing); and
- Composing and thinking skills.

The linguistic forms of written English discourse are different in many ways from that of spoken English discourse. Written English is based on the sentence, paragraph, and text. Furthermore, complex written sentences replace the chains of coordinately linked phrases and clauses of oral language to suit a neutral and formal style. Just as in speaking, composition differs substantially from one culture to another and the conventions of writing also differ (Connor, 2002). Due to this difference, writing instruction should be based on an examination of the forms of authentic English and should be linked to reading (Carrell, 1996; Nation, 2009). Furthermore, it is important that teachers establish an appropriate balance of instruction to foster the development of language skills (vocabulary and grammar) and other skills, especially higher-level thinking skills, so that ELLs' writing contains a logical flow of ideas. Finally, writing tasks should be at the same level of learners' cognitive development even though there is often a discrepancy between learners' cognitive level and second language skills.

SPONTANEOUS WRITING FOR FLUENCY

Writing about daily life is a low-stakes, low anxiety form of writing practice. Encouraging students to write on a regular basis for real communication motivates them to express themselves in words. For instance, a student can write in English to an English-speaking pen pal who is learning the student's native language, such as Spanish. This also provides an opportunity for the native-speaking Spanish student to write back in Spanish, making this a reciprocally rewarding experience for both students. Students can also write to other students in other classes about what happened in each other's classroom. As long as the writing is understandable, no correction of writing errors is necessary. However, depending on students' ages and English proficiency levels, the teacher should set a reasonable goal of word count to provide guidance for these activities.

ONE-PAGE GRAMMAR FOR ACCURACY

Error correction is a reality in teaching writing to learners. ELLs' writing errors might seem to be chaotic at first glance; and yet, research shows that these errors are often systematic and reflect their developing grammar in a second language (Corder, 1967; Ferris, 2011). The most common errors in ELLs' writing range from misuse of punctuation and words to grammatical morphemes (such as the articles *a, an, the*; the third person singular *-s;* and the copula *be*) and tenses. An efficient way to deal with these learners' writing errors is to provide them with a checklist of the most commonly made mistakes in their own writing called a "one-page grammar." The checklist might need to be personalized or could be applicable to students with similar proficiency levels or the same native language backgrounds. To use the checklist, the teacher can number each item and reference the numbers when giving feedback to a learner's writing. The numbers can direct students' attention to the type of errors in their own writing without directly providing the correction. This procedure transforms students from passively receiving feedback to actively participating in the process of improving their own grammar in English.

BLENDING READING AND WRITING FOR GENRE WRITING

As mentioned earlier, ELLs tend to approach the task of learning a second language analytically. Writing instruction that is categorized, for example by focusing on specific genres, can be useful for learners to develop the required writing skills. Focus on form, or the linguistic features of each genre, is also important as ELLs are also learning how to use the surface features of the target language.

The English language arts writing standards of the CCSS clearly state that narratives, expository writing, and arguments are the key genres required for reading and writing instruction for students at all levels, from kindergarten to high school, with differentiated requirements (National Governors Association Center for Best Practices & Council of Chief State School Officers, 2010a). Appendix C of the same document provides annotated samples of students' writing that match up to the standards specified for each grade level. Table 2.3 shows an example of an annotated sample of a narrative written by a second grader that illustrates the standards (National Governors Association Center for Best Practices & Council of Chief State School Officers (2010b, p. 12).

This sample narrative also includes the general linguistic feature of narratives (Derewianka, 1990, p. 42):

1. Specific, individual participants (*I, my sister, my mom and dad*)
2. Use of action verbs (*running, cry, bleeding, lying, put, found …*) mainly and feeling words (*felt, was surprised*)
3. Past tenses (*happened, were (running), did … cry, was (bleeding), put …*)
4. Linking words of time (*So that night … and in the morning*).
5. Descriptive language (*Boy! Did we cry …*)
6. First person or third person point of view (*I, my*)

To teach students to write a narrative similar to the example, the teacher can plan a unit using three to four short stories at a similar reading level about things that happened in the past. These stories should also share most of the same linguistic features described above. The teacher can annotate each story to highlight the linguistic features. Then the teacher can provide specific guidelines or rubrics for students to write in the same style and manner as the example shown in Table 2.4. The rubric should be explained with one of the short stories that students read in this unit to provide specific examples of what each item means.

STUDENT SAMPLE: GRADE 2, NARRATIVE

This narrative was produced in class, and the writer likely received support from the teacher.

My first tooth is gone

I recall one winter night. I was four. My sister and I were running down the hall and something happend. It was my sister and I had run right into each other. Boy! did we cry. But not only did I cry, my tooth was bleeding. Then it felt funny. Then plop! There it was lying in my hand. So that night I put It under my pillow and in the morning I found something. It was not my tooth it was two dollars. So I ran down the hall, like I wasen't supposed to, and showed my mom and dad, They were suprised because when they lost teeth the only thing they got is 50¢.

Annotation

The writer of this piece

- **establishes a situation in time and place appropriate for what is to come.**
    - *I recall one winter night. I was four, My sister and I were running down the hall and something happend.*
- *recounts a well-elaborated sequence of events using temporal words to signal event order.*
    - *My sister and I were running down the hall and something happend. ... But not only did I cry ... Then it felt funny. Then plop! There it was lying in my hand.*
- **includes details to describe actions, thoughts, and feelings.**
    - *Boy! did we cry.*
    - *Then it felt funny.*
    - *So I ran down the hall, like I wasen't supposed to, and showed my mom and dad*
- **provides a sense of closure.**
    - *They were suprised because when they lost teeth the only thing they got is 50¢.*
- **demonstrates growing command of the conventions of standard written English.**
    - *This piece illustrates the writer's largely consistent use of beginning-of-sentence capitalization and end-of-sentence punctuation (both periods and exclamation points). The pronoun / Is also capitalized consistently, and almost all the words are spelled correctly. The writer sets off a parenthetical element with commas and uses an apostrophe correctly.*

Figure 2.3 This figure is an example of student work sample: grade 2 narrative.

Table 2.4 **Example rubric.**

RECOUNT RUBRIC—SECOND GRADE		
1. Title: Describe what happened in a phrase		
2. Story:		
One or two sentences:	When did it happen?	____
One or two sentences:	What were you doing when it happened?	____
One or two sentences:	What were others doing when it happened?	____
Two to three sentences:	What happened exactly?	____
	What were the details?	____
One or two sentences:	What happened next?	____
One or two sentences:	How did you or others feel?	____
3. Mechanics:		
Does each sentence start with a capital letter?		____
Does each sentence end with punctuation?		____
Does each sentence have a subject?		____
Do most sentences have a verb in past tense?		____
Are there words and phrases about time?		____

SUMMARY

This chapter focused on teaching the language arts to ELL students. The chapter began with a real case scenario. This chapter then described the characteristics of each of the four language arts domains: listening, speaking, reading, and writing. We have discussed how these four language skills are interdependent rather than discrete. We have also discussed how oral language proficiency has a strong impact on ELLs' text-level literacy skills (Wright, 2015) and why it is important for teachers to provide opportunities for language learners to develop all four skills simultaneously in order to attain high levels of proficiency in English. We have also described the unique challenges that ELLs face in acquiring each of the four language skills and some best practices to overcome the difficulties and to meet the needs of these students in each of the four areas. We have also provided examples of specific strategies that can be used for teachers to help ELLs strengthen their proficiency in each of the four language domains (i.e., strategies for teaching listening, speaking, reading, and writing). Additionally, we have emphasized the importance of the English language arts to all areas of the curriculum and how they should be integrated throughout the curriculum as much as possible.

REFERENCES

Aliki. (2000). *William Shakespeare and the Globe*. New York, NY: HarperCollins.

Anderson, N. J. (2014). Developing engaged second language readers. In M. Celce-Murcia, D. M. Brinton, & M. A. Snow (Eds.), *Teaching English as a second or foreign language, 4th ed.* (pp. 170–188). Boston, MA: National Geographic Learning.

Arrington, C. N., Kulesz, P. A., Francis, D. J., Fletcher, J. M., & Barnes, M. A. (2014). The contribution of attentional control and working memory to reading comprehension and decoding. *Scientific Studies of Reading, 118*(5), 325–346.

Baltas, J. G., & Nessel, D. (1999). *Easy strategies & lessons that build content area reading skills*. New York, NY: Scholastic.

Brown, H. D. (2015). *Teaching by principles: An interactive approach to language pedagogy*. White Plains, NY: Pearson Education.

Bradlow, A. R., Pisoni, D. B., Akahane-Yamada, R., & Tohkura, Y. (1997). Training Japanese listeners to identify English /r/and /l/: IV. Some effects of perceptual learning on speech production. *The Journal of the Acoustical Society of America, 101*(4), 2299–2310.

Carle, E. (2012). *Have you seen my cat?* New York, NY: Simon and Schuster.

Carney, J. A. F. (2010). *Little things*. Retrieved from http://www.poemhunter.com/poem/little-things-23/

Carrell, P. L. (1996). Text as interaction: Some implications of text analysis and reading research for ESL composition. In B. Leeds (Ed.), *Writing in a second language: Insights from first and second language teaching and research* (pp. 40– 47). Boston, MA: Addison-Wesley.

Carrell, P. L., Devine, J., & Eskey, D. (1988). *Interactive approaches to second language reading*. Cambridge, England: Cambridge University Press.

Corder, S. P. (1967). The significance of learner's errors. *International Review of Applied Linguistics in Language Teaching, 5*(4), 161–170.

Cummings, J. (2008). BICS and CALP: Empirical and theoretical status of the distinction. In B. Street & N. H. Hornberger (Eds.), *Encyclopedia of language and education (2nd ed.) Volume 2: Literacy* (pp. 71–83). New York, NY: Springer Science Business Media LLC.

Connor, U. (2002). New directions in contrastive rhetoric. *TESOL Quarterly, 36*(4), 493–510.

dePaola, T. (1979). *Strega Nona*. New York, NY: Aladdin.

Derewianka, B. (1990). *Exploring how texts work*. Newtown, AU: Primary English Teaching Association.

Derwing, T. M., & Munro, M. J. (2015). *Pronunciation fundamentals: Evidence-based perspectives for L2 teaching and research*. Philadelphia, PA: John Benjamins.

Echevarría, J., & Graves, A. (2011). *Sheltered content instruction: Teaching English learners with diverse abilities* (4th ed.). Boston, MA: Pearson Education.

Echevarría, J., Vogt, M. E., & Short, D. J. (2013). *Making content comprehensible for English learners: The SIOP Model*. Boston, MA: Pearson.

Ediger, A. M. (2014). Teaching second/foreign language literacy to school-age learners. In M. Celce-Murcia, D. M. Brinton, & M. A. Snow (Eds.), *Teaching English as a second or foreign language*, 4th ed. (pp. 154–169). Boston, MA: National Geographic Learning.

Eggins, S. (2004). *An introduction to systemic functional linguistics* (2nd ed.). New York, NY: Bloomsbury.

Ferris, D. R. (2011). *Treatment of error in second language student writing* (2nd ed.). Ann Arbor, MI: The University of Michigan Press.

Fisher, D., & Frey, N. (2008). Homework and the gradual release of responsibility: Making "responsibility" possible. *English Journal, 98*(2), 40–45.

Frey, N., & Fisher, D. (2009). The release of learning. *Principal Leadership, 9*(6), 18–22.

Friends. (2016, March 11). Seasons (Episodes by seasons). Retrieved from https://www.youtube.com/show/friends

Froese, S. (2013, March 17). A day at the beach. Retrieved from http://bluebell-books.blogspot.com/2013/03/a-day-at-beach-by-sharon-froese.html

Fromkin, V. A., Rodman, R., & Hyams, N. (2011). *An introduction to language,* (9th ed.). Boston, MA: Wadsworth.

Genesse, F., Linholm-Leary, K., Saunders, W. M., & Christian, D. (2006). *Educating English language learners: A synthesis of research evidence*. New York, NY: Cambridge University Press.

Gilbert, J. B. (2008). *Teaching pronunciation: Using the prosody pyramid.* New York, NY: Cambridge University Press.

Goldenberg, C. (2008, Summer). Teaching English language learners: What the research does—and does not—say. *American Educator*, 8–44.

Goodman, K. S. (1967). Reading: A psycholinguistic guessing game. *Literacy Research and Instruction, 6*(4), 126–135.

Goodman, K. S., & Goodman, Y. (1978). *Reading of American children whose language is a rural dialect of English or a language other than English* (Final Report No. C–0003–0087). Washington, DC: National Institute of Education.

Grabe, W. (1991). Current developments in second language reading research. *TESOL Quarterly, 25*(3), 375–406.

Grabe, W., & Stoller, F. L. (2014). Teaching reading for academic purposes. In M. Celce-Murcia, D. M. Brinton, & M. A. Snow (Eds.), *Teaching English as a second or foreign language* (4th ed.; pp. 189–205). Boston, MA: National Geographic Learning.

Graves, M. F., August, D., & Mancilla-Martinez, J. (2013). *Teaching vocabulary to English language learners.* New York, NY: Teachers College Press.

Hall, D., Jarrold, C., Towse, J. N., & Zarandi, A. L. (2015). The developmental influence of primary memory capacity on working memory and academic achievement. *Developmental Psychology, 51*(8), 1131–1147.

Hymes, D. (1972). On communicative competence. In J. B. Pride & J. Holmes (Eds.), *Sociolinguistics: Selected Readings* (pp. 269–293). Harmondsworth, England: Penguin Books.

Li, N. (2015). A book for every teacher: Teaching to English Language Learners. Charlotte, NC: Information Age.

Lightbown, P. M., & Spada, N. (2013). *How languages are learned* (4th ed.). Oxford, England: Oxford University Press.

Lukin, A. (2008). Reading literary texts: Beyond personal responses. In Z. Fang & M. J. Schleppegrell (Eds.), *Reading in secondary content areas: A language-based pedagogy* (pp. 84–103). Ann Arbor, MI: University of Michigan Press.

Moss, B., Lapp, D., & O'Shea, M. (2011). Tiered texts: Supporting knowledge and language learning for English learners and struggling readers. *English Journal, 100*(5), 54–60.

Moyer, A. (2013). *Foreign accent: The phenomenon of non-native speech.* New York, NY: Cambridge University Press.

Nation, I. S. P. (2009). *Teaching ESL/EFL reading and writing*. New York, NY: Routledge.

National Governors Association Center for Best Practices & Council of Chief State School Officers. (2010a). Common Core State Standards for English language arts and literacy. Washington, DC: Authors.

National Governors Association Center for Best Practices & Council of Chief State School Officers. (2010b). Common Core State Standards for English language arts and literacy in history/social studies, science, and technical subjects: *Appendix C: Samples of student writing*. Washington, DC: Authors.

Page, P., & Petit, M. (Eds.). (2005). *Romeo and Juliet (Picture this! Shakespeare*). Hauppauge, NY: Barron's Educational Series.

Pearson, P. D., & Gallagher, M. C. (1983). The instruction of reading comprehension. *Contemporary Educational Psychology, 8*(3), 317–344.

Pinter, A. (2013). Teaching young learners. In A. Burns & J. C. Richards (Eds.), *The Cambridge guide to pedagogy and practice in second language teaching* (pp. 103–111). New York, NY: Cambridge University Press.

Peregoy, S. F., & Boyle, O. F. (2013). *Reading, writing, and learning in ESL: A resource book for teaching K–12 English learners,* (6th ed.). Boston, MA: Pearson.

Polacco, P. (1994). *Pink and Say.* New York, NY: Philomel Books.

Pressley, M. (2002). Metacognitive and self-regulated comprehension. In A. Farstrup & S. Samuels (Eds.), *What research has to say about reading instruction* (pp. 291–309). Newark, NJ: International Reading Association.
Richards, J. C. (1985). *The context of language teaching.* New York, NY: Cambridge University Press.
Schleppegrell, M. J. (2004). *The language of schooling: A functional linguistic perspective.* Mahwah, NJ: Lawrence Erlbaum Associates.
Scrivener, J. (2011). *Learning teaching: The essential guide to English language teaching* (3rd ed.). London, England: Macmillan Education.
Shakespeare, W. (2004). *Romeo and Juliet.* New York, NY: Simon & Schuster.
Short, D., & Echevarría, J. (2016). *Developing academic language with the SIOP model.* Boston, MA: Pearson.
Stahl, M. (2014). A courtroom in the classroom. Retrieved from http://www.read-works.org/passages/courtroom-classroom
Williams, J. (2005). *Teaching writing in second and foreign language classrooms.* Boston, MA: McGraw-Hill.
Wright, W. E. (2015). *Foundations for teaching English language learners: Research, theory, policy, and practice.* Philadelphia, PA: Caslon.
Zeffirelli, F., Hussey, O., Whiting, L., & Shakespeare, W. (1995). *Romeo and Juliet.* Videocassette. Paramount Pictures Corporation, Hollywood, CA.
Zwiers, J., O'Hara, S., & Pritchard, R. (2014). *Common core standards in diverse classrooms: Essential practices for developing academic language and disciplinary literacy.* Portland, MA: Stenhouse.

POST-READING ACTIVITIES

1 Complete this table in a separate document:

LIST THE CHALLENGES ELLS ENCOUNTER FOR EACH OF THE FOLLOWING DOMAINS	LIST STRATEGIES YOU COULD USE TO ADDRESS THE CHALLENGES
Reading	
Writing	
Listening	
Speaking	

2 List at least ten strategies used by strong readers to comprehend text (refer to Table 2.2, "Strategies Used by Good Readers to Comprehend Text," to check your work).

3 Reflect on how you could integrate English Language Arts into all content areas.

CHAPTER 2

READING 2.2 OVERVIEW

This section provides a synopsis of the work of Jim Cummins, who studied and analyzed the characteristics of young people who were exposed to two language environments. The purposes and procedures associated with Cummins's two types of language skills—Basic Interpersonal Communication Skills (BICS) and Cognitive Academic Language Proficiency (CALP)—are explained. In addition, Cummins's four quadrants for instructional support are clearly defined and outlined. Readers will learn that the level of cognitive demand on English Language Learners will vary based on their schema.

PRE-READING ACTIVITIES

1. How do you think students' proficiency in their home language influences learning content in English?
2. How would you describe the difference between basic interpersonal skills and academic language proficiency?
3. What instructional choices could you make to support English Language Learners who are at varying levels of language acquisition and contextual understanding?

TEACHING FOR ENGLISH LANGUAGE DEVELOPMENT

ANETE VÁSQUEZ

This section explains the very practical implications of research in the phenomenon of bilingualism for classroom teachers as it relates to a context where many ELLs are learning English as their second, third, or even fourth language. One very important objective of this section is to help teachers understand how they can positively and purposefully mediate an ELL's language development in English.

A very prevalent concept of academic English that has been advanced and refined over the years is based on the work of Jim Cummins (1979; 1980; 1986; 1992; 2001). Cummins analyzed the characteristics of children growing up in two language environments. He found that the level of language proficiency attained in both languages, regardless of what they may be, has an enormous influence on and implications for an ELL's educational success. One situation that teachers often discover about their ELLs is that they arrived in the United States at an early age or were born in the United States but did not learn English until commencing school. Once they begin attending school, their chances for developing their home language are limited, and this home language is eventually superseded by English. This phenomenon is often referred to as limited bilingualism or subtractive bilingualism. Very often ELLs in this situation do not develop high levels of proficiency in either language. Cummins has found that ELLs with limited bilingual ability are overwhelmingly disadvantaged cognitively and academically from this linguistic condition. However, ELLs who develop language proficiency in at least one of the two languages derive neither benefit nor detriment. Only in ELLs who are able to develop high levels of proficiency in both languages did Cummins find positive cognitive outcomes.

The upshot of this line of research in bilingualism seems counterintuitive for the lay person, but it does conclusively show that, rather than providing ELLs with more English instruction, it is important to provide ELLs with instruction in their home language. By reaching higher levels of proficiency in their first language, an ELL will be able to transfer the cognitive benefits to learn English more effectively.

Of course, we don't live in a perfect world, and it is not always feasible to provide instruction in an ELL's home language, so it behooves all teachers to be cognizant of the types of language development processes that ELLs undergo. Cummins (1981) also posited two different types of English language skills. These he called BICS and CALP. The former, basic interpersonal communication skills (BICS), correspond to the social, everyday language and skills that an ELL develops. BICS is very much context-embedded in that it is always used in real-life situations that have real-world connections for the ELL, for example in the playground, at home, shopping, playing sports, and interacting with friends. Cognitive academic language proficiency (CALP), by contrast, is very different from BICS in that it is abstract, decontextualized, and scholarly in nature. This is the type of language required to succeed at school or in a professional setting. CALP, however, is the type of language that most ELLs have the hardest time mastering exactly because it is not everyday language.

Even after being in the United States for years, an ELL may appear fluent in English but still have significant gaps in their CALP. Teachers can be easily fooled by this phenomenon. What is needed is for teachers in all content areas to pay particular attention to an ELL's development in the subject-specific language of a school discipline. Many researchers (Hakuta et al., 2000) agree that an ELL may easily achieve native-like conversational proficiency within two years, but it may take anywhere between five and ten years for an ELL to reach native-like proficiency in CALP.

Since Cummins's groundbreaking research, there has been a lot of work carried out in the area of academic literacy. An alternative view of what constitutes literacy is provided by Valdez (2000), who supports the notion of *multiple literacies*. Scholars holding this perspective suggest that efforts to teach academic language to ELLs are counterproductive since it comprises multiple dynamic and ever-evolving literacies. In their view, school systems should accept multiple ways of communicating and not marginalize students when they use a variety of English that is not accepted in academic contexts (Zamel & Spack, 1998).

However, one very important fact remains. As it stands now, in order to be successful in a school, all students need to become proficient in academic literacy.

A third view is one that sees academic literacy as a dynamic interrelated process (Scarcella, 2003), one in which cultural, social, and psychological factors play an equally important role. She provides a description of academic English that includes a phonological, lexical (vocabulary), grammatical (syntax, morphology), sociolinguistic, and discourse (rhetorical) component.

Regardless of how one defines academic literacy, many have criticized teacher education programs for failing to train content-area teachers to recognize the language specificity of their own discipline and thus being unable to help their students recognize it and adequately acquire proficiency in it (Bailey et al., 2002; Kern, 2000).

Ragan (2005) provides a simple framework to help teachers better understand the academic language of their content area. He proposes that teachers ask themselves three questions:

- What do you expect ELLs to know after reading a text?
- What language in the text may be difficult for ELLs to understand?
- What specific academic language should be taught?

Another very useful instructional heuristic to consider when creating materials to help ELLs acquire academic literacy was developed by Cummins and is called Cummins' Quadrants. In the quadrants, Cummins (2001) successfully aligns the pedagogical imperative with an ELL's linguistic requirements. The four quadrants represent a sequence of instructional choices that teachers can make based on the degree of contextual support given to an ELL and the degree of cognitive demand placed on an ELL during any given instructional activity. The resulting quadrants are illustrated in Table 2.5.

Table 2.5 **Cummins' quadrants.**

Quadrant I: High context embeddedness, and Low cognitive demand (easiest)	Quadrant III: High context embeddedness, and High cognitive demand
Quadrant II: Low context embeddedness, and Low cognitive demand	Quadrant IV: Low context embeddedness, and High cognitive demand (most difficult)

Quadrant I corresponds to pedagogic activities that require an ELL to use language that is easy to acquire. This may involve everyday social English and strategies that have a high degree of contextual support (i.e. lots of scaffolding, visual clues, and manipulatives to aid understanding, language redundancies, repetitions, and reinforcements) or this may include experiential learning techniques, task-based learning, and already familiarized computer programs. Activities in this quadrant also have a low degree of cognitive demand (i.e. are context embedded). In other words, they are centered on topics that are familiar to the ELL or that the ELL has already mastered and do not require abstract thought in and of themselves.

Quadrant IV corresponds to pedagogic activities that require the ELL to use language that is highly decontextualized, abstract, subject-specific, and/or technical/specialized. Examples of these include lectures, subject-specific texts, and how-to manuals. The topics within this quadrant may be unfamiliar to the ELL and impose a greater cognitive demand on the ELL. Academic language associated with Quadrant IV is difficult for ELLs to internalize because it is usually supported by a very low ratio of context-embedded clues to meaning (low contextual support). At the same time, it is often centered on difficult topics that require abstract thought (high cognitive demand). It is important for the teacher to (1) elaborate language, as well as (2) provide opportunities for the ELL to reflect on, talk through, discuss, and engage with decontextualized oral or written texts. By doing this the teacher provides linguistic scaffolds for the ELL to grasp academically.

Quadrants II and III are pedagogic "go-between" categories. In Quadrant II, the amount of context embeddedness is lessened, and so related development increases the complexity of the language while maintaining a focus on topics that are easy and familiar for the ELL. In Quadrant III, language is again made easier through the escalation of the level of context embeddedness to support and facilitate comprehension. However, Quadrant III instruction allows the teacher to introduce more difficult content-area topics.

When a teacher develops lesson plans and activities that are situated within the framework of Quadrant I and II, the ELL engages in work that is not usually overwhelming. In low-anxiety classrooms, ELLs feel more comfortable to experiment with their language to learn more content. As an ELL moves from level 1 of English language development (preproduction) to level 3 (speech emergence), a teacher may feel that the time is right to progress to creating lesson plans and activities that fit pedagogically into Quadrants III and IV. A gradual progression to Quadrant III reinforces language learning and promotes comprehension of academic content. According to Collier (1995):

> A major problem arising from the failure of educators to understand the implications of these continuums is that ELLs are frequently moved from ESOL classrooms and activities represented by Quadrant I to classrooms represented by Quadrant IV, with little opportunity for transitional language experiences characterized by Quadrants II and III.

> Such a move may well set the stage for school failure. By attending to both language dimensions (level of contextual support and degree of cognitive demand) and planning accordingly, schools and teachers can provide more effective instruction and sounder assistance to second-language learners. (p. 35).

The degree of cognitive demand for any given activity will differ for each ELL, depending on the ELL's prior knowledge of the topic.

REFERENCES

Bailey, A. L., Butler, F. A., Borrego, M., LaFramenta, C., and Ong, C. (2002). Towards a characterization of academic language. *Language Testing Update*, 31: 45–52.

Collier, V. P. (1995). Acquiring a second language for school. *Directions in Language and Education*, 1 (4). Washington, DC: National Clearinghouse for Bilingual Education.

Cummins, J. (1979). Cognitive/academic language proficiency, linguistic interdependence, the optimum age question and some other matters. *Working Papers on Bilingualism*, 19: 121–129.

Cummins, J. (1980). The cross-lingual dimensions of language proficiency: Implications for bilingual education and the optimal age issue. *TESOL Quarterly*, 14 (2): 175–187.

Cummins, J. (1986). Empowering minority students: A framework for intervention. *Harvard Educational Review*, 56 (1): 18–36.

Cummins, J. (1992). Bilingual education and English immersion: The Ramírez report in theoretical perspective. *Bilingual Research Journal*, 16: 91–104.

Cummins, J. (2001). *Negotiating identities: Education for empowerment in a diverse society.* Los Angeles: California Association for Bilingual Education.

Hakuta, K., Butler, Y. G., and Witt, D. (2000). *How long does it take English learners to attain proficiency?* Santa Barbara: University of California Linguistic Research institute Policy Report (2000–2001).

Kern, R. (2000). *Literacy and language teaching.* Oxford: Oxford University Press.

Ragan, A. (2005). Teaching the academic language of textbooks: A preliminary framework for performing a textual analysis. *The ELL Outlook.* Retrieved 13 August, 2007, from www.coursecrafters.com/ELL-Outlook/2005/nov_dec/ELLOutlookITIArticle1.htm.

Scarcella, R. (2003). *Academic English: A conceptual framework.* Technical Report 2003–1. Irvine, CA: University of California Linguistic minority Research institute. Retrieved July 2, 2007, from www.ncela.gwu.edu/res-about/literacy/2_academic.htm.

Valdez, G. (2000). Nonnative English speakers: Language bigotry in English mainstream classes. *Associations of Departments of English Bulletin*, 124 (Winter): 12–17.

Zamel, V. and Spack, R. (1998). *Negotiating academic literacies: Teaching and learning across language and cultures.* Mahwah, NJ: Lawrence Erlbaum.

POST-READING ACTIVITIES

1. What does the acronym BICS represent? What does it assess?
2. What does the acronym CALP represent? What does it assess?
3. Summarize your understanding of Cummins's Quadrants (refer to Table 2.5, "Cummins's Quadrants," to check your work).

CHAPTER 3

ADVANCED ENGLISH LANGUAGE LEARNERS

INTRODUCTION

Student English Language Learners (ELLs) who are also classified as high ability, high potential, or gifted are exceptional learners. This population can present a unique level of challenge for preservice or new teachers. Educators must be able to assess and identify these students so they can provide meaningful and appropriate instructional strategies and learning activities.

The first article provides readers with strategies to teach English Language Arts (ELA) Standards in a manner that celebrates high-ability learners from diverse cultures. The authors discuss how the standards determine outcomes, but that educators determine the most appropriate ways to teach. The authors also provide information on ELLs who are proficient in their native language, possess special skills, and contribute rich cultural perspectives to the learning community. Furthermore, they explain why recognition of the strengths of high-ability ELLs can contribute to the American education system.

The second reading provides a clear and thorough description of the qualities, descriptors, strategies, and actions that should be implemented when working with high-potential

ELLs. Although some students may not have fully developed their basic interpersonal communication skills, the authors suggest that bilingualism may be beneficial in content area learning. Examples are provided to help the reader visualize the effectiveness of the strategies.

The two selected readings are intricately linked because they expose the reader to an exceptional group of learners, identify effective strategies, and discuss the benefits of bilingualism in American schools. Preservice and new teachers will find value in the content of the selections because they will learn how to work with this population in a way that is meaningful, relevant, and productive.

READING 3.1 OVERVIEW

High-ability English Language Learners (ELLs) are an exceptional population.

> The ELA [English Language Arts] Standards provide a support framework for high-ability ELLs that acknowledge their cognitive ability, appreciate cultural diversity, and advance academic and personal satisfaction, rather than presenting an obstacle to be conquered because of students' limited English knowledge and skills. (Phelps 2013, 1)

After reading this article, preservice and new teachers will have a clear understanding of the ELA strands, how to support ELLs with literacy acquisition, how to differentiate instruction to meet the needs of gifted ELLs, and how to celebrate culture through the standards. Readers will also be introduced to ways they can advocate for this exceptional group.

PRE-READING ACTIVITIES

1. List the five strands embedded in each section of the K–5 Common Core State Standards (CCSS).
2. What ideas do you have for differentiating instruction for high-ability ELLs?
3. Reflect on ways that you could advocate for this population of students.

IMPLEMENTING ENGLISH LANGUAGE ARTS STANDARDS TO CELEBRATE HIGH-ABILITY LEARNERS FROM DIVERSE CULTURES

BY DR. CONNIE L. PHELPS

After decades of collaborative work, the National Governors Association and Council of Chief State School Officers released K–12 instructional standards known as the Common Core State Standards (CCSS), intended to develop literacy and college and career readiness when students graduate from high school (NGA & CCSSO, 2010). The English Language Arts (ELA) Standards can present a challenge for high-ability English language learners (ELL). Because the ELA Standards specify only required outcomes, teachers have the flexibility to determine how to implement the standards for linguistically diverse and exceptional needs students who are held to the same expectations as native English language speakers (NGA & CCSSO, 2010). The ELA Standards provide a supportive framework for high-ability ELLs that acknowledge their cognitive ability, appreciate cultural diversity, and advance academic and personal satisfaction, rather than presenting an obstacle to be conquered because of students' limited English knowledge and skills.

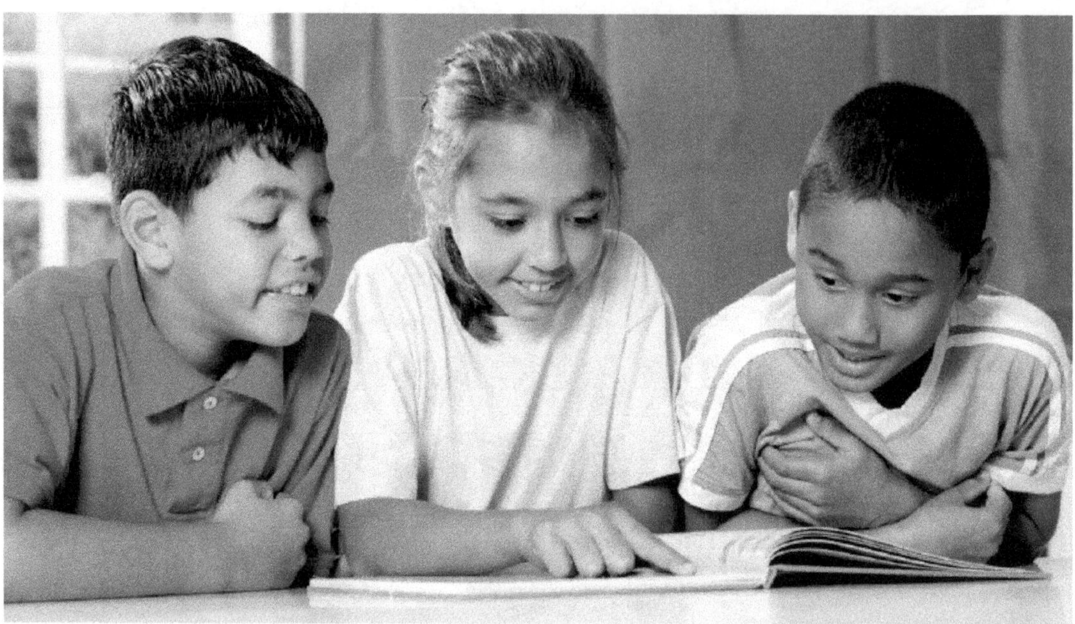

UNDERSTANDING THE ENGLISH LANGUAGE ARTS STANDARDS

Divided into three main sections, ELA Standards are comprehensive for grades K–5, are content-specific for grades 6–12, and include three appendices. Each section addresses reading, writing, speaking, listening, and language strands in grades K–5; College and Career Readiness Standards also anchor the grades 6–12 section (Common Core State Standards Initiative, 2012). Competencies in the ELA Standards require students in grades K–12 to: (a) demonstrate independence to become self-directed learners; (b) build strong content knowledge across a wide range of subjects; (c) adapt communication in response to an audience, task, purpose, and discipline; (d) comprehend as well as critique as listeners and speakers; (e) value evidence to support interpretation of a text; (f) use technology and digital media thoughtfully in language arts; and (g) understand diverse perspectives and cultures that are different than their own (Common Core State Standards Initiative, 2012).

Key design features of the five ELA Strands address reading (text complexity and growth of comprehension); writing (text types, responding to reading and research); speaking and listening (flexible communication and collaboration); and language (conventions, effective use, and vocabulary). The three appendices provide supplementary material on reading, writing, speaking, listening, and language with a glossary of key terms (Appendix A); text exemplars for grade levels with performance tasks

(Appendix B); and annotated samples demonstrating adequate performance at grade levels (Appendix C) (NGA & CC-SSO, 2010). To achieve academically and develop gifts and talents within the framework of the ELA Standards, high-ability ELLs may need assistance from the educational community.

SUPPORTING ENGLISH LANGUAGE LEARNERS IN ELA STANDARDS

Ethnic backgrounds, first language and English language abilities, academic experiences, and socioeconomic status can vary widely for high-ability ELLs. For example, assessment in core subjects may assist ELLs who speak their first language relatively well by identifying the prerequisite knowledge and skills needed to gain proficiency. Because ELLs often speak their first languages proficiently, possess special skills and talents, and contribute rich cultural practices and perspectives, they also need recognition of these strengths and know that they can enrich American schools and society (LaFond, 2012).

High-ability ELLs need assistance from teachers who are prepared, qualified, and eager to work with this exceptional population. Proactive teachers who view the unique abilities and skills of ELLs positively rather than as language barriers to academic success are key in this educational journey. ELLs need school experiences with a variety of language experiences in a literacy-rich environment. Teachers who deliver college and career readiness education through best practices and additional resources that are well-understood to ELLs support their attainment of ELA Standards. These practices include classroom discussion and interaction, ongoing assessment and feedback, and capable English language speakers who model and guide proficiency in ELA Standards (LaFond, 2012).

DIFFERENTIATING ELA STANDARDS FOR HIGH-ABILITY ELLS

Effective practices that differentiate assessment, curriculum, instruction, and environment for high-ability ELLs found in the professional standards of gifted education are also embedded within ELA Standards. Preassessment of high-ability ELLs based on their advanced cognitive functioning is critical when differentiating instruction in ELA Standards. Implementing ELA Standards flexibly rather than with rigid adherence to grade-level expectations balances formal academic learning and differentiated instruction within a contextually supportive environment. Identifying student skills and interests helps by creatively matching reading materials with their background knowledge, preferences, and motivation (Reis, 2009).

For example, master teacher Colleen Mitchell at Village Elementary School in Emporia, KS, found gifted ELLs in her classes possessed excellent social skills, but they lacked English language skills. Attaining ELA Standards is a slow process, as it can take an ELL 5–7 years to attain English language proficiencies. To provide language practice, Colleen arranged for gifted ELLs—and their parents who knew about butterfly migration—to participate as citizen scientists in *Journey North* to track monarch butterfly migration to and from Mexico (Annenberg Learner, 2013). Participants released butterflies and received some from back from other parts of the United States and North America!

Practices that encourage talent development, challenge higher level thinking skills, and modify curriculum by incorporating college and career readiness strategies into individual learning plans for gifted ELLs are recommended practices. Diverse ELL gifted learners need challenging curriculum that acknowledges and demonstrates their above-average abilities and strengths in ELA Standards. Opportunities for accelerated and enriched learning experiences in a stimulating environment support their social and emotional growth, develop leadership potential, and encourage their academic achievement (National Association for Gifted Children [NAGC], 2008). An excellent resource, *Using the Common Core State Standards for English Language Arts With Gifted and Advanced Learners* (VanTassel-Baska, 2013), describes and demonstrates ELA Standards with specific examples and meaningful experiences.

ADVOCATING FOR ACADEMIC SUCCESS WITHIN THE ELA STANDARDS

In addition to understanding ELA Standards, the exceptional needs of ELLs, and differentiating instructional practices, the following recommendations can help parents and educators pave the way toward success as advocates for ELL children:

1. Participate in the school's activities. Take advantage of seminars and other programs offered at school to expand your own knowledge base.

2. Have the ELL advocate for him- or herself. Work with the child to determine how to talk with a teacher respectfully about his or her needs.
3. Ask for help, if necessary, to advocate for an ELL. If language becomes a barrier, find someone who can help communicate effectively with an ELL's teacher.
4. Educate teachers about an ELL's unique needs and cultural heritage. Participate in parent-teacher conferences and other events (Stambaugh & Chandler, 2012).

¡Colorín Colorado! (WETA, 2011) is a bilingual web-based service and educational initiative whose mission is to find research-based best teaching practices to help diverse and exceptional ELLs succeed through reading activities. The name of the web-based service is derived from a playful phrase frequently used to end stories in Spanish-speaking countries. Its equivalent is "that's end of the story" or "they lived happily ever after," which is a wonderful metaphor for the joy found in creating satisfying and memorable cultural experiences through ELA Standards.

CELEBRATING DIVERSE ELL CULTURES THROUGH ELA STANDARDS

The challenge to helping high-ability ELLs gain ELA Standards proficiency requires sensitivity, patience, and commitment. American schools have achieved a rich and diverse cultural history by integrating the language and cultural practices of diverse learners and their families into the richly textured and colorful tapestry of our national heritage (Castellano, 2003). High-ability ELLs need a supportive instructional environment that helps them gradually take the risks needed to practice and perfect English language skills. However, a smile or the beaming face of a high-ability ELL who connects with the English language tells a story without any words: The effort exerted is worthwhile and the intrinsic reward is great.

REFERENCES

Annenberg Learner. (2013). *Monarch butterfly: Journey north.* Retrieved from http://www.learner.org/jnorth/monarch/

Castellano, J. A. (2003). *Special populations in gifted education: Working with diverse gifted learners.* Boston, MA: Pearson.

National Governors Association Center for Best Practices, & Council of Chief State School Officers. (2010). *Common Core State Standards for English Language Arts.* Retrieved from http://www.corestandards.org/the-standards

LaFond, S. (2012). *Common Core and ELLs: An* overview *(Part I).* Retrieved from http://www.corestandards.org/assets/application-for-english-learners.pdf

National Association for Gifted Children. (2008). *Common Core State Standards: Research support for differentiating for gifted and talented students.* Retrieved from http://www.nagc.org/index2.aspx?id=8986

Reis, S. M. (2009). *Joyful reading: Differentiation and enrichment for successful literacy learning.* San Francisco, CA: John Wiley & Sons.

Stambaugh, T., & Chandler, K. L. (2012). *Effective curriculum for underserved gifted students.* Waco, TX: Prufrock Press.

VanTassel-Baska, J. (Ed.). (2013). *Using the Common Core State Standards for English Language Arts with gifted and advanced learners.* Waco, TX: Prufrock Press.

WETA. (2011). *¡Colorín Colorado!* Retrieved from http://www.colorincolorado.org/about

AUTHOR'S NOTE

Connie L. Phelps, Ed.D., directs the gifted special education program, teaches gifted program courses, and supervises gifted practica experiences at Emporia State University. Phelps received her Ed.D. from the University of Arkansas, Fayetteville. She serves as Chair of NAGC's Professional Development Network.

POST-READING ACTIVITIES

1. Write down your current understanding of the ELA Standards.
2. Which practices are recommended for working with diverse ELL gifted learners?
3. List four ways you can advocate for your ELL students.

CHAPTER 3

READING 3.2 OVERVIEW

This journal article provides preservice and new teachers with knowledge that is essential for identifying and working with high-potential English Language Learners (ELLs). The authors present essential qualities, descriptions, strategies, and actions that can be implemented with gifted students from any language background. The strategies presented are beneficial for all linguistically responsive educators.

PRE-READING ACTIVITIES

1. How would you describe sociolinguistic consciousness? Write down your initial thoughts.
2. Describe how you would learn about your high-achieving ELL's language background, experiences, and proficiency levels.
3. Reflect on strategies you could implement to provide an appropriate level of challenge and support to gifted ELLs.

MEETING THE LINGUISTIC NEEDS OF HIGH-POTENTIAL ENGLISH LANGUAGE LEARNERS

WHAT TEACHERS NEED TO KNOW

BY NIELSEN PEREIRA AND LUCIANA C. DE OLIVEIRA

The population of English language learners (ELLs) in general education classrooms has been increasing over the last few decades. However, ELLs are still underrepresented in gifted programs and teachers struggle to provide these students with adequate educational experiences. What do teachers need to know about high-potential ELLs? What research-based strategies can be used with these students regardless of their language background? Teachers need to know the distinction between everyday and academic languages and about English language proficiency levels. There are strategies and tools that linguistically responsive teachers can use in educating high-potential ELLs.

Issues related to the education of high-potential ELLs have been discussed among researchers and policy makers for many years (Bernal, 1974; Marland, 1972). In 1972, the Marland Report highlighted that "highly gifted

Nielsen Pereira and Luciana C. de Oliveira, "Meeting the Linguistic Needs of High-Potential English Language Learners What Teachers Need to Know," *Teaching Exceptional Children*, vol. 47, no. 4, pp. 208-215.

children can be identified in all groups within society" (p. 8). However, many of the issues concerning the education of high-potential ELLs remain unresolved, and finding effective ways to educate these students is an important task that researchers and practitioners in gifted education have yet to fully address. Although much of the emphasis in consideration of high-potential ELLs has been on identification procedures to address underrepresentation (Lohman, Korb, & Lakin, 2008), Callahan (2005) urged educators of the gifted to consider ways to improve and guide the delivery of instruction of gifted students from underrepresented populations. Indeed, providing teachers with the tools they need to deliver quality educational experiences to ELLs once they have been placed in a gifted-and-talented program is paramount. A number of specific strategies have been identified in the literature as essential for teachers to use with ELLs (de Oliveira, 2011; de Oliveira & Shoffner, 2009). These strategies are used to differentiate instruction so that ELLs learn content and the English language simultaneously.

> Outstanding talents are present in children and youth from all cultural groups, across all economic strata, and in all areas of human endeavor. (U.S. Department of Education, 1993, p. 26)

ESSENTIAL KNOWLEDGE FOR TEACHERS OF HIGH-POTENTIAL ELLS

The current federal definition of learners with gifts and talents states,

> [Students who are gifted] give evidence of high achievement capability in areas such as intellectual, creative, artistic or leadership capacity, or in specific academic fields, and who need services or activities not ordinarily provided by the school in order to fully develop those capabilities. (No Child Left Behind Act of 2001 [NCLB], 2002, p. 526)

Previous federal definitions (Marland, 1972; U.S. Department of Education, 1993) included reminders that giftedness is a phenomenon that can be found across all groups within society. Nowhere in these definitions is there a requirement for students with gifts and talents to have minimum levels of English proficiency. However, teachers who may have had very little preparation for working with ELLs may have to redefine or broaden their conceptions of giftedness in order to identify and educate high-potential ELLs. We argue that giftedness can be found in all linguistic groups. Thus, adjusting identification procedures for students with gifts and talents who speak English as a second language is paramount and should continue to be a focus of research. Equally important, however, is to adjust the content and instruction provided in gifted-and-talented programs to meet the needs of high-potential ELLs, whether they have been identified as gifted or not.

DISPROPORTIONATE REPRESENTATION

Students who speak a language other than English at home compose approximately 21% of the population of children ages 5 to 17 years in the United States (U.S. Census Bureau, 2010). The greatest numbers of ELLs are found in southern states, such as California, Florida, and Texas, and in states with heavily populated urban areas, such as Illinois and New York (National Clearinghouse on English Language Acquisition [NCELA], 2010). However, states such as Arkansas, Colorado, Delaware, Georgia, Indiana, Kentucky, North Carolina, Tennessee, and Vermont, to name a few examples, have experienced more than 200% growth in the numbers of ELLs in their schools from 1997 to 2008 (NCELA, 2010). These numbers indicate that the increase in the ELL population is a phenomenon that affects schools across the United States. Despite the increasing percentages of ELLs in schools, they remain underrepresented in gifted programs.

Yoon and Gentry (2009) examined the racial and ethnic representation in gifted programs and concluded that Hispanic students were underrepresented in 43 out of 50 states. Asian and Pacific Islander students were overrepresented in 41 out of 50 states, and White students were moderately overrepresented in 26 out of 50 states. Given that the ELL population in the United States will very likely continue to increase, according to recent immigration numbers (Batalova & McHugh, 2010), finding effective ways to educate high-ability ELLs remains an important task. With the number of such students increasing, there is an expectation of an increase in this group's representation in gifted programs. Thus, although the focus of research has been on methods of identification that work with ELLs, teachers must also be equipped to work with ELLs regardless of their language background. Often ELLs are able to use the English language to communicate with others, but they may not be proficient in academic language usage.

> *Teachers can support ELLs by providing challenging materials that will support their content and English language development simultaneously.*

ACADEMIC LANGUAGE

The academic language of school differs from the everyday language used for communication (Schleppegrell, 2004). The everyday language students use to interact with peers and teachers in social situations was originally conceptualized as "basic interpersonal communication skills" (BICS; Cummins, 1979). The academic language necessary to grasp concepts in the different content areas was originally described as "cognitive academic language proficiency" (CALP; Cummins, 1979). Understanding these differences can allow educators to help ELLs navigate language difficulties they may face in schools. Cummins argued the distinction between BICS and CALP is that the majority of students acquire BICS more rapidly in order to communicate. The majority of this language acquisition occurs informally. Learning the academic language, however, becomes a challenge that most children and youth have to face in school; ELLs face this challenge while also learning a second language for communication purposes. Research has shown that proficiency in oral English takes between 3 and 5 years for ELLs, whereas proficiency in in academic English can take 4 to 7 years (Hakuta, Butler, & Witt, 2000). Providing adequate educational experiences to ELLs includes teaching them the content necessary to perform well in standardized assessments (i.e., CALP) as well as the language they need in everyday communication (i.e., BICS). Learning a second language can be a slow process (Hakuta et al., 2000), and ELLs may struggle with specific content areas if they have not acquired BICS. Therefore, many researchers defend bilingualism as a way to help students learn the content area and develop English as well their first language (Escamilla, Chavez, & Vigil, 2005; Hakuta et al., 2000). High-potential ELLs should receive instruction that allows them to learn English as they learn the same content as other students. Instruction should include advanced educational opportunities. Teachers can support ELLs by providing challenging materials that will support their content and English language development simultaneously. However, teachers should keep in mind a student's level of English proficiency in order to offer educational experiences at adequate levels of challenge.

LEVELS OF LANGUAGE PROFICIENCY

Proficiency levels can provide valuable information to teachers on how to plan for instruction of ELLs. States are required to collect language proficiency data on all kindergarten-through-12th- grade (K-12) students classified as ELLs. The most commonly used instrument is ACCESS (Assessing Comprehension and Communication in English State-to-State; World-Class Instructional Design and Assessment [WIDA],

2014). ACCESS is a large-scale English language proficiency assessment given to K-12 students who have been identified as ELLs. It is given annually in WIDA Consortium member states to monitor students' progress in acquiring academic English. States are required to have academic standards for English language proficiency, and many states use the WIDA academic standards. However, states such as California and New York have developed their own academic standards for English language proficiency and may use different instruments to assess student language proficiency. A student's English proficiency level is most commonly reported as a score, and like most proficiency tests, a certain level of performance is expected of students scoring at different proficiency levels. The Teachers of English for Speakers of Other Languages (TESOL) English Language Proficiency Standards Framework (TESOL, 2006) defines five language proficiency levels with information on students' language performance (see Table 8.1).

Table 3.1 **TESOL Language proficiency levels.**

LEVEL	LANGUAGE PERFORMANCE EXPECTATIONS
Level 1 (starting)	Respond to some simple communication tasks
	Use language to communicate around basic needs
Level 2 (emerging)	Respond to more varied communication tasks
	Use high-frequency and common vocabulary words and expressions in oral or written short sentences but often with errors that impede communication
Level 3 (developing)	Adapt English language skills to meet immediate communication and learning needs
	Use more general and specialized vocabulary and syntax
	Able to communicate with others on familiar matters and to understand and be understood in many basic social situations
	May exhibit many errors of convention that impede communication but retain much of its meaning
Level 4 (expanding)	Able to use English in concrete and abstract situations as a means for learning in academic content areas, although may exhibit minor errors of conventions that do not impede communication
	Understand and use specialized academic vocabulary and expressions and construct sentences with varying linguistic complexity and lengths in oral and written communication
Level 5 (bridging)	Communicate effectively with various audiences and recognize implicit meanings
	Speak, understand, read, write, and comprehend in English without difficulty and use technical academic vocabulary and expressions
	Use sentences with varying linguistic complexity and lengths in extended oral and written communication
	Oral and written language is comparable to English-speaking peers

Note. TESOL = Teachers of English for Speakers of Other Languages. Adapted from "TESOL Pre-K-12 English language proficiency standards framework," by Teachers of English to Speakers of Other Languages, 2006.

High-potential ELLs at Level 1, 2, or 3 of English proficiency may require instructional modifications in order to participate in advanced programs. Students at Level 4 or 5 of English proficiency, however, have acquired a level of English proficiency that allows them to use English in academic settings. Thus, teachers may find it easier to identify potential in these students. Information on the English language proficiency of all ELLs should be available to teachers in order for them to develop appropriate expectations for these students. Proficiency level descriptions provide general information on students' abilities and skills; therefore, it is important for teachers to also get to know each of their individual ELL students' abilities and skills.

LINGUISTICALLY RESPONSIVE TEACHING FOR HIGH-POTENTIAL ELLS

The National Association for Gifted Children (NAGC) *Pre-K-Grade 12 Programming Standards* (NAGC, 2010) include a culturally responsive curriculum as one of the ways educators can respond to the increasingly multicultural nature of schools and gifted programs. Villegas and Lucas (2002) defined basic principles of culturally responsive teaching, including respecting cultural diversity, learning about students' backgrounds, understanding how students learn and promoting student learning, and being capable of advancing equity in schools. More recently, Lucas and Villegas (2011) expanded on the idea of culturally responsive teaching and introduced the term *linguistically responsive teaching*. Linguistically responsive teaching includes respect for and positive attitudes toward linguistic diversity, ability to identify the language demands of classroom discourse and tasks, and application of key principles of second-language learning in the classroom. In Table 3.2, we provide an overview of the qualities, actions, and strategies employed by linguistically responsive teachers (LRTs).

Advocating for greater equity is especially important for ELLs, who can be overlooked for identification for gifted-and-talented programming (Harris, Plucker, Rapp, & Martinez, 2009). LRTs, in contrast, hold high expectations for content learning while providing support students need to understand and use the academic language, which is generally learned from teachers and textbooks. Difficulty with written language may be misinterpreted by some teachers who assume that fluency in spoken language indicates general fluency in the academic language ELLs are developing (Lucas & Villegas, 2011). LRTs, however, understand the need for direct teaching of academic language necessary for ELLs to perform at levels commensurate with their abilities.

Table 3.2 **Qualities, strategies, and actions of linguistically responsive teachers.**

QUALITY	DESCRIPTION	STRATEGIES AND ACTIONS
Sociolinguistic consciousness	Knowledge of how language use and language attitudes are influenced by sociocultural and sociopolitical factors (e.g., race, ethnicity, socioeconomic status, and identity)	Use examples that are relevant to students' culture (s). Encourage students to discuss differences between their own culture and the "dominant" culture.
	Understanding of the connection between language, culture, and identity	Bring books and stories or folktales from students' cultures that have the same themes as those in their reading books. Share important historical events from students' countries of origin.
	Understanding the ineffectiveness of learning English at the expense of leaving one's home language or dialect	Encourage parents and students to use their first language. Ask students to share essential vocabulary in their first language. This might motivate English-speaking students to learn a foreign language.
Value for linguistic diversity	Respect for and interest in diverse students' home languages	Ask ELLs to share essential vocabulary in their first language.
	Providing positive attitudes toward students' languages to encourage them to engage in school learning	Learn and use some vocabulary or key words and phrases in students' first languages.
Learning about ELLs' language backgrounds, experiences, and proficiencies	Differentiation of instruction according to the language proficiency levels of ELLs	Provide ELLs (especially those at Levels 4 and 5 of English proficiency) with opportunities to develop advanced language proficiency. Use instructional strategies presented in Table 3 to adapt instruction for ELLs.
Advocating for ELLs	Actively addressing the learning of ELLs and work to improve their educational experiences (Athanases & de Oliveira, 2011)	Go beyond your own classroom context to ensure ELLs receive equitable opportunities in school. Highlight the potential of ELLs when a deficit view is brought up in meetings or other circumstances.
	Awareness that ELLs can have gifts and talents.	Use information, such as definitions of giftedness highlighting that giftedness exists across all cultural groups, to advocate for the needs of ELLs.

(Continued)

Table 3.2 ***(Continued)***

QUALITY	DESCRIPTION	STRATEGIES AND ACTIONS
Identifying the language demands of classroom discourse and tasks	Identifying the language demands beyond just vocabulary	Identify challenging linguistic forms and functions.
	Providing the background knowledge ELLs need to understand a lesson	Provide additional background during a social studies lesson to a student moving to the United States from another country.
Applying key principles of second-language learning	Conversational language proficiency is fundamentally different from academic language proficiency.	ELLs may be able to use their everyday language to talk about the weather (e.g., "It's nice and sunny today") but may need additional support to discuss climate change (e.g., "Changes in weather pattern may lead to climate changes in a particular region of the globe").
	ELLs need comprehensible input just beyond their current level of competence.	Do not need to simplify instruction; instead, modify it to meet the needs of your students. Keep in mind that high-potential ELLs may learn the English language at a faster pace.
	Social interaction for authentic communicative purposes fosters ELL learning.	Provide opportunities for ELLs to communicate with other students, who can serve as role models of language. Build interactive opportunities among all students (Wong-Fillmore & Snow, 2005).
	Skills and concepts learned in the first language transfer to the second language.	Differentiate instruction by teaching high-potential ELLs more nuanced ways to complete simple tasks. A student who can already tell time in his or her first language can learn new terms and ways of expressing time in English, rather than learning the concept of telling time for the first time.
Scaffolding instruction to promote ELLs' learning	Instructional support essential for ELLs' learning of both academic content and English (or another language) in the school context (Walqui & van Lier, 2010)	Examples of scaffolding include activating prior knowledge, using multimodal materials and various written texts, employing different collaborative learning activities, using extralinguistic supports, supplementing and modifying written text and oral language, and providing clear and explicit instructions.

Note. ELL = English language learner.

These essential qualities of LRTs identified by Lucas and Villegas (2011) describe some orientations, knowledge, and skills that classroom teachers need to develop for teaching ELLs. The framework identifies specific qualities that *all* educators can develop in order to work with ELLs. Table 3.3 provides an overview of instructional strategies that teachers can employ when working specifically with high-potential ELLs, based on the essential qualities of LRTs and previous research on ELLs and their teachers (de Oliveira, 2011; de Oliveira & Pereira, 2008; de Oliveira & Shoffner, 2009; Pereira & Gentry, 2013).

Table 3.3 **Strategies used by linguistically responsive teachers.**

STRATEGY	EXAMPLES
Build language-rich environments	Provide ELLs with opportunities to listen, read, speak, and write in English
	Provide ELLs with opportunities to develop advanced language proficiency
Pay attention to language	Speak clearly—enunciate
	Use steps in giving directions and repeat key points
	Paraphrase
	Pause often
Modify, don't simplify, instruction	Modify how you present information to students, not *what* you present
	Present challenging content
	Ask questions when you present information
	Model the expected performance
Provide opportunities for ELLs to communicate with other students	Plan activities where ELLs can interact with their fluent peers
	Provide role models of language (including bilingual fluent peers)
	Plan heterogeneous groups
Create opportunities for ELLs to understand and process the material	Plan for teacher-directed (in front of classroom) instruction
	Include individual, pair, and group activities
	Plan for reading from textbooks (either with the help from the teacher or as an individual activity)
Use multimodal strategies	Use oral and written language
	Use visual (e.g., pictures, flash cards, graphs, manipulatives) and auditory (e.g., video, music) materials
	Use direct experience (field trips, walks around school)
	Use nonverbal communication (body movements and expressions)
Identify the language demands in texts you assign	Identify what is challenging in the texts you assign—beyond vocabulary
	Identify the background knowledge ELLs need
	Discuss how textbooks are organized
Establish language and content objectives	Consider what you expect ELLs to learn about language and content
Scaffold ELLs' academic language and content learning	Involve ELLs in all classroom activities
	Provide temporary assistance so that ELLs are able to complete a task on their own

STRATEGY	EXAMPLES
Make connections to students' language(s) and culture(s)	Use examples that are relevant to students' culture(s) Use students' home language(s) as resource in the classroom

Note. ELL = English language learner.

Although at first glance some of the strategies in Table 3 may appear to be examples of how to simplify instruction to help ELLs learn the English language or understand directions and the materials, that is not the case. The goal of using these strategies is to differentiate instruction in ways that allow ELLs to learn the content and the English language simultaneously. For example, teachers can facilitate learning by planning for appropriate language models. A teacher working with high-potential ELLs can make sure students learn basic and advanced vocabulary simultaneous to building a language-rich environment. The focus with high-potential students would be on developing advanced language proficiency.

> High-potential ELLs often have the ability to learn a second language at a faster pace but need teachers who will challenge them and provide structured opportunities to develop academic language proficiency.

Providing opportunities for ELLs to interact with fluent English-proficient (FEP) students is also crucial. For example, Level 5 ELLs might be able to help other ELLs who are not as proficient in English by translating directions and content for Level 1 or Level 2 students. However, Level 5 students also need to interact with FEP students who are better models for learning the English language. Those interactions also provide opportunities for high-potential ELLs to be challenged, especially in classrooms in which teachers often need to use simplified language because of students at lower levels of English proficiency.

LRTs plan lessons for ELLs that include language objectives. Those can include teaching how to use different types of discourse or learning vocabulary specific to certain content areas. A math teacher, for instance, can point out the difference between a table (piece of furniture) and a table including numerical values. Teachers should plan to explicitly teach any language aspects that might present challenges to ELLs, such as the organization of the various sections of a textbook or of different types of discourse. High-potential ELLs can benefit greatly from using such strategies as they often have the ability to learn a second language at a faster pace but need teachers who will challenge them and provide structured opportunities to develop academic language proficiency.

CONCLUSION

The information presented should provide practitioners with essential knowledge for teachers of high-potential ELLs and key strategies that work with children of all language backgrounds. Many scholars in the field of gifted education have advocated for differentiating instruction to meet the needs of gifted learners, and that differentiation should be used with all learners (Borland, 2008; Gentry, 2014; Peters, Matthews, McBee, & McCoach, 2014). Teachers should differentiate for ELLs and provide support for continued development of language. The best examples of strategies that work with ELLs are those developed for use in English as a Second Language classes. Understanding language proficiency and the development of academic language can help teachers plan for instruction that is responsive to the needs of high-potential ELLs simultaneous to the provision of advanced work. The same academic rigor should be expected of ELLs with gifts and talents as well as those English-speaking students with gifts and talents. Teachers who use strategies of linguistically responsive teaching are better prepared to help high-potential ELLs succeed in school.

REFERENCES

Athanases, S. Z., & de Oliveira, L. C. (2011). Toward program-wide coherence in preparing teachers to teach and advocate for English language learners. In T. Lucas (Ed.), *Teacher preparation for linguistically diverse classrooms: A resource for teacher educators* (pp. 195–215). New York, NY: Routledge.

Batalova, J., & McHugh, M. (2010). *DREAM vs. reality: An analysis of potential DREAM Act beneficiaries.* Washington, DC: Migration Policy Institute.

Bernal, E. M. (1974). Gifted Mexican-American children: An ethno-scientific perspective. *California Journal of Educational Research, 25,* 261–273.

Borland, J. H. (2008). Identification. In J. A. Plucker & C. M. Callahan (Eds.), *Critical issues and practices in gifted education* (pp. 261–280). Waco. TX: Prufrock Press.

Callahan, C. M. (2005). Identifying gifted students from underrepresented populations. *Theory Into Practice, 44.* 98–104.

Cummins, J. (1979). Cognitive/academic language proficiency, linguistic interdependence, the optimum age question and some other matters. *Working Papers on Bilingualism, 19,* 121–129.

de Oliveira, L. C. (2011). In their shoes: Teachers experience the needs of English language learners through a math simulation. *Multicultural Education, 19*(1), 59–62.

de Oliveira, L. C., & Pereira, N. (2008). "Sink or Swim:" The challenges and needs of teachers of English language learners. *INTESOL Journal, 5*(1), 77–86.

de Oliveira, L. C., & Shoffner, M. (2009). Addressing the needs of English language learners in an English education methods course. *English Education, 42*(1), 91–111.

Escamilla, K., Chavez. L., & Vigil, P. (2005). Rethinking the "gap:" High stakes testing and Spanish-speaking students in Colorado. *Journal of Teacher Education,* 56, 132–144.

Gentry, M. (2014). T*otal school cluster grouping and differentiation: A comprehensive, research-based plan for raising student achievement and improving teacher practices* (2nd ed.). Waco, TX: Prufrock Press.

Hakuta. K., Butler, Y. G., & Witt, D. (2000). *How long does it take English-language learners to attain proficiency?* Berkeley: University of California Linguistic Minority Research Institute. Retrieved from http://escholarship.org/uc/item/13w7m06g

Harris, B., Plucker, J. A., Rapp, K. E., & Martinez, R. S. (2009). Identifying gifted and talented English language learners: A case study. Journal for the Education of the Gifted, 32, 368–442.

Lohman, D. F., Korb, K. A., & Lakin, J. M. (2008). Identifying academically gifted English-language learners using nonverbal tests: A comparison of the Raven, NNAT, and CogAT. *Gifted Child Quarterly, 52,* 275–296.

Lucas. T., & Villegas. A. M. (2011). A framework for preparing linguistically responsive teachers. In T. Lucas (Ed.), *Teacher preparation for linguistically diverse classrooms: A resource for teacher educators* (pp. 55–72). New York. NY: Routledge.

Marland, S. P., Jr. (1972). *Education of the gifted and talented: Report to the Congress of the United States by the U.S. Commissioner of Education and background papers submitted to the U.S. Office of Education.* Washington, DC: Government Printing Office. Retrieved from http://www.eric.ed.gov/PDFS/ ED056243.pdf

National Association for Gifted Children. (2010). *Pre-K-Grade12 gifted programming standards. Retrieved from* http://www.nagc.org/ GiftedEducationStandards.aspx

National Clearinghouse on English Language Acquisition. (2010). *NCELA state Title III information system.* Retrieved from http:// www.ncela.us/t3sis

No Child Left Behind Act of 2001, Pub. L. No. 107–110, 12 115, Stat. 1425 (2002).

Pereira, N., & Gentry, M. (2013). A qualitative inquiry into the experiences of gifted English language learners in midwestern schools. *Journal of Advanced Academics, 24,* 164–194.

Peters, S. J., Matthews, M. S., McBee, M. T., & McCoach, D. B. (2014). *Beyond gifted education: Designing and implementing advanced academic programs.* Waco, TX: Prufrock Press.

Schleppegrell, M. J. (2004). The *language of schooling: A functional linguistics perspective.* Mahwah, NJ: Lawrence Erlbaum.
Teachers of English to Speakers of Other Languages. (2006). *TESOL Pre-K-12 English language proficiency standards framework.* Alexandria, VA: Author.
U.S. Census Bureau. (2010). *Language use.* Retrieved from http://www.census.gov/hhes/socdemo/language/
U.S. Department of Education. (1993). *National excellence: The case for developing America's talent.* Washington, DC: Government Printing Office.
Villegas, A. M., & Lucas, T. (2002). Preparing culturally responsive teachers: Rethinking the curriculum. *Journal of Teacher Education, 53,* 20–32.
Walqui, A., & van Lier, L. (2010). *Scaffolding the academic success of adolescent English language learners: A pedagogy of promise.* San Francisco, CA: WestEd.
Wong-Fillmore, L., & Snow, C. (2005). What teachers need to know about language. In C. T. Adger, C. E. Snow, & D. Christian (Eds.), *What teachers need to know about language* (pp. 7–54). Washington, DC: Center for Applied Linguistics.
World-Class Instructional Design and Assessment. (2014). ACCESS *for ELLs summative assessment.* Retrieved from http://www.wida.us/assessment/ACCESS/
Yoon, S., & Gentry, M. (2009). Racial and ethnic representation in gifted programs: Current status of and implications for gifted Asian American students. *Gifted Child Quarterly, 53,* 121–136.

Nielsen Pereira, *PhD, Assistant Professor of Gifted. Creative, and Talented Studies Department of Educational Studies College of Education, Purdue University.* **Luciana C. de Oliveira.** *PhD. Associate Professor, Department of Teaching and Learning, Teachers College, Columbia University.*

Address correspondence concerning this article to Nielsen Pereira. Purdue University, 100 N. University St, BRNG 5110, West Lafayette, IN 47906
(e-mail: npereira@purdue.edu).

TEACHING Exceptional Children, *Vol. 47, No. 4, pp.* 208–215.

POST-READING ACTIVITIES

1 On a separate document, complete this table using your own words:

QUALITY	DESCRIPTIONS	STRATEGIES
Sociolinguistic consciousness		

2 On a separate document, complete this table using your own words:

QUALITY	DESCRIPTIONS	STRATEGIES
Learning about background, experiences, and proficiencies		

3 Compare effective strategies to ineffective ones and explain the differences.

CHAPTER 4

SOCIOECONOMIC STATUS

INTRODUCTION

Socioeconomic status (SES) is commonly defined as the position of a person in society based on level of education completed, income, and occupation. SES is generally separated into three "classes," although overlap is possible. These three classes include upper, middle, and low socioeconomic status. Two readings are presented in this chapter to explain how capital can influence education; how low SES may negatively affect learners; the characteristics of such learners; and possible solutions for addressing the issue.

The authors of the first reading, "Socioeconomic Status: Its Broad Sweep and Long Reach in Education," present theory, methods, and research to explain how SES is conceptualized in educational institutions. They provide a research base that has its foundational underpinnings in 1966 and continues through the twenty-first century. Strengths and implications of the research are addressed. In addition, a solution to minimize the achievement gap is offered. Caveat: This is a controversial reading and is included in this anthology to prompt rich discussions.

The second reading, "Urban Students in High-Poverty Schools: Information and Support Strategies for Educators," clearly describes the characteristics that this population of students encounter. The authors provide a clear and detailed list of attributes associated with students who live in underprivileged areas. They propose meaningful, research-based intervention strategies to support this population.

Both readings in this section will expose the future educator to the realities of working with students who come from low SES backgrounds. It is essential to understand where students come from, the challenges they may face, and the strategies that teachers can use to support them. The theories, methods, research, and practical ideas presented in the readings provide critical foundational knowledge to the teacher candidate.

READING 4.1 OVERVIEW

The selected chapter from the book *Handbook of Research on Schools, Schooling and Human Development* is titled "Socioeconomic Status: Its Broad Sweep and Long Reach in Education." The research included is focused on thematic perspectives, the influence of socioeconomic status (SES) on student success rates, SES differences among schools, and proposed approaches for minimizing the achievement gap. The authors write about the strengths and weaknesses of prior and current research on this topic. They also emphasize the critical influence preschool can have on student success rates.

PRE-READING ACTIVITIES

1. What do you think is the biggest predictor of student success?
2. In your own words, define the term *socioeconomic stratification.*
3. To what extent do you think attendance at a preschool affects a student's academic achievement?

READING 4.1

SOCIOECONOMIC STATUS

ITS BROAD SWEEP AND LONG REACH IN EDUCATION

BY DORIS R. ENTWISLE, KARL L. ALEXANDER, AND LINDA S. OLSON

Studies of the social inequality *in* schooling or *because* of schooling began with the Coleman Report (Coleman et al., 1966), which responded to Section 402 of the Civil Rights Act of 1964. It said:

> The Commissioner shall conduct a survey and make a report to the President and the Congress ... concerning the lack of availability of equal educational opportunities for individuals by reason of race, color, religion, or national origin in public educational institutions at all levels in the United States, its territories and possessions, and the District of Columbia. (p. iii)

Focusing attention on six racial and ethnic groups, the survey addressed four major questions: (a) the extent of racial and ethnic segregation in public schools; (b) whether the schools offer equal educational opportunities to these groups in terms of school characteristics like library size, teacher characteristics, and so on; (c) how much students of various groups learn as measured by standardized test performance; and (d) whether relationships

Doris R. Entwisle, Karl L. Alexander and Linda S. Olson, "Socioeconomic Status: Its Broad Sweep and Long Reach in Education," *Handbook of Research on Schools, Schooling & Human Development*, ed. Judith L. Meece and Jacquelynne S. Eccles, pp. 237-255.

exist between students' achievement and the kinds of schools they attend. Over 700 pages in length, the Report, dated July 2, 1966, analyzed over 645,504 "instruments returned."

The Report's major conclusion (p. 304) was a bombshell. It announced that the proportion of variance in students' achievement accounted for by "school facilities," like school and teacher characteristics, is "vanishingly small," but large contributions come from "student body characteristics," that is, from students' family backgrounds and related factors; that is, socioeconomic status. This conclusion, so different from what was expected, triggered a shower of reanalyses that culminated several years later in Mosteller and Moynihan's (1972) reaffirmation of the Report's major findings.

Many large studies since the Coleman Report (e.g., Jencks & Phillips, 1998; Lee, 2002) continue to show gaps in achievement favoring richer children over their poorer counterparts, or favoring Whites over Blacks. These gaps, visible even for children in the earliest grades, get larger with age. Because of this "fan spread," even a slight edge in achievement in the early years predicts greater gaps with age (Alexander, Entwisle, & Bedinger, 1994; Alexander, Entwisle, & Dauber, 2003; Consortium for Longitudinal Studies, 1983; Ensminger & Slusarcick, 1992; Entwisle & Hayduk, 1982, 1988; Harnqvist, 1977; Husén & Tuijnman, 1991; Kerckhoff, 1993; Kraus, 1973; Luster & McAdoo, 1996).

No doubt, as we will discuss in more detail later, reasons for this persistence in stratification are multiple. First, the average socioeconomic status (SES) of the school where children begin first grade is probably not much different from the average SES of the school where they finish. Second, parents' plans for their children's education are in place long before high school, and these plans—or the lack of them—tend to reflect parents' own social structural locations. Third, the basic curriculum in reading and reckoning is cumulative, especially in the early years. Starting in first grade, reading and math skills are built up step by step, and doing well one year helps children do well the next, not only because they know more to start with, but also because their doing well leads parents and teachers to hold high expectations for them. In fact, over four decades ago, noting the persistence in children's achievement levels, Bloom (1964) wrote: "All subsequent learning in the school is affected and in large part determined by what the child has learned ... by the end of grade 3" (p. 110; see also Husén, 1969; Kraus, 1973). Still, no national study in the United States has yet directly linked school experience in the primary grades to educational outcomes in young adulthood, although Kerckhoff (1993) shows such long-term ties in Great Britain.

Subsequent to the Coleman Report, and perhaps because of continuing skepticism about its validity, sociologists investigated mainly the organization of high schools, how curriculum tracking relates to inequalities in test scores or years of completed education (e.g., Sewell & Hauser, 1975). The many fewer studies along the same lines in elementary schools focused on ability grouping within classrooms. Most such research in the 1970s, however, dealt with educational achievement as a stepping stone to status attainment; that is, with social stratification more generally (see Sewell & Hauser, 1975). In this tradition, family SES was essentially modeled as a unitary force, as an attribute indicating the quality of the home environment. The mechanism(s) or processes by which its effects on schooling came about, for the most part, were not on the agenda.

Except for the cross-cultural work in "child socialization" and early work in sociolinguistics, other researchers did not pay much attention to SES either. Writing about the survival of people in urban slums from a "cross-cultural perspective," however, Hess (1970) contrasted the life circumstances of the middle class to those of the "lower class" urban poor. He saw aspects of American social structure as significant in the *early* acquisition of behavior, given the extreme contrasts between the lives of the poor and the middle class (see pp. 464–465). He also recognized that middle-class parents have more facility in dealing with ideas and in verbalizing motives and that parents orient children toward roles in society based on their own class position. Moreover, in the laboratory he showed that in teaching their 4-year-old children, welfare mothers employed strategies different from those of professional mothers. Mothers on welfare describe school to their 4-year-old children in terms of the school's authority system rather than, like professional mothers, in terms of the child's problems with learning (Hess & Shipman, 1965). Also, lower status parents teach children to be passive, and their language is directive rather than oriented toward problem solving.

In these same early years, developmental sociolinguists took a different approach, trying to link cultural and regional differences between dialects to differences in children's school success. Early on, some U.S. researchers attributed cognitive deficits to dialect differences. Bernstein's (1967, 1971) group in the UK likewise pointed to "restricted" codes as characteristic of lower-class parents' speech in contrast to the "elaborated" codes characteristic of middle-class parents. Restricted codes were thought to undercut lower-class children's cognitive development (Bernstein, 1967, 1971) in much the same way as dialect differences.

The "dialect" and "code" approaches were soon and soundly rejected, however, especially in the face of Lambert and MacNamara's (1969) brilliant studies. In Montreal, Francophone (lower class) children consistently did poorly in school compared to Anglophone (middle class) children, and language differences were presumed to be at issue. However, when middle-class Anglophone children were schooled entirely in French speaking schools starting in kindergarten, by fourth grade these children did just as well in all school subjects as their counterparts who attended English-speaking schools (Lambert & Tucker, 1972). This work made it clear that the correlates of social class rather than language structure hobble poorer children's learning in school. Around the same time in the United States, research on placebo effects in education, especially the studies directed at teachers' higher expectations for middle-class children, suggested other ways social class effects could be mediated. Rist's (1970) ethnography of a kindergarten class, for instance, describes classroom seating patterns with the poorest (worst-dressed) children seated at a table the most distant from the teacher, and the better-dressed seated successively closer.

THEMATIC PERSPECTIVES

In the 1970s, research on SES and children's schooling was redirected and reformulated by Bourdieu's ideas about "cultural capital" and by Elder's use of life course models. Even when not explicitly referenced, these two advances underlie much of the current U.S. research on SES and schooling.

Pierre Bourdieu (Bourdieu & Passeron, 1977) proposed that social inequalities are maintained through parents' cultural capital. Among many other things, this concept implies that the more parents share the school's standards, the easier it is for parents to help their children do well in school. Cultural capital includes most of what is implied by "taste." It recognizes socially stratified linguistic patterns, like those Hess noted earlier, but embraces much more, such as parents' "savvy" about the workings of schools and society, children's exposure (or lack of it) to "high culture" like classical music and art, and parents' worldviews and outlook as bound up with their social class positions. Like Hess, Bourdieu emphasizes how parents' social roles lead to differences in problem solving strategies and expectations about children's social roles. His ideas underlie a series of insightful studies in sociology (see especially, Lareau, 1996, 2002).

A shift to life course studies, the other major advance, is best represented by Elder's (1974) *Children of the Great Depression*. This particular work and its extensions generally side-step issues of schooling but use social class as a fulcrum to explain not only change in a wide range of outcomes like level of schooling, but also outcomes such as worldviews, marriage timing, and the likelihood of "success" more generally. The book emphasizes how changes in family circumstances brought about by historical events (the Depression) affect human development over the long term. The core assumption of the life course perspective—that developmental processes and outcomes are constantly changing and shaped by the life trajectories children follow—has increasingly directed attention to cultural identities and SES as *bundles* of variables that impact children's life trajectories, including their schooling. Elder was among the earliest to examine the impact of social change on development over the life course and to emphasize plasticity in behaviors and attitudes throughout life (Elder, 1998).

The idea that long-term trajectories are key to understanding educational outcomes is now a dominant theme in school attainment research in the United States (Oakes, 1985; Stevenson, Schiller, & Schneider, 1994). For example, we now know that adolescents more often fail a grade if their mothers are on welfare early in the child's life (Furstenberg, Brooks-Gunn, & Morgan, 1987), or that economically disadvantaged children in first grade are more likely to drop out of school in adolescence (Alexander, Entwisle, & Kabbani, 2003; Ensminger & Slusarcick, 1992; Reynolds, 1992), or that SES in first grade can be a better predictor of status at age 22 than first-grade test scores (Entwisle, Alexander, & Olson, 2005).

The best evidence so far on the benefits of a longitudinal approach to schooling, however, comes from long-term follow-ups of randomized experiments evaluating preschools (e.g., Barnett, 1995; Darlington, Royce, Snipper, Murray, & Lazar, 1980; Lazar & Darlington, 1982) and of participants in the Panel Study of Income Dynamics (Garces, Thomas, & Currie, 2002). Compared to their control-group counterparts without preschool, low-income children who attended the Perry Preschool in the 1960s were less likely to be retained in grade or placed in special education as they progressed up through the grades. They had higher achievement scores at age 14, and their advantage continued into adulthood: they have higher literacy scores at age 19, and by age 27 more of them have high school degrees or a GED (71% versus 54%), more earned at least $2,000 per month (29% versus 7%), more owned their own homes (36% versus 13%), and more had stayed off welfare (41% versus 20%) (Schweinhart, Barnes, & Weikart, 1993). Still, exactly how preschooling or additional income early in life improves children's life chances is hard to specify. The wide range of studies that have begun to tackle these issues are the focus of the next section.

SOCIOECONOMIC STATUS AND THE FAMILY CONTEXT

To review the full range of influences correlated with parents' status and class standing that could affect children's schooling is a much larger task than this chapter can undertake. Our review is necessarily selective, and to start, a few words are needed about "social class."

The terms *social class* or *socioeconomic status* are used almost interchangeably in developmental research. Social class comparisons often involve "middle class," as compared with "working class/blue collar" or "disadvantaged/poverty." "Poverty" implies family income at or below the federal government's poverty line, most often judged by whether children are eligible for subsidized meals at school. The U.S. poverty rate, based solely on money income, is updated annually to reflect changes in the Consumer Price Index and is adjusted for family size. For example, the poverty threshold for a family of four was $8,414 in 1980, $17,029 in 1999 (Table 681, U.S. Census Bureau, 2001). According to the 2007 figures, it is now $20,614 for a family of four (Table 688, U.S. Census Bureau, 2007). Eligibility for subsidized meals at school is either "full" for children in families with incomes equal to 130% or less of the current poverty level, or "partial" for those with incomes from 131% to 180% of poverty level. More generally, "social class" or "SES" can be measured by even one variable, like parent income or education level, or job prestige level, either alone or in some combination. These definitions tend to be specific to each study unless they are based entirely on poverty status (Entwisle & Astone, 1994).

A great deal of effort is currently devoted to specifying the correlates of a child's social class or SES—things other than parent income or education—that could be important for schooling. In this connection note that race/ethnicity and SES overlap: 34% of African American children and 29% of Hispanic children were in the lowest 20% of the population as the 21st century began (Lee & Burkam, 2002).

Most people in the United States have only a fuzzy recognition of status boundaries, perhaps because of the American ethic of egalitarianism. Language, however, signals social status even for persons who will not consciously admit status boundaries, and it defines the character of social relations between people as well. A listener can correctly judge the social class of a speaker from 10 to 15 seconds of recorded speech (Harms, 1961). Teachers use such cues to distinguish middle-class children from children whose families are variously labeled "blue collar," "working class," "disadvantaged," or "poor" (Williams, 1970).

Language differences are not easily ignored even when people try very hard to do so. Such judgments, at a level that may be below a teacher's awareness, *can* bias other judgments. Bikson (1974) showed, for example, that teachers "hear" sentences spoken by Anglo children to be of the same length as sentences spoken by minority group children despite the fact that the sentences spoken by the minority group children are about twice as long as those spoken by Anglo children. Such unconscious biases may lead a teacher to expect one child to learn to read easily and expect another child to have difficulty in learning to read. Such status-linked judgments also can have far-reaching consequences, especially early in a child's school career, because such judgments, even when unconscious, cause a child to sense that he or she is held in low or high esteem. Moreover, social differentiations of speech and of nonverbal cues like body language are primary and ever-present.

THINGS MONEY CAN BUY

Probably the most researched correlate linked to social class is income. Study after study links it and other measures of family economic status to the amount of schooling children obtain (e.g. Elder, 1974; Garfinkel & McLanahan, 1986; Haveman & Wolfe, 1994; McLoyd, 1989, 1990). There is no doubt that family income can predict much of the variance in school outcomes. For example, we know that children living in poverty for at least one year are 6% less likely than those not raised in poverty to graduate from high school (Haveman & Wolfe, 1994). Moreover, the strong relationship between family income and children's school outcomes begins early. Children from advantaged homes arrive at first grade with their verbal and math skills at a higher level than those of children from disadvantaged homes (Huston, 1994; Lee & Burkam, 2002; Smith, 1972; West, Denton, & Germano-Hausken, 2000).

Books, games, computers, family trips to museums, zoos, science centers, historical sites, and sporting events, summer camp attendance and tutoring as well as the purchase of bicycles, musical instruments, and hobby equipment are often mentioned as resources that higher SES families are better able to provide (Heyns, 1978; Saxe, Guberman, & Gearhart, 1987; Schneider & Coleman, 1993; Entwisle & Alexander, 1995), and data are consistent with the coupling of economic resources and these kinds of learning materials in higher SES homes (Entwisle, Alexander, & Olson, 1997). Baltimore children on meal subsidy in 1990, for example, were less likely to have a daily newspaper, magazines, encyclopedias, or an atlas in the home, and also less likely to have a computer than those not on subsidy (38% versus 17%). During the first few grades, children on subsidy were also less likely than those not on subsidy to go to state or city parks, the zoo or science center, fairs or carnivals, or to take trips or vacations. But none of these resources by itself is essential, and in her monograph *Things Money Can't Buy*, Mayer (1997) makes a strong case that income by itself, or material goods that money can buy, is not the main factor explaining the correlation between family income and children's success in school—money does not buy either the material or psychological well-being that children require to succeed. Mayer points out that doubling low income families' income would reduce the dropout rate only from 17.3% to 16.1%, perhaps because things families purchase as their incomes increase—cars, restaurant meals—are not what help children do well. In fact, things that can help children in school, like books and family trips, cost so little that it is the family's "taste" rather than money income that governs family activities. Children's opportunities *are* unequal, but income inequality is not the primary reason. Children do better in school because they have parents who love to do math or to read and who have other *noneconomic* characteristics. Income is a good indicator of family lifestyles, consumption patterns, and cultural or social opportunities, however.

Heyns (1978) earlier saw income as the means through which families express their willingness to commit resources directly to children, and emphasized the importance of cultural activities, independent of family income, for children's schooling.

CORRELATES OF INCOME AND EDUCATION

A substantial body of research now demonstrates the many ways that class-related family resources other than money influence schooling. For example, compared to working-class parents, middle-class parents more often advocate for their children at school (Baker & Stevenson, 1986; Hess, 1970; Lareau, 1987, 1992, 2002; Useem, 1991), and seek out stronger schools and academic programs (Entwisle, Alexander, & Olson, 2006). Middle-class parents also give their children a sense of entitlement, telling them that teachers can be questioned or that school personnel will be helpful (Hess & Shipman, 1965; Lareau, 1987, 2002). Social class provides parents with unequal resources to comply with teachers' requests for parental participation. Thus, even though middle-class and working-class parents tend to have the same educational values, working-class parents are more likely to turn over responsibilities for education to teachers, while middle-class parents see education of their children as a joint enterprise with teachers. Middle-class parents also read more to their children, more often initiate contact with teachers, attend more school events, and consort with other children's parents more often than do working-class parents. In fact, the class position of parents predicts their overall level of school involvement.

Resources in neighborhoods are another dimension of family SES (see Sampson, 1992; Wilson, 1987). Research on neighborhoods and children's schooling so far relates mainly to poverty, often taking the form of qualitative studies of parenting styles that facilitate children's cognitive growth (see Brooks-Gunn, Duncan, & Aber, 1997a, 1997b). For instance, Furstenberg et al. (1999) find that some poor families in Philadelphia who are not able to move to better neighborhoods nevertheless manage to send their adolescents to parochial schools. Even among these highly disadvantaged families, parents with a little more education tend to have more positive social networks and more institutional connections in the neighborhood than those with less education. *Only about one tenth* of the variation in academic competence, even among severely disadvantaged adolescents in Philadelphia, is explained by low family income, welfare dependence, or low parent education. Furstenberg et al. (1999) say "Psychological competence [of parents] is part of the picture, but not as important as social resources that connect the child to the community" (p. 132). Like

Lareau (1987), they emphasize the role of social class in promoting access to other social institutions.

Neighborhoods can also influence children through other means (Entwisle, Alexander, & Olson, 1997). With family SES taken into account, gains that Baltimore children make on achievement tests over summer periods when schools are closed are significantly higher in neighborhoods where poverty rates were lower. Controlling on students' meal subsidy level and parents' education, children's achievement gains in summers correlate positively with the percentage of families above the poverty line in their neighborhoods and inversely with schools' meal subsidy rates. In other words, when the resources provided by the school are cut off, the resources in neighborhoods can in part replace them.

Other recent research brings us back to the importance of class-related features of speech and language, reminiscent of the early work on speech as a signal of social class differences. Lareau (2002) emphasizes parents' use of reasoning rather than directives. Hart and Risley (1995) note that professional parents speak over 2,000 words per hour to their toddlers; this compares to 600 words per hour spoken by parents on welfare to their toddlers. By age 4 a typical child of professionals would have heard 45 million words compared to 13 million for welfare children. Middle-class parents are also more likely than working-class parents to start conversations or to use language in ways that provide entrée to the larger world (see Rothstein, 2004).

Language relates to SES differences in childrearing patterns as well. Working-class toddlers get two reprimands for every expression of encouragement by parents, while toddlers of professionals get an average of six encouragements per reprimand (Hart & Risley, 1995). Similarly, in middle school, parents' use of encouragement and praise predicts favorable track placements (Dornbusch & Glasglow, 1995).

Some of the earlier research is especially revealing about social class differences in how parents teach problem solving, such things as generating and testing hypotheses, willingness to defer solutions, ability to verbalize crucial elements in a problem, and general tolerance of uncertainty. In several studies of verbal interaction between mothers and their children as mothers attempt to guide the children in solving problems, compared to lower-class mothers, middle-class mothers take more actions that will help their children to become successful problem solvers (Bee, Van Egeren, Streissguth, Nyman, & Leckie,1969; Hess & Ship-man, 1965; Rackstraw & Robinson, 1967). Bee et al. note that the middle-class mother allows her child to work at his or her own pace, offering general structuring suggestions on how to search for a problem's solution and telling the child what he or she is doing that is *correct*. The lower-class mother, by contrast, makes more controlling and disapproving comments, and makes more highly specific suggestions that do not emphasize basic problem-solving strategies. In trying to solve problems, positive instances are more helpful than negative instances. When the middle-class mother emphasizes what is correct, she effectively blocks off a number of alternatives whose exploration would be fruitless. Hess and Shipman (1965) also note that lower-class mothers do not permit their children enough time to formulate alternative hypotheses. Middle-class mothers show more tentativeness and see more alternatives to explain behavior. Middle-class mothers are also more receptive and responsive to their children's questions, tend to evade questions less, and to give more accurate and more informative answers (Rackstraw & Robinson, 1967). Middle-class speakers are also more apt to use mitigating forms: "You might want to ... ," "I would do ... ," "Perhaps we should ... ," rather than "Do this" or "Don't do that."

The imprint of status and class standing runs much deeper than parents knowing the ropes of the local school system or their use of language, however. Parents' expectations for their children, which are derived from their own worldviews, correlate strongly with SES and predict the specific actions taken to help children learn. Compared to parents with lower expectations, those who expect their first graders to get high marks read to their children more, see the child's school records more often, ensure that their children borrow books from the library in summer, and take their children on more summer trips (see Entwisle, Alexander, & Olson, 1997, 2000). All these examples differ across social class boundaries (see Lareau, 2002). Moreover, parents who have high expectations encourage their children to have high expectations for themselves (Entwisle & Hayduk, 1982), and children with higher expectations take part more often in class, by raising their hands, for example (Entwisle & Webster, 1972). Parents' expectations are an important source of consistency in children's social contexts. For example, parents' expectations for how far their children will go in school persist: at ages 6 and 13, $r = .49$; at ages 6 and 16, $r = .44$ (Entwisle et al., 1997).

Most of the research covered so far pertains to the home context and early schooling. A natural question is the extent to which SES resources early in life predict outcomes over the long term. The next section reviews some evidence on this question. Much of the evidence comes from the Beginning School Study (BSS), one of the first longitudinal studies to examine the long-term impact of early school experiences.

THE BEGINNING SCHOOL STUDY

Initiated in 1982, the Beginning School Study (BSS) followed 790 students randomly selected from Baltimore public schools, from the beginning of first grade (age 6) up to the present (age 28). Two-thirds of these students were on meal subsidy when their formal schooling began (see Entwisle, Alexander, & Olson, 1997 for a fuller description of the BSS sample and study design).

TIMING OF SES RESOURCES

To estimate the long-term impact of socioeconomic status (SES) early in life on children's ultimate school attainment, information on the BSS panel collected at age 6 (beginning first grade) was used to forecast educational attainment at age 22 for a randomly selected panel of Baltimore students (Entwisle, Alexander, & Olson, 2005). Their model can be represented by one equation (see Figure 4.1 with SES taken as a measure of the social resources available to children as they start first grade). (In this example, SES is a composite of both parents' education level, both parents' occupational status, plus the child's eligibility for meal subsidy.) Other independent predictors in the equation are race, gender, parent psychological support, neighborhood poverty level, the child's temperament/disposition, and two indicators of the child's cognitive skills (a standardized test score composite and a composite of first grade marks in reading and math, see Figure 4.1).[1] This equation states that children's educational attainment by age 22 varies directly in response to the eight variables measured at age 6: race, gender, family SES, neighborhood, parents' psychological support, temperament/disposition, and cognitive skills (Duncan, Brooks-Gunn, Yeung, & Smith, 1998; Entwisle et al., 1997; Furstenberg, Cook, Eccles, Elder,

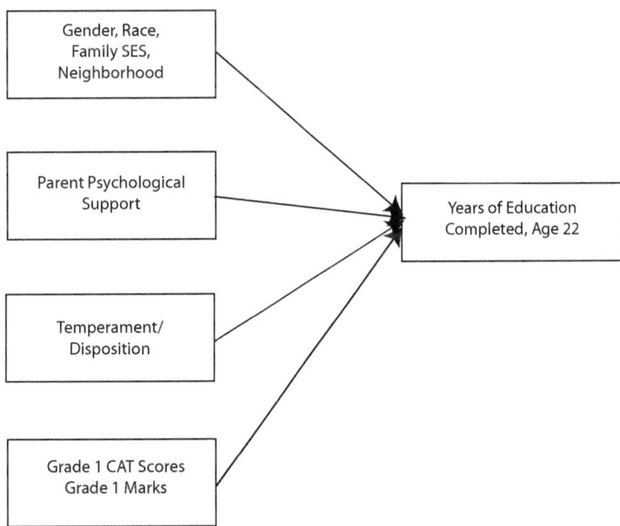

Figure 4.1 Conceptual model of grade 1 predictors of years of education completed at age 22.

& Sameroff, 1999; Hart, Atkins, & Fegley, 2003; Sampson, Morehoff, & Gannon-Rowley, 2002; Wilson, 1996).

Many attainment studies use measures obtained in adolescence to predict educational attainment in adulthood (see e.g., Haveman & Wolfe, 1994), but in the age 6 model described above, effects of predictors measured at age 6 are assessed 16 years later. Assessing the effect of students' individual social resources *before they could have been much affected by the experience of schooling* identifies SES resources present when schooling starts and distinguishes these resources from those produced by the school. Estimating separate effects for SES and parents' psychological support before school begins has the advantage of separating the psychological capital of parents as a resource from their SES as a resource (Entwisle & Alexander, 1996). (Note that the influence of SES is measured *net* of the influence of other variables in the equation, such as test scores.)

When children start first grade their SES, race, gender, and neighborhood are predetermined. Parents' initial expectations for their children's school performance crystallize either prior to or concurrent with entry into first grade (see Entwisle et al., 1997; Entwisle & Hayduk, 1982; Finn & Cox, 1992). Demographics and family resources are known to influence children's development prior to first grade and to predict children's earliest standardized test scores and marks. Children's temperament/disposition also can predict their cognitive status by first grade (see Entwisle et al., 2005).

For the panel of Baltimore students, the model estimates the contribution of students' SES *when they start school* to their educational attainment and level of schooling 16 years later (age 22), controlling for sex, race, and other predictors in the equation. By age 22, about half of the panel had either dropped out or obtained a high school degree, and the rest had gone on to postsecondary schooling, either sub-baccalaureate or 4-year college. By age 22, then, we have a complete picture of the paths children took upon finishing compulsory education and then over the years immediately after leaving high school.

The model in Figure 4.1, estimated by OLS, explains 42% of the variance in educational attainment by age 22. All the age 6 variables (except test scores) *directly* predict years of school completed.

Table 4.1 shows that by age 22, female students have higher educational attainment than their male peers. Also, African Americans are doing better than Whites, and living in a poor neighborhood undercuts schooling (standardized coefficient of -.11). The latter effect is comparable in size to that of every other predictor except family SES. Family SES has by far the largest direct path (standardized coefficient of .40), and so stands out as the most powerful predictor of the amount of education 6-year-olds in this panel attained by age 22.

Table 4.1 **OLS regression model to explain effects of demographic, parental, and personal predictors on educational attainment at age 22.**

	YEARS OF EDUCATION AT AGE 22			
Gender	.10*	.10*	.10*	.10*
Race (African American, White)	.06+	.08*	.09*	.10*
Family SES Index	.42*	.42*	.41*	.40*
Poor/Non-Poor Neighborhood	–.11*	–.11*	–.12*	–.11*
Parent Psychological Support Index	.21*	.14*	.12*	.11*
Temperament/Disposition		.17*	.15*	.13*
Composite CAT Score, Spring 1983			.06	.02
Composite Marks, End Grade 1				.09+
R^2	.39	.42	.42	.42

Note. Standardized Regression Coefficients, $N = 521$. Estimates are weighted to account for attrition in the sample between grade 1 and age 22 (sample attrition is 20%).
+ $p \leq .10$. * $p \leq .05$.

COMPARISON WITH A HIGH SCHOOL MODEL

The next question is whether the size of the SES coefficient estimated with data secured at age 6 is the same as the size of a coefficient estimated with data secured later in life. A highly similar study of high school sophomores' attainment 15 years later (Alexander & Eckland, 1975) shows a much smaller direct effect of SES (.14) and their model explains only a little more variance in attainment (44% versus 42%) than the first-grade model does. One difference between the two models is that Alexander and Eckland include several more predictors, variables like class rank and curricular choices in high school, which can be seen as intermediate outcomes. In fact, much of the influence of SES in the Alexander and Eckland model flows *through* variables like class rank and curricular choices, showing that school processes are an important link between family SES level and ultimate educational attainment. The importance of this comparison of the two models is that we see in the second model how SES is converted into other resources as children go though school. In the high school model, SES even has a *smaller direct path* to educational attainment than do the school-related variables like educational expectations or curriculum.

The difference in the size of direct effect of SES (.40 versus .14), depending on whether data are secured at age 6 or in adolescence, bears directly on questions of model specification raised by Haveman and Wolfe (1994) and Alexander and Cook (1982). The direct path coefficient for SES in the high school model is far smaller than the *total* effect of SES, which is the sum of the *direct path and all the indirect paths*, and these examples suggest why. Much of the influence of SES is converted to other school outcomes like rank in class or curricular choices as children progress through school.

Many different kinds of studies now suggest that supplementing SES resources early in life, even before preschool, is very effective for boosting attainment (e.g., Barnett, 1995; Gomby, Larner, Stevenson, Lewit, & Behrman, 1995). We see why: SES resources present early in life are continuously being converted into other resources, like class standing or achievement, and probably many other things not included in the high school model, perhaps problem-solving strategies, self-confidence, not being held back, and so on.

The two models presented above that compare the direct impact of SES measured at age 6 to its direct impact when measured in high school make a strong case for supplementing children's SES resources as early in life as possible. Students' achievement in high school necessarily reflects SES influence on earlier outcomes.

In what has been said up to here, SES has been taken to signify a measure of *each child's* home context, parents' SES assets, and its correlates. Children's other main social context is the school, and schools *as institutions* respond to the SES of their individual students. Curriculum tracks or "ability" groups, for example, often turn out to be mainly "SES groups." Likewise, a curriculum track labeled "college preparatory" in a low SES school may have little in common with a track by the same name in a high SES school. The next section looks into how students' SES relates to school organization, how schools are organized relative to the average SES of their student bodies.

SES AND WITHIN SCHOOL TRACKS

Following the Coleman Report, sociologists and others concerned with equity in schooling turned, as we said, mainly to studies of curriculum tracking and course taking. The evidence is clear that poor children are disproportionately placed in low ability groups in elementary schools and in non-college-bound tracks in high schools, and further that these placements in lower tracks and ability groups lead to lower achievement and negative attitudes and behaviors (Kao & Thompson, 2003). Moreover, even within tracks, low-income students disproportionately take low level and remedial classes related to low-skill jobs. While tracking practices in high school became less standardized toward the end of the 20th century (Lucas, 1999), they are still much in evidence in the United States.

The large majority of U.S. middle schools also track students (Braddock, 1990), but research on tracking in middle schools is less extensive than that in high schools (e.g., Eccles, Midgley, & Adler, 1984; Eccles, Midgley, Wigfield, et al., 1993; Feldman & Elliott,

1990; Reynolds, 1992). Still, in middle school many students are first aware of formal tracking, a key organizational change for them (Braddock, Wu, & McPartland, 1988; Hoffer, 1992, 1994). Middle school tracks generally have effects like those attributed to high school tracks, in that students in low tracks tend to learn less than those in high tracks (Catsambis, 1992; Fulgini, Eccles, & Barber, 1995; Hallinan, 1992).[2] Whether middle school tracking affects *ultimate* outcomes is not altogether clear except that taking algebra and (usually) a foreign language in middle school are prerequisites for most college tracks in high school. Many low-income or minority group parents, who tend not to have gone to college themselves, are unaware of this critical fork in the road. Often, schools are reluctant to inform parents and students about track placements and their potential effects (Eccles & Harold, 1996). As a consequence then, often low SES parents are not informed or misinformed about tracking.

Despite the generally held view that the United States possesses a more "open" system than does Great Britain, the similarities between middle school choices in the United States and the British 11+ exams is plain (Entwisle, Alexander, & Olson, 2006). All in all, tracking and course taking patterns work to the overall disadvantage of low-income students in high school and middle school. What is not generally recognized, however, is that practices in elementary school not generally seen as "tracking" *are* probably much more harmful for low-income or minority students, and they feed into the middle school tracks. These practices include retention, special education, and ability grouping within classrooms, especially in first grade. Each of these administrative decisions effectively creates a "track" and the evidence is overwhelming that students who are retained, placed in special education, or in low ability groups are of lower SES than children not so placed.

Research *directly* on curriculum tracking, grade-school retention, and special education placement from a school organizational perspective is rare. For this reason, we will draw heavily on the Baltimore Beginning School Study (BSS) in what follows. Much of the information on retention and special education tracking presented here is from Entwisle, Alexander, and Olson (1997) and Alexander, Entwisle, and Dauber (2003).

For the most part, elementary schools have a simple flat plan of organization—a string of self-contained classrooms with individual teachers—so their structure has prompted relatively little sociological research. Nevertheless, because elementary schools reflect the characteristics of the neighborhoods in which they are located, the BSS showed that primary school students were tracked *between* schools by SES (Dauber, Alexander, & Entwisle, 1993; Entwisle & Alexander, 1993). Then, first grade children were held back or placed in special education. Thus, tracks were created *within* schools, but these groupings were not perceived as tracks. Nevertheless, these tracks presented different and lesser curricula, and poor or disadvantaged children were much more likely to occupy these tracks than were better-off children.

GRADE RETENTION

When the Beginning School Study started, there were only rough estimates of the number of children held back (retained) each year in the United States because there were no national data on grade retention until the early 1990s. However, using Census data, Hauser and his colleagues (Hauser, 2001; Hauser, Pager, & Simmons, 2000; Heubert & Hauser, 1999) identified children who are a year or more older than was typical for their grade in school and then focus on patterns of overage enrollments. Combining complex information from several sources, Hauser (2001, p. 160) estimated a cumulative retention rate through middle school (ages 12–14) of about 17 to 18% for children who began school in the late 1980s. For certain children, mainly those of low SES, however, rates were much higher. To give an example, Bianchi (1984), using Census data, estimated retention rates for students in poverty households, where the head is a high school dropout, at about 50% for boys and 40% for girls. Likewise, among National Educational Longitudinal Study (NELS88; Smith-Maddox, 1999) eighth graders in the lowest SES quartile, over 31% were held back versus about 8% of children in the highest quartile (National Center for Education Statistics, 1990). Similarly, by the sixth year of the BSS, among low SES students, 59% of the boys and 43% of the girls had been retained at least once.

Early studies of grade retention also suggested that rates vary inversely with age, with first graders showing the highest rates. For 15 states for which data were available, first grade retention averages over 11%, and retentions are around 7% per year for grades 2 through 6 (Shepard & Smith, 1989). Grade specific rates in the 7 to 8% range for elementary children are consistent with cumulative retention rates on the order of 50% in many areas of the country. Beginning School Study data reflected the same patterns: over 17% of BSS first-graders were held back (23% of low SES students), a rate more than twice that for any later year (see also Fine, 1991).

The causes and consequences of retention are not well understood, mainly because most research on retention ignores children's preretention status even though students who are retained have many problems *before* retention.[3] About 84% of BSS first-graders who were retained were on meal subsidy, compared to 63% of those who were not retained. Also, compared to never-retained, the average reading comprehension scores of first-graders who would be retained later that year were about one standard deviation lower than those of other children when they began first grade. Retainees were more likely than the never retained to come from a one-parent than a two-parent home (58% versus 39%) and their mothers were less likely to have completed high school. Retainees were also absent about 50% more often, less popular with peers, less involved in classroom activity, and less well-behaved in class. The scheduling of BSS children's retentions matched the severity of their difficulties: those with the lowest California Achievement Test scores at the beginning of first grade were held back that year, those with the next lowest scores were held back in their second year, and so on (Alexander et al., 1994; see also Reynolds, 1992; Shepard & Smith, 1989). In the BSS panel, by the end of third grade, 43% of those on subsidy had been retained compared with only 17% of students not on subsidy.

From the perspective of school organization, retention effectively creates a separate school track for multiple reasons and has unintended consequences for children. First, retained children are separated from their age mates, moved away from their peer group. Second, retained children are "off-time" in the rigidly age-graded system of the elementary school, usually permanently. Also, compared to their classmates, grade repeaters are taller, heavier, and have fewer deciduous teeth. For example, the average BSS girl in fourth grade who had been retained once, was 7 pounds heavier (about 10%) than her "on-time" classmates. Additionally, by taking the same grade twice, retained children are exposed to a less advanced curriculum than their age-mates. Because they are often assigned to the lowest reading group before being retained, they are doubly disadvantaged in reading (Alexander, Entwisle, & Legters, 1998). Lastly, retained children often have incomplete school records because they miss testing sessions and move more often. Of four California Achievement Tests routinely involving BSS children in the first 2 years of school, 44% of retainees missed at least one test compared to only 9% of the other children. Missing tests creates gaps in school records that put retained students at a further disadvantage, because these gaps in themselves are a kind of "labeling."

It is also important to point out that higher retention rates allow schools to look better on standardized tests because the least capable students (those who are retained) take easier tests than their age-mates who are promoted. First grade repeaters who would take Grade 2 level tests if they were on time, take Grade 1 achievement tests in their second year of school after they have been retained, for instance. Schools also have a better looking profile on standardized tests when retained students miss tests or their tests are "lost," because then proportionately more low scores are left out of the school average.

To summarize, the Beginning School Study showed that the largest percentage of children who will ever be retained are retained in their first and second years of school. Grade retention effectively placed children in a curriculum track that slowed down their academic development. With no national data on retention at the time, neither the public nor policy analysts appreciated how prevalent early retention was or how misleading evaluations of its effects were, especially for low income students.

SPECIAL EDUCATION PLACEMENT

Special education placement is less common than retention but still far from rare (Heller, 1982; Karweit, 1992; Leinhardt & Pallay, 1982). Following the passage of Public Law 94–142 in 1975, the proportion of children in federally funded special education programs jumped from about 8% of public school students to just under 12% by 1992 to 1993 (U.S. Department of Education 1995, p. 346). In 2003 to 2004, the rate was almost 14%, and children with mild learning handicaps showed the biggest jump between 1976 to 1977 and 2001 to 2002. The proportion of learning disabled rose from 1.8% to 6.0% of the total enrollment in public schools (U.S. Department of Education, 2006).

Children with special learning needs can be placed in separate classes, but the majority are now mainstreamed for all but 1 or 2 hours a day. Even so, special education is a "track" that is obvious to students and to teachers, and the consequences of being placed in special education can be almost as serious as the consequences of retention. Also, most children placed in special education tend to remain there for their school careers (Edgar, Heggelund, & Fisher, 1988; Walker et al., 1988).

From the Beginning School Study, we learned that special education placement was often the next step taken if retention is not effective in getting children up to satisfactory performance levels at the start of elementary school. Of the 42 first-grade retainees who remained in Baltimore schools for at least 8 years, 38 were also in special education for that entire period (Alexander et al., 1994).

MULTIPLE TRACKS

Analysts generally treat retention, special education, and ability-grouping as three isolated events, but ignoring children's placement in multiple tracks could easily disguise or misrepresent the effects of placements. For a child to be in a low reading group, and then retained, is a different experience from being placed only in a low reading group.

The large majority of BSS students (69%) had no low placements in first grade (Entwisle & Alexander, 1993; Alexander & Entwisle, 1996b); however, this percentage varied by SES—39% of low SES students had at least one low placement compared with 29% of higher SES students. Overall, 22% were in the lowest reading group, 16% were held back at year's end, and 13% received special education services. The other side of the coin is that over half (53%) of higher SES students were in the highest reading group compared with only a third (32%) of the low SES students. Also, 21% of low SES students were retained in first grade compared with only 6% of the higher SES group. Of those who experienced any of these placements, over half (60%) had one low placement, but 48% of low SES students compared with only 18% of higher SES students had multiple low placements.

The multiple low placements were in all possible combinations. For example, almost three fourths of children in low first grade reading groups were eventually held back, half of them in first grade. By the end of the sixth grade, 35% of those who had been in low first grade reading groups were retained a second time. In comparison, *none* of the children in high reading groups repeated first grade and 88% did not repeat any grade. Children in low groups in first grade were also more likely than other children to receive special education services later: more than half the children in low reading groups in first grade were receiving special education services in sixth grade, compared to only 6% of children in the high group in first grade (Alexander & Entwisle, 1996b).

Change in reading group level from one grade to the next could signal lack of reliability in initial assignments, because BSS children in both the lowest and highest first grade reading groups were found at *all* second grade reading levels. Just 45% of BSS children remained in the same level of reading group in first and second grade, with 34% predicted to stay in the same group by chance alone. Movement between years is generally downward, however. While 87% of BSS first-graders were in high or middle groups, only 69% of those same children were in high or middle groups in second grade. The lowest group enlarged the most—from 13% to 31%. The downward trend in group placement between years is partly a consequence of the high rate of retention in first grade. That is, when the least successful students are retained, the "low" group in second grade must be filled from the ranks of the children left to choose from (those who are promoted). In this way, a high retention rate has implications for children *not* retained by consigning more of them to lower reading groups in the following years. Altogether, 37% of BSS children were in a low reading group in year one or year two, or both.

Prior to BSS, only a few studies in the United States followed a single cohort of children from first grade up through the later grades (e.g., Ensminger & Slusarcick, 1992; Pedersen, Faucher, & Eaton, 1978; Stroup & Robins, 1972), but all find evidence of long-term consequences of early tracking. *Other things equal*, BSS children's first grade reading group rank predicted their standardized achievement scores in reading and math at least up to the fourth grade (see Pallas, Entwisle, Alexander, & Stluka, 1994). Children's reading group rank had larger effects on their test scores than their reading marks did, and some rank effects on scores also were direct, that is, independent of marks (see Entwisle et al., 1997, p. 90).

The tracks within schools created by retention and special education are especially problematic because these "tracks" are far below the level of public consciousness.

The majority of retention and special education assignments are made early in children's school careers, actually in the first 2 years, when their full significance may not be appreciated. By the end of second grade, for example, roughly one quarter (27%) of BSS children had either been held back or placed in special education. The evidence is now overwhelming that retention is a significant correlate of high school dropout (see e.g., Allensworth & Nagoka … Cairns, Cairns, & Neckerworth, 1989; Ensminger & Slusarcick 1992; Roderick, 1994; Rumberger, 2001).

SCHOOL CALENDARS[4]

Long summer vacations may exacerbate early tracking related to children's socioeconomic status. Results from the Beginning School Study (BSS) also examined growth in children's achievement during the academic year and summer months. Scores that come from tests given at the start and end of the *academic* year (September to June) show that children's annual gains in test scores have two components. Between September and June, children who come from low SES homes gain as much on standardized tests as do children from higher SES homes (Entwisle et al., 1997) …). More specifically, in *winters* over the first 5 years of school, BSS children from low SES homes gained a total of 193 points on CAT tests of verbal comprehension while those from higher SES homes gained about the same amount—191 points. (In math, gains are 186 points for each SES subsample, respectively, over the same five winter periods.) During winter periods when school was in session the low SES and higher SES children thus gained the same amounts on standardized tests. In *summers*, by contrast, the *total* gains in verbal comprehension over the same 5-year period are only 1 point for the low SES but 47 points for the higher SES children (summer math gains total 8 points for low SES and 25 points for higher SES children, respectively). During summers when school is closed, higher SES youth continue to gain in reading and in math but lower SES children do not.

The idea that SES predicts children's learning mainly over the summer when school is closed is not new and has been demonstrated in nationally representative data as well as in localized samples (e.g., see Borman & Boulay, 2004; Downey, von Hippel, & Broh, 2004; Entwisle & Alexander, 1992, 1994; Entwisle, Alexander, & Olson, 1997; Cooper, Borman, & Fairchild … Heyns, 1978; Murnane, 1975). The "summer learning" data show that SES resources have episodic effects. Thus, not only the nature of SES resources but the presence of *other* resources can make a difference in evaluating the impact of SES resources. When school is in session, resources children need for learning are available to everyone, so all children gain. In the summer, however, without the benefit of school resources, low SES students stop gaining. The resources available to them from their homes and neighborhoods are not sufficient to promote their continued growth, while high SES students who have plentiful resources at home continue to gain. This information is important for social and educational policy because it shows that resources from *other* entities like the school can replace resources lacking in the family, at least over the elementary years and earlier, judging from the Perry Preschool and other randomized experiments on preschool. It may be important to work out the boundary conditions on this substitutability. The comparison of the grade 1 and high school models in the last section would argue that high school is a much less optimum time to supplement SES resources than are the preschool years.

SES DIFFERENCES BETWEEN SCHOOLS

Family SES, as we have just seen, predicts track placement and functioning within schools. It also predicts differences between schools. A school's SES—the collective SES of the student body—has as much impact on achievement growth of high school students as does their family SES (Rumberger & Palardy, 2005). We suspect that SES tracking between schools far surpasses within-school tracking as a force affecting schooling.

Elementary schools appear to have the same general structure because the topics covered in their curricula look much the same across grades and across schools. With the exception of grouping within classes, as we have noted, society perceives them as "untracked"—one program fits all. However, the BSS provided considerable evidence showing SES differences between public schools in Baltimore. The elementary schools there and elsewhere (see Kahlenberg, 2006), differ strongly by the average family SES level of their student bodies.

The small size of elementary schools in Baltimore and elsewhere, plus curriculum focused on basic academic skills, helps support the myth that not until middle school does "tracking" begin. Quite the opposite is true, however. In Baltimore, the variation in SES level *between* elementary schools actually outstripped that between secondary schools. In 1990 to 1991, for example, the proportion of Baltimore children participating in the subsidized meal program varied across *all* elementary schools on average from 5% to 100%, but varied only from 8% to 65% across high schools (Baltimore City Public Schools, 1991). This greater SES variation across elementary schools is mainly a consequence of their small catchment areas which differ sharply by family income level. Neighborhoods differ in terms of the SES of the families that inhabit them and therefore the elementary schools within these neighborhoods also differ by SES.

The correspondence between average SES levels of neighborhoods and schools in Baltimore can be seen in data on the average number of students on meal subsidy in a school and measures of neighborhood SES. The rank order correlations in first grade between meal subsidy level of students across schools and neighborhood indicators are as follows: average school subsidy level correlates .86 with median household income of the neighborhood, .66 with percentage of workers in the neighborhood with high status jobs, and .83 with neighborhood poverty level.

BSS students who lived in the better-off neighborhoods began school with higher test scores than students who lived in the poorer neighborhoods. Of the 20 schools randomly selected to participate in the BSS, the school with the fewest (11%) students on meal subsidy enrolled children whose average California Achievement Test score in reading comprehension at the beginning of first grade was 302 and average math concepts score was 316. However, in the school with most students (90%) on meal subsidy, reading scores averaged 265 (37 points lower, about 0.9 SD's) and math scores averaged 273 (43 points lower, about 1.3 SD's). The rank-order correlations between the percentage of first grade students on meal subsidy in the 20 BSS schools and students' average reading and math California Achievement Test scores when they began first grade are .65 in reading and .72 in math.

The achievement test differences across BSS schools when children began first grade enlarged as they progressed up through the grades. By the end of year 5, the difference in standardized test scores between children in the highest and lowest SES schools was 66 points in reading and 48 points in math.

The figures for *all* Baltimore City elementary schools show these same patterns during the period of the Beginning School Study (see Baltimore City Public Schools, 1988). In schools with 50% or fewer students on meal subsidy, children were reading at grade level 3.19 by the end of Grade 2 and at over one year above grade level (7.15) by the end of Grade 5. In schools where 89% or more of students were on subsidy, children were reading at half a year below grade level at the end of Grade 2, and slightly below grade level at the end of grade 5. The gap in reading achievement between the highest and lowest SES schools in Baltimore increased between the end of Grade 2 and Grade 5 from about two-thirds of a grade level to one and one-third grade levels 3 years later.

Other studies also reveal strong patterns of SES stratification across elementary schools. One of the earliest was the Coleman Report (1966) based on a nationwide sample of over 400,000 children, which documented greater school-to-school variability in standardized test scores for children in their elementary years (grades 1, 3, 6) than for children in their secondary years (grades 9 and 12). In fact, variation across schools in reading scores is almost 60% greater at grade 3 than at Grade 12 and in math over 100% greater. Similar stratification by SES characterizes schools in Britain where, as here, primary schools are also much smaller than secondary schools. Teachers' salaries, the proportion of oversize classes, expenditures for fuel and the like, all vary *more* across primary schools than do the equivalent indices across secondary schools (Central Advisory Council for Education, 1967, pp. 618–619).

SOCIOECONOMIC STRATIFICATION AND SCHOOL CONTEXTS

That students' track placement in high school is not simply a consequence of their prior achievement or ability is well-known (Alexander, Cook, & McDill, 1978; Heyns, 1978; Jencks et al., 1972). The perceived single curriculum of the elementary school, however, has tended to conceal tracking between elementary schools. This variation in SES of the student body, not surprisingly, is associated with differences in how elementary schools function, as most parents know. In fact, parents of BSS children used many strategies to get their children into "high SES" schools. In the poorest areas especially, they turned to private (mainly parochial) schools. Similar findings were reported by Furstenberg and colleagues (1999) in Philadelphia. To place children into better schools, some parents resorted to stating that a child was living at one address (perhaps that of an aunt) while actually living at another.

From the Beginning School Study, we learned that this parental concern was justified because not only do the marks teachers give, but also teachers' ratings of children's noncognitive traits, correspond to the SES level of the student body. When first-grade teachers rated BSS students' temperament/disposition, in the school where only 11% of children were on meal subsidy, they rated pupils about one standard deviation higher than did teachers in the school where 90% of children were on subsidy. The rank-order correlation (inverse) between school meal subsidy level and teachers' average ratings of students' temperament/disposition is .71. Moreover, in schools with high percentages of children on subsidy, some children were rated "off the scale," that is, three SDs below their school's mean on temperament/disposition. No student was rated off the scale in the more affluent schools.

The picture involving SES and school functioning becomes more distinct the longer children are in school. Less than half (47%) of BSS children who started first grade in a school where more than 90% of children were on subsidy had reached fifth grade 5 years later because 53% had either been retained or designated to receive special education services. By contrast, 77% of those who started first grade in schools where 50% or less of the children were on subsidy were in fifth grade 5 years later.

Clearly, *where* children started elementary school effectively placed them on a track. Baltimore School Study children of high SES had relatively high test scores as they entered first grade and were grouped together. Children of low SES levels had relatively lower test scores in first grade, and they were grouped together. The same schools then reported the highest and lowest scores at the end of elementary school. For BSS children, correlations are .41 and .55 respectively, between initial California Achievement Test scores in reading and math in the fall of first grade and scores on higher levels of the same tests at the end of elementary school.

The stratified outcomes *later* in the educational pipeline also can be forecast surprisingly well from the stratification patterns visible in elementary school (see also Alexander & Entwisle, 1996b; Kerckhoff, 1993). Baltimore School Study children with the highest test scores at the end of elementary school were more likely to take algebra and a foreign language in middle school, and so to get the needed prerequisites to move into college preparatory programs in high school. Those with low scores at the end of elementary school were not found in these courses (Dauber, Alexander, & Entwisle, 1996). For example, 62% of BSS children placed in the lowest reading group in one first grade classroom took "low level" English in sixth grade. Likewise, 51% of the children retained in first grade are in "low math" in sixth grade.

SOCIOECONOMIC STRATIFICATION AND SCHOOL TRANSITIONS

We discussed earlier the BSS teachers' perceptions of children's noncognitive attributes correlated with the SES level of the school the children attend. This section takes up a different set of issues: the variation in the organizational structure of elementary schools associated with SES of the student body.

Elementary schools (N = 118) in Baltimore in 1982 generally had grade structures that covered five or six grades plus kindergarten and perhaps prekindergarten, but at least 10 other organizational patterns existed (K–3; PK–K; PK–2, PK–3; 3–5, 4–6, 1–5; K–8; PK–8; K–12). One serious problem with nonstandard grade structures is that they require students to make "extra" transitions. For example, children in PK–2 or PK–3 schools had to transfer to another elementary school to complete grades 3, 4, and 5. In Baltimore the elementary schools with nonstandard grade patterns had proportionately more children on subsidy (80% versus 67%), and most of these schools (10 out of 14) were located in the poorest Baltimore City neighborhoods (over 40% of residents in poverty). Making extra school transitions was thus a burden imposed more often upon low than upon higher SES children. School transitions are difficult hurdles for children of all ages (Alexander, Entwisle, & Dauber, 1994; Anderman & Mueller, ...; Eccles, 2004; Hamre & Pianta, ...; Simmons & Blyth, 1987; Vernon-Feagans, Gallagher,

& Kainz, . . .). Among BSS students, retention rates over the first 5 years of school were significantly higher (50% versus 35%) for students who did not stay in the same elementary school throughout the 5-year period (Entwisle et al., 1997).

Another kind of transition is also more common for low than for higher SES youth. Low SES families tend to move often, and these moves often require children to transfer between schools at times that interfere with their schooling (McLanahan & Sandefur, 1994). Nationally, in 1994, among families with annual incomes less than $10,000, 30% had attended three different schools by 3rd grade compared to 10% of children with annual incomes over $25,000 (see Rothstein, 2004). School moves can have other negative consequences. Teachman and colleagues (Teachman, Paasch, & Carver, 1996) reported that *all* of the benefits of attending Catholic schools for youth in the NELS88 sample can be explained by the negative relationship between family moves and attendance at parochial schools.

Baltimore School Study data revealed similar patterns. Of those who made two or more school moves in their elementary years, 88% were on meal subsidy compared to 65% of those who did not move. In addition, these moves were made *within* the school year almost twice as often as in the summer (between school years). In Year 4 of the study, for example, of 92 within-system moves, 57 (62%) were within-year transfers (see Entwisle et al., 1997).

Off-time moves are difficult because children must adjust to a new neighborhood, new school, new teacher, new classmates, and a new physical plant with few or no institutional supports to help. Even orderly transitions like that from elementary to middle school are disruptive and challenging, but because these moves are expected, the school and family are at least partially mobilized to smooth the student's way, with allowances made for need to readjust to new rules and a new curriculum. It is hard for teachers to accommodate students who make unscheduled moves in the middle of the year, however. The curriculum and the pace at which it is covered usually differ from one school to the next (Barr & Dreeben, 1983). Also, new students disrupt the teaching schedule and create a feeling of restlessness and upheaval in the classroom. With many students coming and going all year long, as happens in poverty areas, teachers find it necessary almost continuously to "reteach," "backtrack," and in other ways try to catch up new students to the class (Lash & Kirkpatrick, 1990).

The links between meal subsidy, household moves, and deficits in school performance are clear. Baltimore School Study children who moved two or more times within the system *began* first grade with California Achievement Test scores from 25% to 50% of a standard deviation below those of children who did not move later on. Those who moved the most also started school with other serious problems. Conduct marks at the beginning of first grade for *future* frequent movers (3 or more moves), for example, were low: 45% needed improvement versus 20% of the children who did not move. Even in the first year the frequent movers were absent more (18 days compared to 12), and retention rates over the first 5 years of school were significantly higher (50% versus 35%) for those who moved.

Data on household moves, daunting as they are, still fail to capture the full complexity of poor children's school transitions. The mobility histories of the BSS youth in just one school, where grade structure (PK–3) required that students move after third grade to complete elementary school, show that of the 69 BSS youngsters who started first grade in this school, where the meal subsidy rate was over 90%, less than one-fifth went through their elementary years in a completely orderly way (see Entwisle et al., 1997).

SCHOOL-TO-SCHOOL TRACKS

Kerckhoff's (1993) longitudinal analysis of British schooling shows that SES patterns persist from infant school to points in life well past secondary school (age 23). Little of the research on middle or high school transitions in the United States at this time focused on the ways in which school organizational structures or student SES levels mesh over transitions between schools (Alexander & Entwisle, 1996a; Becker, 1987). Still, when children enter or leave a school, effects of SES tend to be most apparent (see Dauber et al., 1996; Simmons & Blyth, 1987). At the beginning of middle school, for example, the SES background of BSS youth predicted placements in math better than it predicted changes in placements during the middle school years. Why? Probably because higher SES parents were more effective as advocates for their children (Lareau, 1987), and were more aware of the tracking in middle school. Fifth-grade test scores, marks, and retention histories, which all correlate with SES, as well as SES itself, predicted placement decisions for BSS youth at the start of middle school.

An earlier transition into first grade may be even more telling because SES predicts children's cognitive status when they start school (Duncan, Brooks-Gunn, et al., 1998). As we said, children from disadvantaged homes start kindergarten with lower cognitive skills than their better-off counterparts (Lee & Burkam, 2002). They have much smaller vocabularies than children from higher SES homes (Hart & Risley, 1995; U.S. Department of Education, 2003). These deficits put children from low SES families at higher risk for retention in first grade than children from better off families (Alexander, Entwisle, & Dauber, 2003; Reynolds 1992; Shepard & Smith, 1989; Zill, 1996).

Whether tracking effects are cumulative, that is, whether tracks mesh over transitions, cannot be fully addressed with the BSS data, but retention in elementary school predicted remedial placements of BSS students in middle school, and those in remedial tracks learned less than did those in other tracks due to a less demanding curriculum (Entwisle, Alexander, & Olson, 2006). Also, high middle school tracks led to a college track in high school, while remedial tracks were much less likely to do so.

SUMMARY OF LESSONS FROM BSS

To summarize decades of research on the BSS, children's academic histories start long before age 6, and are carried along in more ways than by test scores or marks. The "sorting and selecting" by SES into elementary school tracks or preschools sets the stage for placements that follow (e.g., Alexander, Entwisle, & Dauber, 1994; Ensminger & Slusarcick, 1992; Entwisle & Alexander, 1993; Entwisle, Alexander, & Olson, 1997; Entwisle & Hayduk, 1988; Kerckhoff, 1993; Peterson, DeGracie, & Ayabe, 1987; Stroup & Robins, 1972). First grade track assignments, for example, predict test scores and dropout in middle school (Alexander, Entwisle, & Horsey, 1997; Cairns et al. 1989; Ensminger & Slusarcick, 1992; Lloyd, 1978). Other things equal, low SES children are more often in "low" tracks in elementary school, whether in low ability groups, retention or receiving special education services (Alexander, Entwisle, & Dauber, 1994; Bianchi, 1984; Entwisle & Alexander, 1988). By middle school, family SES was also converted into a tracking advantage: In high SES middle schools, higher family SES increased the odds of BSS students getting into an advanced track rather than a "regular" track by almost 5 to 1, while prior test scores increased the odds by 3 to 1 (Entwisle, Alexander, & Olson, 2006).

The idea of an ongoing envelope surrounding the path of attainment is useful for determining the points at which a trajectory may be modified (see Alexander, Entwisle & Dauber, 2003; Alexander, Entwisle & Horsey, 1997; Kerckhoff, 1993). The channeling force of trajectories is *not* constant over the entire schooling period. Baltimore School Study research suggests that family SES produces more deflections at educational transition points, such as at the beginning of first grade, when middle school begins or ends, or when students apply for college, rather than from year-to-year (Dauber et al., 1996; Entwisle & Alexander, 1993). Altering a trajectory is most effective at the start, however, when children begin school, because initial trajectories tend to persist (Entwisle, Alexander, Cadigan, & Pallas, 1987; Lazar & Darlington, 1982). Also, parents' expectations boost achievement gains more over first grade than later (Duncan et al., 1998; Entwisle, Alexander, & Olson, 1997, 2004; Entwisle & Hayduk, 1982). Schools are highly selective by SES, and in the BSS panel, between-school tracking effects far exceed within-school tracking effects (Entwisle, Alexander, & Olson, 2006).

We need more research on students' and parents' knowledge about SES tracking, especially in the preschool and elementary years. Informed decisions by parents presuppose familiarity with all the options, knowledge of both the short-and long-term consequences of placements, and open lines of communication between parents and schools. However, parents' input into placement decisions is not necessarily "good news" (Gamoran, 1992). Unless knowledge about school differences in program quality is distributed across all families, parent input may actually increase educational inequality (see Baker & Stevenson, 1986; Lareau, 1987).

OUTLOOK FOR THE FUTURE

Research on schools and schooling in the United States has probably overemphasized the importance of individual choices and underemphasized the role of institutional arrangements. Curriculum tracking in high schools may be on the wane (Lucas, 2001) but tracking in preschools and elementary schools is probably accelerating because of the growing inequality in family incomes. Also important is the tendency to gloss over early SES tracking, and to mislabel it as a "retention problem" or as a "minority problem" or "as a school readiness problem."

The American educational system is often perceived as more "open" than the British. Coleman (1993), for example, characterized the U.S. educational system as one with little or no differentiation at any stage, with all children exposed to the same educational environment. Still, we see SES matching of elementary schools with neighborhoods, SES tracking by way of retention and special education in elementary schools, and the strong persistence of educational trajectories starting at age 6. Also, although there are exceptions (see Rosenbaum, 2001), U.S. research on school tracking overlooks possible ways that *early* tracking may affect the substantial fraction of youth not bound for 4-year colleges. The largely buried systems of tracking within and between elementary schools, especially retention, that channel noncollege bound students along separate pathways need to be made more transparent.

Retention in elementary school, far more than academic performance, predicts school dropout (Alexander, Entwisle, & Kabbani, 2001; Cairns et al., 1989; Ensminger & Slusarcick, 1992). It also predicts placement in remedial sections in middle school (Entwisle, Alexander, & Olson, 2006), which is another step toward dropout. Aside from dropouts, 85% of BSS youth in remedial sections in middle school did not go on to *any* form of postsecondary education. In predicting age 22 educational attainment of BSS panel members, retention, middle school tracks, tracking in high school, and SES all proved more important than early test scores. School tracking channels students, opening doors for some, closing doors for others (e.g., Oakes, 1988, 1989–1990). As in Kerckhoff's (1993) study in Great Britain, SES tracking in the BSS panel started at the beginning of elementary school, and persisted across levels of schooling.

From our perspective, patterns of SES tracking are imposed on schools by forces both external and internal to the school. For instance, the test score advantage of higher SES children when they start school, together with the SES clustering of neighborhoods and grade schools, comes from outside the school. Socioeconomic status tracking within schools comes from the high correlation between SES and test scores inside the school. Whether youth are tracked by scores, ability groups, retention, or special education placement, they are tracked by SES as well.

Countering these strong trends, about 40 American school districts now are trying to employ SES as a factor in student assignment (see Kahlenberg, 2006). In LaCrosse, Wisconsin, for instance, no elementary school can have less than 15% or more than 45% of students eligible for meal subsidy. It is important that SES integration can achieve racial integration as a by-product because, as Kahlenberg says, the learning deficits that accompany racial segregation are partly offset by reducing SES segregation (Orfield, 1978). Much of course depends on the details of individual integration plans. Kahlenberg (2006) explains: "Proponents of socioeconomic integration should be under no illusion that conservatives will support such plans as a matter of public policy ... many conservatives do not like plans promoting socioeconomic integration any more than they like policies aimed at racial integration" (p. 4). Our own opinion is that SES integration will lead to higher levels of achievement the earlier it is undertaken, preferably in preschool.

Some commentators forecast declines in social inequality over the 21st century (Gamoran, 2001). The likelihood of this reduction, we think, depends on attenuating the *early* influence of SES on children's preschooling. Debate in the past has centered on whether poverty affects children's schooling through parents' altered norms and "tastes" for nonnormative behavior (e.g., welfare dependence, chronic joblessness, and the like), or whether poverty affects children for structural reasons, through continuing social and economic disadvantage (Tienda, 1991). This dichotomy may be off the mark, however, because the resources schools provide seem sufficient to prompt the same amount of growth in children of *all* SES levels, and sometimes even greater growth by poor children when schools are in session (Downey et al., 2004).

TIMING OF SES RESOURCES

Questions about when in children's lives social resources matter most are not new, nor are they the exclusive province of academics. In 1949, Rogers and Hammerstein put folk wisdom to song in *South Pacific*:

> You've got to be taught
>
> Before it's too late
>
> Before you are six, or seven, or eight.

Still, scientific reassurance about benefits from preschools has been a long time coming, whether from the Perry Preschool Project, the Panel Study of Income Dynamics, or Reynolds's Chicago Study. A majority of children are now enrolled in early childhood programs (in Head Start, preschools, nursery schools, prekindergarten, and other programs). But in these schools, tracking by SES is the rule (see U.S. Department of Education, 2006, Table 2.8). Of the 57% of 3- to 5-year-olds enrolled in early childhood education in 2005, for instance, in all ethnic groups the nonpoor children outnumbered the poor: White 61% versus 45%; Black 68% versus 65%; Hispanic 48% versus 36%. Generally, program quality in preschools tends to correlate with SES (see Currie, 2001).

The lack of preschool facilities for disadvantaged youngsters prior to kindergarten is a major way that tracking by family income takes an early hold upon children from disadvantaged backgrounds. We believe a few extra test points conferred by attending a good preschool could help protect economically disadvantaged children against low placements or retention in the first couple of grades (see Entwisle, 1995), because a number of longitudinal studies show that less advantaged children do profit from preschool (e.g., the Head Start evaluations by Consortium, 1983; Lazar & Darlington, 1982; Reynolds, Wang, & Walberg, 2001). Moreover, a number of randomized studies now confirm that attending preschool away from home helps children before they start first grade (see Barnett, 1995).

Sawhill (1999) estimates that universal preschool would translate into higher academic achievement, higher rates of high school graduation, better health for participants, lower crime rates, and less dependence on welfare, which would save the government $13,000 to $19,000 per child above the cost of sending that child to preschool. The original Head Start programs were exceedingly variable in content, even in the ages of the children they enrolled, but for this very reason the benefits children derived from these programs are strong testimony to the importance of school attendance per se rather than to the details of programs or settings.

To wait until high school to counteract effects of SES segregation is to wait too long. Children start school with positive views of themselves. At age 6 it is hard to measure what would correspond to a child's self-image, but in first grade the academic self-images of BSS students were unrelated to their parents' economic resources. This seeming sturdiness of young children's self-images, however, is soon tested by school organizational patterns. In first grade, children's marks, instructional level, and first grade placements like retention all reflect the SES patterns of their school. More children are held back in schools where children are of low SES, and marks are lower on average, so eventually these low marks and other school evaluations undermine students' self-image. Baltimore School Study children retained in first grade, for instance, had less favorable self-images than nonretained children by middle school (Alexander, Entwisle, & Dauber, 1994).

Society confuses uneven growth trajectories with a reduced ability to grow. Even though BSS children of all SES levels gained the same amount on standardized tests when school was in session, parents and teachers of children in low SES schools held lower expectations for those children. Also, teachers gave those children lower marks than higher SES children, and many more of the lower SES children were held back.

Of the many ways to improve the school climate in poor neighborhoods, we believe the main one is to correct the mistaken public perception that elementary schools are falling down on the job. Children's families and the public at large need to be made aware that the early deficits in test scores of poor children as they start first grade come from the lack of resources *before* first grade. Compelling evidence in Atlanta (Heyns, 1978), Baltimore (Entwisle, Alexander, & Olson, 1997), and nationally (Downey et al., 2004) shows that *when schools are in session* they tend to offset SES differences in test score gains. During the school year, low SES children gain as much from attending elementary school as higher SES children do—schools are counteracting family disadvantage when children are attending school.

How can this be in the face of the evidence reviewed earlier about variation in school quality related to SES? Downey et al. (2004) explain the paradox as follows: Low SES children in "disadvantaged" schools get a bigger boost from attending a low SES school than the boost higher SES children get from attending a high SES school, despite the (probably) poorer quality of the lower SES schools, because of the *extreme* lack of resources in their home environments.

We have come a long way since the Coleman report, if not in improving children's life chances, at least in beginning to understand how SES fits into the picture. Even the timing issue—when SES resources matter most—has been a challenge. The evidence on negative effects of retention and special education placement in the Lazar and Darlington (1982) reanalysis of Head Start evaluations was largely overlooked until recently, as was the evidence showing that in first grade low SES children get more of a boost when school is in session than do high SES children. A key development, now in the wings, is school integration by SES. That trend, plus the emphasis on preschooling, can bode well for the future.

We believe the optimum approach for improving the life chances of disadvantaged children is to provide more preschools. It is rare for a policy decision that involves education to be as firmly grounded in scientific evidence as is the long-term value of preschool *and* its economic efficiency. Investment in preschooling, as we have said, confers benefits far into adulthood. The softer side of this policy, less often noticed, is its potential for increasing children's sense of well-being, and what that could mean for the functioning of schools and families.

AUTHOR NOTE

Preparation of this chapter was supported by the National Science Foundation #SES-0451711, Spencer Foundation #200600005, and a Mellon Fellowship to Doris Entwisle.

NOTES

1 See Entwisle, Alexander, and Olson (2005) for a fuller description of this analysis.

2 See Hoffer (1992, 1994). Overall, grouping by ability does not appear to be an improvement over mixed groupings.

3 See Allensworth and Nagoaka …

4 For additional studies on school calendars and academic achievement, see Harris, Borman, and Fairchild …

REFERENCES

Alexander, K. L., & Cook, M. A. (1982). Curricula and coursework: A surprise ending to a familiar story. *American Sociological Review, 47*, 626–640.

Alexander, K. L., Cook, M. A., & McDill, E. L. (1978). Curriculum tracking and educational stratification. *American Sociological Review, 43*, 47–66.

Alexander, K. L., & Eckland, B. K. (1975). Contextual effects in the high school attainment process. *American Sociological Review, 40*, 402–416.

Alexander, K. L., & Entwisle, D. R. (1996a). Educational tracking during the early years: First grade placements and middle school constraints. In A. C. Kerchoff (Ed.), *Generating social stratification: Toward a new research agenda* (pp. 83–113). Boulder, CO: Westview Press.

Alexander, K. L., & Entwisle, D. R. (1996b). Early schooling and educational inequality: Socioeconomic disparities in children's learning. In J. Clark (Ed.), *James S. Coleman* (pp. 63–79). Hampton, England: Falmer Press.

Alexander, K. L., Entwisle, D. R., & Bedinger, S. D. (1994). When expectations work: Race and socioeconomic differences in school performance. *Social Psychology Quarterly, 57*, 283–299.

Alexander, K. L., Entwisle, D. R., & Dauber, S. L. (1994). *On the success of failure: A reassessment of the effects of retention in the primary grades.* New York: Cambridge University Press.

Alexander, K. L., Entwisle, D. R., & Dauber, S. L. (2003). *On the success of failure: A reassessment of the effects of retention in the primary grades* (2nd ed.). New York: Cambridge University Press.

Alexander, K. L., Entwisle, D. R., & Horsey, C. (1997). From first grade forward: Early foundations of high school dropout. *Sociology of Education, 70*, 87–107.

Alexander, K. L., Entwisle, D. R., & Kabbani, N. (2001). The dropout process in life course perspective: Early risk factors at home and school. *Teachers College Record, 103*, 760–822.

Alexander, K. L., Entwisle, D. R., & Kabbani, N. (2003). Grade retention, social promotion, and "Third Way" alternatives. In A. J. Reynolds, M. C. Wang, & H. J. Walberg (Eds.), *Early childhood programs for a new century* (pp. 197–238). Washington, DC: Child Welfare League of America.

Alexander, K. L., Entwisle, D. R., & Legters, N. (1998, August). *On the multiple faces of first grade tracking.* Paper presented at the annual meeting of the American Sociological Association, San Francisco, CA.

Baker, D. P., & Stevenson, D. L. (1986). Mothers' strategies for children's school achievement: Managing the transition to high school. *Sociology of Education, 59*, 156–166.

Baltimore City Public Schools. (1988). *School profiles: School year 1987–88.* Baltimore, MD: Office of the Superintendent of Public Instruction.

Baltimore City Public Schools. (1991). *Maryland school performance program report, 1991, school system and schools—Baltimore City.* Baltimore, MD: Author.

Barnett, W. S. (1995). Long-term effects of early childhood care and education on disadvantaged children's cognitive development and school success. *The Future of Children, 5*, 25–50.

Barr, R., & Dreeben, R. (1983). *How schools work.* Chicago: University of Chicago Press.

Becker, H. (1987). *Addressing the needs of different groups of early adolescents* (Report No. 16). Baltimore, MD: Johns Hopkins University, Center for Research on Elementary and Middle Schools.

Bee, H., Van Egeren, L. F., Streissguth, A. P., Nyman, B. A., & Leckie, S. (1969). Social class differences in maternal teaching strategies and speech patterns. *Developmental Psychology, 1*, 726–734.

Bernstein, B. (1967). Elaborated and restricted codes: An outline. *International Journal of Applied Linguistics, 33*, 126–133.

Bernstein, B. (1971). A sociolinguistic approach to socialization: With some reference to educability. In J. Gumperz & D. Hymes (Eds.), *Directions in sociolinguistics* (pp. 465–497). New York: Holt, Rinehart & Winston.

Bianchi, S. M. (1984). Children's progress through school: A research note. *Sociology of Education, 57*, 184–192.

Bikson, T. K. (1974). *Minority speech as objectively measured and subjectively evaluated.* Paper presented at the American Psychological Association meeting, New Orleans, LA.

Bloom, B. B. (1964). *Stability and change in human characteristics.* New York: Wiley.

Borman, G. D., & Boulay, M. (2004). *Summer learning: Research, policies, and programs.* Mahwah, NJ: Erlbaum.

Bourdieu, P., & Passeron, J.C. (1977). *Reproduction in education, society, culture.* Beverly Hills, CA: Sage.

Braddock II, J. H., Wu, S. C., & McPartland, J. (1988). *School organization in the middle grades: National variations and effects* (Report No. 24). Baltimore, MD: Johns Hopkins University, Center for Research on Elementary and Middle Schools.

Braddock, J. (1990). Tracking the middle grades: National patterns of grouping for instruction. *Phi Delta Kappan, 71,* 445–449.

Brooks-Gunn, J., Duncan, G., & Aber, J. L. (1997a). *Neighborhood poverty: Context and consequences for children* (Vol. 1). New York: Russell Sage.

Brooks-Gunn, J., Duncan, G., & Aber, J. L. (1997b). *Neighborhood poverty: Context and consequences for children* (Vol. 2). New York: Russell Sage.

Cairns, R. B., Cairns, B. D., & Neckerman, H. J. (1989). Early school dropout: Configurations and determinants. *Child Development, 60,* 1437–1452.

California Achievement Test. (1979). *California achievement tests: Norms tables, level 18, forms C and D.* Monterey, CA: CTB/McGraw Hill.

Catsambis, S. (1992, March). *The many faces of tracking middle school grades: Between- and within-school differentiation of students and resources.* Paper presented at the Society for Research on Adolescence Meeting, Washington, DC.

Central Advisory Council for Education. (1967). *Children and their primary schools.* London: Her Majesty's Stationery Office.

Coleman, J. S. (1993). Foreword. In A. C. Kerckhoff (Ed.), *Diverging pathways: Social structure and career deflections* (pp. xiii–xvii). New York: Cambridge University Press.

Coleman, J. S., Campbell, E. Q., Hobson, C. J., McPartland, J., Mood, A., Weinfeld, F. D., & York, R. L. (1966). *Equality of educational opportunity.* Washington, DC: U.S. Government Printing Office.

Consortium for Longitudinal Studies. (1983). *As the twig is bent: Lasting effects of preschool programs.* Hillsdale, NJ: Erlbaum.

Currie, J. (2001). Early childhood education programs. *Journal of Economic Perspectives, 15,* 213–238.

Darlington, R. B., Royce, J. M., Snipper, A. S., Murray, H. W., & Lazar, I. (1980). Preschool programs and later school competence of children from low-income families. *Science, 208,* 202–204.

Dauber, S. L., Alexander, K. L., & Entwisle, D. R. (1993). Characteristics of retainees and early precursors of retention in grade: Who is held back? *Merrill-Palmer Quarterly, 39,* 326–343.

Dauber, S. L., Alexander, K. L., & Entwisle, D. R. (1996). Tracking and transitions through the middle grades: Channeling educational trajectories. *Sociology of Education, 69,* 290–307.

Dornbusch, S. M., & Glasgow, K. L. (1995). The structural context of family-school relations. In A. Booth & J. F. Dunn (Eds.), *Family-school links* (pp. 35–44). Mahwah, NJ: Erlbaum.

Downey, D. B., Von Hippel, P. T., & Broh, B. (2004). Are schools the great equalizer? Cognitive inequality during the summer months and the school year. *American Sociological Review, 69,* 613–635.

Duncan, G. J., Brooks-Gunn, J., Yeung, W. J., & Smith, J. K. (1998). How much does childhood poverty affect the life chances of children? *American Sociological Review, 63,* 406–423.

Eccles, J. S. (2004). Schools, academic motivation, and stage-environment fit. In R. M. Lerner & L. Steinberg (Eds.), *Handbook of adolescent psychology* (2nd ed., pp. 125–153). New York: Wiley.

Eccles, J. S., & Harold, R. D. (1996). Family investment in children's and adolescents' schooling. In A. Booth & J. F. Dunn (Eds.), *Family school links* (pp. 3–34). Mahwah, NJ: Erlbaum.

Eccles, J. S., Midgley, C., & Adler, T. (1984). Grade-related changes in the school environment: Effects on achievement motivation. In J. G. Nicholls (Ed.), *The development of achievement motivation* (pp. 283–331). Greenwich, CT: JAI Press.

Eccles, J. S., Midgley, C., Wigfield, A., Buchanan, C. M., Reuman, D., Flanagan, C., & MacIver, D. (1993). Development during adolescence: The impact of stage–environment fit on young adolescents' experience in school and families. *American Psychologist, 48*, 90–101.

Edgar, E., Heggelund, M., & Fisher, M. (1988). A longitudinal study of graduates of special education preschools: Educational placement after preschool. *Topics in Early Childhood Special Education, 8*, 61–74.

Elder Jr., G. H. (1974). *Children of the great depression: Social change in life experience.* Chicago: University of Chicago Press.

Elder Jr., G. H. (1998). The life course and human development. In W. Damon & R. M. Lerner (Eds.), *Handbook of child psychology: Vol. 1. Theoretical models of human development* (pp. 939–991). New York: Wiley.

Ensminger, M. E., & Slusarcick, A. L. (1992). Paths to high school graduation or dropout: A longitudinal study of a first-grade cohort. *Sociology of Education, 65*, 95–113.

Entwisle, D. R. (1995). The role of schools in sustaining benefits of early childhood programs. *The Future of Children, 5*, 133–144.

Entwisle, D. R., & Alexander, K. L. (1988). Factors affecting achievement test scores and marks received by Black and White first graders. *The Elementary School Journal, 88*, 449–471.

Entwisle, D. R., & Alexander, K. L. (1992). Summer setback: Race, poverty, school composition, and mathematics achievement in the first two years of school. *American Sociological Review, 57*, 72–84.

Entwisle, D. R., & Alexander, K. L. (1993). Entry into schools: The beginning school transition and educational stratification in the United States. *Annual Review of Sociology, 19*, 401–423.

Entwisle, D. R., & Alexander, K. L. (1994). Winter setback: School racial composition and learning to read. *American Sociological Review, 59*, 446–460.

Entwisle, D. R., & Alexander, K. L. (1995). A parent's economic shadow: Family structure versus family resources as influences on early school achievement. *Journal of Marriage and the Family, 57*, 399–409.

Entwisle, D. R., & Alexander, K. L. (1996). Further comments on seasonal learning. In A. Booth & J. F. Dunn (Eds.), *Family-school links: How do they affect educational outcomes?* (pp. 125–136). Mahwah, NJ: Erlbaum.

Entwisle, D. R., Alexander, K. L., Cadigan, D., & Pallas, A. M. (1987). Kindergarten experience: Cognitive effects or socialization? *American Educational Research Journal, 24*, 337–364.

Entwisle, D. R., Alexander, K. L., & Olson. L. S. (1997). *Children, schools and inequality.* Boulder, CO: Westview Press.

Entwisle, D. R., Alexander, K. L., & Olson. L. S. (2000). Summer learning and home environment. In R. D. Kahlenberg (Ed.), *A notion at risk: Preserving public education as an engine for social mobility* (pp. 9–30). New York: Century Foundation Press.

Entwisle, D. R., Alexander, K. L., & Olson. L. S. (2004). The first grade transition in life course perspective. In J. T. Mortimer & M. J. Shanahan (Eds.), *Handbook of the life course* (pp. 229–250). New York: Kluwer Academic/Plenum.

Entwisle, D. R., Alexander, K. L., & Olson. L. S. (2005). First grade and educational attainment by age 22: A new story. *American Journal of Sociology, 110*, 1458–14502.

Entwisle, D. R., Alexander, K. L., & Olson. L. S. (2006). Educational tracking within and between schools: From first grade through middle school and beyond. In A. Huston & M. Ripke (Eds.), *Developmental contexts in middle childhood* (pp. 173–197). New York: Cambridge University Press.

Entwisle, D. R., & Astone, N. M. (1994). Some practical guidelines for measuring youth's race/ethnicity and socioeconomic status. *Child Development, 65*, 1521–1540.

Entwisle, D. R., & Hayduk, L. A. (1982). *Early schooling: Cognitive and affective outcomes.* Baltimore, MD: Johns Hopkins Press.

Entwisle, D. R., & Hayduk, L. A. (1988). Lasting effects of elementary school. *Sociology of Education, 61*, 147–159.

Entwisle, D. R., & Webster Jr., M. (1972). Raising children's performance expectations. *Social Science Research, 1*, 147–158.

Feldman, S. S., & Elliott, G. R. (1990). *At the threshold: The developing adolescent*. Cambridge, MA: Harvard University Press.

Fine, M. (1991). *Framing dropouts: Notes on the politics of an urban public high school*. Albany, NY: State University of New York Press.

Finn, J. D., & Cox, D. (1992). Participation and withdrawal among fourth-grade pupils. *American Educational Research Journal, 29*, 141–162.

Fulgini, A. J., Eccles, J. S., & Barber, B. L. (1995). The long-term effects of seventh-grade ability grouping in mathematics. *Journal of Early Adolescence, 15*, 58–89.

Furstenberg Jr., F. F., Brooks-Gunn, J., & Morgan, S. P. (1987). *Adolescent mothers in later life*. New York: Cambridge University Press.

Furstenberg Jr., F. F., Cook, T. D., Eccles, J., Elder Jr., G. H., & Sameroff, A. (1999). *Managing to make it*. Chicago: University of Chicago.

Gamoran, A. (1992). The variable effects of high school tracking. *American Sociological Review, 57*, 812–828.

Gamoran, A. (2001). American schooling and educational inequality: A forecast for the 21st century [Special issue]. *Sociology of Education*, 135–153.

Garces, E., Thomas, D., & Currie, J. (2002). Longer-term effects of head start. *Poverty Research News, 6*, 3–5.

Garfinkel, I., & McLanahan, S. S. (1986). *Single mothers and their children: A new American dilemma*. Washington, DC: Urban Institute Press.

Gomby, D. S., Larner, M. B., Stevenson, C. S., Lewit, E. M., & Behrman, R. E. (1995). The long-term outcomes of early childhood programs: Analysis and recommendations. *The Future of Children, 5*, 6–24.

Hallinan, M. T. (1992). The organization of students for instruction in the middle school. *Sociology of Education, 65*, 114–127.

Harms, L. S. (1961). Listener judgments of status cues in speech. *Quarterly Journal of Speech, 47*, 164–168.

Harnqvist, K. (1977). Enduring effects of schooling: A neglected area in educational research. *Educational Researcher, 6*, 5–11.

Hart, B., & Risley, T. R. (1995). *Meaningful differences in the everyday experience of young American children*. Baltimore, MD: Brookes.

Hart, D., Atkins, R., & Fegley, S. (2003). Personality and development in childhood. *Monographs of the Society for Research in Child Development, 68*, 1–108.

Hauser, R. M. (2001). Should we end social promotion? Truth and consequences. In G. Orfield & M. Kornhaber (Eds.), *Raising standards or raising barriers? Inequality and high stakes testing in public education* (pp. 151–178). New York: Century Foundation.

Hauser, R. M., Pager, D. I., & Simmons, S. J. (2000, October). *Race-ethnicity, social background, and grade retention*. Paper presented at the National Invitational Conference "Can Unlike Children Learn Together? Grade Retention, Tracking, and Grouping," Alexandria, VA.

Haveman, R. H., & Wolfe, B. L. (1994). *Succeeding generations: On the effects of investments in children*. New York: Russell Sage Foundation.

Heller, K. A. (1982). Effects of special education placement on educable mentally retarded children. In K. A. Heller, W. H. Holtzman, & S. Messick (Eds.), *Children in special education: A strategy for equity* (pp. 262–299). Washington, DC: National Academy Press.

Hess, R. D. (1970). Social class and ethnic influences on socialization. In P. H. Mussen (Ed.), *Carmichael's manual of child psychology* (pp. 457–558). New York: Wiley.

Hess, R. D., & Shipman, V. C. (1965). Early experience and the socialization of cognitive modes in children. *Child Development, 36*, 869–888.

Heubert, J. P., & Hauser, R. M. (1999). *High stakes: Testing for tracking, promotion, and graduation*. Washington, DC: National Academy Press.

Heyns, B. (1978). *Summer learning and the effects of schooling*. New York: Academic.

Hoffer, T. B. (1992). Middle school ability grouping and student achievement in science and mathematics. *Educational Evaluation and Policy Analysis, 14*, 205–227.

Hoffer, T. B. (1994, August). *Cumulative effects of secondary school tracking on student achievement.* Paper presented at the annual meeting of the American Sociological Association, Los Angeles.
Husén, T. (1969). *Talent, opportunity and career.* Stockholm, Sweden: Almqvist & Wiksell.
Husén, T., & Tuijnman, A. (1991). The contribution of formal schooling to the increase in intellectual capital. *Educational Researcher, 20,* 17–25.
Huston, A. C. (1994). Children in poverty: Designing research to affect policy. *Social Policy Report, Society for Research in Child Development, 8,* 1–12.
Jencks, C., & Phillips, M. (1998). The Black–White test score gap: An introduction. In C. Jencks & M. Phillips (Eds.), *The Black–White test score gap* (pp. 1–54). Washington, DC: Brookings Institution Press.
Jencks, C., Smith, M., Ackland, H., Bane, M. J., Cohen, D., Gintis, H., et al. (1972). *Inequality: A reassessment of the effect of failure and schooling in America.* New York: Basic Books.
Kahlenberg, R. D. (2006). *A new way on school integration.* New York: Century Foundation Press.
Kao, G., & Thompson, J. S. (2003). Racial and ethnic stratification in educational achievement and attainment. In K. Cook & J. Hagen (Eds.), *Annual review of sociology* (Vol. 29, pp. 417–442). Palo Alto, CA: Annual Reviews.
Karweit, N. (1992). Retention policy. In M. Alkin (Ed.), *Encyclopedia of educational research* (pp. 1114–1118). New York: Macmillan.
Kerckhoff, A. C. (1993). *Diverging pathways: Social structure and career deflections.* New York: Cambridge Press.
Kraus, P. E. (1973). *Yesterday's children.* New York: Wiley.
Lambert, W. E., & MacNamara, J. (1969). Some cognitive consequences of following a first-grade curriculum in a second language. *Journal of Educational Psychology, 60,* 86–96.
Lambert, W. E., & Tucker, G. R. (1972). *The St. Lambert program of home-school language switch, grades K through five.* Montreal, Canada: McGill University.
Lareau, A. (1987). Social class differences in family-school relationships: The importance of cultural capital. *Sociology of Education, 60,* 73–85.
Lareau, A. (1992). Gender differences in parent involvement in schooling. In J. Wrigley (Ed.), *Education and gender equality* (pp. 207–224). London: Falmer Press.
Lareau, A. (1996). Assessing parent involvement in schooling: A critical analysis. In A. Booth & J. F. Dunn (Eds.), *Family school links* (pp. 57–64). Mahwah, NJ: Erlbaum.
Lareau, A. (2002). Invisible inequality: Social class and child rearing in Black families and White families. *American Sociological Review, 67,* 747–776.
Lash, A. A., & Kirkpatrick, S. L. (1990). A classroom perspective on student mobility. *Elementary School Journal, 91,* 171–191.
Lazar, I., & Darlington, R. (1982). Lasting effects of early education: A report from the Consortium for Longitudinal Studies. *Monographs of the Society for Research in Child Development, 47,* ix–139.
Lee, J. (2002). Racial and ethnic achievement gap trends: Revising the progress toward equity. *Educational Researcher, 31,* 3–12.
Lee, V., & Burkam, D. T. (2002). *Inequality at the starting gate: Social background differences in achievement as children begin school.* Washington, DC: Economic Policy Institute.
Leinhardt, G., & Pallay, A. (1982). Restrictive educational settings: Exile or haven? *Review of Educational Research, 54,* 557–578.
Lloyd, D. N. (1978). Prediction of school failure from third-grade data. *Educational and Psychological Measurement, 38,* 1193–1200.
Lucas, S. R. (2001). Effectively maintained inequality: Education transitions, track mobility, and social background effects. *American Journal of Sociology, 106,* 1642–1690.
Lucas, S. R. (1999). *Tracking inequality: Stratification and mobility in American high schools.* New York: Teachers College Press.
Luster, T., & McAdoo, H. (1996). Family and child influences on educational attainment: A secondary analysis of the High/Scope Perry preschool data. *Developmental Psychology, 32,* 26–39.
Mayer, S. E. (1997). *What money can't buy: Family income and children's life chances.* Cambridge, MA: Harvard University Press.

McLanahan, S. S., & Sandefur, G. (1994). *Growing up with a single parent: What hurts, what helps.* Cambridge, MA: Harvard University Press.

McLoyd, V. (1989). Socialization and development in a changing economy: The effects of paternal income and job loss on children. *American Psychologist, 44,* 293–302.

McLoyd, V. C. (1990). The impact of economic hardship on Black families and children: Psychological distress parenting, and socioemotional development. *Child Development, 61,* 311–346.

Mosteller, F., & Moynihan, D. P. (1972). *On equality of educational opportunity.* New York: Vintage.

Murnane, R. J. (1975). *The impact of school resources on the learning of inner city children.* Cambridge, MA: Ballinger.

National Center for Education Statistics. (1990). *Dropout rates in the United States: 1989.* (NCES 90-659). Washington, DC: U.S. Department of Education, Office of Educational Research and Improvement.

Oakes, J. (1985). *Keeping track: How schools structure inequality.* New Haven, CT: Yale University Press.

Oakes, J. (1988). Tracking in mathematics and science education: A structural contribution to unequal schooling. In L. Weis (Ed.), *Class, race and gender in American education* (pp. 106–125). Albany, NY: SUNY Press.

Oakes, J. (1989–1990). Opportunities, achievement and choice: Women and minority students in science and mathematics. *Review of Research in Education, 16,* 153–222.

Orfield, G. (1978). *Must we bus? Segregated schools and national policy.* Washington, DC: Brookings Institution Press.

Pallas, A. M., Entwisle, D. R., Alexander, K. L., & Stluka, M. F. (1994). Ability-group effects: Instructional, social or institutional? *Sociology of Education, 67,* 27–46.

Pedersen, E., Faucher, T. A., & Eaton, W. W. (1978). A new perspective on the effects of first-grade teachers on children's subsequent adult status. *Harvard Educational Review, 48,* 1–31.

Peterson, S. E., DeGracie, J. S., & Ayabe, C. R. (1987). A longitudinal study of the effects of retention/promotion on academic achievement. *American Educational Research Journal, 27,* 107–118.

Rackstraw, S. J., & Robinson, W. P. (1967). Social and psychological factors related to variability of answering behavior in five-year-old children. *Language and Speech, 10,* 88–106.

Reynolds, A. J. (1992). Grade retention and school adjustment: An explanatory analysis. *Educational Evaluation and Policy Analysis, 14,* 101–121.

Reynolds, A. J., Wang, M. C., & Walberg, H. J. (2001). *Early childhood programs for a new century.* Washington, DC: Child Welfare League of America, Inc.

Rist, R. (1970). Student social class and teacher expectations: The self-fulfilling prophecy in ghetto education. *Harvard Educational Review, 40,* 411–451.

Roderick, M. (1994). Grade retention and school dropout: Investigating the association. *American Educational Research Journal, 31,* 729–759.

Rosenbaum, J. (2001). *Beyond college for all: Career paths for the forgotten half.* New York: Russell Sage Foundation.

Rothstein, R. (2004). *Class and schools.* Washington, DC: Economic Policy Institute.

Rumberger, R. W. (2001, January). *Why students drop out of school and what can be done.* Paper prepared for the Civil Rights Project at Harvard University's Graduate School of Education and Achieve. Cambridge, MA.

Rumberger, R. W., & Palardy, G. J. (2005). Does segregation still matter? The impact of student composition on academic achievement in high school. *Teachers College Record, 107,* 1999–2045.

Sampson, R. J. (1992). Family management and child development: Insights from social disorganization theory. In J. McCord (Ed.), *Advances in criminology theory: Vol 3. Fact, frameworks, and forecasts* (pp. 63–93). New Brunswick, NJ: Transaction.

Sampson, R. J., Morenoff, J. D., & Gannon-Rowley, T. (2002). Assessing "neighborhood effects": Social processes and new directions in research. *Annual Review of Sociology, 28,* 443–478.

Sawhill, I. (1999). Kids need an early start: Universal preschool education may be the best investment Americans can make in our children's education–and our nation's future. *Blueprint Magazine,* (Fall) 37–39.

Saxe, G. B., Guberman, S. R., & Gearheart, M. (1987). Social processes in early number development (Serial No. 216). *Monographs Social Research Child Development.* Malden, MA: Blackwell.

Schneider, B. L., & Coleman, J. S. (1993). *Parents, their children, and schools.* Boulder, CO: Westview.

Schweinhart, L. J., Barnes, H. V., & Weikart, D. P. (1993). *Significant benefits: The High Scope/Perry preschool study through age 17.* Ypsilanti, MI: High Scope Educational Research Foundation.

Sewell, W. H., & Hauser, R. M. (1975). *Education, occupation, and earnings.* New York: Academic.

Shepard, L. A., & Smith, M. L. (1989). *Flunking grades: Research and policies on retention.* London: Falmer Press.

Simmons, R. G., & Blyth, D. A. (1987). *Moving into adolescence: The impact of pubertal change and school context.* Hawthorn, NY: Aldine de Gruyter.

Smith, M. S. (1972). Equality of educational opportunity: The basic findings reconsidered. In F. Mosteller & D. Moynihan (Eds.), *On equality of educational opportunity* (pp. 230–342). New York: Vintage Books.

Smith-Maddox, R. (1999). The social networks and resources of African American eighth graders: Evidence from the National Educational Longitudinal Study of 1988. *Adolescence, 34*(133), 169–183.

Stevenson, D. L., Schiller, K. S., & Schneider, B. (1994). Sequences of opportunities for learning. *Sociology of Education, 67*, 184–198.

Stroup, A. L., & Robins. L. N. (1972). Elementary school predictors of high school dropout among black males. *Sociology of Education, 45*, 212–222.

Teachman, J. D., Paasch, K., & Carver, K. (1996). Social capital and dropping out of school early. *Journal of Marriage and the Family, 58*, 773–783.

Tienda, M. (1991). Poor people and poor places: Deciphering neighborhood effects on poverty outcomes. In J. Huber (Ed.), *Macro-micro linkages in sociology* (pp. 244–262). Maberry, CA: Sage.

U.S. Census Bureau. (2001). *Statistical abstract of the United States: 2001.* Washington, DC: Author.

U.S. Census Bureau. (2007). *Statistical abstract of the United States: 2007.* Washington, DC: Author.

U.S. Department of Education. (1995). *The condition of education 1995.* (Technical Report No. NCES 95-273). Washington, DC: U.S. Department of Education, National Center for Education Statistics.

U.S. Department of Education. (2003). *Digest of educational statistics.* Retrieved from http://nces.ed.gov/programs/digest/d03

U.S. Department of Education. (2006). *The condition of education 2006.* (NCES 2006-071). Washington, DC: U. S. Government Printing Office, National Center for Educational Statistics.

Useem, E. L. (1991). Student selection into course sequences in mathematics: The impact of parental involvement and school policies. *Journal of Research on Adolescence, 1*, 231–250.

Walker, D. K., Singer, J. D., Palfrey, J. S., Orza, M., Wenger, M., & Butler, J. (1988). Who leaves and who stays in special education: A 2-Year follow-up study. *Exceptional Children, 54*, 393–402.

West, J., Denton, K., & Germino-Hausken, E. (2000). *America's kindergartners: Findings from the Early Childhood Longitudinal Study, Kindergarten Class of 1998–99, Fall 1998.* (NCES 2000-070). Washington, DC: U.S. Department of Education, National Center for Education Statistics.

Williams, F. (1970). Psychological correlates of speech characteristics: On sounding disadvantaged. *Journal of Speech and Hearing Research, 13*, 472–488.

Wilson, W. J. (1987). *The truly disadvantaged: The inner city, the underclass, and public policy.* Chicago: University of Chicago Press.

Wilson, W. J. (1996). *When work disappears: The world of the new urban poor.* New York: Knopf.

Zill, N. (1996). Family change and student achievement: What we have learned, what it means for schools. In A. Booth & J. Dunn (Eds.), *Family-school links: How do they affect educational outcomes?* (pp. 139–174). Mahwah, NJ: Erlbaum.

POST-READING ACTIVITIES

1. What were the results of the Coleman Report (Coleman et al. 1966)?
2. Can you summarize the Beginning School Study?
3. What can you do to minimize the achievement gap in your own classroom?

CHAPTER 4

READING 4.2 OVERVIEW

Students who attend urban, high-poverty schools are affected by unique challenges. The authors of this article address some of the challenges and describe characteristics that are often associated with this population of learners. In addition, the authors include suggestions for research-based interventions that can address the needs of this specific group. The intervention strategies are explained and examples are provided. The purpose of the article is to provide the reader with ideas for academic, social, and behavioral support to help students in urban, high-poverty schools reach their full potential.

PRE-READING ACTIVITIES

1. Write down the characteristics that you believe contribute to learning challenges for students in urban, high-poverty schools.
2. Identify issues you believe that students in urban, high-poverty schools encounter in the learning environment.
3. What strategies do you already know about that could facilitate the learning of students in such an environment?

READING 4.2

URBAN STUDENTS IN HIGH-POVERTY SCHOOLS

INFORMATION AND SUPPORT STRATEGIES FOR EDUCATORS

BY MARY M. CHITTOORAN AND SUSAN E. CHITTOORAN

Schools in large central cities—those with a population of 250,000 or more—have seen a marked increase in the enrollment of children who pose unique academic and behavioral challenges for educators. According to the Congressionally mandated report, *The Condition of Education 2008* (National Center for Education Statistics), there are significant racial, ethnic, and linguistic disparities in enrollment among urban and nonurban schools. For example, of the 20% of school-age children who speak a language other than English at home, most attend urban schools. Forty-five percent of all students in schools with high minority enrollments (i.e., where 75% or more are minority) are enrolled in urban (versus suburban and rural) schools.

While many urban schools serve students from middle- and high-income families, the focus of this handout will be on urban, high-poverty schools, those where 75% of students are eligible for free or reduced-price lunches. An estimated 45% of students in urban settings are low-income; nationally, 69% of students in high-poverty districts are enrolled in urban schools. There

Mary M. Chittooran and Susan E. Chittooran, "Urban Students in High-Poverty Schools: Information and Support Strategies for Educators," *Communiqué*, vol. 38, no. 6, pp. 32-33.

are notable racial and ethnic differences in the enrollment of students in high-poverty, urban schools; for example, 44% of blacks, 46% of Hispanics, and 27% of American Indians/Alaska Natives attend such schools, compared with 9% of whites and 17% of Asian/Pacific Islanders.

Children in high-poverty, urban schools present educators with an array of challenges that they are typically not trained to address. The situation is exacerbated when there is a cultural mismatch between students and their teachers. For example, some statistics suggest that while more than 30% of students are from minority groups, only about 10% of their teachers are persons of color. Teacher retention in urban, low-income schools is a growing problem, with some sources reporting that up to 30% of new teachers in large urban schools leave their positions within the first 3 years of teaching. Teachers in urban schools in high-poverty areas are particularly susceptible to burnout. Numerous reasons for this phenomenon have been cited, including high-stress environments, teaching conditions that differ markedly from those they had expected, lack of academic preparation, and an inability to meet the needs of their students.

CHARACTERISTICS OF STUDENTS IN URBAN, HIGH-POVERTY SCHOOLS

While the following characteristics do not apply to all students in urban, high-poverty schools, they are more frequently associated with such schools than with those in relatively wealthy, nonurban areas.

- Chronic, generational poverty as well as short-term, situational poverty; the latter may be occasioned by job loss, unemployment, divorce, or death of family members
- Relatively poor functioning on measures of physical and emotional health, intellectual development, and academic achievement
- Significant social–behavioral problems, including extreme violence and aggression
- High proportion of culturally diverse populations
- Disproportionate number of homeless children and families
- Large numbers of students for whom English is a second language
- High percentage of children who qualify for (but may not necessarily receive) special education services
- Meals that are lacking in both quantity and nutritional quality

- Poor healthcare and irregular well-child or follow-up medical care
- Home environments that are unsanitary, unsafe, or offer inadequate supervision of children
- Dangerous neighborhoods characterized by violence and vandalism
- Crowded schools, high student–teacher ratios, and stressed and alienated faculty
- Inadequate funding, facilities, and resources, even though per pupil expenditures are higher for urban, high-poverty schools than for suburban schools

SCHOOL-BASED INTERVENTIONS

Studies have indicated that comprehensive, integrated approaches are most effective at addressing the complex needs of urban students in high poverty areas. Following are some suggestions for educators.

ESTABLISH A SAFE, CARING SCHOOL CLIMATE

Educators can build a school climate that is characterized by warmth, respect, and acceptance for all children. In fact, programs such as the Safe and Responsive Schools Project (see Recommended Resources) have shown that positive school climates that address violence proactively reduce the need for peer mediation programs. Schools can provide a safe place for students who lack safety in the world outside. Educators should address labeling, stereotyping, and discrimination and can use proactive approaches to ensure that all children feel included. Predictable routines can help introduce structure into lives that may otherwise be chaotic.

USE NONDISCRIMINATORY ASSESSMENT

The accurate assessment of students' strengths and weaknesses is critical to developing and implementing academic and behavioral interventions. Such assessment must not penalize students for behaviors that may be due to their impoverished status or that may be appropriate for their cultural backgrounds. Culturally competent assessment requires that professionals use measures that are culturally and linguistically appropriate (e.g., assessment in students' native language), include interpreters and translators for children and their families, and consider cultural norms that may differ from the mainstream (e.g., limited direct interactions with authority figures; Banks & Banks, 2009).

DIFFERENTIATE INSTRUCTION

The great diversity of students in urban settings requires that educators be prepared to differentiate (individualize) instruction so that all students' needs are met. Culturally responsive teaching methods (Gay, 2000) and an equity pedagogy (Banks & Banks, 2009) help educators incorporate their students' cultural backgrounds into instruction and ensure that *all* students, regardless of their backgrounds, have the opportunity to reach their potential.

Some examples of culturally relevant teaching strategies include using appropriate cultural names and labels, celebrating the accomplishments of key figures from a variety of cultural groups, and developing useful class assignments (e.g., having students draw maps of their neighborhoods to help them learn map skills).

TEACH APPROPRIATE SOCIAL BEHAVIORS

Educators can actively teach children prosocial behaviors that may not have been taught at home and that may help them build the social networks that are critical to school success. A variety of social skills training programs such as *Skillstreaming* (McGinnis, 2005), simulations, and role-plays may be used to teach behaviors such as taking turns, sharing information, and expressing anger appropriately.

CONSIDER STUDENTS' LANGUAGE

Educators must be especially careful when it comes to children who do not speak standard English, either because they speak another language or because they speak with accents or use unique dialects. Language differences are not to be viewed as deficits, and assessment and instruction must take such differences into consideration. For example, children can be taught to use language that is appropriate in school settings without having their own language or speech patterns diminished in any way or being told that the way they and their families speak in the home is incorrect or undesirable.

PROVIDE ADEQUATE NUTRITION

Teachers and administrators can provide families with information about programs that offer free and reduced-price meals for eligible children, both during the school year and the summer months. Schools can also help parents who lack the requisite reading and writing skills to access such resources and complete applications for these services. Educators must remain sensitive to parents who prefer not to avail themselves of such services because of pride or shame at having to accept charity. Sometimes families are more comfortable accessing services through culturally specific agencies.

OFFER COMPREHENSIVE HEALTH SERVICES

Medical intervention and preventive healthcare services must be provided for students. The school nurse or other personnel may need to dispense medications when families cannot be relied upon to do so, or when medication must be taken during the school day. Teachers may have to keep extra pairs of glasses or toothbrushes on hand for children who lack supplies. Schools may need to provide students access to well-child or immunization programs. Collaboration with community health agencies is often the most efficient way to ensure adequate healthcare is available to families in the school community; such agencies may set up clinics within school buildings to provide easy access. School personnel should also be aware of appropriate referral sources for no-cost or minimal cost healthcare in the community, such as free clinics.

INVOLVE FAMILIES

Studies have shown that parent involvement results in improved academic and behavioral outcomes for children, yet getting parents in urban, high-poverty schools involved may be one of the greatest challenges facing educators. The situation may be exacerbated in the case of parents who are culturally diverse, lack education, or do not speak English. Some ideas that have facilitated parent involvement include skills-based workshops; parenting groups; GED, ESL, or computer classes; day care for younger children; and transportation to medical appointments.

BUILD SCHOOL-COMMUNITY PARTNERSHIPS

Unlike wealthier schools, urban, high-poverty schools often are not connected to the communities of which they are a part. Local agencies and businesses can help forge links between these schools and their communities. For example, resources may be provided by corporate sponsors, hospitals and clinics, political action groups, and faith-based organizations. Local universities can form professional development school partnerships with urban schools, offer mentoring services, and provide opportunities for university students to serve as role models for children in urban, high-poverty schools. Colleges and universities could also donate computers and offer technical support and resources to local schools. Teacher education institutions (particularly those located in urban areas) could implement programs that are designed to prepare teachers for the challenges and the rewards of urban teaching.

NETWORK WITH OTHER EDUCATORS

One way to help teachers in high-stress environments is to link them with others who are engaged in the same kind of work. Educators can be encouraged to share their experiences, talents, and resources with others and may benefit from interacting with others who have successfully navigated the challenges of urban teaching.

SUMMARY

Students in urban, high-poverty schools bring with them unique challenges. Meeting their needs is the collective responsibility of schools and the communities in which they are located. Educators must provide these students with academic, social, and behavioral support so they are helped to achieve their potential. Such efforts will ultimately result in successful outcomes, not only for students, but also for their families.

REFERENCES

Banks, J. A., & Banks, C. M. (2009). *Multicultural education: Issues and perspectives* (7th ed.). New York: Wiley.

Gay, G. (2000). *Culturally responsive teaching: Theory, research, and practice.* New York: Teachers College Press.

McGinnis, E. (2005). *Skillstreaming in the elementary school: Lesson plans and activities.* Champaign, IL: Research Press.

National Center for Education Statistics. (2008). *The condition of education 2008* (Report NCES 2008031). Washington, DC: Author. Available: http://nces.ed.gov/pubsearch/pubsinfo.asp?pubid=2008031

RECOMMENDED RESOURCES: PRINT

Brown, D. F. (2002). *Becoming a successful urban teacher.* Portsmouth, NH: Heinemann.

Duhon-Sells, R. (2004). *Best practices for teaching students in urban schools.* Mellen Studies in Education, No. 100. Lewiston, NY: The Edwin Mellen Press.

Kozol, J. (1992). *Savage inequalities: Children in America's schools.* New York: Harper Perennial.

Payne, R. (2005). *A framework for understanding poverty* (3rd ed.). Highlands, TX: aha! Process, Inc.

Weiner, L. (2006). *Urban teaching: The essentials.* New York: Teachers College Press.

RECOMMENDED RESOURCES: ONLINE

Children's Defense Fund: http://www.childrensdefense.org
Council of the Great City Schools: http://www.cgcs.org
ERIC Clearinghouse on Urban Education: http://www.eric.ed.gov
National Center for Culturally Responsive Education Systems (NCCRESt): http://www.nccrest.org
National Center for Education Statistics: http://nces.ed.gov
National Coalition for Parent Involvement in Education (NCPIE): http://www.ncpie.org
National Institute for Urban School Improvement: http://www.urbanschools.org
Rethinking Schools Online: http://www.rethinkingschools.org
Safe and Responsive Schools Project: http://www.unl.edu/srs

Mary "Rina" M. Chittooran, PhD, NCSP, is on the faculty of Saint Louis University in St. Louis, MO, where she teaches courses in multicultural issues. **Susan E. Chittooran**, MSSW, is a policy analyst for the Women's Bureau, U.S. Department of Labor in New York City.

POST-READING ACTIVITIES

1. List ten characteristics of students enrolled in urban, high-poverty schools.
2. Identify one form of assessment and one instructional strategy; each must be culturally relevant.
3. Why is family involvement important? Based on the reading, how can you encourage such participation?

CHAPTER 5

AUTISM

INTRODUCTION

According to the Centers for Disease Control and Prevention (2016), "Autism Spectrum Disorder (ASD) is a developmental disability that can cause significant social, communication and behavioral challenges." Preservice and new teachers must have a thorough understanding of what a spectrum disorder is, how it can affect learning, and the best practices for working with this diverse population of students.

The first piece will introduce readers to the term *spectrum disorders*; the types of disorders; and the symptoms associated with each. Potential and unlikely causes of ASD are explored. In addition, the authors address the implications that the growing population of students with ASD may have on schools and families. Research-based best practices for teaching this group are described in rich detail. This reading lays the foundation for how to teach ASD students and is followed by an article that puts theory into practice.

The second reading is a case study that was conducted on an eleven-year old student attending a summer reading intervention program. The research includes a report of the diagnostic assessments administered, an analysis of the data, significant findings, and a summary of the intervention.

Readers will learn how an effective plan was created to introduce a student with ASD—who was fixated on one book—learn how to navigate a wider variety of texts. Students who have ASD are considered exceptional.

> The term exceptional children includes children who experience difficulties in learning as well as those whose performance is so superior that modifications in curriculum and instruction are necessary to help them fulfill their potential. Thus, exceptional children is an inclusive term that refers to children with learning and/or behavior problems, children with physical disabilities or sensory impairments, and children who are intellectually gifted or have a special talent. The term students with disabilities is more restrictive than exceptional children because it does not include gifted and talented children. (Heward 2017, para. 1)

These readings were chosen as part of this anthology to introduce preservice and new teachers to this diverse group of students and to provide them with strategies to best meet the needs of this growing population.

REFERENCES

Centers for Disease Control and Prevention. 2016. *Autism Spectrum Disorder (ASD).* Retrieved from https://www.cdc.gov/ncbddd/autism/facts.html

Heward, W. L. 2017. *Who Are Exceptional Children?* Retrieved from https://www.education.com/download-pdf/reference/22828/

CHAPTER 5

READING 5.1 OVERVIEW

In this reading, the authors describe autistic spectrum disorders (ASDs), possible causes, and implications on schools. The article includes clear and comprehensive descriptions of the most popular research-based educational methods for teaching students with ASD. These practices include Applied Behavior Analysis (ABA); Developmental, Individual Difference, Relationship-Based model (DIR); the Picture Exchange Communication System (PECS); social stories; and Treatment and Education of Autistic and Communication Related Handicapped Children (TEACCH). This piece was chosen to introduce preservice and new teachers to methods for working with students who have ASD. It will lay the foundation for teaching students on the spectrum using innovative and diverse practices.

PRE-READING ACTIVITIES

1. Describe your current understanding of the term *autism spectrum disorders.*
2. There has been an increase in the prevalence of students with ASD. What implications could that have on schools?
3. List best educational practices that you could implement when working with students on the spectrum.

RESEARCH-BASED EDUCATIONAL PRACTICES FOR STUDENTS WITH AUTISM SPECTRUM DISORDERS

READING 5.1

BY JOSEPH B. RYAN, ELIZABETH M. HUGHES, ANTONIS KATSIYANNIS, MELANIE MCDANIEL AND CYNTHIA SPRINKLE

Autism spectrum disorder (ASD) has become the fastest growing disability in the United States, with current prevalence rates estimated at as many as 1 in 110 children (CDC, 2010). This increase in the number of students identified with ASD has significant implications for public schools. The most popular research-based educational practices for teaching this population, explored in the pages that follow, include Applied Behavior Analysis (ABA); the Developmental, Individual-Difference, Relationship-Based model (DIR/Floortime); the Picture Exchange Communication System (PECS); social stories; and Treatment and Education of Autistic and Communication Related Handicapped Children (TEACCH).

In 1990, while amending the Education for All Handicapped Children Act, Congress expanded the number of disability categories eligible to receive special education services in public schools by including autism. Autism is a developmental disability that significantly affects an individual's verbal and nonverbal communication as well as social interaction. It is typically

Joseph B. Ryan, et al., "Research-Based Educational Practices for Students With Autism Spectrum Disorders," *Teaching Exceptional Children*, vol. 43, no. 3, pp. 56-64.

evident before age 3 and adversely impacts a child's educational performance. Other characteristics commonly associated with autism include:

(a) engagement in repetitive activities and stereotyped movements, (b) poor *eye* contact, (c) difficulty socializing with others, (d) resistance to changes in daily routines, and (e) unusual responses to sensory experiences such as loud noises (Individuals With Disabilities Education Act [IDEA], 2008). Although the intelligence quotient (IQ) distribution for specific types of autism resembles that of the general population, there appears to always be significant differentiation between written and oral language skills, marked emotional difficulties recognized by parents and teachers but not by the students themselves, and sensory problems similar to persons who function at a much lower cognitive level (Barnhill, Hagiwara, Myles, & Simpson, 2000). As a result, children with autism, regardless of whether they are high or low functioning, have difficulty with peer relationships and understanding social situations (Kasari, Freeman, Bauminger, & Alkin, 1999).

AUTISTIC SPECTRUM DISORDERS

Autism is a disorder that adversely affects a child's communication, socialization, and interests prior to age 3, with the average onset at 15 months (Hutton & Caron, 2005). One aspect of *autism* that distinguishes it from other disabilities is that the term refers to a spectrum or multiple types of similarly related disorders. Hence, the disability is more commonly referred to as autism spectrum disorder (ASD), with symptoms ranging from mild cognitive, social, and behavioral deficits to more severe symptoms in which children may suffer from intellectual disabilities and be nonverbal. There are five sub-types of ASD.

AUTISTIC DISORDER

Approximately one third (35%–40%) of children with autism are nonverbal (Mesibov, Adams, & Klinger, 1997).

The majority of students diagnosed with autism have IQ scores categorizing them with intellectual disability, with only one third (25%–33%) having an IQ in the average or above-average range (Heflin & Alaimo, 2007).

ASPERGER'S SYNDROME

Individuals with Asperger's syndrome typically do not exhibit delays in the area of verbal communication, and often develop large vocabularies. However, they do show impairments in their ability to understand nonverbal communication or the pragmatics of language. As a result, even though many individuals may be very high functioning cognitively (e.g., Temple Grandin, an internationally renowned author) they often experience significant social skill deficits.

CHILDHOOD DISINTEGRATIVE DISORDER (CDD)

CDD is a very rare disorder (1/50,000) that typically affects males. It is characterized by a period of normal development followed by an onset of autism-related symptoms, including marked losses of motor, language, and social skills. Symptoms may appear as early as age 2, although most develop the symptoms between 3 and 4 years of age (National Institute of Mental Health, 2008).

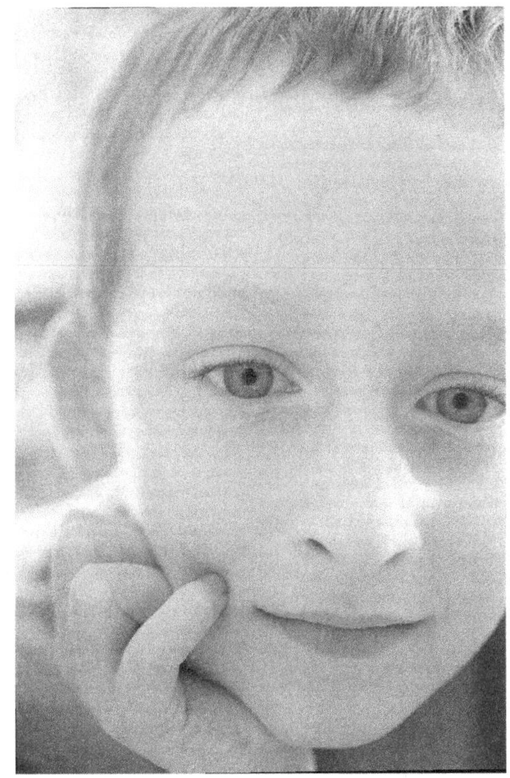

RETT SYNDROME

In contrast to CDD, Rett's is a rare genetic disorder (1/15,000) that almost exclusively affects females. The disorder is characterized by a period of normal development followed by a deceleration of head growth accompanied by an increase in autism-related symptoms (between 6 and 18 months). Other symptoms include regression in mental and social development, loss of language, seizures, and loss of hand skills that results in a constant hand-wringing motion (Heward, 2009).

PERVASIVE DEVELOPMENTAL DISORDER NOT OTHERWISE SPECIFIED (PDD-NOS)

PDD-NOS is most commonly used to describe children who exhibit at least one characteristic of an ASD subtype, but do not meet all of the specific diagnostic criteria (American Psychiatric Association, 2000). As a result, children who suffer from a qualitative difference from their peers in communication, socialization, or interests and activities may receive a diagnosis of PDD-NOS.

INCREASE IN PREVALENCE RATES OF ASD

Perhaps the most alarming aspect of ASD for school systems has been the dramatic and continued increase in prevalence rates of ASD across the United States over the past 2 decades. When a new disability first becomes eligible for special education services, it is often anticipated prevalence rates will rise as school systems begin to actively screen children for the disability. This increase in numbers of children served should be expected within the first several years, as was seen with the increased prevalence of traumatic brain injury (TBI), which was added as a disability category the same year as autism. However, after 2 years, the growth rate for children identified with TBI began to plateau, while the prevalence rate for children with ASD has continued to grow nearly 2 decades later (Newschaffer, Falb, & Gurney, 2005).

In 1992, the year following ASD eligibility under IDEA, only 5,415 students with ASD were declared eligible for IDEA services (U.S. Department of Education, 1995), representing less than one percent (.1%) of all students with disabilities. A decade later the number of students receiving special education services for ASD reached 97,204 (1.66% of all students with disabilities; U.S. Department of Education, 2003) an increase of 1,708%. In comparison, the percentage increase for all disabilities during this same period was just 30.38%. By the last count, the prevalence rate has continued to increase, surpassing a quarter million students (292,818), and now accounts for 4.97% of all students with disabilities (U.S. Department of Education, 2008). This represents a dramatic increase of 201.24% since 2002, and a 5,307.53% increase since the category was first established. The Centers for Disease Control and Prevention

(CDC)'s Autism and Developmental Disabilities Monitoring Network estimated that approximately 1 in 110 children may have ASD (CDC, 2010).

CAUSES OF AUTISM

The etiology of ASD is currently unknown. The combination of skyrocketing prevalence rates and lack of knowledge regarding the cause of ASD has sent concerned parents and educators searching for answers through both traditional (e.g., news media and professional journals) and informal (e.g., World Wide Web blogging) informational outlets. Unfortunately, this has sometimes resulted in further confusion as consumers are left to sift through a combination of research, speculation, and misinformation for answers. Given that ASD is a spectrum of disorders, it is very likely there are multiple causes (Halsey, Hyman, & the Conference Writing Panel, 2001); current research focuses on both biological and environmental factors. From a biological or genetic perspective, researchers have observed structural and chemical differences in the brain of children with ASD as early as the first trimester's development of the fetus (Halsey et al., 2001). These findings, coupled with increased prevalence rates among family members with a history of the disorder, add credence to possible genetic causes.

Related to the biological theory is the controversial view that ASD is caused by a compromised immune system resulting from exposure to vaccinations. As a result, there has been significant concern over the use of childhood vaccinations, specifically those containing thimerosal, a mercury-based preservative. The National Institutes of Health (NIH), the American Academy of Pediatrics, and several other medical organizations stress there is no research to support this link (Halsey et al., 2001). Medical professionals emphasize that most vaccinations developed after 2001 no longer contain thimerosal, and caution that the increasing trend of parental refusal to vaccinate their children has resulted in increased outbreaks of the potentially fatal childhood diseases these vaccinations were *designed to prevent. Still*, there is a continued call for research to further explore if certain children are more susceptible to developing degenerating types of ASD after being administered vaccinations, especially because the age at which many vaccinations are administered correlates with the onset of the degenerative forms of ASD.

Although there is also concern that ASD may result from environmental toxins, there has been no empirical research to support this claim. Heflin and Alaimo (2007) cautioned that although it has been observed that specific geographical areas have been shown to contain higher concentrations of ASD, this may be the result of families either (a) moving to areas that provide better educational services for their children with ASD, or (b) these locales are more effective at screening and identifying the disorder.

IMPLICATIONS FOR SCHOOLS

The continued increase of students identified with ASD has placed significant stressors on public schools and the educators that serve them. Points of contention between parents and school districts include (a) eligibility and services provided, (b) educational placement (e.g., least-restrictive environment), and (c) instructional methodologies (Yell, Katsiyannis, Drasgow, & Herbst, 2003; Zirkel, 2002).

In respect to eligibility and services, Yell and Drasgow (2000, p. 213) recommended that (a) school districts ensure timely eligibility decisions based on evaluations by professionals with experience in ASD, (b) educators develop individualized education programs (IEPs) that address all the areas of need identified in the evaluation, and (c) services identified in the IEP result in meaningful educational benefit to the student (e.g., districts must monitor student progress toward IEP goals and objectives). In accordance with federal law, districts must place students with disabilities in integrated settings to the maximum extent appropriate and adopt empirically validated instructional strategies and programs. In addition, using empirically validated methodologies is particularly important given the emphasis of the No Child Left Behind Act of 2001 on incorporating evidence-based methodologies and related provisions in IDEA regarding services outlined in a student's IEP (see Simpson, 2005). Specifically, IEPs require "a statement of the special education and related services and supplementary aids and services, based on peer-reviewed research to the extent practicable" (IDEA, 20 U.S.C. & 1414 [d] [1] [A] [i] [IV]).

Unfortunately, given the number of non-evidence-based interventions currently marketed for the treatment of ASD (e.g., facilitated communication, holding therapy, secretin therapy), selecting efficacious interventions can be a challenging proposition for both the lay and professional consumer alike. Table 5.1 summarizes the most popular research-based educational practices for teaching students with ASD, a good starting point for educators seeking effective interventions.

Table 5.1 **Evidence-based interventions for students with autism spectrum disorders.**

INTERVENTION	PROGRAM DESCRIPTION	DEMONSTRATED EFFICACY	INTERNET LINK
Developmental, Individual-Difference, Relationship-Based Model (DIR/Floortime; Wieder & Greenspan, 2001)	Through challenging yet child-friendly play experiences, clinicians, parents, and educators learn about the strengths and limitations of the child, therefore gaining the ability to tailor interventions as necessary while strengthening the bond between the parent and child and fostering social and emotional development of the child. *Time requirement:* 14–35 hours per week	Increased levels of: • Social functioning • Emotional functioning • Information gathering *For ages:* Approximately 2–5 years	www.icdl.com This Interdisciplinary Council on Developmental and Learning Disorders site allows professionals to learn more about the DIR/Floortime model, DIR institutions and workshops, and current research regarding DIR/Floortime.
Discrete Trial Training (DTT; Lovaas, 1987)	Intervention that focuses on managing a child's learning opportunities by teaching specific, manageable tasks until mastery in a continued effort to build upon the mastered skills. *Time requirement:* 20–30 hours per week across settings	Increased levels of: • Cognitive skills • Language skills • Adaptive skills • Compliance skills *For ages:* Approximately 2–6 years	www.helpingtogrow.istores.com www.aba.insightcommerce.net www.adaptivechild.com These commercial sites provide opportunities to purchase programs and adaptive equipment.
Lovaas Method (Lovaas, 1987)	Intervention that focuses on managing a child's learning opportunities by teaching specific, manageable tasks until mastery in a continued effort to build upon the mastered skills. *Time requirement:* 20–40 hours per week	Increased levels of: • Adaptive skills • Cognitive skills • Compliance skills • Language skills • IQ • Social functioning *For ages:* Approximately 2–12 years	www.lovaas.com Official site for Lovaas Institute that provides detailed information about Lovaas method, success stories, services, and products available.

(Continued)

Table 5.1 ***(Continued)***

INTERVENTION	PROGRAM DESCRIPTION	DEMONSTRATED EFFICACY	INTERNET LINK
Picture Exchange Communication System (PECS; Bondy & Frost, 1994)	Communication system developed to assist students in building fundamental language skills, eventually leading to spontaneous communication. The tiered intervention supports the learner in learning to identify, discriminate between, and then exchange different symbols with a partner as a means to communicate a want. *Time requirement:* As long as the child is engaged, typically 20–30 minutes per session	Increased levels of: • Speech and language development • Social-communicative behaviors *For ages:* Approximately 2 years-adult	www.PECS.com Official site; provides information regarding PECS training courses, consultation, certification, and products.
Social stories (Gray & Garand, 1993)	Personalized stories that systematically describe a situation, skill, or concept in terms of relevant social cues, perspectives, and common responses, modeling and providing a socially accepted behavior option. *Time requirement:* Time requirements vary per story; approximately 5–10 min prior to difficult situation	Increased levels of: • Prosocial behaviors *For ages:* Approximately 2–12 years	www.thegraycenter.org This site provides information about resources available through the Center, including products on how to make and use social stories. The site also provides general information about autism and research that supports the use of social stories.
Treatment and Education of Autistic and Communication related handicapped CHildren (TEACCH; Schopler & Reichler, 1971)	Intervention that supports task completion by providing explicit instruction and visual supports in a purposefully structured environment, planned to meet the unique task needs of the student. *Time requirement:* Up to 25 hours per week (during the school day)	Increased levels of: • Imitation • Perception • Gross motor skills • Hand-eye coordination • Cognitive performance *For ages:* Approximately 6 years-adult	www.teacch.com The site is operated through a division of the University of North Carolina Department of Psychology and provides links to regional centers, programs and services, as well as access to current research and publications supporting the method.

EVIDENCE-BASED EDUCATIONAL PROGRAMS FOR STUDENTS WITH ASD

APPLIED BEHAVIOR ANALYSIS (LOVAAS/DISCRETE TRIAL TRAINING)

In 1957, noted behaviorist B. F. Skinner extended the concept of operant conditioning and rewarding positive behaviors to verbal behavior—meaning behavior is under the control of consequences mediated by other people. Skinner's research shaped the way researchers and educators alike looked at behavior. His research became a catalyst for further investigation into how theories of behavior, referred to as *applied behavior analysis* (ABA), could be used within educational settings. Generally speaking, ABA is a systematic process of studying and modifying observable behavior through a manipulation of the environment (Chiesa, 2004). The theory characterizes the components of any behavior by an A-B-C model: the antecedent to the behavior (A; stimulus/event that occurs prior to the behavior), the behavior itself (B; child's action in response to a stimulus), and the consequence (C; outcome or result of the behavior). In recent years, the principles of this theory of behavior have been used to create a behavior modification program sharing the same name, designed for the treatment of individuals with cognitive and behavioral deficits, including ASD.

Clinical psychologist Ivar Lovaas first provided evidence of the effectiveness of ABA programs for children with ASD. In this seminal study (Lovaas, 1987), one group of children less than 4 years old received an intensive treatment of ABA called discrete trial training (DTT) over a span of 2 to 3 years. DTT is an instructional strategy in which a specific task (also called a trial) is isolated and taught by being repeatedly presented to the student. Responses are recorded for each command and the trial is continued until the student demonstrates mastery of the task. Specifically, DTT consists of (a) presenting a discriminative stimulus to the student (e.g., teacher asks student what sound the letter *p* makes), (b) occurrence or approximation of target response from the student (e.g., student attempts to make the *p* sound), (c) delivery of reinforcing consequence (e.g., teacher claps hands and smiles replying with the proper sound of the letter *p*), and (d) specified intertrial interval (e.g., teacher repeats request after specific lapsed time).

In order to promote success, ABA programs require consistent, intense, sometimes almost constant feedback and correction of a child's behavior. Therefore, intense one-on-one instruction is recommended at the beginning of the intervention (e.g., 20–30 hours per week), and parent participation is crucial to help ensure learned behaviors generalize across environments (e.g., home and school). As the new behavior replaces the old behavior and becomes more automatic, the parent or teacher implementing the intervention must methodically lessen interaction and feedback with the child during the targeted behavior.

The DIR model serves as a framework to understand the developmental profile of an infant or child and the family.

Lovaas (1987) reported that nearly half *(47%)* of the children in the ABA program achieved higher functioning in comparison to only 2% of the control group not receiving treatment. Though this particular study was criticized for questionable research practices, it has since been replicated with similar results (Cohen, Amerine-Dickins, & Smith, 2006; Howard, Sparkman, Cohen, Green, & Sanislaw, 2005). This body of research includes several studies which reported half (50%) of the children with ASD treated with ABA prior to age 4 showed significant increases in IQ, verbal ability, and/or social functioning (Lovaas, 1987). Even those who did not show dramatic improvements had significantly better improvement than matched children in the control groups. In addition, some children who received ABA therapy were eventually able to attend classes with their nondisabled peers. This research suggests intensive ABA interventions implemented early in a child's development can result in long-term positive outcomes. ABA and DTT have an extensive body of research that supports its use in academic and behavior interventions for children with ASD (Simpson, 2004) as well as other intellectual disabilities (Iwata et al., 1997), and are considered to be scientifically based practices for treating individuals with ASD (Simpson, 2005).

DEVELOPMENTAL, INDIVIDUAL-DIFFERENCE, RELATIONSHIP-BASED APPROACH MODEL/FLOORTIME

The Developmental, Individual Differences, Relationship-Based model (DIR; Wieder & Greenspan, 2001) is a comprehensive, interdisciplinary approach to treating children with disabilities, specifically those with ASD. It focuses on the child's individual developmental needs, including social-emotional functioning, communication skills, thinking and learning processes, motor skills, body awareness, and attention span. The DIR model serves as a framework to understand the developmental profile of an infant or child and the family by developing relationships and interactions between the child and parent. It enables caregivers, educators, and clinicians to plan an assessment and intervention program that is tailored to the specific needs of the child and their family. It is not necessarily an intervention, but rather a method of analysis and understanding that helps organize the many intervention components into a comprehensive program (Wieder & Greenspan, 2001).

A vital element of the DIR model is Floortime (Wieder & Greenspan, 2001). Floortime serves both as an intervention and as a philosophy for interacting with children. It aims to create opportunities for children to experience the critical developmental stages they are lacking through intensive play experiences. It can be implemented as a procedure within the home, school, or as a part of a child's different therapies. A Floortime program initially involves one-on-one experiences between the parent or caregiver and the child. These experiences are typically 20-to 30-minute periods when parents literally get on the floor with their children and interact and play in a way that challenges typical behaviors (e.g., repetitive movements, isolation, inappropriate play) and encourages appropriate, interactive play and socialization through parent-directed modeling and prompting.

This intervention aims to train parents and teachers to engage the emotions of even the most withdrawn toddler by entering the child's world. School systems sometimes incorporate aspects of this model into their programs but generally do not make this their primary means of educating young children with ASD. Controlled research supporting Floortime is limited, but supports a positive outcome for children with ASD. A pilot study using the PLAY Project Home Consultation program (see http://www.playproject.org/), a training program for parents of young children with ASD incorporating Floortime (Wieder & Greenspan, 2001), found that nearly half (45.5%) of the children made significant functional developmental progress through the program and reported a 90% approval rating from parents involved in the program (Solomon, Necheles, Ferch, & Bruckman, 2007).

With its strong emphasis on social and emotional development, the Floortime model (Wieder & Greenspan, *2001)* may be a natural complement to a behavioral teaching program. Further research is needed promoting Floortime, but it is currently being used successfully by families who prefer a play-based therapy as a primary or secondary treatment, especially for toddlers and preschoolers (Wieder & Greenspan, 2001).

PICTURE EXCHANGE COMMUNICATION SYSTEM

Typical learners are constantly communicating needs, wants, and desires through socially acceptable verbal expressions and physical gestures that may not come naturally to individuals with ASD. An increasingly common intervention used to enhance communication skills of children with ASD is the Picture Exchange Communication System (PECS; Bondy & Frost, 1994). PECS is a multitiered program that promotes communication through the exchange of tactile symbols and objects. Symbols may include photographs, drawings, pictures of objects, or objects that a child is taught to associate with a desirable toy, person, or activity.

The three instructional phases of PECS teach a child to (a) request an item or activity by giving a corresponding picture, symbol, or object to his/her partner, (b) generalize the activity by bringing the request symbol to the partner who may be located in different areas of the room, and (c) discriminate between two different request symbols before bringing it to the partner (Lund & Troha, 2008). The six-phase PECS program extends beyond discrimination of two symbols to the discrimination of many symbols and incorporates more complex language exchange between interventionist and student (Bondy & Frost, 1994).

PECS (Bondy & Frost, 1994) requires the instructor to teach the child to request a desired activity through modeling (i.e., demonstration of desired behavior). The child is prompted by the teacher to use the tactile symbols to make a specific request (e.g., student points to picture of glass of water to express desire for a drink). It is important to create symbols that are significant and personal to the child, which will accurately communicate what the child is requesting. The child is positively reinforced for correctly using the appropriate symbols and essentially associates the symbol with a desired activity. This in turn increases the probability the child will continue to use the symbol to request that specific activity (e.g., water break) in the future. It is equally important that the child is corrected whenever the symbols are used incorrectly (e.g., the child screams for drink), therefore decreasing the chances that an inappropriate method of communication will be repeated.

The various tiers of PECS (Bondy & Frost, 1994) gradually increase in complexity as tasks become more difficult Although verbal and gestural prompting (e.g., pointing) may be necessary at the beginning of each phase, it should be faded as the student demonstrates mastery of the skill (e.g., teacher refrains from asking the child which picture will ask for water once the child consistently uses the object correctly). Teaching the child to generalize the behavior learned is critical for the behavior to be functional and applicable to daily life. Behavior generalization is naturally incorporated into

PECS during the second stage when the partner physically moves farther away from the child, and during the third stage when the child is taught to discriminate between different symbols (e.g., glass of water and glass of milk).

Research supports PECS (Bondy & Frost, 1994) as a promising practice for teaching individuals with ASD how to more appropriately communicate requests (Carr & Felce, 2006; Ganz & Simpson, 2004; Simpson, 2005). Due in part to the prescribed order of teaching, PECS may be very beneficial for individuals who are either nonverbal or have limited communication skills. Lund and Troha (2008) also provided preliminary evidence that a modified version of PECS using objects as symbols in the place of pictures may be used successfully to facilitate communication skills for children who have the comorbid condition of ASD and blindness.

SOCIAL STORIES

Social stories (Gray & Garand, 1993) provide a brief descriptive story for children to help them better understand specific social situations. *Social* stories describe "a situation, skill, or concept in terms of relevant social cues, perspectives, and common responses in a specifically defined style and format" (The Gray Center for Social Learning and Understanding, n.d.). The goal of social stories is not to change an individual's behavior but rather to expose the individual to a better understanding of an event, thereby encouraging an alternative and proper response. Less formally, the teacher and student may create personalized stories that explicitly inform the child what to expect in a given situation that has proven to be difficult in the past (e.g., riding the school bus, participating in an assembly), and in turn how the child should act in the particular situation. Social stories can be used either to encourage replacement of a child's maladaptive behaviors (e.g., screaming to get a teacher's attention) or to promote prosocial behaviors (e.g., introducing yourself to person entering a room; Spencer, Simpson, & Lynch, 2008).

Social stories are typically presented to the child before the situation occurs as a way to help rehearse the scenario. For example, if a child has difficulty riding the school bus, the teacher and student could develop a social story regarding how the student should board and ride the bus, and why that behavior is necessary. The story should also include positive behaviors that the child does well, other events that may serve as behavioral triggers (e.g., other children violating student's personal space), and how the individual could best respond to each situation (Sansosti, Powell-Smith, & Kincaid, 2004; Scattone, Wilczynski, Edwards, & Rabian, 2002). In addition to reading the story, the child may require prompting during social situations, and may need to practice the skill presented in the story. Recognition of appropriate behavior by the student is vital, reinforcing appropriate behaviors with an ultimate goal of self-regulation and management (Spencer et al., 2008).

Social stories should be written and illustrated at a level in keeping with the cognitive ability of the student they serve. Gray developed clear guidelines (see The Gray Center for Social Learning and Understanding, n.d.) for developing a story, which typically ranges from 5 to 10 sentences. Stories should: (a) define a specific target behavior of concern, (b) identify an appropriate replacement behavior, (c) be written from the child's perspective, (d) include pictures or drawings to help the child relate to the desired behavior, and (e) include a ratio of one directive sentence for every two to five sentences that are either descriptive, perspective, or both.

Specifically, *directive* sentences define the goal of the story and provide responses or behaviors the student is expected to perform. *Descriptive* sentences provide details regarding the event, setting, thoughts, or actions of people in a similar situation. *Perspective* sentences are usually related to consequences or outcomes of the situation and describe how other people may react or feel based on the action or inaction of the main character of the story. Additionally, stories may include *affirmative* sentences that provide statements of social value (Ali & Frederickson, 2006; Sansosti et al., 2004), *control* sentences that reinforce the student's method of self-regulation and affirm the right to choose, and *cooperative* sentences that provide names of responsive people who may assist in the student's efforts or may be impacted by their choices. Some of the sentences may also have blanks for the student to fill in (Ali & Frederickson, 2006). As with any good story, a title, introduction, body, and conclusion are important elements (Quilty, 2007). The format of the social story should be predictable. It should not merely be a list of tasks, but should describe behaviors rather than simply directing the child.

Although the research is not yet extensive, the use of social stories is considered a promising behavioral intervention for children with ASD (Simpson, 2005), helping to increase desirable prosocial behaviors such as hand washing, delayed echolalia, following directions, and using a quiet voice (as reviewed by Sansosti et al., 2004); and to decrease undesirable, maladaptive behaviors such as calling out in class (Crozier & Tincani, 2005), hitting, screaming, falling from a chair, and crying while completing homework (Adams, Gouvousis, VanLue, & Waldron, 2004). Although full confirmation supporting the efficacy of social stories for children with ASD is premature until larger scale research studies are conducted, early findings appear to be very promising.

Social stories can be used either to encourage replacement of a child's maladaptive behaviors … or to promote prosocial behaviors.

TREATMENT AND EDUCATION OF AUTISTIC AND COMMUNICATION RELATED HANDICAPPED CHILDREN (TEACCH)

The TEACCH program has been used to educate children with ASD for over 3 decades. Based on Eric Schopler's work in the 1970s (e.g., Schopler & Reichler, 1971), TEACCH uses structured teaching, which highlights the use of visual supports, to maximize the independent functioning of a child with ASD and/or other related disorders (Hume & Odem, 2007). TEACCH is composed of four critical, structured teaching components: (a) physical structure and organization of the work space, (b) schedules indicating details about the required task, (c) work systems depicting detailed expectations of the individual during the task, and (d) task organization explicitly describing the learning task. The TEACCH system requires the environment to be arranged to meet the unique needs of the child in a given situation. For example, if a child is expected to perform specific homework tasks, the TEACCH program requires the desk area at home be set up in a way that prompts the child to self-monitor personal behavior while working through the tasks necessary to complete the homework assignment (e.g., take out homework, put name on page, read directions, ask for assistance, put completed homework in folder, place folder in book bag). TEACCH may also be used with older students to help prepare them for the workplace by maximizing task independence. For example, a worker whose task it is to sort and stack different materials can use TEACCH to remain on task and efficiently perform the responsibilities required with minimum supervision.

TEACCH requires that the child receive explicit instruction on how to maximize the use of the physical work space through either physical or visual prompts. The adult supervisor may model how the organized space is used to cue different performance steps and monitor the individual as these tasks are being mastered. Primary reinforces are frequently used to increase desired behavior (e.g., verbal praise, recognition, time for desired activity). Staff should prompt and reward the student as necessary, decreasing prompts as the student becomes more self-sufficient and requires less adult supervision.

Although there have been no large-scale studies to date investigating TEACCH, it has been found to be a promising intervention for students with ASD (Simpson, 2005). Studies have demonstrated increases in fine and gross motor skills, functional independence, on-task behavior, play behavior, imitation behavior, and other functional living skills, while reducing the need for teacher prompts (Hume & Odom, 2007; Tsang,

Shek, Lam, Tang, & Cheung, 2007). TEACCH has demonstrated efficacy for children with ASD across various ages and ability levels.

FINAL THOUGHTS

Identifying effective interventions to use with children who have ASD can be challenging for educators and parents alike, especially when various fads and "quick-fix" solutions may receive as much if not more press than evidence-based approaches. The current emphasis on implementing evidence-based interventions leads educators and parents to seek out programs supported by data from empirical research. Although there is a growing body of quality research available on effective interventions for children with ASD, it is still fairly limited, especially given the increasing prevalence rates and wide range of educational, verbal, and social skill deficits associated with this disability.

REFERENCES

Adams, L., Gouvousis, A., VanLue, M., & Waldron, C. (2004). Social story interventions: Improving communication skills in a child with autism spectrum disorder. *Focus on Autism and Other Developmental Disorders, 19,* 87–94.

Ali, S., & Frederickson, N. (2006). Investigating the evidence base of social stories. *Educational Psychology in Practice, 22,* 355–377.

American Psychiatric Association. (2000). *Diagnostic and statistical manual of mental disorders* (3rd ed. text rev.). Arlington, VA: Author.

Barnhill, G., Hagiwara, T., Myles, B. S., & Simpson, R. L. (2000). Asperger syndrome: A study of the cognitive profiles of 37 children and adolescents. *Focus on Autism and Other Disabilities, 15,* 146–153.

Bondy, A., & Frost, L. (1994). The picture exchange communication system. *Focus on Autistic Behavior,* 9(3), 1–19.

Carr, D., & Felce, J. (2006). Brief report: Increase in production of spoken words in some children with autism after PECS teaching to Phase III. *Journal of Autism and Developmental Disorders, 37,* 780–787.

Centers for Disease Control and Prevention. (2010, November). Prevalence of autism spectrum disorders. *MMWR Surveillance Summaries,* 56(SS-1), 1–28. Retrieved from http://www.cdc.gov/mmwr/indss_2007.html

Chiesa, M. (2004). *Radical behaviorism: The philosophy & the science.* Boston, MA: Authors Cooperative.

Cohen, H., Amerine-Dickins M., & Smith, T. (2006). Early intensive behavioral treatment: Replication of the UCLA model in a community setting. *Journal of Developmental & Behavioral Pediatrics, 27,* 145–155.

Crozier, S., & Tincani, M. (2005). Using a modified social story to decrease disruptive behavior of a child with autism. *Focus on Autism and Other Developmental Disabilities, 20,* 150–157.

Ganz, J., & Simpson, R. (2004). Effects on communicative requesting and speech development of the picture exchange communication system in children with characteristics of autism. *Journal of Autism and Developmental Disorders, 34,* 395–409.

Gray, C. A., & Garand, J. D. (1993). Social stories. Improving responses of students with autism with accurate social information. *Focus on Autistic Behavior, 8,* 1–10.

The Gray Center for Social Learning and Understanding. (n.d.). *What are social stories*? Zeeland, MI: Author. Retrieved from http://www.thegraycenter.org/social-stories/what-are-social-stories

Halsey N., Hyman S., & the Conference Writing Panel. (2001). Measles-mumps-rubella vaccine and autistic spectrum disorders. *Pediatrics,* 107(5), 84–107

Heflin, J. L., & Alaimo, D. F. (2007). *Students with autism spectrum disorder.* Upper Saddle River, NJ: Pearson/Merrill Prentice Hall.

Heward, W. L. (2009). *Exceptional children: An introduction to special education* (9th ed.). Upper Saddle River, NJ: Pearson/Merrill Prentice Hall.

Howard, J. S., Sparkman, C. R., Cohen, H. G., Green, G., & Sanislaw, H. A. (2005). A comparison of intensive behavior analytic and eclectic treatments for young children with autism. *Research in Developmental Disabilities, 26,* 359–383.

Hume, K., & Odom, S. (2007). Effects of an individual work system on the independent functioning of students with autism. *Journal of Autism and Developmental Disorders. 37,* 1166–1180.

Hutton, A. M., & Caron, S. L. (2005). Experience of families and children with autism in rural New England. *Focus on Autism and Other Developmental Disabilities, 20,* 180–190.

Individuals With Disabilities Education Act of 2004, 20 U.S.C. §§ 1414 *et seq.* (2008).

Iwata, B., Bailey, J., Neef, N., Wacker, D., Repp. A., & Shook, G. (Eds.). (1997). *Behavior analysis in developmental disabilities (1968–1995).* Bloomington, IN: Society for the Experimental Analysis of Behavior.

Kasari, C., Freeman, S. F. N., Bauminger, N., & Alkin, M. C. (1999). Parental perspectives on inclusion: Effects of autism and Down syndrome. *Journal of Autism and Developmental Disorders, 29,* 297–305.

Lovaas, O. I. (1987). Behavioral treatment and normal educational and intellectual functioning in young autistic children. *Journal of Consulting and Clinical Psychology,* 55, 3–9.

Lund, S., & Troha, J. (2008). Teaching young people who are blind and have autism to make requests using a variation on the picture exchange communication system with tactile symbols: A preliminary investigation. *Journal of Autism and Development Disorders, 38,* 719–730.

Mesibov, G. B., Adams, L. W., & Klinger, L. G. (1997). *Autism: Understanding the disorder.* New York, NY: Plenum.

National Institute of Mental Health. (2008). *Autism spectrum disorders (pervasive developmental disorders).* Retrieved from http://www.nimh.nih.gov/health/publications/autism/index.shtml

Newschaffer, C. J., Flab, M. D., &. Gurney, J. G. (2005). National autism prevalence trends from the United States special education data. *Pediatrics, 115,* 277–282.

Quilty, K. M. (2007) Teaching paraprofessionals how to write and implement social stories for students with autism spectrum disorders. *Remedial and Special Education, 28,* 182–189.

Sansosti, F., Powell-Smith. K., & Kincaid, D. (2004). A research synthesis of social story interventions for children with autism spectrum disorder. Focus *on Autism and Other Developmental Disorders, 19,* 194–204.

Scattone, D., Wilczynski, S. M., Edwards, R. P., & Rabian, B. (2002). Decreasing disruptive behaviors of children with autism using social stories. *Journal of Autism and Developmental Disorders, 32,* 535–542.

Schopler, E., & Reichler, R. J. (1971). Developmental therapy by parents with their own autistic child. In M. Rutter (Ed.], *Infantile autism: Concepts, characteristics, and treatment* (pp. 206–227). London, United Kingdom: Churchill-Livingston.

Simpson, R. L. (2004). Finding effective intervention and personnel preparation practices for students with autism spectrum disorder. *Exceptional Children, 70,* 135–149.

Simpson, R. L. (2005). Evidence-based practices and students with autism spectrum disorders. Focus *on Autism and Other Developmental Disabilities, 20,* 140–149.

Skinner, B. F. (1957). *Verbal behavior.* East Norwalk, CT: Appleton-Century-Crofts.

Solomon, R., Necheles, J., Ferch, C., & Bruckman, D. (2007). Pilot study of a parent training program for young children with autism: The PLAY project home consultation program. *Autism: The International Journal of Research and Practice, 11*, 205–224.

Spencer, V. G., Simpson, C. G., & Lynch, S. A. (2008). Using social stories to increase positive behaviors for children with autism spectrum disorders. *Intervention in School & Clinic, 44*, 58–61.

Tsang, S., Shek, D., Lam, L., Tang., F., & Cheung, P. (2007). Brief report: Application of the TEACCH program on Chinese pre-school children with autism—Does culture make a difference? *Journal of Autism and Developmental Disorders, 37*, 390–396.

U.S. Department of Education. (1995). *Seventeenth annual report to Congress on the implementation of the Individuals with Disabilities Education Act.* Washington, DC: Author. Retrieved from http://www2.ed.gov/pubs/OSEP95AnlRpt/index.html

U.S. Department of Education. (2003). *Twenty-fifth annual report to Congress on the implementation of the Individuals with Disabilities Education Act.* Washington, DC: Author. Retrieved from http://www.ed.gov/about/reports/annual/osep/2003/index.html

U.S. Department of Education. (2008). *Individuals with Disabilities Education Act (IDEA) data.* Retrieved from http://www.ideadata.org/PartBdata.asp

Wieder, S., & Greenspan, S. (2001). The DIR (developmental, individual-difference, relationship-based) approach to assessment and intervention planning. *Bulletin of ZERO TO THREE: National Center for Infants, Toddlers, and Families*, 21(4), 11–19.

Yell, M. L., & Drasgow, E. (2000). Litigating a free appropriate public education: The Lovaas hearings and cases. *The Journal of Special Education, 33*, 205–214.

Yell, M. L., Katsiyannis, A., Drasgow, E., & Herbst, M. (2003). Developing legally correct and educationally appropriate programs for students with autism spectrum disorders. *Focus on Autism and Other Developmental Disabilities, 18*, 182–191.

Zirkel, P. A. (2002). The autism case law: Administrative and judicial rulings. *Focus on Autism and Other Developmental Disabilities, 17*, 84–93.

Joseph B. Ryan *(South Carolina CEC), Associate Professor of Special Education, School of Education, Clemson University, South Carolina.* **Elizabeth M. Hughes** *(South Carolina CEC), Doctoral* Student, *Curriculum and Instruction; School of Education, Clemson University, South Carolina.* **Antonis Katsiyannis** *(South Carolina CEC), Professor of Special* Education, *School of Education, Clemson University, South Carolina.* **Melanie McDaniel** *(Tennessee CEC), Graduate Student. Speech and Language Pathology, School of Medicine, Vanderbilt University, Nashville, Tennessee.* **Cynthia Sprinkle** *(South Carolina CEC), Substitute Teacher. Hart Academy. Hartwell, Georgia.*

Correspondence concerning this article should be addressed to Joseph Ryan, Department of Special Education, 102 Tillman Hall, Clemson University, Clemson, SC 29634-0702 (e-mail: Jbryan@clemson.edu).

TEACHING Exceptional Children, *Vol. 43, No. 3, pp. 56–64.*

POST-READING ACTIVITIES

1. On a separate document, complete this table using your own words.

EVIDENCE-BASED EDUCATIONAL PROGRAM	PURPOSE
Applied Behavior Analysis (ABA)	
Developmental, Individual-Difference, Relationship-Based Model (DIR)	

2. List the three instructional phases of the Picture Exchange Communication System.

3. How could you use social stories with a student on the spectrum?

CHAPTER 5

READING 5.2 OVERVIEW

In this reading, we are introduced to Mackenzie, an eleven-year-old student who has been diagnosed with Autism Spectrum Disorder (ASD). Upon her arrival at a summer university reading clinic, she explains how she would only read one specific book. The practice of becoming attached to one piece of text is not uncommon among individuals diagnosed with ASD. The authors explain other common symptoms of spectrum disorders. They present Mackenzie's case study and include her evaluation, diagnostic findings, and a description of the intervention plan. This chapter was chosen to introduce preservice and new teachers to diverse ways to help students navigate a variety of texts.

PRE-READING ACTIVITIES

1. Write down your current knowledge of spectrum disorders.
2. What methods would you use to evaluate a student's fluency and comprehension?
3. What strategies would you employ to engage readers on the autism spectrum?

READING 5.2

I READ ONLY DOG BOOKS!

ENGAGED READING FOR STUDENTS ON THE AUTISTIC SPECTRUM

BY BARBARA ANN MARINAK, LINDA B. GAMBRELL, AND JACQUELYNN A. MALLOY

Mackenzie announced her arrival at our summer reading clinic by proclaiming, "I read only dog books!" Not a problem we thought, there are lots of dog books in a wide variety of genres; fiction, nonfiction, poetry, newspaper articles, magazines, and so forth. However, we quickly discovered what Mackenzie really meant: "I read only THIS dog book!" And this dog book was *Dog Heroes of September 11th: A Tribute to America's Search and Rescue Dogs* by Nona Kilgore Bauer (2006), a stunning text published by Kennel Club Books. Like many students diagnosed with Autistic Spectrum Disorder (ASD), fifth-grader Mackenzie was attached to this one book, read it hundreds of times, and had memorized most of the text. Understanding Mackenzie's proclamation suddenly made our job more challenging. Mackenzie was attending the reading clinic to receive a comprehensive reading evaluation and intervention for delayed reading comprehension. Clearly, if we were going to earn Mackenzie's trust, we had to begin where she was—with the rescue dogs of 9/11.

The following chapter celebrates the hard work and determination of Mackenzie, an 11-year-old student diagnosed with ASD. Mackenzie spent the summer in our university reading clinic. This case study presents an overview of ASD, data from her Evaluation report, our diagnostic findings, and a summary of the intervention program designed to prepare Mackenzie for middle school. Included in the instructional program and conclusions, readers will find a description of the methods that proved helpful as Mackenzie learned to navigate a wide variety of text including Book Blessing (Marinak, Gambrell, & Mazzoni, 2012), chunking, text mapping (Williams, Hall, & Lauer, 2004), the Q-Matrix (Wiederhold, 1998), Text Impression (McGinley & Denner, 1987), and summary paragraph (Pressley, 1989).

PERSPECTIVES ON READING AND AUTISM SPECTRUM DISORDER

Autism is a complex developmental disability that typically appears during the first 3 years of life and affects a person's ability to communicate and interact with others. Autism is defined by a certain set of behaviors and is a "spectrum disorder" in that it affects individuals differently and to varying degrees. There is no known single cause for autism. The term "spectrum" is crucial to understanding autism because of the wide range of intensity, symptoms and behaviors, types of disorders, and considerable individual variation. Children with autism spectrum disorders may be nonverbal and asocial, as in the case of many with "classic" autism, or Autistic Disorder. On the other end of the spectrum are children with a high-functioning form of autism characterized by idiosyncratic social skills and play (Autism Society, 2012).

In the *Diagnostic and Statistical Manual* (American Psychological Association, 2000), these diagnostic categories are outlined under the heading of Pervasive Developmental Disorders. In the *Diagnostic and Statistical Manual*, the disorders are defined by deficits in three core areas: social skills, communication, and behaviors and/or interests. Types of autism spectrum disorders, or pervasive developmental disorders, include: autistic disorder, Asperger syndrome, childhood disintegrative disorder, Rett syndrome, and pervasive developmental disorder—Not Otherwise Specified. In March 2012, the Centers for Disease Control and Prevention issued their autism prevalence report. The report concluded that the prevalence of autism has risen to one in every 88 births in the United States and almost 1 in 54 boys (Centers for Disease Control and Prevention, 2012).

Autism is characterized by what is clinically described as a deficit in social reciprocity. Social reciprocity may include a range of back-and-forth actions, such as gestures, sounds, play, attention, and conversation. Further, ritualistic and obsessive behaviors are often present: for example, a child may insist on lining up toys rather than playing with them. Other characteristics seen in children with ASD can include hyperlexia (intense fascination with letters or numbers and an advanced ability to read words), hypergraphia (intense fascination with writing letters) and significantly delayed inferential comprehension (Autism Society, 2012).

In addition, many at-risk readers, including those with ASD, exhibit low reading motivation (O' Connor & Klein, 2004). As Gambrell notes, motivation "makes the difference between learning that is superficial and learning that is deep and internalized" (Gambrell, 1996, p.15). Therefore, if we were going to provide effective diagnostic instruction for Mackenzie, it was critical for us to instruct in ways that supported not only her skill to read but her will to read. Hence, our work included the pedagogical practices necessary to support her reading engagement.

CASE STUDY

BACKGROUND

Mackenzie came to us at age 11 with a significant history. She was an only child living with her adoptive mother. During her time at the reading clinic, Mackenzie's adoptive parents were separated and her father no longer resided in the home. Mackenzie did spend time with her father through supervised visitations. Mackenzie was adopted from a Chinese orphanage when she was 13 months old. Mackenzie's mother shared that in the orphanage there was one nurse for every 50 children. During this time, Mackenzie was propped fed, meaning that the nurse would cut off a bottle's nipple and prop it on a pillow. The milk would drain into Mackenzie's mouth. She never learned how to suck as an infant due to this feeding technique. As a result of this, Mackenzie has had over a dozen dental surgeries due to the decay-inducing pooling of liquid this feeding technique placed on her developing teeth.

Mackenzie's mother also reported that at age 2, Mackenzie received support services from United Cerebral Palsy for developmental speech delay, occupational therapy for fine motor control, and therapy for sensory overload. In addition, Mackenzie experienced chronic ear infections as a preschooler with a transient hearing loss. At the time of reading clinic, however, Mackenzie's overall health was good.

SCHOOL HISTORY

According to Mackenzie's school records, she received speech and Language services since kindergarten. According to an initial evaluation report, Mackenzie was diagnosed with autistic spectrum disorder (ASD) in third grade. According to the psychologist who completed the Wechsler Intelligence Scale for Children—Fourth Edition, Mackenzie presented a unique set of thinking and reasoning abilities and noted that her overall intellectual functioning was difficult to summarize by a single score of the Wechsler Intelligence Scale for Children—Fourth Edition. Her full scale IQ computed to an 81 (below average). Mackenzie's verbal reasoning abilities, as measured by the Verbal Comprehension Index, were in the average range (VCI = 96).

However, Mackenzie's nonverbal reasoning abilities, as measured by the Perceptual Reasoning Index, were in the borderline range (PRI=73). The Perceptual Reasoning Index is designed to measure fluid reasoning in the perceptual domain with tasks that primarily assess nonverbal fluid reasoning and perceptual organization abilities. Her ability to sustain attention, concentrate, and exert mental control was also in the borderline range (WMI = 74). And finally, Mackenzie's ability to process simple or routine visual material without making errors, as measured on the Processing Speed Index, was in the average range (PSI = 97).

Other data leading to the diagnosis of ASD, specifically Asperger syndrome (American Psychological Association, 2000), included a pragmatic disorder characterized by repetitive use of language, little or no eye contact, lack of interest in peer relationships, lack of spontaneous play, persistent fixation on objects, and difficulty changing routines schedules or her opinions.

Interestingly, the psychologist summarized her report by noting that Mackenzie's verbal reasoning abilities are much more developed than her nonverbal reasoning abilities. Her strength lies in making sense of complex verbal information and using verbal abilities to solve novel problems. Her weakness exists in the ability to process complex visual information by forming spatial images of part-whole relationships and/or by manipulating parts to solve novel problems.

In the area of reading achievement, Mackenzie performed better on correctly applying phonetic decoding rules when reading a series of nonsense words (pseudoword decoding standard score = 106) compared to tasks that require her to correctly read a series of printed words (Word reading standard score = 97). Her ability to read sentences and paragraphs and answer questions about what was read (reading comprehension = 78) was decreased when compared to the two previously mentioned subtests. According to the school psychologist, her reading composite standard score (88) may not be the most accurate measure of her reading skills.

INTERESTS AND ATTITUDES

According to Mackenzie's mother, she is very interested in animals. She enjoys training dogs for agility and obedience. She has done service dog work with the American Red Cross. She is currently involved in horseback riding. Mackenzie is also very involved with her pets at home, which include one dog, two cats, and two fish. She is interested in all types of land and sea animals. She also enjoys identifying birds and their habitats. Mackenzie's mother commented that she resists instructional help. She does not like to leave the regular education classroom setting to receive support because she is worried about missing the information discussed while she is gone. Her mother also stated that, "Mackenzie doesn't understand that she doesn't understand."

At home, Mackenzie likes to be read to. Her mother added that she believes Mackenzie is learning to like to read and hopes that she becomes enthusiastic about reading for pleasure and begins "to treasure the time spend reading". According to her mother, Mackenzie needed to improve her reading comprehension, her use of graphic organizers, her ability to interpret unknown words, her interpretation of test questions, the use of textbooks, and grasping, transferring and retaining knowledge from text. Mackenzie's mother feels that her daughter is increasingly becoming more frustrated with comprehension and hopes it becomes a less exasperating task.

When asked about how she feels as a reader, Mackenzie commented that she is an "okay" reader. Mackenzie believes that she needs to learn how to pronounce words and understand what she is reading to become a better reader. She stated that she believes that reading is an "okay" way to spend her time.

DIAGNOSTIC READING EVALUATION

A diagnostic reading evaluation in the early days of reading clinic revealed significant scatter between word recognition and comprehension abilities. Three measures of word identification were administered to Mackenzie. The word identification subtest from the Woodcock Reading Test-Revised (WRMT-R) and the Slosson Oral Reading Test-Revised (SORT-R3) are measures of isolated word recognition. Word recognition in isolation was also examined on the graded word lists from the Qualitative Reading Inventory-5 (QRI-5) (Leslie & Caldwell, 2010). Mackenzie's word identification grade equivalents on the WRMT-R, the SORT-R3, and the QRI-5 were significantly discrepant above her grade level. Her grade equivalent was 7.1 on the WRMT-R, 8.7 on the SORT-R3, and upper middle school on the QRI-5.

Two measures of comprehension were administered to Mackenzie; the passage comprehension subtest from the WRMT-R and graded passages from the QRI-5

(Leslie & Caldwell, 2010). Mackenzie's passage comprehension grade equivalent on the WRMT-R of 3.9 was significantly discrepant from her grade placement of 5.9. On the QRI-5, Mackenzie's required look-backs in order to answer questions at the independent and/or instructional levels on all types of texts regardless of how it was read (oral/silent). Without the opportunity to look back, Mackenzie's performance was at the frustration level on all passages administered (Grades 2, 3, 4, and 5).

With look backs, Mackenzie's comprehension on the QRI-5 (Leslie & Caldwell, 2010) was 1 year below grade placement. Specifically, Mackenzie demonstrated ability at the instructional level at a midfifth grade range for both narrative and expository text read orally and silently with look-backs. Mackenzie was independent at a midthird grade level for expository text read silently with look-backs.

An error pattern was noted on Mackenzie's comprehension responses. All comprehension errors were on implicit questions. In summary, and consistent with patterns seen in children with ASD, Mackenzie exhibited word identification ability significantly above her grade placement and comprehension below her grade placement.

Mackenzie's psychological evaluation and reading diagnostic revealed a reading pattern of literacy delays typically seen in children with ASD. Mackenzie indicated significantly delayed inferential comprehension, difficulty in self-reflection, monitoring meaning, clarifying, and summarizing.

The nature of ASD as a disorder of social pragmatics and delayed expressive language presents obstacles for educators. Children with ASD are often impaired in their ability to demonstrate knowledge and/or understandings. Hence, assessing present levels of performance and learning needs is a challenge. Research indicates that explicit instruction and ongoing performance assessments are critical in order to grow reading comprehension (Vacca, 2007). Therefore, while completing the diagnostic reading evaluation, we spent time with the only book Mackenzie said she would read—*Dog Heroes of September 11th: A Tribute to America's Search and Rescue Dogs* (Bauer, 2006). Mackenzie was able to read and retell virtually the entire book. She had memorized most of the canine biographies and was comfortable sharing her knowledge. As a way of assessing Mackenzie's familiarity and comfort with graphic organizers, we asked her to share information about her favorite dog using a Retelling Pyramid (Pressley, 1989). Without hesitation, Mackenzie declared that if she had to select a favorite dog, Riley was her pick. We all know Riley too! This beautiful, calm golden retriever being transported to the top of debris that was the North Tower in a Stokes basket is a familiar photograph from the search rescue effort—second only perhaps to the image of the three firefighters raising the American flag at Ground Zero. Figure 5.1 displays Mackenzie's Retelling Pyramid about Riley, the hero dog who graces the cover of *Dog Heroes of September 11th: A Tribute to America's Search and Rescue Dogs.*

Riley
What is your hero dog's name?
Golden Retriever
Two words describing the breed of this hero dog.
World Trade Center
Three words describing where this hero dog searched.
to trust their dogs
Four words to describe what the handlers had to learn
Transported in a Stokes basket
Five words describing how Riley got to the debris that was the North Tower

Figure 5.1 Retelling pyramid.

After the reading evaluation was completed, a period of diagnostic instruction began. Based on Mackenzie's background and assessment data, as well our review of the research related to ASD and reading comprehension, several goals were formulated for her time in reading clinic. This included providing her with as much choice as possible and inviting her into collaborative literacy experiences with high interest text.

Mackenzie's instruction was designed to grow her silent reading comprehension with both fiction and informational text. Specifically, in order to promote transition between texts and to encourage Mackenzie to take risks, every instructional session included the use of both fiction and informational text. The following section summarizes instruction from several fiction and informational texts selected by Mackenzie during reading clinic. From our observations and formative data, intervention recommendations were developed to support Mackenzie transition to middle school. Based on this case study and the body of research that grounded our instruction, the strategic recommendations that conclude this chapter have implications for engaging ASD students with similar comprehension needs.

INSTRUCTIONAL OBSERVATIONS: FICTION TEXT

An early instructional goal for Mackenzie was related to the reading of fiction text. She was asked to identify the elements of fiction, including characters, setting, problem, events, resolution, and theme. Mackenzie was able to identify all the elements of story but had difficulty defining each. A story grammar with definitions was reviewed and posted for her reference.

The technique of book blessing (Marinak, Gambrell, and Mazzoni, 2012) was used throughout reading clinic to afford Mackenzie an informed choice of text. This method enables the teacher to "bless" a collection of books, introducing each with an enticing preview. Mackenzie's first Book Blessing was arranged for fiction and included several rescue dog titles. Mackenzie appeared to be delighted with the "blessed" choices and after carefully listening to a book talk about each, selected *My Dog, My Hero* by Betsy Byars, Laurie Myers, Betsy Duffey, and Loren Long (2000). The book contains various fictional stories about dogs that do heroic things for their families, neighbors, and communities.

Before reading each chapter, a Text Impression (McGinley & Denner, 1987) was used to frontload vocabulary and encouraged Mackenzie to begin discussing the possible content. Mackenzie was very effective with Text Impression for this fiction title. She was able to offer logical predictions based on the words provided.

During silent reading, text was chunked to promote discussion. We began with a 4–5 page segment. However, it quickly became evident that the text was not appropriately chunked for Mackenzie's needs. Though she appeared to silently read the assigned pages, she struggled with comprehension questions. As we continued reading *My Dog, My Hero*, diagnostic instruction indicated that an appropriate segment for Mackenzie was 2–3 paragraphs.

Comprehension questions posed to Mackenzie were generated using the Q-Matrix (Wiederhold, 1998). The Q-Matrix is designed to engage students in question answering and question writing. It is comprised of 36 question stems that can be applied to text. The stems are arranged in a cognitive hierarchy. When applied to text, stems 1–12 can generate literal questions, stems 13–24 can generate inferential questions, and stems 25–36 can generate extended questions.

Though we would eventually release responsibility for writing Q-Matrix questions to Mackenzie, we provided the questions during the early days of instruction. Because *My Dog, My Hero* followed a predictable pattern (each chapter is a fictional biography of a hero dog), three consistent questions were used to guide and monitor Mackenzie's comprehension; "Who is the hero of the story?"; "What were his/her heroic actions?"; and, "How did people respond to the hero dog's actions?" Mackenzie had difficulty responding to the questions, especially the inferential inquiry related to people's responses to the dogs. Repeated use of the Q-Matrix was seen as critical in order to increase Mackenzie's ability to ask and answer literal, inferential, and extended questions.

After reading, the elements of fiction were reviewed with Mackenzie using a story map. A story map is an organizer that graphically represents the elements of fiction (characters, setting, problem, events, resolution, and theme). Prior to the introduction of this organizer, we asked Mackenzie to provide an oral retelling of the each chapter. We noted that the oral retellings were sparse and contained information from

Mackenzie's extensive prior knowledge and not from the text. After prompted to retell using the text, Mackenzie was able to complete the story map.

The next Book Blessing whereby Mackenzie was invited to select her second fiction book, included more fiction dog books and a few folktales. To our surprise, Mackenzie selected The *Korean Cinderella* by Shirley Climo (1996). She explained that she liked the pictures in the book, but when asked, indicated that she had not read many folktales. Another Text Impression was used to introduce the following words; *Korea, stepmother, rags, sandal, magistrate, bride, and marriage*. Mackenzie had more difficulty with this Text Impression, likely due to her lack of background knowledge with this story. She was initially not willing to offer prediction but eventually concluded that the story might be about a wedding in Korea and a stepmother who dies.

Mackenzie's comprehension was monitored after she silently read 2–3 paragraph chunks in *The Korean Cinderella*. A new graphic organizer was introduced to support Mackenzie's ability to self-monitor predictions. A Predict and Support chart (Pressley, 1989) was selected due to Mackenzie's difficulty using text-based information. Predict and Support helps students make predictions about what they will be reading and then support their predictions with excerpts from the text.

During reading, Mackenzie initially resisted stopping at prearranged chunks to offer predictions. She often needed keywords in order to accurately find support for her predictions. As the text concluded, Mackenzie became more effective at making and monitoring predictions independently. However, she continued to struggle with locating text support for her predictions. In addition, when faced with an inaccurate prediction or a prediction that could not be substantiated within the text, Mackenzie was unwilling or unable to revise her original thinking.

Mackenzie was again asked several questions generated from the Q-Matrix. In addition, she was introduced to question writing. Mackenzie had little difficulty writing literal questions. As anticipated, writing and responding to inferential questions proved to be a struggle. Mackenzie was unclear as to what an inference was and was frustrated responding to any questions that were not literal.

In order to begin teaching inferencing, we reduced Mackenzie's text chunk from 2–3 paragraphs to 3–4 carefully selected sentences. In addition, we used the following script to explain inference:

> An inference is reading between the lines. It is a word that means a conclusion or judgment. If you infer that something has happened, you do not see, hear, feel, smell, or taste the actual event. But from what you know, it makes sense to think that it has happened. You make inferences every day and most of the time you do so without thinking about it. Suppose you in your yard and you hear barking.

> You see nothing, but you *infer* that there is a dog approaching. We all know the sound of a dog barking. We know that these sounds *almost always* mean there is a dog is nearby. But there could be some other reason, and therefore another explanation, for the sounds. Perhaps your neighbor has their television on and the sound is a dog on the TV. Or maybe someone is playing a recording of a barking dog. Making *inferences* means choosing the most likely explanation from the facts at hand. (Cuesta College, 2012, p. 1)

Following this instruction, we returned to *The Korean Cinderella* and reduced the text load from which Mackenzie was to infer. With a chunk of 3–4 sentences, Mackenzie was able to begin offering logical inferences.

After reading each chunk of *The Korean Cinderella*, Mackenzie added information to a story map. In addition to using the story map to retell the text, Mackenzie was introduced to a character map. A character map was selected because like the Q-Matrix, this graphic organizer scaffolds inferential comprehension. The character map requires students to identify a main character, qualities that describe that character, and examples of those qualities from the text. Mackenzie was able to identify the main character. She was also able to describe the character's actions. Consistent with comprehension patterns seen in students with ASD, Mackenzie had difficulty inferring the character's attributes as represented by the actions. For example, Mackenzie could find examples of a character being unkind (yelling, denying a request, etc.) but was unable to describe the actions as unkind. With prompting and careful study of the actions she selected, Mackenzie was able to offer the attributes *hardworking, sad,* and *lonely*. Interestingly, Mackenzie was not able to offer character attributes without the scaffold of specific text examples.

Mackenzie enjoyed *The Korean Cinderella* and selected another Cinderella tale, *The Rough-Face Girl* by Rafe Martin (1998), from her third Book Blessing (Marinak, Gambrell, & Mazzoni, 2012). Planning for strategic redundancy, we once again frontloaded vocabulary and discussion using a Text Impression. *Wigwam, marry, daughters, rough, moccasins, cruel, hardhearted, beautiful, ugly, miserable, lonely, proud, ashamed,* and *worn* were provided. This Text Impression resulted in Mackenzie being much more engaged during prereading discussion and more accurate in her predictions. Based on this Text Impression, Mackenzie offered that the story would be about a Native American girl who has a miserable sister and might marry a special man.

As with previous fiction texts, Mackenzie silently read 2–3 paragraphs followed by discussion. She was asked inferential questions based on 3–4 sentence chunks. Mackenzie was able to logically infer and provide text support throughout the entire book. In fact, Mackenzie's risk-taking grew so significantly that she began offering spontaneous inferences. One such example included an inference she offered based on an illustration. The picture contained a woman guarding a wigwam with her arms crossed and a frown on her face. Mackenzie stated that, "the woman must not want anyone in the wigwam because she looks angry."

After reading, Mackenzie continued to practice writing her own questions using the Q-Matrix. She was able to ask: "Who is the Invisible Being?" and "Why would the Invisible Being marry the sisters?" The two "who" questions were literal. However, the "why would" question was inferential. This is was the first inferential question Mackenzie was able to generate on her own. She also knew the answer and provided text support for her conclusion.

As with the previous fiction texts, Mackenzie completed a story map. She proved to be quite effective in her ability to retell the story using the story grammar structure. As with *The Korean Cinderella*, Mackenzie was asked to complete a character map for *The Rough-Face Girl*. Mackenzie successfully located text examples about the two sisters, but once again, required prompting to infer the character's attributes.

Table 5.2. **Definitions and Guiding Questions for the Informational Text Elements**

INFORMATIONAL ELEMENTS	DEFINITION	GUIDING QUESTIONS
Author's purpose	The intent of the author	Did the author write the text to entertain, inform and/or persuade the audience regarding the selected topic? Why did the author write this book/selection? What information did the author want to convey?
Major ideas	The key points the author wants the reader to understand	What are the major ideas of the book/selection? How are the major ideas presented?
Supporting details	The information that supports and clarifies the major ideas	What are the supporting details for each major idea? How are the supporting details presented?
Aids	The variety of pictorial, graphic, typographic and structural representations used to convey information	What aids does the author use to convey meaning? What information is included in the aids (major ideas, supporting detail, vocabulary)?
Vocabulary	Technical words that are needed for full understanding of the text	What key vocabulary words are used to convey major ideas? What vocabulary words are used in the supporting details?

INSTRUCTIONAL OBSERVATIONS: INFORMATIONAL TEXT

Observing that Mackenzie benefitted from the structure of a story grammar, a similar framework was provided for informational text. Where Mackenzie had some familiarity with the elements of a story grammar, she did not know the elements of informational text. Instruction was provided in author's purpose, major idea(s), supporting detail(s), vocabulary, and aids to understanding (Marinak & Gambrell, 2007). Table 5.2 contains the definitions and guiding questions that were used to introduce Mackenzie to the elements of informational text. As with the elements of a story grammar, the elements of informational text were posted for Mackenzie's reference.

In order to continue nurturing Mackenzie's reading engagement, Book Blessing (Marinak, Gambrell, & Mazzoni, in press) was also used with informational text. Her first informational Book Blessing included a variety of titles related to dogs. Mackenzie selected *Rosie: A Visiting Dog's Story* by Stephanie Calmenson (1998). Before reading, we began with a KWL chart (Ogle, 1986) to encourage and scaffold Mackenzie's anticipations. Mackenzie was asked to describe everything she knew about visiting dogs while we scribed. Given her interest in service dogs, Mackenzie was able to generate a great deal of information about visiting dogs. We then employed the Q-Matrix to support her creation of questions. Mackenzie was asked to think about what she wanted to learn about Rosie. Her questions were added to the W column of the KWL chart and included: "What does Rosie do as a job? How does she do her job? How did she learn to do her job?" and "Where does Rosie like to go?"

Rosie: A Visiting Dog's Story was chunked and discussed using the same methods that proved effective for Mackenzie during her reading of fiction. Mackenzie read 3–4 paragraph chunks and responded to inferential questions that drew on 3 to 4 sentences. After each chunk of text, Mackenzie also considered possible information to add to the KWL chart. The "W" questions Mackenzie created proved to be effective prompts as she added new information to the KWL. She correctly answered each of her "W" questions.

After reading, Mackenzie was introduced to one of the informational text structures she would work with during reading clinic. Given that she was preparing to enter middle school, four major informational text structures and corresponding signal words informed Mackenzie's diagnostic instruction using informational text. Table 5.3 contains a summary of these structures. *Rosie: A Visiting Dog's Story* is written in a time order text structure; however, the three major ideas related to sequence in this text must be inferred. Mackenzie required modeling and prompting to comprehend that *puppy hood, training,* and *working* were the three time periods in the book.

However, once the major ideas were added to the text map, Mackenzie had little difficulty contributing several supporting details for each of the major ideas.

Table 5.3. **Four major text structures and signal words.**

TEXT STRUCTURE	DEFINITION	SIGNAL WORDS
Enumeration	A major idea is supported by a list of details and examples.	for instance, for example such as, to illustrate another
Time order	A major idea is supported by details. Both major ideas and supporting details must be in a particular sequence.	first, next, last Before, after Finally, following
Compare and contrast	The supporting details of two or more major ideas indicate how those concepts are similar or different.	but, different from same as, similar to as opposed to instead of, however compared with, both, while
Cause and effect	The supporting details give the causes of a major idea or the supporting details are the results produced by the major idea.	because of, as a result of in order to, effects of therefore, consequently if ... then

Another critical goal for Mackenzie was to invite her into a wide variety of informational texts. Following *Rosie, A Visiting Dog's Story*, Mackenzie's Book Blessing was expanded to include newspapers, magazines, and web-based resources. Mackenzie was intrigued by the options stating, "You mean I can read things other than books?" Her second informational selection was a newspaper article called *A Friendly, Dedicated Cop* (Darvish, 2012). Mackenzie was becoming increasingly successful using Text Impressions to frame her anticipations. Using the words *career*, *enforcement*, *detecting*, *explosives*, and *retirement*, Mackenzie predicted that the article was going to be about a bomb-sniffing service dog that worked with the police department.

Mackenzie was interested in the newspaper article and wanted to read the six paragraphs without interruption. After reading, she used the Q-Matrix to create numerous questions, including two that were inferential. Her questions included: "Why is Nitro in the newspaper? What did Nitro do that made him so special? How might Nitro have been trained?" and "How are Nitro and Rosie similar?" Mackenzie independently went back into both the newspaper article and *Rosie: A Visiting Dog's Story.* It was also noted that while Mackenzie persisted in answering some of the questions without text support, she was more willing to revise her answers after consulting the book and article.

Once again, given the demands of middle school that Mackenzie would soon be facing, we felt an urgency to teach Mackenzie how to summarize. Given the success she exhibited using a Retelling Pyramid for her favorite 9/11 rescue dog, we selected a more rigorous summarization method. Capitalizing on her familiarity and comfort with the elements of information text, and the brevity of *A Friendly, Dedicated Cop,* we introduced to Mackenzie to the summary paragraph (Pressley, 1986). This method was employed after Mackenzie provided a verbal retelling of the newspaper article. The summary paragraph uses a very predictable 1–3–1 structure: 1 sentence of introduction including the title; 3 sentences of important information including major idea(s) and supporting details explained with key vocabulary; and, 1 sentence of conclusion explaining the author's purpose. Mackenzie was frustrated with the summarization process. She had difficulty making decisions about which supporting details to include as well as inferring the author's purpose. However, with modeling and prompting, Mackenzie was able to complete a summary paragraph of the newspaper article. We continued using the summary paragraph with texts that gradually increased in length and complexity.

RECOMMENDED STRATEGIES AND PRACTICES

Given her difficulty transitioning, the sixth-grade day would likely be challenging for Mackenzie. Her Individualized Education Plan for middle school included full inclusion with learning support as needed. Consequently, the diagnostic intervention carried out during reading clinic was designed to ascertain a manageable and effective cadre of reading methods that could be used by all of Mackenzie's teachers. While strategic redundancy and consistency is helpful for all students, it is critical for ASD students. Therefore, in order to help Mackenzie move from subject to subject (and text to text), some degree of strategic similarity was crucial. In other words, she needed to engage with text using structures and methods she was familiar with and that had proven effective. The following section summarizes the methods that allowed Mackenzie to grow more confident and proficient in reading comprehension. The five methods comprised the final recommendations forwarded to her middle school team.

CHOICE: BOOK BLESSING

Chandler-Olcott and Kluth (2009) advocate for the full inclusion of ASD students in general education classrooms. They passionately argue that all students benefit from participating in diverse classrooms. Chandler-Olcott and Kluth (2009) caution, however, that an expanded definition of literacy must be employed when planning instruction for ASD students. This expanded definition includes attending to the social and pragmatic needs of autistic students *before* providing specific strategy instruction. We concurred with this recommendation when considering choice as the first important attribute of Mackenzie's intervention plan.

Choice is widely acknowledged as a method for enhancing motivation. Numerous studies support the idea that literacy choices enhance both motivation and achievement (Guthrie & Davis, 2003; Turner & Paris, 1995). Allowing ASD students to make even a minimal task choice can enhance subsequent interest in the activity. In addition, providing student choices can result in increased effort commitment to reading, and ease transitioning (Chandler-Olcott and Kluth, 2009)

When using the Book Blessing (Marinak, Gambrell, & Mazzoni, 2012) technique, the teacher gathers 10 to 15 books and reading materials from a range of reading levels and shares some interesting tidbit of information that will make children want to know the rest of the story. Typically, 8 to 12 books can be briefly shared at each 5-minute Book Blessing session. Here are some things to consider as you select books each week.

1 Have a range of genres represented. Typically you should have approximately 40% informational text, 40% narrative or story text, with the remaining 20% representing such genres as poetry, newspapers, magazines, joke books, and riddle books. For students with ASD, early Book Blessings will most likely be comprised of only high interest titles. However, it is recommended that Book Blessings be gradually varied in order to broaden the reading interests of students with ASD.

2 Gather the children together and tell them that you have a bag or basket of books that you want to share with them because you think they may want to read some of these books, articles, etcetera.

3 Briefly introduce each text, giving the title and author, and perhaps commenting on the topic, cover illustration, or author as you tell about or read "just a little bit" from each text. For example, sometimes just reading the first paragraph of a book is enough to make children want to read the book. Or, you might comment that you like all the books by a particular author. If you have read the book yourself, you might want to just tell a few things you remember about the book.

4 After you have introduced the books, put them on the reading table, in book baskets, or in the classroom library—and watch them disappear.

FRONTLOAD VOCABULARY: TEXT IMPRESSION

Numerous studies exploring reading comprehension and students with ASD have indicated a necessity to activate prior knowledge and frontload vocabulary using a consistent and structured method (Carr & Thompson, 1996; O'Connor & Klein, 2004). We selected Text Impression for Mackenzie due to its applicability with any type of text and the use of vocabulary to frame anticipations. Text Impression is a thinking-reading strategy that uses important or interesting vocabulary to guide predictions.

To implement Text Impression, present 6–14 important and/or interesting words from the book or selection before reading. Introduce them on a white board, one by one. After presenting each word, pose questions such as: "What do you know? Now, what do you know? What do you think this book or selection will be about? What do you expect to read about if these words are in the book or selection?" and "How does this word change your prediction?" During your discussion, note how the predications change and evolve as words are introduced. As the text is being read, remind students that a few words can create many different ideas and that it is okay if their predications don't exactly match the text.

TEXT STRUCTURE INSTRUCTION: THE ELEMENTS AND STRUCTURES OF INFORMATIONAL TEXT

Formative data revealed that Mackenzie had little experience reading informational text and was unfamiliar with the text structures. Research clearly supports the necessity of text structure instruction for at-risk readers. In several studies, Williams and her colleagues documented comprehension gains in at-risk readers. Findings demonstrated that at-risk readers are sensitive to text structure and improved their comprehension of informational text following explicit text structure instruction (Williams, Hall, & Lauer, 2004; Williams, Hall, Lauer, Stafford, DeSisto, & deCani, 2005). In addition to gains in reading comprehension following text structure instruction, studies have also found evidence that such structural knowledge can be transferred to new learning demands (Broer, Aarnoutse, Kieviet & van Leeuwe, 2002; Palincsar & Duke, 2004). For example, Palincsar and Duke (2004) found that children learn to value and use the features of informational text following instruction. Teaching with and about informational text promotes general literacy knowledge as well as subject matter knowledge in the content areas.

We taught Mackenzie the elements of informational text and began introducing her to the four major text structures. However, time in reading clinic was brief and she would require a great deal more exposure to these frameworks. We recommended that the elements and structures displayed in Tables 5.2 and 5.3 be used to support Mackenzie during language arts instruction and content area reading.

INFERENCING AND QUESTIONING: Q-MATRIX

Teaching ASD students to ask and answer questions and to respond to inferential inquiry is a need well grounded in the research (Miles & Simpson, 2001; Rogers & Mvles, 2001; Vacca, 2007). Using explicit modeling, we taught Mackenzie what an inference was and how to respond to inferential questions. Then, to continue growing her ability to comprehend inferential inquiry, we used the Q-Matrix to begin engaging her in writing inferential questions about the text she was reading.

When introducing Mackenzie to the concept of an inference, we explicitly modeled how to respond to inferential comprehension questions. We designed questions that could not be answered with verbatim responses and/or use pronoun referents. We posed inferential questions based on information that was indirectly stated in the text or that could be deduced from relationships not directly stated (Center on Teaching and Learning, 2012)

The Q-Matrix (Wiederhold, 1998) provided a predictable structure to support Mackenzie's ability to begin writing questions. It includes 36 question stems that can be applied to text. The stems are arranged in a cognitive hierarchy. When applied to text, stems 1–12 can generate literal questions, stems 13–24 can generate inferential questions, and stems 25–36 can generate evaluative questions.

When using the Q-Matrix, first model how the stems can generate questions. Note that the words in the stems can be used in the question as they appear on the matrix. In this case, book language is added to the end of the stem to complete the question. However, in some cases, the words on the stems should be "pulled apart" to insert book language to complete the question. The full Q-Matrix might seem overwhelming to some readers. The Q-Matrix can be used more selectively by allowing students to choose one stem for a reading selection. The teacher can also focus the use of the stems by assigning one stem or several stems during a discussion.

SUMMARIZATION: SUMMARY PARAGRAPH

The final method recommended in Mackenzie's intervention plan was the summary paragraph. Summarizing is a challenge for many at-risk students, but it is especially difficult for students with ASD. Research suggests that due to the pragmatic process of moving from retelling to summarizing, a simple visual structure can prove helpful

(Broun, 2004; Chandler-Olcott & Kluth, 2009; Vacca, 2007). We selected the summary paragraph because the 1–3–1 framework was simple, visual, and could be modified based on whatever Mackenzie was reading.

Begin use of the summary paragraph with a discussion that summarization involves deciding which information is important enough to include and which information can be excluded. The summary paragraph provides a model for the number and types of sentences that should be included in a summary. Figure 5.2 contains a template for the summary paragraph. The content of the required sentences can be revised based on the text being summarized.

Name————————————Summary of ————————————

Summary Paragraph

A suggested framework for the construction of a summary paragraph is:

- 1 sentence of introduction (including title)
- 3 sentences of important information (major idea(s) and supporting details) explained with key vocabulary
- 1 sentence of conclusion (author's purpose)

Summary Paragraph = 5 sentences

Figure 5.2 Summary paragraph.

CONCLUSION

As summer came to an end it was now time to review Mackenzie's case report with her receiving instructional team. The group welcomed our findings and celebrated Mackenzie's hard work and success over the summer. After reading clinic, Mackenzie was more willing to read books about a variety of topics and exhibited greater perseverance as she explored these more challenging texts. In the early weeks of the school year, her language arts teacher provided an update. She explained that Mackenzie announced her arrival in middle school with the proclamation, "I read only THIS dog book!" Thanks to our experience, her new team was able to honor Mackenzie's passion while inviting her into a new world of middle school reading. A subsequent email to us explained that

Mackenzie was not the only dog lover in her section. *Dog Heroes of September 11th: A Tribute to America's Search and Rescue Dogs* (Bauer, 2006) became a new favorite of her peers—as did the remarkable young lady who shared it!

NOTE

1 The authors would like to thank Jennifer K. Solomon for her dedication to Mackenzie.

RESOURCES: CHILDREN'S BOOKS

Bauer, N. K. (2006). *Dog heroes of September 11: A tribute to America's search and rescue dogs.* Allenhurst, NJ: Kennel Club Books.

Byars, B., Myers, L., Duffey, B., & Long. L. (2000). *My dog, my hero.* New York, NY: Henry Holt.

Calmenson, S. (1998). *Rosie: A visiting dog's story.* New York, NY: Sandpiper Books.

Climo, S. (1996). *The Korean Cinderella.* New York, NY: HarperCollins.

Darvish, A. R. (2012). A friendly dedicated cop. Retrieved from http://www.thefreelibrary.com/POLICE+PATROL+DOGS+LEARN+NEW+SKILLS

Martin, R. (1998). *The rough-face-girl.* New York, NY: Puffin Books.

REFERENCES

American Psychological Association. (2000). *Diagnostic and statistical manual of mental disorders DSM-IV-TR.* New York, NY: American Psychological Association.

Autism Society of America. (2012). *Autism.* Retrieved from http://www.autismsociety.org/about-autism/

Broer, N., Aarnoutse, C., Kieviet, F., & Van Leeuwe, J. (2002). The effects of instructing the structural aspects of text. *Educational Studies, 28*(3), 213–238.

Broun, L. T. (2004). Teaching students with autistic spectrum disorders to read: A visual approach. *Teaching Exceptional Children, 36,* 36–40.

Carr, S. C., & Thompson, B. (1996). The effects of prior knowledge and schema activation strategies on the inferential reading comprehension of children with and without learning disabilities. *Learning Disability Quarterly, 19,* 48–61.

Center on Teaching and Learning. (2012). *Comprehension.* Retrieved from http://reading.uoregon.edu/big_ideas/comp/comp_dr_1.php

Centers for Disease Control and Prevention. (2012). *Autism spectrum disorders: Data and statistics.* Retrieved from http://www.cdc.gov/ncbddd/autism/data.html

Chandler-Olcott, K., & Kluth, P. (2009). Why everyone benefits from including students with autism in literacy classrooms. *The Reading Teacher, 62*(7), 548–557.

Cuesta College. (2012). *Making inferences and drawing conclusions.* Retrieved from http://academic.cuesta.edu/acasupp/AS/309.HTM

Gambrell, L. (1996). Creating classroom cultures that foster reading motivation. *The Reading Teacher, 50,* 4–25.

Guthrie, J., & Davis, M. (2003). Motivating struggling readers in middle school through an engagement model of classroom practice. *Reading & Writing Quarterly, 19*(1), 59–85.

Leslie, L., & Caldwell, J. (2010). *Qualitative Reading Inventory-5*. New York, NY: Allyn & Bacon.

Marinak, B. & Gambrell, L. (2007). Choosing and using informational text for instruction in the primary grades. In B. Guzzetti (Ed.), *Literacy for the new millennium* (pp. 141–154). New York, NY: Praeger Books.

Marinak, B., Gambrell, L., & Mazzoni, S. (2012). *Maximizing motivation for literacy learning, K-6*. New York, NY: Guilford.

McGinley, W., & Denner, P. (1987). Story impressions: A prereading/writing activity. *Journal of Reading, 31*(3), 248–253.

Miles, B., & Simpson, R. L. (2001). Effective practices for students with Asperger syndrome. *Focus on Exceptional Children, 34*(3), 1–14.

O'Connor, I. M., & Klein, P. D. (2004). Exploration of strategies for facilitating the reading comprehension of high-functioning children with autistic spectrum disorder. *Journal of Autism and Developmental Disorders, 34*(2), 115–127.

Ogle, D. (1986). KWL: A teaching model that develops active reading of expository text. *The Reading Teacher, 40*, 564–570.

Palincsar, A., & Duke, N. (2004). The role of text and text-reader interactions in young children's reading development and achievement. *The Elementary School Journal, 105*(2), 183–197.

Pressley, M. (1989). Strategies that improve children's memory and comprehension of text. *The Elementary School Journal, 90*, 3–12.

Rogers, M. F., & Mvles, B. S. (2001). Using social stories and comic strip conversations to interpret social situations for an adolescent with Asperger Syndrome. *Intervention in School & Clinic, 36*(5), 310. Retrieved from Questia database: http://www.questia.com/PM.qst?a=o&d=5001003694

Turner, J., & Paris, S. (1995). How literacy tasks influence children's' motivation for literacy. *The Reading Teacher, 48*(8), 662–673.

Vacca, J. S. (2007). Autistic children can be taught to read. *International Journal of Special Education, 22*(3), 54–61.

Wiederhold, C. W. (in consultation with Kagan, S.). (1998). *Cooperative learning & higher-level thinking: The Q-Matrix*. San Clemente, CA: Kagan.

Williams, J., Hall, K., & Lauer, K. (2004). Teaching expository text structure to young at-risk learners: Building the basics of comprehension instruction. *Exceptionality, 12*(3), 129–144.

Williams, J., Hall, K., Lauer, K., Stafford, B., DeSisto, L., & DeCani, J. (2005). Expository text comprehension in the primary classroom. *Journal of Educational Psychology, (97)*4, 538–550.

POST-READING ACTIVITIES

1. In your own words, define the term *spectrum*.

2. On a separate document, complete this table using your own words.

DIAGNOSTIC READING ASSESSMENT	PURPOSE
Woodcock Reading Test-Revised (WRMT-R)	
Slosson Oral Reading Test-Revised (SORT-R3)	
Qualitative Reading Inventory-5 (QRI-5)	

3. Based on the reading, list effective strategies for engaging readers on the autistic spectrum.

CHAPTER 6

EMOTIONAL DISTURBANCE

INTRODUCTION

According to the Individuals with Disabilities Education Act (IDEA), emotional disturbance (ED) is categorized as an exceptionality. It is defined as:

Emotional disturbance: A condition exhibiting one or more of the following characteristics over a long period of time and to a marked degree that adversely affects a child's educational performance:

a. An inability to learn that cannot be explained by intellectual, sensory, or health factors.

b. An inability to build or maintain satisfactory interpersonal relationships with peers and teachers.

c. Inappropriate types of behavior or feelings under normal circumstances.

d. A general pervasive mood of unhappiness or depression.

e. A tendency to develop physical symptoms or fears associated with personal or school problems. The term includes schizophrenia. The term does not apply to children who are socially maladjusted, unless it is determined that they have an emotional disturbance.

(Retrieved from https://www.scasd.org/cms/lib5/PA01000006/Centricity/Domain/114/13_categories_of_exceptionality_as_defined_by_IDEA.pdf)

The two studies presented in this section explore how diversity may be an influential factor when assessing the academic achievement of students with ED. The authors of the first reading explored the academic characteristics of students from varying socioeconomic backgrounds who have been identified as having ED. They examined levels of performance on high-stakes assessments and suspension rates. Results of the study and implications for intervention research are provided.

The next study compared the development of oral reading fluency among general education students and those with ED or a learning disability. The authors describe how data was collected and analyzed and identify common trends. This reading builds on the first study, based on the scale of the study and number of participants.

Both readings in this section will introduce preservice and new teachers to the characteristics of students who are classified as having ED. Readers will learn about academic and social attributes that may influence achievement. The studies were chosen to emphasize the prevalence of this exceptionality and to provide meaningful and appropriate interventions for this diverse population of learners.

CHAPTER 6

READING 6.1 OVERVIEW

In this article, Siperstein and Bountress explore the academic characteristics of students who are considered exceptional under the category of emotional disturbance (ED). One hundred forty ED students from communities with varied socioeconomic status (SES), high-stakes testing scores, and rates of suspension were studied. The authors used the Woodcock-Johnson III assessment to measure literacy and mathematic achievement. They also employed state testing scores to analyze relative academic achievement. Readers will learn about the implications of intervention practices and eligibility practices for students with ED in diverse schools.

PRE-READING ACTIVITIES

1. How would you define emotional disturbance (ED)? Write down your initial thoughts.
2. Predict the relationship between the academic characteristics of students with ED and the SES of the school.
3. Describe how you would promote academic success for students with ED.

SCHOOL CONTEXT AND THE ACADEMIC ACHIEVEMENT OF STUDENTS WITH EMOTIONAL DISTURBANCE

BY ANDREW L. WILEY, GARY N. SIPERSTEIN, KAITLIN E. BOUNTRESS, STEVEN R. FORNESS, AND FREDERICK J. BRIGHAM

ABSTRACT: *The authors examined the academic characteristics of 140 elementary-aged students served under the category of emotional disturbance (ED) from schools that differed in income level, performance on state testing, and suspension rates. School income accounted for a large amount of the variance in the reading and math achievement of students with ED as measured by the Woodcock-Johnson III. However, relative academic performance (as measured by performance on state testing compared with same-school peers and teacher ratings of academic competence) was similar across school income levels. Implications for intervention research and eligibility practices for students with ED are discussed.*

There are currently almost a half million children and youth in the United States served in special education under the category of emotional

Andrew L. Wiley, et al., "School Context and the Academic Achievement of Students With Emotional Disturbance," *Behavioral Disorders*, vol. 33, no. 4, pp. 198-210.

disturbance (ED; U.S. Department of Education, 2007). These students experience some of the worst educational outcomes of any student group, including academic underachievement, low grades, grade retention, failure to graduate, dropout, and suspension/expulsion (Bullis & Cheney, 1999; Greenbaum et al., 1996; Kauffman, 2005; Kortering & Blackorby, 1992; Wagner, 1995; Walker, Ramsey, & Gresham, 2004). Historically, school-based interventions for students with ED have focused primarily on improving behavior (Lane, 2004), largely because problem behavior is the most conspicuous characteristic of ED (Sabornie, Cullinan, Osborne, & Brock, 2005). Recently, however, there has been a heightened interest in interventions that directly address the academic deficits of this population as a result of federal mandates requiring schools to demonstrate high levels of student achievement for all students (Mooney, Denny, & Gunter, 2004), as well as research suggesting that effective academic interventions can also reduce the problem behavior of students with ED (e.g., Gunter & Reed, 1997; Jolivette, Wehby, & Hirsch, 1999; Nelson, Johnson, & Marchand-Martella, 1996). Although some promising academic interventions for students with ED have been identified, additional and more rigorous research is clearly needed (Gunter & Reed, 1998; Lane, 2004; Mooney, Epstein, Reid, & Nelson, 2003; Ruhl & Berlinghoff, 1992).

To identify effective academic interventions and supports for students with ED, it is critical that we understand and take into account their academic characteristics and needs. Most research to date suggests that students with ED exhibit moderate to severe academic deficits across subject areas (e.g., Nelson, Benner, Lane, & Smith, 2004; Reid, Gonzalez, Nordness, Trout, & Epstein, 2004). Furthermore, these academic deficits tend to remain stable or worsen over time (e.g., Anderson, Kutash, & Duchnowski, 2001; Greenbaum et al., 1996; Mattison, Hooper, & Glassberg, 2002; Nelson et al., 2004; Reid et al., 2004). Given the emphasis on impaired educational performance in the federal definition for ED, findings showing that students with ED have low academic achievement scores should not be surprising.

What has in fact proven surprising and difficult to explain is the substantial variability in academic achievement that exists for students with ED (Reid et al., 2004; Trout, Nordness, Pierce, & Epstein, 2003). Aggregated data mask significant within-group differences in the academic functioning of students with ED. For example, in their meta-analysis of research on the academic status of students with ED compared with students without disabilities, Reid and colleagues (2004) calculated a wide range of effect sizes for the studies they reviewed (–3.37 to +0.5). Moreover, an omnibus test for heterogeneity of effect sizes was significant, indicating that there were greater than expected differences across studies in the academic achievement of students with ED.

Further evidence that students with ED are heterogeneous with regard to their academic functioning is provided by national data recently collected from a stratified sample of more than 2000 elementary and secondary students served in special education under the category of ED (Wagner, Kutash, Duchnowski, Epstein, & Sumi, 2005). Among students with ED, 61% scored in the bottom quartile on the Passage Comprehension subtest of the Woodcock-Johnson III (WJ-III), 25% in the second quartile, 9% in the third quartile, and 5% in the top quartile. On the Calculation subtest, 43% were in the bottom quartile, 25% in the second quartile, 19% in the third quartile, and 8% in the top quartile. Findings such as these suggest that to obtain an accurate understanding of the academic characteristics of students with ED, we must closely examine the heterogeneity within the population.

Heterogeneity of student characteristics within disability categories has been identified as one of the most critical issues that must be addressed in identifying research-validated special education practices. Forness (2005) stated that the pursuit of evidence-based practice for students with ED may be a "chimerical endeavor" if we don't first account for the "admixture of research participants in school-identified categories of special education" (p. 318). The uncertainty that within-category variability introduces into intervention research led Odom and colleagues (2005) to conclude that "researchers cannot address a simple question about whether a practice in special education is effective; they must specify for whom the practice is effective and in what context" (p. 139, emphasis added). In other words, significant variability in the academic achievement of students with ED raises serious questions about whether results from intervention research can be generalized to all students with ED served in public schools.

Researchers have examined numerous factors that might explain differences in the achievement of students with ED. For example, several studies have found a relationship between special education placement and achievement for students with ED. Students with ED served in more restrictive settings have been found to have larger academic deficits than students with ED served in less restrictive settings (e.g., Browne, Stotsky, & Eichorn, 1977; Glassberg, 1994; Lane, Wehby, Little, & Cooley, 2005; Meadows, Neel, Scott, & Parker, 1994). Subject area has also been found to explain variation in achievement (e.g., Lee, Elliot, & Barbour, 1994; Rosenblatt & Rosenblatt, 1999). For example, Greenbaum and colleagues (1996) found that students with ED performed significantly lower in math than reading. Some researchers have examined within-child factors that contribute to variability in the academic performance of students with ED. Nelson and colleagues (2004), for instance, found that math deficits were larger for older (older than 12 years) versus younger (12 years old and younger) students with ED. However, very few studies have provided the necessary information to allow meaningful analysis of other within-child factors (e.g., gender, ethnicity; Reid et al., 2004).

With the exception of some preliminary work on teacher instructional behaviors and classroom context (Sutherland, Lewis-Palmer, Stichter, & Morgan, 2008), research has seldom considered the role of school context in explaining variability in the academic characteristics of students with ED. It is likely that aspects of school context such as community, institutional, and individual factors exert a major influence on how schools approach the eligibility process and whom schools serve in special education under the category of ED.

School personnel, in allocating limited instructional resources, must balance the objective of determining which students in their building exhibit the greatest learning and behavior problems with the objective of determining which eligibility criteria those students do or do not meet (Gerber & Semmel, 1984; MacMillan & Siperstein, 2002). Importantly, judgments about the severity of student problems (and who qualifies for services) are based, at least in part, on comparisons to the performance of the average child in the school. Moreover, determinations regarding who is served as ED are influenced not only by perceptions of student problems but also by other challenges, pressures, and priorities that confront school personnel at the local level as they try to provide services and supports to students with behavioral and learning problems.

Therefore, to the extent that the average student can be characterized by the school context, and to the extent that other influences on the eligibility process vary by school context, differences in school context are likely to be associated with differences in who is served for ED. In this regard, one aspect of school context that is likely to be of paramount importance is the socioeconomic level of the school. Abundant research has shown a strong relationship between socioeconomic status (SES) and the academic achievement of children and youth in the general population (McLoyd, 1998; Sirin, 2005; White, 1982). Children who live in poverty generally score from 0.5 to 1.5 standard deviations below children who do not live in poverty on standardized tests of academic achievement (Brooks-Gunn & Duncan, 1997). Thus, school SES plays a major role in determining the backdrop of average student performance against which eligibility decisions are made.

The purpose of the present study, therefore, was to directly examine the relationship between school SES and the academic characteristics of students with ED. Furthermore, because SES is only one aspect of school context, we also focused on other school characteristics, such as the academic achievement and the rate of disciplinary actions at the school. We hypothesized that schools that vary in terms of income level, academic performance, and disciplinary problems also vary in whom they serve as ED and that, as a result, students with ED are markedly different school to school. Thus, we examined the way schools that vary in terms of income level, academic performance, and disciplinary problems differ in how they define *emotional disturbance* and what it means to be ED.

METHOD

SCHOOL CONTEXT

To describe the school context in which students are served as ED, we focused on school income level, school academic performance, and suspension rate. All school data were obtained from the Massachusetts Department of Education. School data are collected and reported annually (in both print and electronic formats) by the Massachusetts Department of Education to meet state and federal reporting requirements.

School income level. School income level/SES for each school was determined by the percentage of students in the building who met the criteria for free or reduced lunch. Student eligibility for free or reduced lunch is determined based on household size and income level. Students are eligible for reduced lunch if their household income (based on size) is equal to or less than 180% of the federal poverty guidelines; students are eligible for free lunch if their household income is less than 130% of the federal poverty guidelines. The 2006–2007 poverty guideline for a family of four, for example, is a total annual household income of $20,000. Eligibility for free and reduced lunch has been used extensively as a measure of school SES (Ensminger et al., 2000).

School academic performance. Results from the Massachusetts Comprehensive Assessment System (MCAS) were used to represent the overall academic performance of schools. The MCAS is administered annually to 3rd-through 10th-grade students to measure progress toward statewide educational goals. Performance on the MCAS is reported for schools as the percentage of students in each grade scoring in ranges labeled *advanced, proficient, needs improvement,* and *warning/failing* in each of the subject areas tested in that grade (e.g., English/language arts, math, science, social studies). For the present study, the percentage of fourth-grade students scoring advanced or proficient on the English/language arts section of the MCAS was used as a measure of the academic performance of the school.

School suspension rate. Out-of-school suspension (OSS) rates were recorded for each school. The OSS rate is reported as the percentage of students at the school who received one or more out-of-school suspension in one school year. The OSS rate was selected as a school context variable for several reasons. First, it provides information about the frequency and severity of problem behaviors exhibited by students at the school. The student who is referred for services in a school with high overall levels of problem behavior may be very different from the student who is referred for services in a school that experiences substantially less problem behavior (Brigham & Kauffman, 1996). Of equal importance is the fact that differences in OSS rates reflect important context-related differences in how schools respond to and address student behavior. The OSS rates are driven by individual factors (e.g., teacher and administrator attitudes, beliefs, levels of experience, stakeholder pressures) and organizational factors (climate, resource availability, leadership, discipline policies) as much or more than the frequency and severity of student problem behavior at the school (Christie, Nelson, & Jolivette, 2004).

STUDENTS WITH ED

Participants were 140 students in Grades K though 6 served in special education under the category of ED (see Table 6.1 for demographic information). Students were included only if their current individualized education plan confirmed that ED was the primary special education eligibility category.[1] At the time of the study, these students were served in 36 schools. The schools represented the full range of school income, school academic performance, and suspension rates. The percentage of students eligible for free and reduced lunch at these schools ranged from 2% to 95% (*M* = 44.21%, *SD* = 33.48%). The percentage of fourth-grade students scoring advanced or proficient ranged from 16% to 88% (*M* = 46.29%, *SD* = 21.19%). Finally, the percentage of all students at each school receiving one or more OSS ranged from 0% to 19% (*M* = 3.32%, SD = 4.31%).

Table 6.1 **Participant demographics.**

STUDENTS WITH ED (*N* = 140) (%)	
Gender	
Male	84
Female	16
Race	
Caucasian	59
African-American	19
Hispanic	17
Asian	2
Other	3
Eligible for free/reduced lunch	
Yes	68
No	32

ASSESSMENT OF ACADEMIC ACHIEVEMENT

Measures of academic achievement compared with national norms consisted of two math subtests (Calculation and Applied Problems) and two reading subtests (Letter Word Identification and Passage Comprehension) of the WJ-I1I (Woodcock, McGrew, & Mather, 2001). Results for each subtest are reported as standard scores (*M* = 100, *SD* = 15). The WJ-III has high concurrent validity with other major individual tests of academic achievement, and test-retest reliabilities for all four subtests are strong, ranging from .83 to .92.

Two measures were used to assess the academic functioning of students with ED relative to their school and classroom peers. First, the scores of students with ED on the English/language arts and math sections of the MCAS were used. Student scores, school means, and school standard deviations were used to calculate *Z* scores that represented the difference between the MCAS performance of students with ED and the average MCAS performance of students in their school. English/language arts and math means and standard deviations for each school, grade, and subject were obtained from the public Web site for the state Department of Education. Second, teachers rated students with ED on the academic competence subscale of the Social Skills Rating System–Teacher Version (SSRS-T; Gresham & Eliot, 1990). The SSRS-T rating of academic competence requires teachers to rate students on nine Likert-type items to compare the target student with his or her classmates in academic performance, motivation to succeed, and intellectual functioning. Teacher ratings of academic competence on the SSRS-T are reported as standard scores (*M* = 100, *SD* = 15). The coefficient alpha reliability for academic competence is .95.

PROCEDURE

The WJ-III was administered at the student's school in a quiet area outside the classroom by project staff. The SSRS-T rating of academic competence was completed by the teacher who spent the most instructional time with the student. Of the teachers (*n* = 57) who completed the rating form, 38% were regular education teachers and 62% were special education teachers. Student records were reviewed to obtain demographic information and student scores on the English/language arts and math sections of the MCAS. The MCAS is administered to students beginning in the third grade. Therefore, MCAS scores were available only for third-through sixth-grade students (*n* = 76). Grades were similar for students with ED across school income levels.

RESULTS

To assess the relationship between school context and the academic functioning of students with ED, we conducted a series of multiple regression analyses.[2] First, four parallel regression analyses were conducted in which each of the four WJ-III subtest scores were regressed on all three school context variables (school income, school academic performance, school suspension rates). Next, the three measures of relative academic achievement (teacher ratings, English/language arts MCAS score, math MCAS score) were regressed on the school context variables. In each analysis, school income was entered first. School academic performance and suspension rates were entered second and last to determine the extent to which they predicted unique variance above and beyond school SES. To correct for family-wise error rates, p was set at .007 (.05/7).

Results for the regression models predicting the performance of students with ED on the four subtests of the WJ-III are presented in Table 6.2. For each model, the overall F value was significant. Furthermore, for each analysis, school income contributed significantly to WJ-III subtest scores, but school academic performance did not. Higher school income predicted higher WJ-III scores in every model. The total R^2 for each model ranged from .22 to .29. For interpreting squared correlations in regression analysis, an R^2

Table 6.2 **Regression analyses for school variables predicting Woodcock-Johnson III scores[a].**

WJ SUBTESTS	SCHOOL VARIABLE	B	SE	β	R^2	F
Letter Word	Income	.29	.07	.55***	.22	13.08***
	Academic performance	.01	.10	.01		
	Suspension rate	.56	.44	.13		
Passage Comprehension	Income	.29	.06	.58***	.24	14.29***
	Academic performance	−.01	.09	−.01		
	Suspension rate	.53	.39	.14		
Calculation	Income	.22	.06	.46***	.25	15.08***
	Academic performance	.16	.09	.20		
	Suspension rate	.84	.39	.23*		
Applied Problems	Income	.24	.07	.45***	.29	18.33***
	Academic performance	.19	.10	.22		
	Suspension rate	.69	.42	.17		

[a]For all four regression models, df = 3, 136.
*$p < .05$.
***$p < .001$.

of .01 is a small effect, an R^2 of .10 is a medium effect, and an R^2 of .25 is a large effect (Cohen, Cohen, West, & Aiken, 2003, p. 179). These regression analyses showed that school income was strongly related to the academic achievement of students with ED as measured by a standardized test. The regression models accounted for 22% of the variance in Letter Word Identification, 24% of the variance in Passage Comprehension, 25% of the variance in Calculation, and 29% of the variance in Applied Problems.

In stark contrast to predicting academic performance as measured by the WJ-III, none of the school context variables predicted the MCAS performance of students with ED relative to same-school peers or the academic ratings of students with ED by teachers relative to their same-class peers (see Table 6.3). Overall, school context was not significant in explaining variance in the academic performance of students with ED relative to their school and classroom peers. Unlike academic achievement relative to national norms (WJ-III scores), school context was unrelated to the academic achievement of students with ED relative to their same-school and same-class peers.

Table 6.3 **Regression analyses for school variables predicting relative academic achievement[a].**

RELATIVE ACHIEVEMENT MEASURE	SCHOOL VARIABLE	*B*	*SE*	*β*	R^2	*F*
English/language arts relative to school (MCAS)	Income	−.01	.01	−.24	.05	1.23
	Academic performance	.01	.01	.17		
	Suspension rate	.03	.04	.11		
Math relative to school (MCAS)	Income	.01	.01	.04	.02	.38
	Academic performance	−.01	.01	−.12		
	Suspension rate	.01	.04	.05		
Teacher rating of academic competence	Income	.02	.05	.07	<.01	.33
	Academic performance	.03	.08	.06		
	Suspension rate	.24	.31	.09		

[a]For the regression model predicting teacher ratings of academic competence, $N = 140$, $df = 3, 136$. For the two regression models predicting performance on state testing (ELA and Math) relative to same-school peers, $N = 76$, $df - 3, 72$.

As a follow-up to the regression analyses, we explored the relationship between school context and the academic characteristics of students with ED by focusing on schools at the extreme ends of the SES continuum. We identified two groups of students with ED from the total sample of 140. The first group included students with ED from high-income (HI) schools, whereas the second group included students with ED from low-income (LI) schools. HI schools were defined as those that had 20% or fewer students eligible for free and reduced lunch. LI schools were defined as those that had 70% or more students eligible for free and reduced lunch. Using these criteria, we were able to identify 15 HI schools and 10 LI schools. In our sample, there were 39 students with ED from HI schools and 64 students with ED from LI schools. Table 6.4 presents demographic information for the students with ED from HI and LI schools.

Table 6.4 **Demographics of students with ED from High-Income (HI) and Low-Income (LI) Schools.**

CHARACTERISTIC	STUDENTS WITH ED (*N* = 39) FROM HI SCHOOLS (%)	STUDENTS WITH ED (*N* = 64) FROM LI SCHOOLS (%)
Gender		
Male	86	87
Female	14	13
Race		
Caucasian	87	47
African American	5	25
Hispanic	3	23
Asian	5	0
Other	0	5
Free/reduced lunch		
Yes	15	92
No	85	8

A series of one-way analyses of variance were conducted to compare students with ED from HI schools to students with ED from LI schools on the WJ-III.[3] The differences between the two groups were substantial (see Table 6.5). All of the effect sizes for group differences were very large; the largest effect size was for Applied Problems and Passage Comprehension, followed by Letter Word Identification and

Table 6.5 **Group means for the academic achievement of students with ED, by school context.**

	STUDENTS WITH ED FROM HI SCHOOLS (*N* = 39) *M (SD)*	STUDENTS WITH ED FROM LI SCHOOLS (*N* = 64) *M (SD)*	*F*	ES
Letter Word	102.82 (10.75)	82.97 (18.19)	37.46***	1.24
Passage Comprehension	98.33 (13.27)	79.20 (14.64)	44.36***	1.35
Calculation	102.91 (12.44)	85.69 (15.42)	34.76***	1.21
Applied Problems	108.05 (14.47)	87.47 (15.62)	44.44***	1.35

***$p < .001$.

Calculation. Across all four subtests, students with ED from the HI schools scored in the average range. Conversely, students with ED from LI schools scored in the low range.

Next, we compared students with ED from HI schools to students with ED from LI schools on their relative academic performance (how they compare with students in their schools and classrooms). We first looked at the relative performance (*Z* scores calculated using school means) on state testing (MCAS) of students with ED from HI and LI schools. Twenty students who had MCAS scores (out of 39) were from HI schools, whereas 35 students who had MCAS scores (out of 64) were from LI schools.

No differences were found for the MCAS performance of students with ED from HI and LI schools relative to their same-school peers (see Table 6.6). On average, students with ED from HI schools scored more than a standard deviation (Z = −1.23) below their same-school peers on the English/language arts section of the MCAS, and more than half a standard deviation (Z = −.61) lower on the math section. Students with ED from LI schools scored three fourths of a standard deviation (Z = –.78) lower than same-school peers on English/language arts and almost half a standard deviation lower on math (Z = −.41). Relative to same-school peers, the academic performance deficits of students with ED from HI schools are the same as or possibly larger than the academic performance deficits of students with ED from LI schools. These findings are in sharp contrast to student performance on standardized assessment, where performance is calculated based on national norms.

Table 6.6 **Group means for the relative achievement of students with ED, by school context.**

	STUDENTS WITH ED FROM HI SCHOOLS (*N* = 39) *M* (*SD*)	STUDENTS WITH ED FROM LI SCHOOLS (*N* = 64) *M* (SD)	*F*	SIGNIFICANCE
English/language arts relative to school (MCAS)[a]	−1.23 (1.32)	−0.78 (1.26)	1.53	ns
Math relative to school (MCAS)[a]	−0.61 (1.07)	−0.41 (1.08)	0.45	ns
Teacher rating of academic competence	91.95 (10.56)	90.98 (12.01)	0.17	ns

[a]For English/language arts and math scores on state testing (MCAS), *n* = 20 for the high-income group and *n* = 35 for the low-income group.

Similar to relative performance on the MCAS, there were no differences between the two groups in teacher ratings of academic competence (see Table 6.6). Rating scale means for both groups showed that, on average, the academic performance of students with ED from both HI and LI schools was judged to be approximately two thirds of a standard deviation below their classmates. Overall, despite the dramatic differences between students with ED from HI and LI schools on academic achievement based on national norms, teacher ratings of their academic competence were almost identical for both groups.

DISCUSSION

To be eligible for special education services under the category of ED, a student must exhibit social-emotional problems that "adversely affect educational performance" (Individuals With Disabilities Education Improvement Act, 2004). This impairment criterion has long been criticized for being vague and overly subjective (e.g., Forness & Knitzer, 1992; Kauffman, 2005). Furthermore, the wording of the criterion implies (and has been narrowly interpreted by schools to mean) an adverse impact on academic achievement only, rather than a broader interpretation that would include other aspects of school performance (e.g., interpersonal, affective, vocational; Gresham, 2005). Even when the impairment standard is narrowly interpreted to mean low achievement, no operational criterion exists to guide schools in making this judgment. The absence of clear eligibility criteria is likely a major factor in variability from one school to the next in the characteristics of students served as ED.

The findings of this study clearly demonstrate that the academic characteristics of students served as ED vary markedly from school to school. Overall, we found that across different school contexts, there was significant variability in the academic achievement of students identified by the school as ED. School income level accounted for a large amount of variance (22%–29%) in the academic achievement of students with ED. In fact, when we compared students with ED in the highest income schools with students with ED in the lowest income schools, there was an approximately 20-point average difference in standard scores on individual tests of reading and math. Overall, we found that school context produced a huge range in the academic achievement of students with ED, such that differences of almost 1.5 standard deviations existed between students from LI and HI schools.

These results confirm that the eligibility criteria set forth in the federal definition concerning educational performance are inconsistently applied from one school to the next. Students with ED from LI schools exhibited large academic achievement deficits, scoring in the low range compared with national norms. Students served in special education under the category of ED in LI schools exhibit substantial deficits in academic achievement, conforming to the impairment criterion in the federal definition of ED. On the other hand, students with ED from HI schools were average to above average in their academic achievement compared with national norms. That is, the characteristics of students with ED from HI schools did not align with federal guidelines if "educational impairment" is interpreted to mean academic deficits.

However, variability in the academic achievement of students with ED based on national norms tell only part of the story. We also examined the academic achievement of students with ED based on local norms (i.e., relative to the achievement of their same-school peers who were not ED). We measured the relative achievement of students with ED using teacher ratings and student performance on state testing compared with all same-school, same-grade peers. Strikingly, we found that the relative achievement of students with ED was the same across HI and LI schools. There were no differences between students with ED from LI and HI schools in performance on state testing compared with their same-school peers. In HI schools, students with ED scored on average well more than a standard deviation below their same-school peers on the state test of reading and more than a half standard deviation below on math. Similarly, in LI schools, students with ED scored an average of three fourths of a standard deviation below their same-school peers on reading and just under a half standard deviation below their peers on the state test of math. It should be noted that there was probably a floor effect operating for LI schools. That is, because the average performance of all students on state testing in LI elementary schools was generally low, students with ED could be only so much lower than that. This was also the only area in which we observed any substantial subject area differences in that reading deficits relative to classmates were somewhat more severe than math deficits relative to peers.

These results (the absence of differences between HI and LI schools in relative achievement) present a very different picture from the one provided by looking at the academic achievement of students with ED based on national norms. The heterogeneity in academic achievement that was so pronounced when looking at standard scores on the WJ-III was, in effect, washed away when looking at the relative achievement of students with ED based on local norms. This suggests a certain consistency in how schools operationalize the educational impairment criterion. From the perspective of schools, impaired educational performance for a student with ED means low achievement compared with his or her classmates. Similar findings have been reported for students with learning disabilities (LD). Peterson and Shinn (2002) found that students are identified as LD when their achievement is low relative to their same-school peers. A major finding of our study is that relative achievement is equally important for understanding who schools serve under the category of ED.

Our findings raise many of the same questions for the field of ED that Peterson and Shinn (2002) raised regarding eligibility practices for LD. We must ask ourselves whether it is professionally defensible that school context determines whether a child receives services for ED. School practitioners have long recognized that many students who are not identified as ED in one type of school (e.g., low SES) would likely qualify for services in another type of school (e.g., high SES). Our study confirms this reality and underscores the need to reexamine our practices in special education as they relate to providing services to students with ED.

One interesting serendipitous finding that further sheds light on the unique effect of school context was the large difference between LI and HI schools in the prevalence of students served as ED. In obtaining the sample for the present study, we were able to find many students identified as ED in LI schools, whereas there were very few students identified as ED in HI schools. Specifically, the mean number of participants per LI school was more than twice the mean number of participants per HI school. This finding is consistent with national data showing that LI school districts serve higher percentages of students as ED (Coutinho, Oswald, Best, & Forness, 2002; Oswald, Coutinho, Best, & Singh, 1999).

It is likely that multiple factors contribute to a wide disparity between LI and HI schools in the prevalence of students served in special education under the ED category. In part, the difference reflects a naturally occurring difference in the prevalence of emotional and behavioral disorders exhibited by children from low-SES versus high-SES families (Brooks-Gunn & Duncan, 1997; Costello, Compton, Keeler, & Angold, 2003; Costello, Messer, Bird, Cohen, & Reinherz, 1997; McLoyd, 1998). Another reason why fewer students in HI schools are served under the category of ED could be because their needs are more frequently met in other ways. For example, students with ED may be served by HI schools under other categories of special education (e.g., LD; Duncan, Forness, & Hartsough, 1995) more often than their counterparts in LI schools. Also, it could be that a greater percentage of HI students with ED have access to nonschool mental health services and supports that address their individual needs, thus reducing the need for school-based special education.

This study has several implications for intervention research for students with ED. Our results raise questions about preferred measures of outcome: using progress on standardized tests with national norms versus using progress on closing the gap between students with ED and their classmates without ED. In actual fact, any measure of academic progress may be suspect, given our findings, unless progress is stratified by children in their different educational contexts of high-, middle-, and low-income schools. Moreover, because the population of students served as ED is heterogeneous, we cannot assume that academic interventions demonstrated to be effective for students with ED served in one school context will be effective for students served in a different school context. In addition, our results indicate that primary and secondary prevention efforts should concentrate on students' relative achievement based on local norms (e.g., teacher ratings of academic achievement) as a risk factor for students being identified as ED. Most importantly, the results presented here underscore the need for researchers to thoroughly characterize participants and the context in which they were identified and served as ED. Descriptions of school characteristics may be as important as descriptions of variables such as gender and age when it comes to conducting and analyzing research for students with ED. Positive and negative findings from past intervention research should be reexamined with student variability across school contexts in mind.

A limitation of this study is that student data were not collected at the time students were initially found eligible under the category of ED. Consequently, inferences about variability in student characteristics arising from variability in eligibility practices can be made only retrospectively. On one hand, differences in academic achievement as measured by the WJ-III were large enough to all but rule out the possibility that HI and LI schools use the same standard to establish impairment in educational performance. It is less certain whether relative achievement changed over time (such that, for example, students with ED were achieving the same as their peers at the time they were identified but have fallen behind since). Future research should examine the academic characteristics of students in different school contexts who exhibit risk factors for ED but are not receiving services. This information would enable us to better understand what child or school characteristics are related to service delivery. It would also allow us to examine differences across different school contexts in the magnitude of students who meet eligibility requirements for ED but are not in special education.

CONCLUSION

Recent reform efforts, particularly those prompted by high-stakes assessment for general education, have recognized that individual schools have widely varying student populations and require different resources to promote academic success in their students. Contextual disparities require different schools to modify and supplement instruction from a variety of means (Title I funding, state supplemental dollars, etc.). Paradoxically, special education research and perhaps even services have not kept pace with this recognition of academic differences among schools. Because special education is a federally mandated program and state education codes contain universal definitions and criteria for disability categories, there is a certain presumption that all schools in a state serve a uniform group of children.

This study demonstrated that schools do not serve a uniform group under the category of ED. Students with ED from different types of schools exhibited very different academic characteristics. It appears that schools interpret the impaired educational performance clause of the ED definition to mean low achievement relative to the average achievement of students in their school, not according to a larger standard of low achievement. It may also be that schools differ in the extent to which they consider aspects of performance other than academic achievement (i.e., social-emotional functioning). The implications of these findings for served and unserved students with ED are profound. Recognizing the relationship between school characteristics and the academic achievement of students with ED is necessary if we are to identify and implement effective interventions and policies for these students.

NOTES

1 Permission forms were sent to the parents of elementary school-aged students who were served in special education under the category of ED in those districts. Written parent permission was obtained for 69% of the students who were recruited. Consent rates were similar across all participating school districts.

2 For all models, regression diagnostics (leverage, Cook's D, standardized DFBETA) did not reveal any problems with influential outliers (Hoaglin & Welsh, 1978; Neter, Wasserman, & Kutner, 1989; Pedhazur, 1999). Collinearity diagnostics (condition indices, variance inflation factors, tolerance) did not indicate any linear dependency between the school context (predictor) variables (Fox, 1991; Pedhazur, 1999). Tests of quadratic and interaction terms were not significant (Aiken & West, 1991; Baron & Kenny, 1986; Pedhazur, 1999).

3 A square-root transformation was employed for Letter Word scores to obtain equal group variances; equality of group variances is an assumption underlying analysis of variance (Hinkle, Wiersma, & Jurs, 2003). The reported *F* value is for the comparison of group means on the transformed variable.

4 Effect sizes were calculated for all statistically significant group differences by subtracting the LI mean from the HI group mean and dividing the result by the pooled standard deviation (Lipsey & Wilson, 2001).

REFERENCES

Aiken, L. S., & West, S. G. (1991). *Multiple regression: Testing and interpreting interactions.* Thousand Oaks, CA: Sage.

Anderson, J. A., Kutash, K., & Duchnowski, A. J. (2001). A comparison of the academic progress of students with EBD and students with LD. *Journal of Emotional and Behavioral Disorders, 9,* 106–111.

Baron, R. M., & Kenny, D. A. (1986). The moderator-mediator distinction in social psychological research: Conceptual, strategic, and statistical considerations. *Journal of Personality and Social Psychology,* 57, 1173–1182.

Brigham, F. J., & Kauffman, J. M. (1998). Creating supportive environments for students with emotional or behavioral disorders. *Effective School Practices,* 77(2), 5–35.

Brooks-Gunn, J., & Duncan, G. J. (1997). The effects of poverty on children. *The Future of Children, 7,* 55–71.

Browne, T., Stotsky, B. A., & Eichorn, J. (1977). A selective comparison of psychological, developmental, social, and academic factors among emotionally disturbed children in three treatment settings. *Child Psychiatry and Human Development, 7,* 231–253.

Bullis, M., & Cheney, D. (1999). Vocational and transition interventions for adolescents and young adults with emotional and behavioral disorders. *Focus on Exceptional Children, 31(7),* 1–24.

Christie, C. A., Nelson, C. M., & Jolivette, K. (2004). School characteristics related to the use of suspension. *Education and Treatment of Children, 27,* 509–526.

Cohen, J., Cohen, P., West, S. G., & Aiken, L. S. (2003). *Applied multiple regression/correlation analysis for the behavioral sciences* (3rd ed.). Mahwah, NJ: Erlbaum.

Costello, E. J., Compton, S. N., Keeler, G., & Angold, A. (2003). Relationships between poverty and psychopathology: A natural experiment. *Journal of the American Medical Association, 290,* 2023–2029.

Costello, E. J., Messer, S. C., Bird, H. R., Cohen, P., & Reinherz, H. Z. (1998). The prevalence of serious emotional disturbance: A re-analysis of community studies. *Journal of Child and Family Studies, 7,* 411–432.

Coutinho, M. J., Oswald, D. P., Best, A. M., & Forness, S. R. (2002). Gender and sociodemographic factors and the disproportionate identification of culturally and linguistically diverse students with emotional disturbance. *Behavioral Disorders, 27,* 109–125.

Duncan, B. B., Forness, S. R., & Hartsough, C. (1995). Students identified as seriously emotionally disturbed in day treatment. *Behavioral Disorders, 20,* 238–252.

Ensminger, M. E., Forrest, C. B., Riley, A. W., Kang, M., Green, B. F., & Starfield, B., et al. (2000). The validity of measures of socio-economic status of adolescents. *Journal of Adolescent Research,* 75, 392–419.

Forness, S. R. (2005). The pursuit of evidence-based practice in special education for children with emotional and behavioral disorders. *Behavioral Disorders, 30,* 311–330.

Forness, S. R., & Knitzer, J. A. (1992). A new proposed definition and terminology to replace "serious emotional disturbance" in the Individuals with Disabilities Act. *School Psychology Review, 21,* 12–20.

Fox, J. (1991). *Regression diagnostics.* Thousand Oaks, CA: Sage.

Gerber, M., & Semmel, M. (1984). Teacher as imperfect test: Reconceptualizing the referral process. *Educational Psychologist, 19,* 137–146.

Glassberg, L. A. (1994). Students with behavioral disorders: Determinants of placement outcomes. *Behavioral Disorders, 19,* 181–191.

Greenbaum, P. E., Dedrick, R. F., Friedman, R. M., Kutash, K., Brown, E. C., & Lardieri, S. P., et al. (1996). National Adolescent and Child Treatment Study (NACTS): Outcomes for children with serious emotional and behavioral disturbance. *Journal of Emotional and Behavioral Disorders, 4,* 130–146.

Gresham, F. M. (2005). Response to intervention: An alternative means of identifying students as emotionally disturbed. *Education and Treatment of Children, 28,* 328–344.

Gresham, F. M., & Elliot, S. N. (1990). *Social skills rating system.* Circle Pines, MN: American Guidance Services.

Gunter, P. L., & Reed, T. M. (1997). Academic instruction of children with emotional and behavioral disorders. *Preventing School Failure, 42,* 33–37.

Hinkle, D. E., Wiersma, W., & Jurs, S. G. (2003). *Applied statistics for the behavioral sciences* (5th ed.). New York: Houghton Mifflin.

Hoaglin, D. C., & Welsh, R. E. (1978). The hat matrix in regression and ANOVA. *American Statistician, 32,* 17–22.

Individuals With Disabilities Education Improvement Act of 2004, 31 U.S.C.

Jolivette, K., Wehby, J. H., & Hirsch, L. (1999). Academic strategy identification for students exhibiting inappropriate classroom behaviors. *Behavioral Disorders, 24,* 210–221.

Kauffman, J. M. (2005). *Characteristics of emotional and behavioral disorders of children and youth* (8th ed.). Upper Saddle River, NJ: Merrill Prentice.

Kortering, L. J., & Blackorby, J. (1992). High school dropout and students identified with behavioral disorders. *Behavioral Disorders, 18,* 24–32.

Lane, K. L. (2004). Academic instruction and tutoring interventions for students with emotional and behavioral disorders: 1990 to the present. In R. B. Rutherford, M. M. Quinn, & S. R. Mathur (Eds.), *Handbook of research in emotional and behavioral disorders* (pp. 462–486). New York: Guilford.

Lane, K. L., Wehby, J. H., Little, M. A., & Cooley, C. (2004). Academic, behavioral, and social profiles of students with emotional and behavioral disorders educated in self-contained classrooms and self-contained schools: Part I—Are they more alike than different? *Behavioral Disorders, 30,* 349–361.

Lee, S. W., Elliot, J., & Barbour, J. D. (1994). A comparison of cross-informant behavior ratings in diagnosis. *Behavioral Disorders, 19,* 87–97.

Lipsey, M. W., & Wilson, D. B. (2001). *Practical meta-analysis.* Thousand Oaks, CA: Sage.

MacMillan, D. L., & Siperstein, G. N. (2002). Learning disabilities as operationalized by the schools. In R. Bradley, L. Danielson & D. P. Hallahan (Eds.), *Identification of learning disabilities: Research to practice* (pp. 287–333). Mahwah, NJ: Lawrence Erlbaum Associates.

Mattison, R. E., Hooper, S. R., & Glassberg, L. A. (2002). Three-year course of learning disorders in children classified as behaviorally disordered. *Journal of the American Academy of Child and Adolescent Psychiatry, 41,* 1454–1461.

McLoyd, V. C. (1998). Socioeconomic disadvantage and child development. *American Psychologist, 53,* 185–204.

Meadows, N. B., Neel, R. S., Scott, C. M., & Parker, G. (1994). Academic performance, social competence, and mainstream and nonmainstream students with behavioral disorders. *Behavioral Disorders, 19,* 170–180.

Mooney, P., Denny, R. K., & Gunter, P. L. (2004). The impact of NCLB and the reauthorization of IDEA on academic instruction of students with emotional or behavioral disorders. *Behavioral Disorders, 29,* 237–246.

Mooney, P., Epstein, M. H., Reid, R., & Nelson, J. R. (2003). Status and trends in academic intervention research for students with emotional disturbance. *Remedial and Special Education, 24,* 273–287.

Nelson, J. R., Benner, G. J., Lane, K., & Smith, B. W. (2004). Academic achievement of K-12 students with emotional and behavioral disorders. *Exceptional Children, 71,* 59–63.

Nelson, J. R., Johnson, A., & Marchand-Martella, N. (1996). Effects of direct instruction, cooperative learning, and independent learning practices on the classroom behavior of students with behavioral disorders: A comparative analysis. *Journal of Emotional and Behavioral Disorders, 4,* 53–63.

Neter, J., Wasserman, W., & Kutner, M. H. (1989). *Applied linear regression models* (2nd ed.). Homewood, IL: Irwin.

Odom, S. L., Brantlinger, E., Gersten, R., Horner, R. H., Thompson, B., & Harris, K. (2005). Research in special education: Scientific methods and evidence-based practices. *Exceptional Children, 71,* 137–148.

Oswald, D. P., Coutinho, M. J., Best, A. M., & Singh, N. N. (1999). Ethnic representation in special education: The influence of school-related economic and demographic variables. *Journal of Special Education, 32,* 194–206.

Pedhazur, E. J. (1999). *Multiple regression in behavioral research* (3rd ed.). Orlando, FL: Holt, Reinhart, & Winston.

Peterson, K. M. H., & Shinn, M. R. (2002). Severe discrepancy models: Which explains school identification practices for learning disabilities? *School Psychology Review, 31,* 459–476.

Reid, R., Gonzalez, J. E., Nordness, P. D., Trout, A., & Epstein, M. H. (2004). A meta-analysis of the academic status of students with emotional/behavioral disturbance. *Journal of Special Education, 38,* 130–143.

Rosenblatt, J. A., & Rosenblatt, A. (1999). Youth functional status and academic achievement in collaborative mental health and education programs: Two California care systems. *Journal of Emotional and Behavioral Disorders, 7,* 21–30.

Ruhl, K. L., & Berlinghoff, D. H. (1992). Research on improving behaviorally disordered students' academic performance: A review of the literature. *Behavioral Disorders, 17,* 178–190.

Sabornie, E. J., Cullinan, D., Osborne, S. S., & Brock, L. B. (2005). Intellectual, academic, and behavioral functioning of students with high-incidence disabilities: A cross-categorical meta-analysis. *Exceptional Children, 72,* 47–63.

Sirin, S. R. (2005). Socioeconomic status and academic achievement: A meta-analytic review of research. *Review of Educational Research, 75,* 417–453.

Sutherland, K. S., Lewis-Palmer, T., Stichter, J., & Morgan, P. L. (2008). Examining the influence of teacher behavior and classroom context on the academic and behavioral outcomes for students with emotional and behavioral disorders. *Journal of Special Education, 41,* 223–233.

Trout, A. L., Nordness, P. D., Pierce, C. D., & Epstein, M. H. (2003). Research on the academic status of children with emotional and behavioral disorders: A review of the literature from 1961 to 2000. *Journal of Emotional and Behavioral Disorders, 11,* 198–210.

U.S. Department of Education. (2007). *Twenty-ninth annual report to Congress on the implementation of the Individuals With Disabilities Education Act* Washington, DC: Author.

Wagner, M. M. (1995). Outcomes for youth with serious emotional disturbance in secondary school and early adulthood. *The Future of Children, 5*(2), 90–111.

Wagner, M., Kutash, K., Duchnowski, A. J., Epstein, M. H., & Sumi, W. C. (2005). The children and youth we serve: A national picture of the characteristics of students with emotional disturbances receiving special education. *Journal of Emotional and Behavioral Disorders, 13,* 79–96.

Walker, H. M., Ramsey, E., & Gresham, F. M. (2004). *Antisocial behavior in school: Strategies and best practices* (2nd ed.). Pacific Grove, CA: Brooks-Cole.

White, K. R. (1982). The relationship between socioeconomic status and academic achievement. *Psychological Bulletin, 91,* 461–481.

Woodcock, R. W., McGrew, K. S., & Mather, N. (2001). *Woodcock Johnson III tests of achievement* Itasca, IL: Riverside.

AUTHORS' NOTE

The authors would like to thank all of the participating schools for their time, effort, and invaluable assistance with this study. We would also like to thank Dr. James Earley of the Walker School in Newton, Massachusetts. This research was funded by a grant from the U.S. Department of Education, Office of Special Education Programs (No. H324C040072). The views represented in the report are those of the authors and do not necessarily represent the official views of the Department of Education.

Address correspondence to Andrew Wiley, College of Education, Health, and Human Services, 405 White Hall, Kent State University, Kent, OH 44242, E-mail: awiley5@kent.edu.

POST-READING ACTIVITIES

1. What problems must a student with ED exhibit to qualify for special education services?
2. "Overall, we found that across different school contexts, there was significant variability in the academic achievement of students identified by the school as ED" (Siperstein and Bountress 2008, 8). Describe why you believe the authors made this statement.
3. Brainstorm a list of the most effective ways to increase the academic achievement of students with ED.

CHAPTER 6

READING 6.2 OVERVIEW

Oral reading fluency is the ability to read a piece of text fluently, accurately, quickly, and with expression. It is a significant component of authentic reading comprehension. A large-scale study was conducted to explore the development of oral reading fluency of general education students compared to those classified as having emotional disturbance (ED) or a learning disability. The population included second and third grade students. Oral reading fluency assessments were administered to 185,367 general education students. The same measures were given to 2,146 students identified as having ED and 10,339 with a learning disability. Trends and data were collected, analyzed, and presented in the article.

PRE-READING ACTIVITIES

1. Describe your current understanding of oral reading fluency assessments and measures.
2. Predict the results of the study. Jot your thoughts down and refer to them during a follow-up post-reading activity.
3. Do you think that gender is a factor in the reading proficiency rates for students with ED and learning disabilities? Why or why not?

ORAL READING FLUENCY DEVELOPMENT FOR CHILDREN WITH EMOTIONAL DISTURBANCE OR LEARNING DISABILITIES

BY JEANNE WANZEK, STEPHANIE AL OTAIBA, AND YAACOV PETSCHER

ABSTRACT: *This study used a large statewide database to examine the oral reading fluency development of second-and third-grade students with emotional disturbance or learning disabilities and their general education peers. Oral reading fluency measures were administered to 185,367 students without disabilities (general education), 2,146 students identified with an emotional disturbance, and 10,339 students with a learning disability. Student status and growth trends were examined in a piecewise model at each grade level for the full sample as well as for a subsample with reading difficulties. Data suggested students with disabilities performed significantly below students without disabilities in initial status*

Jeanne Wanzek, Stephanie Al Otaiba and Yaacov Petscher, "Oral Reading Fluency Development for Children With Emotional Disturbance or Learning Disabilities," *Exceptional Children*, vol. 80, no. 2, pp. 187-204.

and growth. The authors also examined gender as a moderator of outcomes for each of the study groups.

Understanding the reading development of students who begin their school careers with weak reading, including students with disabilities, is critical. Beyond the obvious academic difficulties associated with poor reading are important social, emotional, and behavioral issues including a higher risk for high school dropout (Alliance for Excellent Education, 2002), delinquency (Center on Crime, Communities, and Culture, 1997), and future unemployment (National Center for Education Statistics, 2005). Research has shown that some reading difficulties may be intractable (Francis, Shaywitz, Stuebing, Shaywitz, & Fletcher, 1996; Torgesen & Burgess, 1998). Francis and colleagues reported that reading growth for both students with learning disabilities and typically developing students decelerated over time, and described this finding as being consistent with a deficit model of reading development rather than with a lag model in which poor readers catch up over time. The gap existed at initial assessment and was stable over time. Other research consistent with this deficit model has shown that once first graders are well behind their peers in word reading, they rarely catch up (Juel, 1988); this initial gap between poor and strong reading widens over the elementary years (Cunningham & Stanovich, 1997), and becomes increasingly difficult to close (Fletcher & Foorman, 1994). Nevertheless, findings from some more recent studies are consistent with the lag model, showing accelerated growth when students were provided early intervention (e.g., Phillips, Norris, Osmond, & Maynard, 2002; Skibbe et al., 2008).

READING GROWTH OF STUDENTS IN SPECIAL EDUCATION

Reading difficulties, historically, have been the most common reason students receive special education under the specific learning disability (SLD) category (Fletcher, Lyon, Fuchs, & Barnes, 2007), and the number of students classified as having SLD has nearly tripled since 1970 (Swanson & Carson, 1996). Nearly half of all students receiving special education services through the Individuals With Disabilities Education Act (IDEA) do so under the SLD category. The incidence of students identified with emotional disturbance (ED) has also increased, making the ED category the fourth largest among disabilities (U.S. Department of Education, 2011). Like students with SLD, students with ED commonly demonstrate reading deficits (Benner, Nelson, Ralston, & Mooney, 2010; Rice & Yen, 2010).

Students identified with ED or SLD have access to special education services to assist in improving their academic learning outcomes. As educational policies increasingly focus on accountability for growth for all children and specifically require comparison of special education outcomes to general education outcomes, the question is whether it is actually realistic to expect that special education can "normalize" the reading levels of all or most students with disabilities by altering their reading trajectories and accelerating learning to allow them to reach grade-level expectations. Hanushek, Kain, and Rivkin (1998) reported that across Grades 3 to 6, the reading standard scores of students who received special education rose by an average of 0.04 standard deviations per year. Extrapolating their findings suggests that with special education services, a third grader with a disability who is reading at the 20th percentile would likely enter high school reading below the 25th percentile.

The question is whether it is actually realistic to expect that special education can "normalize" the reading levels of all or most students with disabilities by altering their reading trajectories and accelerating learning to allow them to reach grade-level expectations.

Schiller, Sanford, and Blackorby (2008) used Special Education Elementary Longitudinal Study (SEELS) data to compare the reading performance of students with SLD who were receiving reading instruction in either general education or special education settings. In general, oral reading fluency rates were higher for students receiving instruction in general education, but regardless of setting students with SLD did not make gains relative to national norms in reading comprehension. Judge and Bell (2011) examined the Early Childhood Longitudinal Study (ECLS) kindergarten cohort database and found a similar achievement deficit for students with SLD. The authors noted depressed reading achievement from the beginning of school (kindergarten), even prior to identification with SLD. In addition, smaller gains in reading achievement were noted through the grade levels for students with SLD in comparison to students without SLD on measures of early literacy skills and comprehension. Morgan, Farkas, and Wu (2011) also examined ECLS data. They found statistically significant differences in levels of performance at kindergarten between students with SLD and typically developing students, but no differences in slope over the next 5 years.

Reviews of the literature describing the efficacy of interventions for students with ED or SLD have not demonstrated that these interventions have resulted in normalized reading on standardized tests or reaching grade-level benchmarks on criterion-referenced tests (e.g., Reid, Gonzalez, Nordness, Trout, & Epstein, 2004; Rivera, Al Otaiba, & Koorland, 2006; Swanson & Carson, 1996). Swanson and Carson conducted a synthesis of the literature to identify effective interventions for students with SLD. The large average effect sizes for strategy instruction (1.07) and direct instruction (.91) suggested that students receiving these interventions performed about one standard deviation higher than peers who did not receive these interventions, but the authors could not provide evidence that growth was accelerated enough to begin reaching grade-level expectations.

Similarly, Rivera and colleagues (2006) reviewed the literature to describe the efficacy of early reading interventions provided to students with ED. Although effect sizes could not be calculated, a consistent trend emerged indicating that students with ED who received the reading instruction did improve their reading ability from pretest to posttest. Again, the review noted that there was little evidence these interventions helped students with ED reach grade-level expectations in terms of increased standard scores, standard score outcomes within the "normal range," or oral reading fluency rates that met expected grade-level benchmarks. Other literature reviews related to the academic performance of students with ED have found that students' reading performance did not appear to improve over time (e.g., Reid et al., 2004).

Some cross-sectional research comparing the performance of students with SLD or ED has suggested that students with ED showed greater academic performance than students with SLD on several reading measures, including word reading and comprehension (e.g., Epstein & Cullinan, 1983; Luebke, Epstein, & Cullinan, 1989). However, only two longitudinal studies, to our knowledge, directly compared reading achievement of students with ED to students with SLD. In their study, examining a sample of elementary students with ED or SLD, Anderson, Kutash, and Duchnowki (2001) reported that standardized scores for reading achievement only improved for students with SLD, with average standard score improvement from 80.32 to 87.97 over 4 years. By contrast, students with ED remained at a standard score of about 85 over this same timeframe, maintaining growth relative to grade-level peers. Wei, Blackorby, and Schiller (2011) used data from SEELS to examine reading growth trajectories in word reading and comprehension for students in 11 federal disability categories. The findings supported a deficit model, as they showed a decelerating quadratic trend. Although reading growth rates were similar across the disability categories, word reading and comprehension was significantly higher for students with ED than students with SLD.

GENDER AS A MODERATOR OF READING GROWTH

Another recent study of SEELS data examined reading growth for students with ED, and the findings indicated that gender may be an important moderator (Rice & Yen, 2010). Although no gender differences for students with ED were reported in initial reading level, males with ED grew significantly faster than females with ED on measures of letter word identification and passage comprehension. However, Rice and Yen suggested this difference in reading rate might be due to the severity of learning problems among girls with ED, in light of the underidentification of girls with this designation (Cullinan, Osborne & Epstein, 2004).

Other studies have investigated the gender gap in populations of students with and without disabilities. For example, in a recent study examining trends on national and state tests from 2005 to 2009, the Center on Education Policy reported that girls' reading performance was higher than boys in elementary, middle, and high school (Kober, Chudowsky, & Chudowsky, 2010). Several large-scale international studies have also reported gender differences in reading performance favoring girls (e.g., Lynn & Mikk, 2009), particularly among poor readers (Wheldall & Limbrick, 2010).

Given the previous research on reading growth and gender differences, we were interested in longitudinally examining the level and growth in reading for students with ED or SLD and their general education peers. Specifically, we theorized that growth for students with disabilities might be more consistent with a deficit or gap model rather than a lag model, and, given previous findings related to gender differences, we sought to evaluate whether gender was an important moderator. We examined the growth trajectories across two grade levels for all students in these groups as well as the subgroup of students demonstrating deficits in reading.

USING ORAL READING FLUENCY TO UNDERSTAND READING GROWTH

Oral reading fluency is a critically important area to consider because the number of words students read per minute is a metric of reading competence and because it strongly predicts reading comprehension (Fuchs, Fuchs, Hosp, & Jenkins, 2001). Oral reading fluency rates can reliably distinguish between students with SLD and their peers with speech and language delays (Puranik, Petscher, Al Otaiba, Catts, &

Lonigan, 2008) and between students with differing levels of English proficiency with and without SLD (Al Otaiba et al., 2009). Both oral reading fluency level and rate of growth have been shown to predict current (Roehrig, Petscher, Nettles, Hudson, & Torgesen, 2008) and later (Baker et al., 2008; Wanzek et al., 2010) reading performance on statewide tests.

There is a rich history of curriculum-based measures used to track reading performance in order to learn whether growth is sufficient or insufficient to meet grade-level expectations. For example, Deno and colleagues (Deno, Fuchs, Marston, & Shin, 2001) examined oral reading fluency growth rates for 324 students with SLD in Grades 1 through 6. Although students without SLD were growing at rates of 1.01–1.8 words correct per minute per week in Grades 1 through 4, students with SLD grew at rates of .57–.83, with only first-grade growth reaching levels above .58 words correct per week. Deno and colleagues' review of the research on effective reading interventions indicated students with SLD may be able to increase growth to rates of 1.39 words correct per minute per week. There is also evidence that oral reading fluency growth may not be linear (Christ, Silberglitt, Yeo, & Cormier, 2010). The linear and non-linear development of oral reading fluency for students with ED or SLD and the extent to which these students demonstrate accelerated learning in comparison to students in general education has not been examined.

The purpose of the current study was to examine the oral reading fluency development of students receiving special education for ED or SLD and their general education counterparts in second and third grade. Primarily, we wished to learn whether, consistent with a lag model, students in special education accelerate their oral reading fluency rates in the early grades compensating for initial low levels of reading, or whether, consistent with a deficit model, students would demonstrate low initial levels of reading along with insufficient growth to catch up to grade-level expectations. We also examined whether gender was a moderator of reading achievement in these groups of students.

We hypothesized that students in general education would show higher initial levels of oral reading fluency and growth commensurate with expected benchmarks for the grade level, and students with SLD would show the lowest initial levels of reading fluency given their primary disability related to achievement. We anticipated our findings would support a deficit rather than a lag model, with students with ED or SLD demonstrating insufficient growth to catch up to expected grade-level achievement in oral reading fluency, despite receiving special education services. Given the preponderance of research on the importance of gender differences favoring girls in reading achievement, we hypothesized that gender would moderate outcomes and that across all three groups, females would outperform males.

METHOD

PARTICIPANTS

With approval from the Institutional Review Board, we selected students for the present study from the Progress Monitoring and Reporting Network database, the data management and storage database of more than 1.2 million students in Reading First schools in the state of Florida. All students with 2 years of data who began second grade in the school years 2003 through 2008 were included if they were identified with no disability (general education), a primary disability of ED (Florida category of emotional/behavioral disability), or a primary disability of SLD. Across the five cohorts, we identified a total of 197,852 students for the study (185,367 general education students, 2,146 identified with ED, 10,339 identified with SLD). No practically important differences were estimated across the five cohorts of students with regard to initial oral reading fluency status (*d* = .09). At the time of data collection, students in Florida met the state's criteria for emotional/behavioral disability if persistent and consistent emotional or behavioral responses that could not be attributed to age, gender, culture, or ethnicity adversely affected educational performance. According to state guidelines when the data were collected, students were identified with SLD if there was a discrepancy between the student's IQ and academic achievement. Table 6.7 provides demographic data for each of the three study groups.

Table 6.7 **Demographics by Study Group.**

DEMOGRAPHICS	GENERAL EDUCATION	STUDENTS WITH EMOTIONAL DISTURBANCE	STUDENTS WITH SPECIFIC LEARNING DISABILITY
Male	50%	83%	69%
White	31%	31%	34%
Black	37%	53%	33%
Latino	27%	12%	29%
Asian	2%	<1%	<1%
Multicultural	4%	4%	3%
Native American	<1%	<1%	<1%
Free or reduced-price lunch	82%	91%	89%
English language learner	20%	7%	23%

To specifically examine students with reading difficulties, we also selected a subsample of students in each study group that were performing below the 20th percentile on the comprehension subtest of the tenth edition of the Stanford Achievement Test (SAT-10; Harcourt Educational Measurement, 2003) at the end of first grade. A total of 38,763 students performed below the 20th percentile at the end of first grade, 31,691 students in the general education group (17%), 1,137 students in the ED group (53%), and 5,935 students in the SLD group (57%).

MEASURES

ORAL READING FLUENCY

The oral reading fluency subtest (ORF) of the Dynamic Indicators of Early Literacy Skills (DIBELS; Good & Kaminski, 2002) is a test of accuracy and fluency on grade-level connected text. At the time of the study, the state of Florida used DIBELS to monitor reading progress four times per year (September, December, February, April). Trained district and school level teams were responsible for testing and entering scores into the Progress Monitoring and Reporting Network, with state teams following up on testing procedures to ensure interrater reliability.

Student performance on the ORF is measured by having students read three grade-level passages aloud for 1 min. Words omitted, substituted, and hesitations of more than 3 s are scored as errors. The number of correct words per minute from the passage is the oral reading fluency rate. The median score of the three passages is reported. Speece and Case (2001) reported a parallel forms reliability coefficient of .94, and strong predictive validity of reading comprehension has been consistently reported (Roehrig et al., 2008).

SAT-10. The SAT-10 (Harcourt Educational Measurement, 2003) is a group-administered, norm-referenced test. In this study, we used data from the reading comprehension subtest administered at the end of first grade to select students with current reading difficulties in the study groups. The reading comprehension subtest requires the student to read passages and answer multiple-choice questions. The reliability coefficient for internal consistency is .91 for the reading comprehension subtest at Grade 1.

DATA ANALYSES

Examining student trends in oral reading fluency across second and third grade is complicated by the increasing difficulty of passages. Because oral reading fluency growth is not a continuous trajectory across grades, we used an extension of traditional multilevel growth models, known as piecewise growth curve models, to estimate students' oral reading fluency development; this allowed for the simultaneous estimation of a two-rate model for oral reading fluency growth in second and third grade. Two important components in the application of this methodology are worth noting. First, assessing students four times per year on oral reading fluency each year tests both linear and non-linear growth trends. A significant quadratic trend changes the interpretation of the linear term, such that overall growth is described by the extent to which there are periods where learning rates are accelerating (positive quadratic term) or decelerating (negative quadratic term). Second, the data were centered at the first testing time of the second grade year (i.e., September); therefore, the intercept in the model represented the grand mean oral reading fluency rate at the beginning of second grade.

We systematically tested a set of four models, starting with an unconditional means model to test the extent to which variability existed in ORF scores across the eight total time points, then adding in time-coded covariates (linear and nonlinear). Results from the -2 log likelihood test suggested that the addition of the non-linear parameter improved the description of the growth model ($p < 0.01$). This model was followed by the inclusion of the ED and SLD indicators, and the final model included gender as a moderator of the relationships. Nonsignificant variance components at any portion of modeling were fixed to achieve greater power in model estimation. This set of models was then used to describe growth processes for students in each of the study groups (general education, ED, SLD) as well as those who were identified with reading difficulties in each of the groups (below 20th percentile).

An examination of the proportion of missing data revealed that 7% of the data were missing at Time 1, 5% at Time 2, 3% at Time 3, 7% at Time 4, 2% at Time 5, 5% at Time 6, 5% at Time 7, and 8% at Time 8. Despite a low prevalence of missingness, to be conservative, we conducted Little's (1988) test of data missing completely at random. Across all time points, the chi-square test indicated that data were not missing completely at random. Because data were missing more predominantly for students eligible for free or reduced-price lunch and for minority students, we used multiple imputation to correct for an unbalanced design and potential biases in parameter estimation. Multiple imputation was conducted using SAS PROC MI with a Markov Chain Monte Carlo estimation with 10 imputations.

RESULTS

Table 6.8 reports means and standard deviations on ORF for each of the three study groups. In order to demonstrate each group's estimated performance, as well as the expected benchmark performance at each time point and grade level, Figures 6.1 and 6.2 present fitted growth curves for the students in each group. Table 6.9 provides the mean ORF scores, slope coefficients, and standard errors for each group. Rather than providing the mixed model coefficient estimates of intercepts and slopes, which often become burdensome to the reader as the model complexity increases, we summarize the output from the piecewise models as fitted means for each group. The fitted means can be interpreted as the actual predicted mean intercept and slope coefficients for each group rather than a fitted deflection from the grand mean.

Table 6.8 **Oral reading fluency means and standard deviations by study group.**

							SUBSAMPLE: STUDENTS WITH READING DIFFICULTIES					
	GENERAL EDUCATION) (*n* = 185,367)		STUDENTS WITH ED (*n* = 2,146)		STUDENTS WITH SLD (*n* = 10,339)		GENERAL EDUCATION (*n* = 31,691)		STUDENTS WITH ED (*n* = 1,137)		STUDENTS WITH SLD (*n* = 5,935)	
GRADE AND TESTING PERIOD	M	SD	M	SD	M	SD	M	SD	M	SD	M	SD
Second grade												
Fall	59.78	30.96	35.89	28.6	27.33	21.96	33.58	24.81	20.56	18.92	16.99	14.72
Winter 1	73.36	32.87	45.97	32.98	35.13	25.86	41.24	27.11	26.64	21.32	22.04	17.46
Winter 2	86.58	34.27	55.34	35.62	44.71	30.14	51.28	30.37	33.29	24.85	28.98	21.11
Spring	90.75	33.77	62.3	37.48	48.68	30.13	53.28	28.86	38.58	24.77	32.56	21.22
Third grade												
Fall	78.95	32.89	52.15	34.31	40.37	27.95	47.5	29.1	32.5	24.19	26.29	19.43
Winter 1	98.95	33.12	68.5	37.9	57.06	33.08	67.43	32.86	46.86	29.5	40.52	26.23
Winter 2	109.02	33.76	78.19	39.19	67.48	34.85	77.39	33.69	56.83	32.16	50.34	28.53
Spring	110.55	32.71	78.76	36.23	65.6	31.8	74.06	31.06	58.4	29.34	50.3	25.45

Note. ED = emotional disturbance; SLD = specific learning disability.

ORF STATUS AND GROWTH FOR FULL SAMPLE

SECOND GRADE

On average, students who did not have an identified disability correctly read a mean of 59 words correct per minute (wcpm) in the fall of second grade. This second grade fall mean is above the DIBELS ORF benchmark expectation of 44 wcpm, and well above the performance of students identified with ED or SLD ($p < .001$). General education students grew positively over the school year (3.36 wcpm), and increased their rate of learning, evidenced by the positive nonlinear parameter (Grade 2 $\text{slope}^2 = 0.14$).

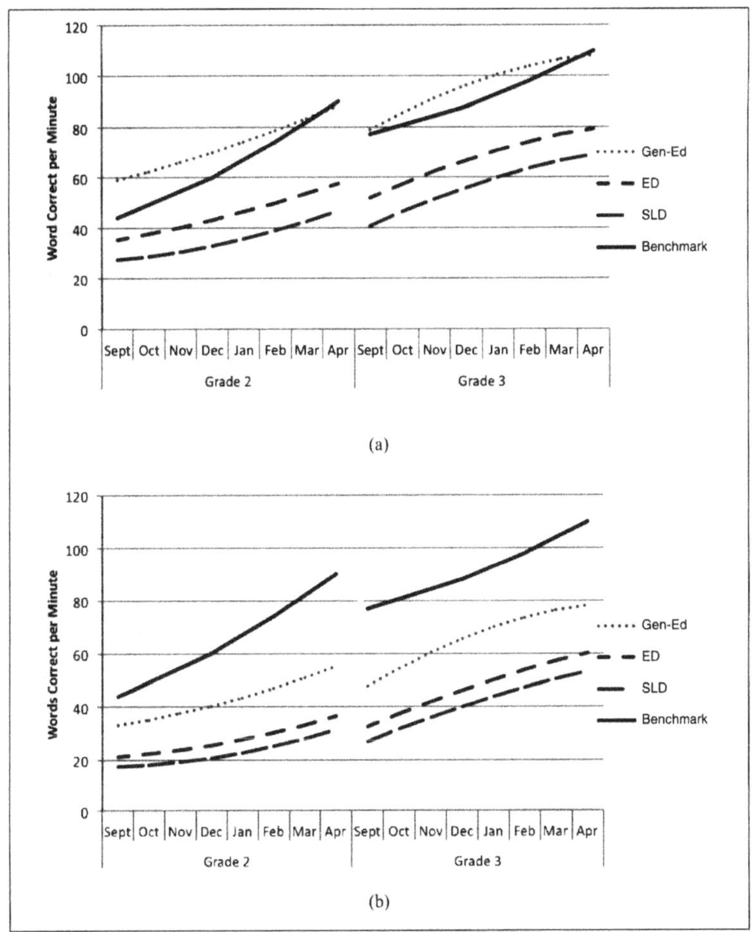

Figure 6.1 Growth trajectories by group for (a) full sample and (b) students with reading difficulties.

Note. Gen-Ed = general education; ED = emotional disturbance; SLD = specific learning disability.

Students identified with ED began second grade with a mean ORF rate of 36 wcpm, or 8 wcpm below the second grade level benchmark, and 23 wcpm less than their general education peers ($p < .001$). Although these students grew at a positive rate in second grade (2.26 wcpm), it was not as steep as the general education students' rate ($p < .001$). However, the rate of acceleration for students with ED was not statistically distinguished from their general education peers (Grade 2 slope^2 = 0.15; $p = .408$) indicating that the rate of acquisition in fluency was similar for both students with ED and general education students. Thus, students with ED did not demonstrate a closing of the gap between their performance and the DIBELS ORF benchmark expectation. Although the benchmark to performance gap was 8 wcpm in the fall of second grade, this gap increased to 24 wcpm by the end of the second grade year.

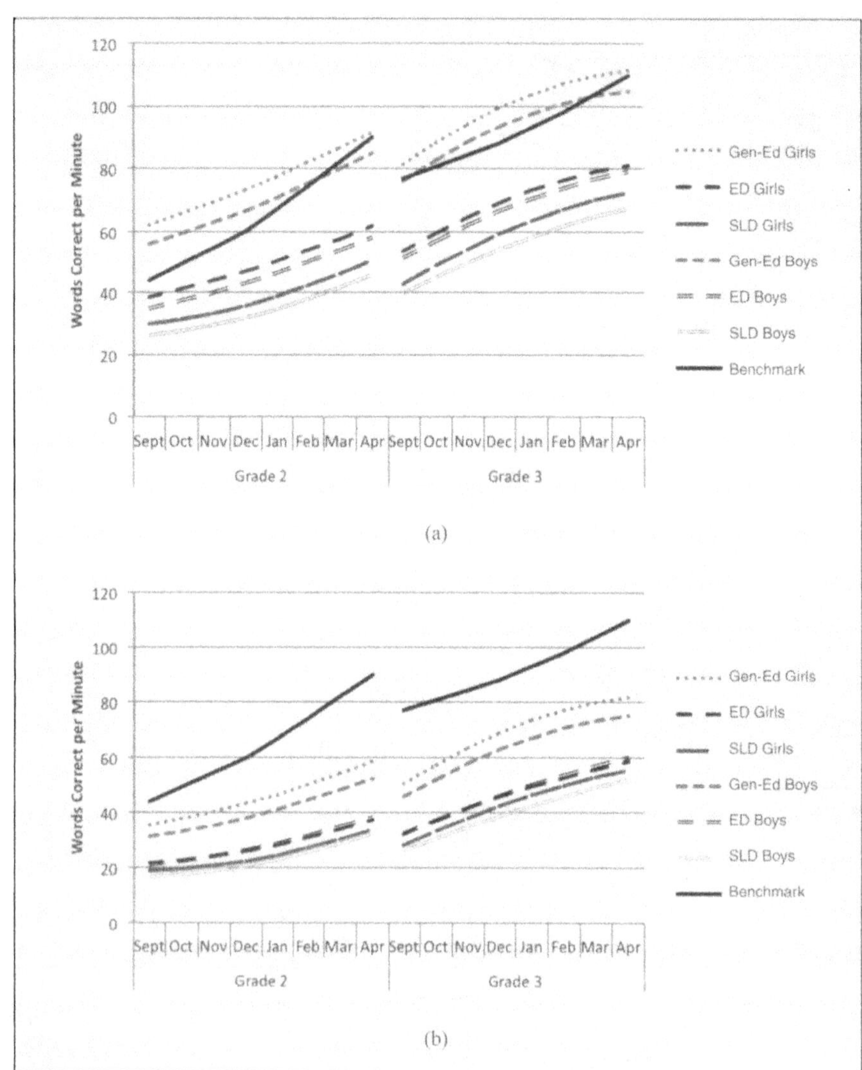

Figure 6.2 Growth trajectories by group and gender for (a) full sample and (b) students with reading difficulties.

Note. Gen-Ed = general education; ED = emotional disturbance; SLD = specific learning disability.

Table 6.9 **Oral reading fluency slopes and intercepts by group.**

		GRADE 2				GRADE 3		
EFFECT	**ESTIMATE**	**SE**	***t*-VALUE**	***p*-VALUE**	**ESTIMATE**	**SE**	***t*-VALUE**	***p*-VALUE**
Full Sample								
Gen ed fall	58.94	0.07	792.05	<.001	78.76	0.04	480.40	<.001
Gen ed slope	3.36	0.02	210.04	<.001	6.71	0.02	147.66	<.001
Gen ed slope^2	0.14	0.00	64.86	<.001	–0.42	0.00	–155.00	<.001
ED fall	35.55	0.63	–37.18	<.001	51.86	0.39	–9.00	<.001
ED*slope	2.26	0.14	–8.01	<.001	5.53	0.20	–0.36	.720
ED*slope^2	0.15	0.02	0.83	.408	–0.26	0.03	4.37	<.001
SLD	27.34	0.36	–88.80	<.001	40.67	0.17	–38.76	<.001
SLD*slope	1.33	0.05	–37.35	<.001	5.55	0.08	10.25	<.001
SLD*slope^2	0.24	0.01	13.49	<.001	0.25	0.01	5.18	<.001
Reading difficulties								
Gen ed fall	33.07	0.15	217.09	<.001	47.74	0.10	152.27	<.001
Gen ed slope	2.02	0.03	60.79	<.001	6.74	0.05	93.03	<.001
Gen ed slope^2	0.19	0.00	42.41	<.001	–0.40	0.01	–71.89	<.001
ED fall	20.94	0.60	–20.19	<.001	32.47	0.45	–6.93	<.001
ED*slope	1.07	0.15	–6.29	<.001	4.81	0.25	–3.92	<.001
ED*slope^2	0.19	0.02	0.09	.926	–0.14	0.04	6.49	<.001
SLD	17.27	0.40	–39.36	<.001	26.83	0.23	–22.56	<.001
SLD*slope	0.59	0.07	–20.03	<.001	4.62	0.11	–6.3	<.001
SLD*slope^2	0.23	0.01	4.82	<.001	–0.14	0.02	12.08	<.001

Note. Column 2 reflects the fitted group means; *SE*, *t*-value, and *p*-value are presented as model estimated coefficients. Gen ed = general education; ED = emotional disturbance; SLD = specific learning disability.

The growth of the students with SLD in second grade largely tracked that of students with ED, and was only differentiated by their intercept levels. Similar to the students with ED, students with SLD grew at a significantly slower linear rate than the general education students in second grade ($p < .001$). In the fall of second grade, students with SLD read at a rate of 27 wcpm, compared to 36 wcpm students with ED ($p < .001$). This gap between the groups remained relatively constant throughout the year, although the students with ED maintained a stronger linear growth rate (2.26 wcpm) than the students with SLD (1.33 wcpm). The rate of acceleration for the students with SLD (Grade 2 slope^2 = .24) counterbalanced this weaker linear growth rate. As a result, the SLD and ED groups of students grew in a similar pattern, and the level of summer drop-off was identical (i.e., 6 wcpm; see Figure 6.1).

THIRD GRADE

The fall of third grade mean for general education students was 79 wcpm, just above the DIBELS ORF fall benchmark of 77 wcpm. Students with ED began third grade reading 52 wcpm, and students with SLD read 41 wcpm, both significantly lower than general education students ($p < .001$). Third grade linear growth for the general education students was estimated at 6.71 wcpm per month, with a negative quadratic coefficient of –.42.

For students with ED, the mean fall score was 25 wcpm below the DIBELS ORF benchmark and 27 wcpm less than general education student performance. By the end of third grade, the students with ED remained at a level of high risk in their oral reading fluency development, despite linear growth that was comparable to the general education students (5.53, $p = .720$), and a rate of deceleration less than the general education students (–0.26; $p < .001$). The mean ORF score for students with ED was 58 wcpm at the end of third grade.

Students with SLD demonstrated significantly slower linear growth than the general education students in third grade (5.55 wcpm, $p < .001$); however, they also demonstrated a lower rate of deceleration (–0.25; $p < .001$). As with the patterns seen in second grade, students with SLD grew similarly to the students with ED in third grade, but were separated by their intercept levels ($p < .001$). The mean third grade fall performance for the students with SLD (41 wcpm) was 36 wcpm below the benchmark, expanding to a 41 wcpm gap by the spring.

STATUS AND GROWTH ON ORF FOR STUDENTS WITH READING DIFFICULTIES

SECOND GRADE

General education students with reading difficulties began second grade reading at 33 wcpm, 25 wcpm less than the full general education sample and 11 wcpm below the expected DIBELS ORF benchmark. These students grew at a linear rate of 2.02 wcpm per month, but accelerated their rate of growth over time.

The students with ED who were also below the 20th percentile in reading comprehension demonstrated a mean ORF score of 21 wcpm at the beginning of second grade, significantly lower than the general education students with reading difficulties ($p < .001$), and grew at a linear rate of 1.07 wcpm per month, which was half the linear rate of the general education students with reading difficulties ($p < .001$). This growth was associated with a 0.20 rate of acceleration, similar to the general education students ($p = .926$).

The students with SLD who were below the 20th percentile on comprehension fared worse than the full group of students with SLD, reading at a rate of 17 wcpm at the beginning of second grade, and growing at a linear rate of 0.59 wcpm with a 0.23 rate of acceleration. The rate of linear growth was significantly slower than the students with reading difficulties in general education ($p < .001$). By the end of the second grade, the mean ORF rate was 32 wcpm, well below the DIBELS ORF benchmark.

THIRD GRADE

The general education students with reading difficulties began third grade at an average ORF level of 48 wcpm, well below the expected benchmark of 77 wcpm, and grew at a rate of approximately 7 wcpm per month, with a negative quadratic trend (–.40), indicating the rate of growth slowed over the course of the school year. By the end of third grade these high-risk readers averaged 78 wcpm.

In the fall of third grade, the mean ORF rate for students with ED and reading difficulties was 32 wcpm. These students showed a linear growth rate in third grade (4.81 wcpm) that was less than the growth for the general education students ($p < .001$). They also demonstrated a deceleration in growth over the year (–0.14); however, this estimate was not as large as the deceleration seen by the general education students with reading difficulties. Students with ED and reading difficulties ended third grade with a mean score of 60 wcpm.

The low readers in the SLD group began third grade with the lowest fluency rate (27 wcpm) of the three groups. Similar to the low readers in the ED group, the students with SLD demonstrated a linear growth rate (4.62 wcpm) significantly lower than the low readers in general education ($p < .001$). The students with SLD and reading difficulties ended third grade with a mean ORF level of 53 wcpm, 25 wcpm lower than the low readers in general education, and 57 wcpm below the DIBELS ORF expected benchmark.

GENDER MODERATION OF STATUS AND GROWTH

We also examined whether gender would moderate the relation between ORF initial status and growth for the study groups. Table 6.10 provides mean ORF scores, slope coefficients, and standard errors for each group by gender for the full sample. (See Figure 6.2 for the growth trajectories for the male and female students in each study group.) On average, male and female students in general education performed at or above benchmark levels for most of second grade; however, levels of ORF were significantly lower for males ($p < .001$). Although female students' linear growth rate was also statistically faster than males ($p < .001$), no practically important growth differences between males and females were observed when comparing the actual fitted mean slopes between gender groups ($d = .11$). This pattern was replicated in third grade, with both gender groups in general education remaining at or above benchmark, and males only being differentiated by the lower initial status ($p < .001$), and not slope. Males and females maintained similar ORF differences when considering ED or SLD designations. Reflecting the general trend displayed in Figure 6.1, students with ED had higher ORF rates than the students with SLD; however, males and females were only differentiated on level of oral reading fluency and not slope.

Table 6.10 **Oral reading fluency slopes and intercepts by group and gender, full sample.**

	GRADE 2				GRADE 3			
EFFECT	**ESTIMATE**	**SE**	***t*-VALUE**	***p*-VALUE**	**ESTIMATE**	**SE**	***t*-VALUE**	***p*-VALUE**
Girls								
Gen ed fall	61.96	0.11	588.7	<.001	81.34	0.06	331.53	<.001
Gen ed slope	3.46	0.02	148.7	<.001	6.86	0.03	90.39	<.001
Gen ed slope^2	0.13	0.00	36.64	<.001	–0.42	0.01	–89.58	<.001
ED fall	38.67	1.63	–14.24	<.001	53.71	0.94	–4.70	<.001
ED*slope	2.55	0.35	–3.36	0.001	5.81	0.49	1.12	0.262
ED*slope	0.13	0.05	0.85	0.395	–0.31	0.08	–0.27	0.790
SLD	29.82	0.56	–57.22	<.001	42.76	0.28	–22.91	<.001
SLD*slope	1.57	0.10	–19.75	<.001	6.12	0.16	8.54	<.001
SLD*slope^2	0.23	0.01	8.17	<.001	–0.31	0.03	–1.37	0.170
Boys								
Gen ed fall	55.95	0.01	8.17	<.001	76.18	0.08	10.47	<.001
Gen ed slope	3.25	0.03	–5.83	<.001	6.56	0.05	–3.16	0.002
Gen ed slope^2	0.15	0.00	1.7	0.090	–0.41	0.01	2.20	0.028
ED fall	34.91	1.77	1.2	0.230	51.49	1.04	0.83	0.406
ED*slope	2.42	0.39	0.12	0.906	5.47	0.55	–0.52	0.602
ED*slope	0.15	0.05	–0.14	0.892	–0.25	0.09	1.02	0.306
SLD	26.22	0.66	3.59	<.001	39.72	0.35	–0.66	0.508
SLD*slope	1.45	0.12	–1.2	0.228	5.29	0.20	–1.60	0.111
SLD*slope^2	0.23	0.02	0.14	0.886	–0.22	0.03	1.82	0.069

Note. Column 2 reflects the fitted group means; *SE*, *t*-value, and p-value are presented as model estimated coefficients. Gen ed = general education; ED = emotional disturbance; SLD = specific learning disability.

When considering only the students scoring below the 20th percentile in reading comprehension, moderator effects were less present than in the full sample. Table 6.11 provides mean ORF scores, slopes, and standard errors for each group by gender for the sample with reading difficulties. (See Figure 6.2 for the growth trajectories for male and female students with reading difficulties in each group.) Male and female students with reading difficulties exhibited differentiation in their ORF levels in both second ($p < .001$) and third grades ($p < .01$) with males' levels lower than females; however, no practically important differences were observed for males and females in the ED ($d = .12$) or SLD ($d = .07$) groups.

Table 6.11 **Oral reading fluency slopes and intercepts by group and gender, students with reading difficulties.**

	GRADE 2				GRADE 3			
EFFECT	**ESTIMATE**	**SE**	***t*-VALUE**	***p*-VALUE**	**ESTIMATE**	**SE**	***t*-VALUE**	***p*-VALUE**
Girls								
Gen ed fall	35.47	0.25	144.32	<.001	50.45	0.15	97.88	<.001
Gen ed slope	2.21	0.05	41.32	<.001	7.08	0.08	61.18	<.001
Gen ed slope^2	0.19	0.01	25.95	<.001	–0.43	0.01	–48.23	<.001
ED fall	21.49	1.45	–9.62	<.001	32.82	1.13	–3.22	0.001
ED*slope	1.06	0.39	–2.97	0.003	4.61	0.56	–2.35	0.019
ED*slope	0.20	0.06	0.26	0.792	–0.15	0.09	2.8	0.005
SLD	18.95	0.80	–20.74	<.001	28.17	0.42	–13.8	<.001
SLD*slope	0.66	0.13	–11.85	<.001	5.26	0.21	–1.29	0.197
SLD*slope^2	0.25	0.02	3.59	<.001	–0.22	0.03	4.61	<.001
Boys								
Gen ed fall	31.37	0.31	–13.17	<.001	45.83	0.20	–2.56	0.010
Gen ed slope	1.88	0.07	–4.87	<.001	6.51	0.10	–2.25	0.025
Gen ed slope^2	0.19	0.01	0.35	0.729	–0.38	0.02	2.81	0.005
ED fall	20.84	1.60	2.17	0.030	32.41	1.23	0.6	0.551
ED*slope	1.07	0.42	0.82	0.412	4.84	0.63	0.72	0.470
ED*slope	0.19	0.06	–0.27	0.789	–0.14	0.10	–0.25	0.802
SLD	16.63	0.92	1.94	0.052	26.31	0.50	1.93	0.053
SLD*slope	0.56	0.16	1.49	0.135	4.37	0.24	–2.27	0.023
SLD*slope^2	0.23	0.02	–1.17	0.241	–0.11	0.04	2.04	0.041

Note. Column 2 reflects the fitted group means; SE, *t*-value, and *p*-value are presented as model estimated coefficients. Gen ed = general education; ED = emotional disturbance; SLD = specific learning disability.

DISCUSSION

The purpose of this study was to examine the ORF level and growth for second-and third-grade students without disabilities and students with ED or SLD. As we hypothesized in relation to a deficit model of reading development, the findings reveal the three groups were distinguished in ORF level at the beginning of second grade and maintained those distinctions throughout second and third grade with no overlap. Both students with ED and students with SLD performed significantly below students without disabilities in oral reading fluency. In addition, as anticipated, students with SLD performed significantly lower than students with ED. Linear growth rates indicated students with disabilities were also growing at significantly slower rates than students without disabilities in general education, with the exception of students with ED in third grade. These data suggest that although the ED and SLD groups were making progress in their reading skills during second and third grade, their rate of growth would not allow them to meet grade-level expectations in reading.

Due to the slower linear rates of growth for the students with ED or SLD, the differences in ORF levels between the students with and without disabilities increased with each grade level. The ED and SLD groups consistently demonstrated below-level reading throughout second and third grade despite receiving special education services for both years. These data add to previous literature suggesting that current special education services do not routinely accelerate growth at a rate that allows students with disabilities to reach grade-level expectations even when these services are provided in the early elementary grades (Hanusheck et al., 1998). By the end of third grade, 455 (21%) students with ED and 1,182 (11%) students with SLD met the expected ORF grade-level benchmarks. Although in most cases the students with ED or SLD demonstrated acceleration in their growth that was superior to students without disabilities, this acceleration was not enough to make up for the overall slower growth rates or for the weaker initial skill level. It is important to note that these data emphasize differences in reading achievement between students with disabilities (ED or SLD) and students without disabilities, and not differences between general education and special education instruction.

To better understand the reading growth of students with disabilities, we examined the students in each of the groups that were demonstrating reading difficulties. Approximately 53% of the students with ED and 57% of the students with SLD were performing below the 20th percentile in reading, in comparison to 17% of the students without disabilities. Even when only examining students with reading difficulties, students without disabilities performed at higher levels and grew at higher rates than students with disabilities. Thus, among students struggling with reading, those with disabilities were not closing the gap with the students without disabilities in general education. All three groups of students with reading difficulties were below expected levels for their grade levels and grew at similar or slower rates than the full sample of students, indicating the trajectories of these students will continue to leave them below grade-level expectations—even for students in general education, which is also consistent with the deficit model of development. The intercept data suggest that students with the most severe reading difficulties were receiving special education services, as would be expected. The services students identified with ED or SLD were receiving was equally effective in increasing oral reading fluency (i.e., similar growth for both groups).

GENDER DIFFERENCES

Our findings indicate gender was a moderator of outcomes for all three groups. Ours is not the first study to find females performing higher than males in reading (Wheldall & Limbrick, 2010). We note that for students without disabilities, the means for both males and females were above the ORF benchmarks. For students with reading difficulties, the lower performance of males was only practically meaningful in the group of students without disabilities (general education). It does appear that schools identified more males than females for special education, with 83% of the ED and 69% of the SLD group in our sample consisting of males. We also note the higher identification of Black students in the ED group, suggesting an overrepresentation of male, Black students identified with ED, which is consistent with the most recent IDEA report (U.S. Department of Education, 2011). However, our data indicated ORF level and growth rate of males and females with reading difficulties in special education was practically similar. Therefore, although more males were identified with a disability in ED or SLD, once in special education males with reading difficulties demonstrated similar progress as females.

PRACTICAL CONSIDERATIONS FOR SPECIAL EDUCATION AND ORAL READING FLUENCY GROWTH

In considering the findings of this study, perhaps a larger question is whether it is appropriate to use typical development to measure the success of students with disabilities, who by definition have demonstrated atypical development (Buzick & Laitusis, 2010). In recent years, a focus on accountability has led to requirements for most students with ED and SLD to be measured against the same academic proficiency guidelines as their typically developing peers without disabilities (No Child Left Behind Act of 2001, 2006). Previous research has noted that schools fail to make adequate yearly progress most often due to the disability subgroup (Eckes & Swando, 2009). It is difficult to judge whether our data suggest a problem with special education (i.e., the services provided were not strong enough to help students reach grade level) or a problem with expectations (i.e., students with disabilities have different growth trajectories than students without disabilities). It is clear that students with ED or SLD begin at lower levels than students without disabilities; one criterion for qualification for special education is underachievement in one or more academic areas. Thus, for students with disabilities to meet grade-level standards they must grow at a faster rate than their peers without disabilities, despite the fact that the students disability has been determined to impact learning. It is possible that without special education the students in this study may have shown lower ORF levels and rates of growth, demonstrating the success of special education to meet student needs and raise achievement rather than suggesting special education was ineffective due to a lack of grade-level achievement for the students with disabilities.

> *For students with disabilities to meet grade-level standards they must grow at a faster rate than their peers without disabilities.*

Clearly it is important to continue to monitor whether students with disabilities are meeting grade-level expectations, particularly in relation to a student's continued need for special education; however, we suggest that monitoring the effectiveness of special education and, equally important, defining the success of students with disabilities requires alternative considerations as a primary focus. As a practical consideration, it is important for educators to ensure high standards and expectations are set for special education and students receive the most efficient and effective intervention in order to accelerate learning. As Deno and colleagues (2001) have previously noted, to define expected development using normative data for a subgroup of special education students would only lead to acceptance of status quo and does not push special educators to improve instruction. However, it may also be inappropriate to define the success of students with disabilities as the ability to meet the same proficiency standards as students without disabilities. We agree with Deno and colleagues that examining student growth rates from current research on effective interventions for students with disabilities may be the most appropriate way to set high standards for special education. As we have noted, current research for students with ED and SLD indicates that student learning can be accelerated beyond what these students achieve without intervention (e.g., Rivera et al., 2006; Swanson & Carson, 1996), but there is little evidence to date that researchers have identified instructional techniques or the intensity of interventions needed to allow most students with disabilities to achieve "normalized" outcomes. The bar for successful student outcomes should be raised first in research by continuing to examine interventions to increase outcomes for students with disabilities beyond current levels and then, in turn, providing practitioners with the resulting knowledge and tools to implement more effective interventions. Raising the bar in research before it is raised in practice provides an evidence-based standard against which practitioners can evaluate the effectiveness of implementation.

LIMITATIONS AND FUTURE RESEARCH

The results of this study are restricted to oral reading fluency development. The patterns of development found in this study among general education, ED, and SLD groups may differ on other reading measures, such as vocabulary or comprehension, or in other content domains. In addition, we relied on school-based identification of ED and SLD to form the groups in this study. This could have increased the error in identification of students. We also collected data prior to implementation of response to intervention methods in the state.

The data we present here are representative of schools that participated in Reading First, and, therefore, should be interpreted with caution as the findings may not generalize to the full population of students. Reading First schools include relatively large numbers of students with low socioeconomic status. Previous research has noted that students' socioeconomic status is moderately related to students' academic achievement (Sirin, 2005).

We were unable to examine the special education interventions that students with ED or SLD received. Research is needed that examines characteristics of and interventions for students who are successful readers after special education in relation to students who demonstrate insufficient growth in special education. Research in this area also would help to address questions related to the development of students with disabilities in various academic areas and better inform the findings of this study. We examined all students across all districts in one state and, thus, the data are representative of average growth across special education services and quality.

SUMMARY

In this study we found that students with ED or SLD were making progress in their reading skills during second and third grade, but did not demonstrate rates of growth that would allow them to meet grade-level expectations in reading, providing additional evidence for the deficit model of reading for students with ED or SLD. Although we maintain that it is important to set goals and monitor student progress towards grade-level expectations, it may be inappropriate to define student success, and therefore the success of special education, based only on students with disabilities meeting the proficiency levels set for students without disabilities. The onus for setting high standards in special education falls first on researchers, who must identify instructional techniques that accelerate learning for students with disabilities, including under ideal conditions, and provide evidence of the effects and growth rates that can be expected in these interventions. We contend that it is this ongoing research that sets the standard for practitioners to judge the effectiveness of interventions implemented in special education, continually raising the bar for our students with disabilities in an evidence-based dynamic.

REFERENCES

Alliance for Excellent Education. (2002). *Every child a graduate: A framework for an excellent education for all middle and high school students*. Washington, DC: Author. Retrieved from http://www.al14ed.org/files/archive/publications/EveryChildAGraduate/every.pdf

Al Otaiba, S., Petscher, Y., Pappamahiel, N. E., Williams-Smith, R., Dyrlund, A., & Connor, C. (2009). Modeling oral reading fluency development in Latino students: A longitudinal study across second and third grade. *Journal of Educational Psychology, 101*, 315–329. http://dx.doi.org/10.1037/a0014698

Anderson, J. A., Kutash, K., & Duchnowski, A. J. (2001). A comparison of the academic process of students with ED and students with LD. *Journal of Emotional and Behavioral Disorders, 9*, 106–115. http://dx.doi.org/10.1177/106342660100900205

Baker, S. K., Smolkowski, K., Katz, R., Hank, F., Seeley, J. R., Kame'enui, E. J., & Beck, C. T. (2008). Reading fluency as a predictor of reading proficiency in low-performing, high-poverty schools. *School Psychology Review, 37*, 18–37.

Benner, G. J., Nelson, J. R., Ralston, N. C., & Mooney, P. (2010). A meta-analysis of the effects of reading instruction on the reading skills of students with or at risk of behavioral disorders. *Behavioral Disorders, 35*, 86–102.

Buzick, H. M., & Laitusis, C. C. (2010). Using growth for accountability: Measurement challenges for students with disabilities and recommendations for research. *Educational Researcher, 39*, 537–544. http://dx.doi.org/10.3102/0013189X10383560

Center on Crime, Communities, and Culture. (1997). *Education as crime prevention* (Occasional Paper Series No. 2.) Retrieved from http://www.prisonpolicy.org/scans/researchbrief2.pdf

Christ, T. J., Silberglitt, B., Yeo, S., & Cormier, D. (2010). Curriculum-based measurement of oral reading: An evaluation of growth rates and seasonal effects among students served in general and special education. *School Psychology Review, 39,* 447–462.

Cullinan, D., Osborne, S., & Epstein, M. (2004). Characteristics of emotional disturbance among female students. *Remedial and Special Education, 25,* 276–290. http://dx.doi.org/10.1177/07419325040250050201

Cunningham, A. E., & Stanovich, K. E. (1997). Early reading acquisition and its relation to reading experience and ability 10 years later. *Developmental Psychology, 33,* 934–945. http://dx.doi.org/10.1037/0012-1649.33.6.934

Deno, S. L., Fuchs, L. S., Marston, D. B., & Shin, J. (2001). Using curriculum-based measurement to establish growth standards for students with learning disabilities. *School Psychology Review, 30,* 507–524.

Eckes, S., & Swando, J. (2009). Special education subgroups under NCLB: Issues to consider. *Teachers College Record, 111,* 2479–2504.

Epstein, M. H., & Cullinan, D. (1983). Academic performance of behaviorally disordered and learning disabled pupils. *The Journal of Special Education, 17,* 303–308. http://dx.doi.org/10.1177/002246698301700306

Fletcher, J. M, & Foorman, B. R. (1994). Issues in definition and measurement of learning disabilities: The need for early intervention. In J. M. Fletcher, & B. R. Foorman (Eds.), *Frames of reference for the assessment of learning disabilities: New views on measurement issues* (pp. 185–200). Baltimore, MD: Brookes.

Fletcher, J. M., Lyon, G. R., Fuchs, L. S., & Barnes, M. A. (2007). *Learning disabilities: From identification to intervention.* New York, NY: Guilford.

Francis, D. J., Shaywitz, S. E., Stuebing, K. K., Shaywitz, B. A., & Fletcher, J. M. (1996). Developmental lag versus deficit models of reading disability: A longitudinal, individual growth curves analysis. *Journal of Educational Psychology, 88,* 3–17. http://dx.doi.org/10.1037/0022-0663.88.1.3

Fuchs, L. S., Fuchs, D., Hosp, M. K., & Jenkins, J. R. (2001). Oral reading fluency as an indicator of reading competence: A theoretical, empirical, and historical analysis. *Scientific Studies of Reading, 5,* 239–256. http://dx.doi.org/10.1207/S1532799XSSR0503_3

Good, R. H., III, & Kaminski, R. A. (Eds.). (2002). *Dynamic indicators of basic early literacy skills* (6th ed.). Eugene, OR: University of Oregon, Institute for the Development of Educational Achievement.

Hanushek, E. A., Kain, J. F., & Rivkin, S. G. (1998, August). *Does special education raise academic achievement for students with disabilities?* (NBER Working Paper No. 6690). Cambridge, MA: National Bureau of Economic Research.

Harcourt Educational Measurement. (2003). *Stanford Achievement Test (10th ed.).* San Antonio, TX: Harcourt Assessment.

Judge, S., & Bell, S. M. (2011). Reading achievement trajectories for students with learning disabilities during the elementary years. *Reading and Writing Quarterly, 27,* 153–178. http://dx.doi.org/10.1080/10573569.2011.532722

Juel, C. (1988). Learning to read and write: A longitudinal study of 54 children from first through fourth grades. *Journal of Educational Psychology, 80, 437–447.* http://dx.doi.org/10.1037/0022-0663.80.4.437

Kober, N., Chudowsky, N., & Chudowsky, V. (2010). *State test score trends through 2008-2009: Slow and uneven progress in narrowing gaps.* Washington, DC: Center on Education Policy.

Little, R. J. A. (1988). A test of missing completely at random for multivariate data with missing values. *Journal of the American Statistical Association, 83,* 1198–1202. http://dx.doi.org/10.1080/01621459.1988.10478722

Luebke, J., Epstein, M. H., & Cullinan, D. (1989). Comparisons of teacher-rated achievement levels of behaviorally disordered, learning disabled, and non-handicapped adolescents. *Behavioral Disorders, 15,* 1–8.

Lynn, R., & Mikk, J. (2009). National IQs predict educational attainment in math, reading and science across 56 nations. *Intelligence, 37,* 305–310. http://dx.doi.org/10.1016/j.intell.2009.01.002

Morgan, P. L., Farkas, G., & Wu, Q. (2011). Kindergarten children's growth trajectories in reading and mathematics: Who falls increasingly behind? *Journal of Learning Disabilities, 44*, 472–488. http://dx.doi.org/10.1177/0022219411414010

National Center for Education Statistics. (2005). *National assessment of educational progress*. Washington, DC: U.S. Department of Education.

No Child Left Behind Act of 2001, 20 U.S.C. §§ 6301 et seq. (2006 & Supp. V. 2011).

Phillips, L. M., Norris, S. P., Osmond, W. C., & Maynard, A. M. (2002). Relative reading achievement: A longitudinal study of 187 children from first through sixth grades. *Journal of Educational Psychology, 94*, 3–13. http://dx.doi.org/10.1037//0022-0663.94.1.3

Puranik, C., Petscher, Y., Al Otaiba, S., Catts, H., & Lonigan, C. (2008). Development of oral reading fluency in children with speech or language impairments: A growth curve analysis. *Journal of Learning Disabilities, 41*, 545–560. http://dx.doi.org/10.1177/0022219408317858

Reid, R., Gonzalez, J. E., Nordness, P. D., Trout, A., & Epstein, M. H. (2004). A meta-analysis of the academic status of students with emotional/behavioral disturbance. *The Journal of Special Education, 38*, 130–143. http://dx.doi.org/10.1177/00224669040380030101

Rice, E. H., & Yen, C. J. (2010). Examining gender and the academic achievement of students with emotional disturbance. *Education and Treatment of Children, 33*, 601–621. http://dx.doi.org/10.1353/etc.2010.0011

Rivera, M. O., Al Otaiba, S., & Koorland, M. A. (2006). Reading instruction for students with emotional and behavioral disorders and at risk of antisocial behaviors in primary grades: Review of literature. *Behavioral Disorders, 31*, 323–337.

Roehrig, A. D., Petscher, Y., Nettles, S. M., Hudson, R. F., & Torgesen, J. K. (2008). Not just speed reading: Accuracy of the DIBELS oral reading fluency measure for predicting high-stakes third grade reading comprehension outcomes. *Journal of School Psychology, 46*, 343–366. http://dx.doi.org/10.1016/j.jsp.2007.06.006

Schiller, E., Sanford, C., & Blackorby, J. (2008). *A national profile of the classroom experiences and academic performance of students with learning disabilities: A special topic report from the special education elementary longitudinal study*. Washington, DC: U.S. Department of Education.

Sirin, S. R. (2005). Socioeconomic status and academic achievement: A meta-analytic review of research. *Review of Educational Research, 75*, 417–453. http://dx.doi.org/10.3102/00346543075003417

Skibbe, L. E., Grimm, K. J., Stanton-Chapman, T. L., Justice, L. M., Pence, K. L., & Bowles, R. P. (2008). Reading trajectories of children with language difficulties from preschool through fifth grade. *Language, Speech, and Hearing Services in Schools, 39*, 475–486. http://dx.doi.org/10.1044/0161-1461 (2008/07-0016)

Speece, D. L., & Case, L. P. (2001). Classification in context: An alternative approach to identifying early reading disability. *Journal of Educational Psychology, 93*, 735–749. http://dx.doi.org/10.1037//0022-0663.93.4.735

Swanson, H. L., & Carson, C. (1996). A selective synthesis of intervention research for students with learning disabilities. *School Psychology Review, 25*, 370–392.

Torgesen, J. K., 6c Burgess, S. R. (1998). Consistency of reading related phonological processes throughout early childhood: Evidence from longitudinal-correlational and instructional studies. In J. Metsala & L. Ehri (Eds.), *Word recognition in beginning reading* (pp. 161–188). Hillsdale, NJ: Erlbaum.

U.S. Department of Education. (2011). *Thirtieth annual report to congress on the implementation of the Individuals with Disabilities Act, 2008*. Washington, DC: Author.

Wanzek, J., Roberts, G., Linan-Thompson, S., Vaughn, S., Woodruff, A. L., & Murray, C. S. (2010). Differences in the relationship of oral reading fluency and high-stakes measures of reading comprehension. *Assessment for Effective Intervention, 35*, 67–77. http://dx.doi.org/10.1177/1534508409339917

Wei, X., Blackorby, J., & Schiller, E. (2011). Growth in reading achievement of students with disabilities, ages 7 to 17. *Exceptional Children, 78*, 89–106.

Wheldall, E. G., & Limbrick, L. (2010). Do more boys than girls have reading problems? *Journal of Learning Disabilities, 43*, 418–429. http://dx.doi.org/10.1177/0022219409355477

ABOUT THE AUTHORS

JEANNE WANZEK (Florida CEC), Assistant Professor, Florida Center for Reading Research and School of Teacher Education, Florida State University, Tallahassee. **STEPHANIE AL OTAIBA** (Texas CEC), Professor, Department of Teaching and Learning, Southern Methodist University, Dallas, Texas. **YAACOV PETSCHER**, Research Associate, Florida Center for Reading Research, Florida State University, Tallahassee.

This research was supported by Grant 1R03HD 060758-01A1 and Grant P50HD052120 from the National Institute of Child Health and Human Development. The content is solely the responsibility of the authors and does not necessarily represent the official views of the National Institute of Child Health and Human Development or the National Institutes of Health.

Address correspondence concerning this article to Jeanne Wanzek, FCRR, Florida State University, 1107 W. Call Street, P. O. Box 306–4304, Tallahassee, FL 32306 (e-mail: jwanzek@fcrr.org).

Manuscript received January 2012; accepted June 2012.

POST-READING ACTIVITIES

1. What is the difference between the deficit model of reading development and the lag model?
2. Revisit your prediction regarding the results of the study. Were you correct? Would you revise your statement now, and if so, how?
3. What did the researchers determine about the influence of gender on oral reading fluency in the populations studied?

CHAPTER 7

HEARING IMPAIRMENTS

INTRODUCTION

In this anthology, you have already read about students who are English Language Learners and those who have special needs. In Chapter 7, you will revisit those topics and read about a new population of exceptional learners: students with a hearing impairment. A *hearing impairment* is a general term that encompasses those who are deaf or hard of hearing (DHH) and those who have mild or moderate hearing loss (MMHL). This diverse group can benefit from research-based instructional strategies that were originally designed for general education students.

In the first article, readers will be introduced to the guided reading approach. Guided reading is an in-class intervention provided to students who exhibit similar reading behaviors. The teacher works with small, homogeneous groups to develop reading proficiency. The authors provide a thorough description of how to implement guided reading for students who are DHH or present other learning challenges.

The authors of the second article interviewed participants who were diagnosed with MMHL to determine common challenges faced in the classroom. Self-determination theory and identity research are discussed. Participants offer strategies that may help facilitate the inclusion of students with MMHL. Educators will learn how to help students (a) achieve a sense of relatedness; (b) increase their sense of competence; and (c) increase their feelings of autonomy (Schirmer and Schaffer 2013, 17).

Both studies in this section are relevant to preservice and new teachers because of the strong likelihood that they may have a hearing-impaired student in their class at some point. According to the Hearing Loss Association of America (2018), almost 15 percent of students in general education classrooms experience some degree of hearing loss. The selected studies will expose the readers to effective, research-based best practices and meaningful recommendations to facilitate the academic and social achievement of this population of diverse learners.

REFERENCES

Hearing Loss Association of America. 2018. *Basic Facts about Hearing Loss*. Retrieved from http://hearingloss.org/content/basic-facts-about-hearing-loss

Schirmer, Barbara. R., and Laura Schaffer. 2013. "Guided Reading Approach: Teaching Reading to Students Who Are Deaf and Others Who Struggle." *Teaching Exceptional Children* 42 (5): 215–252.

CHAPTER 7

READING 7.1 OVERVIEW

Students who are deaf or hard of hearing (DHH) can benefit from research-based instructional strategies that are commonly used in a general education classroom. The authors introduce the guided reading approach for differentiating instruction. "Guided reading is a small group instructional context in which a teacher supports each reader's development of a system of strategic actions for processing new texts at increasingly challenging levels of difficulty" (Fountas and Pinnell 2017). The authors provide research, examples, and a detailed description of how to use the approach with students who are DHH or otherwise present learning challenges.

REFERENCE

Fountas, Irene C., and Gay S. Pinnell. 2017. *Guided Reading: Responsive Teaching across the Grades*. Portsmouth, NH: Heinemann.

PRE-READING ACTIVITIES

1. Describe your current understanding of guided reading.
2. What are leveled books?
3. How would you conduct a guided reading session with a student who is hard of hearing?

GUIDED READING APPROACH

TEACHING READING TO STUDENTS WHO ARE DEAF AND OTHERS WHO STRUGGLE

BY BARBARA R. SCHIRMER AND LAURA SCHAFFER

READING 7.1

Students who are deaf, hard of hearing, English language learners, or learning disabled need daily reading instruction that offers opportunities to learn and to practice strategies for word recognition, fluency, and comprehension. The guided reading lesson structure is flexible enough to be used with any type of reading material and leaves decisions about selection of strategies to teach on any given day up to the teacher. The teacher can provide exactly the level of supportive instruction needed by the students and incorporate evidence-based practices for teaching the skills needed to become successful readers.

When Isabella graduated from her teacher education program, she knew a lot about the importance of teaching the five components of reading instruction recommended by the National Reading Panel (2000)—phonemic awareness, phonics, fluency, vocabulary, and text comprehension—and that these same components are crucial for teaching reading to students who are deaf (Schirmer & McGough, 2005). She also knew quite a

Barbara R. Schirmer and Laura Schaffer, "Guided Reading Approach: Teaching Reading to Students Who Are Deaf and Others Who Struggle," *Teaching Exceptional Children*, vol. 42, no. 5, pp. 52-58.

few strategies for teaching each of these. When she started to organize her classroom for instruction, however, she realized that she did not have a grasp on how to put these components together into a lesson structure that would serve as a framework for daily reading instruction for students who are deaf.

If Isabella's school had adopted SRA Direct Instruction (McGraw-Hill School Education Group, 2010) or Success for All (Success for All Foundation, 2010), she would have been handed a particular lesson structure for literacy instruction. Both of these models require following a scripted lesson format and using specially designed materials. Though SRA Direct Instruction and Success for All and other such models can be highly effective in improving literacy learning (e.g., Carnine, Silbert, Kame'enui, Tarver, & Jungjohann, 2006; Slavin & Madden, 2000), teachers cannot individually decide to select them; these approaches are implemented as schoolwide programs, requiring substantial training of teachers, use of common reading curriculum materials throughout all grade levels by all teachers, and ongoing professional development to ensure fidelity to the steps in the lessons.

Isabella needed to identify a lesson structure into which she could slot evidence-based strategies for explicitly and systematically teaching word recognition, fluency, and comprehension. She also needed a lesson structure that offered the opportunity to teach these strategies at the three crucial points in time for any literacy lesson:

- *Before reading,* when instruction is designed to build the student's knowledge of the words, sentence structures, vocabulary, and content that will be encountered in the upcoming reading material.
- *During reading,* when strategies are focused quite deliberately on providing the support needed for the student to interact effectively with reading material

and to help the reader internalize these strategies so that they can be applied independently with future reading material.
- *After reading,* when activities reinforce the skills taught before and during reading, synthesize what students have learned in order to move toward independence in applying these skills, and extend their ability to think critically and creatively about the ideas in the material.

Isabella sought a model for reading instruction with a strong research base, but also an approach that she could incorporate into her instructional repertoire without a huge investment in new reading materials or training. Fountas and Pinnell's (1996) *guided reading approach* caught her attention; popular among general education teachers, Isabella also found that the guided reading approach is recommended by the Laurent Clerc National Deaf Education Center for use with deaf students (Gallaudet University, 2009). Since introducing the approach, Fountas and Pinnell also continued to develop lists of reading materials categorized across a range of difficulty levels to support reading instruction. This list of *leveled books* has grown continuously since the first lists were published and is now available on a web site to accommodate the constant additions (Fountas & Pinnell, 2009). Having this list of books at progressive levels of difficulty serves to increase the ease of adoption and implementation by teachers.

> *Guided reading has been found to be effective with deaf elementary-level readers in improving reading achievement.*

Though lacking a body of research on efficacy with hearing readers, guided reading has been found to be effective with deaf elementary-level readers in improving reading achievement, given its focus on matching the readability level of the materials to the instructional reading level of the deaf students, explicit and systematic instruction in word recognition and new vocabulary, incorporation of regular fluency activities, and teaching of cognitive strategies for comprehension (Schirmer & Schaffer, in press; see box, "Research on the Guided Reading Approach With Deaf Students"). Further, the approach incorporates evidence-based practices for which there is current consensus:

- Creating a classroom culture that fosters motivation to engage in literacy activities.
- Teaching reading as an authentic activity (for pleasure, for information, for completing a task).
- Providing students with scaffolded instruction in the five key areas of reading instruction (i.e., phonemic awareness, phonics, vocabulary, fluency, and comprehension).
- Giving students ample time to read in class.

- Providing children with high-quality literature across a range of genres.
- Using multiple texts that link and expand vocabulary and concepts.
- Connecting new concepts to background knowledge.
- Balancing student- and teacher-led discussions of texts.
- Using the new literacies of the Internet and technology-based instruction.
- Using a variety of assessment strategies and techniques (Gambrell, Malloy, & Mazzoni, 2007).

What Isabella learned about guided reading can help other teachers in selecting a lesson structure for students, whether students are deaf, hard of hearing, English language learners, learning disabled, or need daily reading instruction that offers opportunities to learn and to practice strategies for word recognition, fluency, and comprehension.

RESEARCH ON THE GUIDED READING APPROACH WITH DEAF STUDENTS

When a state school for the deaf selected the guided reading approach as the main instructional model for teaching deaf students (Schirmer & Schaffer, in press), we set out to investigate the effects of the model on the reading development of students in Grades 1 through 5. Classroom teachers were certified teachers of the deaf with a range of experience from 2 to 30 years. The school describes its curriculum as a regular public school curriculum with modifications in terms of presenting information via American Sign Language and written English. Students, teachers, and staff are assessed regularly with the Sign Language Proficiency Interview (Newell, Caccamise, Boardman, & Holcomb, 1983); teachers and staff receive training as needed to ensure that the campus is barrier-free in terms of communication. School size was approximately 180 students during the first year and 160 students during the second year of intervention; class sizes per grade at the elementary level ranged from 4 to 9 students. In addition to the teacher of the deaf, most classes had at least one teacher aide. Speech and language services were conducted in pull-out sessions with the speech-language clinician.

Within each classroom, students were grouped by reading level, and the classroom teacher conducted the lessons. Guided reading lessons were conducted 3 to 4 times a week during each academic year of the study. The teachers also conducted a *running records* assessment (Clay, 2000) monthly to assess student progress and adjust instruction accordingly. In these assessments, the teacher asked the student to read out loud/in sign (referred to as *storysign*) a new passage at the same reading level as the material used for instruction. During reading, the teacher made a checkmark for each word the student read correctly, notated when the student did not know a word, and wrote the word used by the student when it was a substitution, repetition, omission, or incorrect pronunciation. The teacher also notated the student's reading fluency. The teacher then asked the student to retell the story and appraised the student's inclusion of setting, characters, events, and important details.

Results showed several major patterns:

- Improvement during the guided reading instruction ranged from a half year to 2 years of progress each year of the study for most of the students.
- Achievement dropped precipitously from the end of one school year and the beginning of another school year, particularly for students at the earlier grade levels.
- It took several months of the new school year for students to recapture the level they had achieved at the end of the previous school year.
- Reading achievement levels at the outset were low regardless of grade level, with none of the elementary students at or close to grade level.

Comparing our results to findings with deaf students during the past 2 decades, which have shown that the average deaf student gains one third of a grade equivalent change each school year (Gallaudet Research Institute, 2005; Holt, 1993; Wolk & Allen, 1984), outcomes were better than this average for most of the students in our study. However, it is generally recognized that the goal for reading growth is 1 year of progress for each school year and only a few students came close to this benchmark. Given the low scores at the outset for most of the participants, and the dip that typically took place each summer, progress for most of the participants was far below the benchmark of 1 year of progress per each year of school. Outcomes, though modest, offer incipient evidence for the potential of the guided reading approach in improving the reading achievement of deaf students.

GETTING STARTED WITH THE GUIDED READING APPROACH

The four steps of the guided reading approach (see box) were originally developed by Fountas and Pinnell (1996) as a model for supporting independent and fluent reading for students from kindergarten through Grade 4 and did not incorporate the kinds of concentrated and systematic instruction that struggling readers typically need. By also teaching new vocabulary words before reading and having students read material in segments (rather than a whole book at one sitting), teachers can provide explicit instruction on word recognition, complex syntax, figurative language, new vocabulary, and text structure as needed before, during, and after reading. And, indeed, these modifications are recommended for English language learners and students who are deaf and hard of hearing (Avalos, Plasencia, Chavez, & Rascón, 2007; Schirmer & Schaffer, in press).

The guided reading approach is taught within homogenous groupings of students in order to ensure that all of the students are reading material at their instructional reading levels. When there is a match between current reading level and the readability of the material, instruction can be aimed at the students' *zone of proximal development* (Vygotsky, 1978): the distance between current developmental level, as indicated by independent problem solving, and potential developmental level that is possible with guidance from an adult or in collaboration with a more capable peer. In other words, the material is just difficult enough to offer opportunities to learn and apply new strategies with support from the teacher. It is, therefore, crucial to distinguish between independent, instructional, and frustration level materials.

Independent materials are those that the student can read with essentially no support. These materials are aimed at the student's current developmental level. *Instructional materials* are those that the student can read only with support. *Frustration materials* are those that the student cannot read regardless of the support provided. Frustration materials represent the reader's *zone of distal development,* the distance between his or her current developmental level and furthest potential developmental level. Even with significant support from the teacher, the student is unable to read materials within the zone of distal development. Materials at the reader's frustration level make appropriate read-alouds by the teacher. (See box, "Determining Readability," for guidelines for selecting the appropriate level for instruction.)

STEPS OF THE GUIDED READING APPROACH

Step 1: Group Students and Select Leveled Books. The students are grouped homogenously by instructional reading level. The teacher selects a book that matches the instructional reading level of the students in the group. Each student is provided with a copy of the book to be read.

Step 2: Introduce the Book. The teacher introduces the book by having the students look at the cover, read the title and author, and talk about the topic. In-depth building of background knowledge of the topic may be necessary for struggling readers. Vocabulary words crucial to understanding the story are taught.

Step 3: Ask the Students to Read Silently. The students read the book silently in meaningful segments. The teacher observes, notes student behaviors during reading, and provides support with word recognition, understanding unfamiliar sentence structures, and comprehension when needed. After each segment, the teacher poses a question, encourages the students to self-question, asks for a prediction, or uses another strategy for comprehension monitoring. For struggling readers, reading aloud before silent reading can enable the teacher to pinpoint word recognition difficulties.

Step 4: Discuss. After reading, the students discuss the book. The teacher has the children revisit the text to clarify, find evidence of interpretations, and problem solve confusing or unclear information. The children can then reread a passage independently or with a partner to build fluency.

(Fountas & Pinnell, 1996)

GUIDED READING IN ACTION

Isabella teaches deaf students at a school for the deaf. Some of her students have concomitant disabilities, such as learning and intellectual disabilities. The students are placed in grade levels by chronological age so the reading levels in her classroom range across several grade-equivalent level spans, which her colleagues in other school settings also notice among their students who are deaf and hard of hearing. One of the characteristics of the guided reading approach that Isabella particularly liked was that she could develop a template lesson structure for a week of reading instruction that she could adapt for each reading group. Her template lesson plan included the four steps of the guided reading approach.

One of the characteristics of the guided reading approach that Isabella particularly liked was that she could develop a template lesson structure for a week of reading instruction that she could adapt for each reading group.

For Step 1, she selects a new leveled book for each reading group, making sure to match the book's level to the instructional reading level of the group. (Isabella knows the instructional level of each student in the group because she assesses them regularly. She flexibly varies her grouping of students based on their changing abilities.)

Step 2 incorporates strategies that Isabella teaches before reading. In Isabella's template lesson plan, one full instructional period was dedicated to teaching the new vocabulary that the students would encounter in the reading material because vocabulary development is particularly important for deaf readers. By combining vocabulary teaching with sight word teaching, Isabella could teach two strategies at the same time (i.e., new word concept + automatic recognition of the word in print). While pointing out letter-sound relationships, prefixes and suffixes, and onsets and rimes in these new words, she could teach multiple strategies at the same time (i.e., new word concept + phonic analysis + structural analysis + onset-rime analysis + automatic word recognition).

The other half of Step 2 is to build background knowledge for the book's topic and text structure. In the guided reading approach, this activity can be a brief discussion but if the topic and structure are quite unfamiliar to the students or particularly complex, the teacher can slot more in-depth teaching into this step. Isabella often found that she was able to connect the teaching of new vocabulary with teaching about the topic. And sometimes she was able to coordinate the teaching of the new topic with what she was teaching in science or social studies.

Step 3 provides the opportunity to teach during-reading strategies. Isabella liked to vary the ones she slotted into this step. For comprehension, sometimes she asked questions but other times she asked the students to predict, engage in mental imagery, or generate their own self-questions. For word recognition, she often taught brief mini-lessons on a skill needed to read a specific word, particularly a word essential for understanding the passage. In the guided reading approach, silent reading does not always provide enough information to the teacher about the struggling reader's problems with word recognition and how word recognition difficulties result in comprehension breakdowns. So Isabella typically asked her deaf readers to first read out loud, or—more accurately for deaf students—to storysign. When storysigning during guided reading, the students express ASL conceptually appropriate signs in English word order. She also broke the story into segments because it offered her more opportunity to intervene with a strategy lesson targeted to a word recognition or comprehension difficulty.

DETERMINING READABILITY

A number of factors, within texts and within readers, contribute to readability. Within-text factors include content, structure, cohesiveness, format, typography, literary form and style, vocabulary difficulty, sentence complexity, idea or proposition density, level of abstractness, and organization. Within readers, attitude, motivation, purpose for the reading, cultural background, knowledge of vocabulary, extent of background knowledge of the topic, knowledge of text structure, and ability to identify words contribute to the ease with which the text will be comprehended (Irwin & Davis, 1980; Zakaluk & Samuels, 1988).

The most frequently used tool for determining readability is a *readability formula*. Most formulas rely on two factors. Some use average sentence length and vocabulary difficulty, such as Spache (Spache, 1953; Grades 1–4) and Dale-Chall (Chall & Dale, 1995; Grade 4–adult); others use average sentence length and number of syllables, such as Fry (1989; elementary-adult) and Flesch-Kincaid (Flesch, 1948; Kincaid, Fishburne, Rogers, & Chisson, 1975; upper elementary-secondary). Clearly, these factors do not exhaust all of the possible variables that influence text readability. When used as probability statements or estimates, though, formulas can provide predictive information regarding how easily a text will be understood by the average reader (Fry, 1989). But they will not predict precisely whether a given reader will interact successfully with a particular text.

The use of readability formulas is simple and straightforward, and computer technology has made the process relatively quick. Software is available for most of the formulas and virtually all word-processing programs incorporate readability measures. However, formulas cannot be used in isolation. Although it may be tempting to rely solely on computer software with its aura of scientific validity, formulas must be augmented with other measures for estimating the readability of text (Kotula, 2003).

One approach is for teachers to read the target text themselves, using their own knowledge and understanding of their students to compare against the demands of the text (Dreyer, 1984). A second approach is to give a selection of the text to the student for a trial reading (Rush, 1985). If the student is able to read 98% of the words automatically, with good phrasing and strong comprehension, the material is *independent.* (Some authors use a 95% target, but when the student has to stop and figure out 5 out of every 100 words, the material is not very accessible.) If the student is able to read 90% or fewer of the words automatically, uses word-by-word reading, and has weak comprehension, the material is *frustration. Instructional material* lies between these two points. A third approach is to use a cloze procedure, in which the student is given a reproduced portion of the text from which words have been systematically deleted, usually every fifth word except for the first and last sentences. A fourth suggestion is to develop your own checklist that includes within-reader and within-text factors.

Another approach is to use *leveled books.* Fountas and Pinnell (2009) apply four main criteria in their leveling process:

- *Book and print features* include length (number of pages, words, and lines per page), print (font type, font size, and spaces between words and lines), layout (placement of phrases, sentences, print, and pictures; consistency of layout; use of chapters, headings, and other organizational features), range of punctuation, and illustrations (number and relation to print).
- *Content, theme, and ideas* include familiarity with content, technical nature of content, sophistication of theme, and complexity of ideas.
- *Text structure* includes narrative text (predictability of story structure, description of setting, character development, plot complexity, genre, structure of episodes) and expository text (presentation, organization, and level of information and ideas).
- *Language and literary features* include perspective of author and characters, structure of phrases and sentences, structure of paragraphs and chapters, use of words or phrases as literary devices, and vocabulary (variety of words, number and range of high frequency and interest words, number of multisyllabic words, and word difficulty).

Several options are available for teachers who are not using the Fountas and Pinnell leveled books. Fawson and Reutzel (2000) suggest adapting basal readers. Teachers can work together in using Fountas and Pinnell's criteria to level the basal stories in their reading series or use Fawson and Reutzel's text leveling of several popular basal reading series (including Harcourt Brace, Silver Burdett Ginn, Houghton Mifflin, Scott Foresman, and Scholastic).

Another option is to use the increasingly popular publishers' leveling of their reading packages and theme collections. Some of these publishers use Fountas and Pinnell's leveling and some use their own algorithms.

When using a published leveling system, it is important to recognize that the particular criteria used in leveling may not result in a good match between the book's level and your students' instructional reading needs. For example, Cunningham and his colleagues (2005) analyzed books leveled by Reading Recovery and found that although Reading Recovery lessons incorporate the study of high-frequency words and phonics instruction using onset-rime patterns, "the books they select for their program provide little support for these two instructional components, and the way they level the books provides none at all" (p. 45).

Whatever system you use to determine the readability of the material you select for reading instruction, it is up to you to determine whether the leveling system makes sense in light of the instructional strategies and skills you will be teaching and, if not, to feel free to modify the levels using the other readability measures discussed in this section.

After-reading strategies are incorporated into Step 4. In Isabella's template lesson plan, she included a menu of activities for word recognition, fluency, and comprehension from which she could select during any given lesson. For comprehension, she often asked questions that encouraged critical and creative thinking but she sometimes asked the students to retell or dramatize what they had read, write a narrative or story map summary, or engage in a discussion. For vocabulary and word recognition, she found that worksheets, games, and activities in classroom centers could reinforce skills and information she had taught before reading. For fluency, Isabella often asked the students to reread a section together (i.e., *choral reading*) and other times she paired the students and asked them to alternate rereading a section to each other.

In Isabella's template lesson plan, Step 2 was carried out on Monday and Steps 3 and 4 on Tuesday through Friday, with a new segment of the book being read each day. By Friday, they complete the book and each Monday begin a new book. The lesson structure enables Isabella to systematically and explicitly teach the word recognition, fluency, and comprehension strategies needed by her students to become increasingly more proficient readers.

FINAL THOUGHTS

The guided reading approach offers a lesson structure for teaching literacy to students no matter what their reading ability levels are and the strategies they need to learn and practice. The lesson structure is flexible enough to be used with any type of reading material and leaves decisions about selection of strategies for teaching word recognition, fluency, and comprehension on any given day up to the teacher. The teacher can provide exactly the level of supportive instruction needed by students who are deaf and others who struggle with reading.

Ongoing assessment is a crucial component of the guided reading approach. Because the students' instructional reading level is matched to the readability level of the material, the struggling reader's abilities grow as a result of learning to read materials that are challenging and that present opportunities for applying newly learned skills and strategies. Growth occurs when instructional materials become independent materials, frustration materials become instructional materials, and strategies previously taught become ones the student uses independently.

Because the students' instructional reading level is matched to the readability level of the material, the struggling reader's abilities grow as a result of learning to read materials that are challenging and that present opportunities for applying newly learned skills and strategies.

The selection of the guided reading approach was a good fit for Isabella and the deaf students in her class. She was able to focus instruction on her students' strengths and weaknesses through ongoing assessment and clear benchmarks for their progress. The lesson structure enabled her to select before, during, and after activities that addressed the needs of each student. The approach has provided Isabella with an instructional framework for daily reading instruction into which she can target the word recognition, fluency, and comprehension skills needed by her students.

REFERENCES

Avalos, M. A., Plasencia, A., Chavez, C., & Rascón, J. (2007). Modified guided reading: Gateway to English as a second language and literacy learning. *The Reading Teacher, 61,* 318–329.

Camine, D. W., Silbert, J., Kame'enui, E. J., Tarver, S. G., & Jungjohann, K. (2006). *Teaching struggling and at-risk readers: A direct instruction approach.* Upper Saddle River, NJ: Merrill/Prentice Hall.

Chall, J. S., & Dale, E. (1995). *Readability revisited: The new Dale-Chall readability formula.* Brookline, MA: Brookline Books.

Clay, M. M. (2000). *Running records for classroom teachers.* Portsmouth, NH: Heinemann.

Cunningham, J. W., Spadorcia, S. A., Erickson, K. A., Koppenhaver, D. A., Sturn, J. M., & Yoder, D. E. (2005). Investigating the instructional supportiveness of leveled texts. *Reading Research Quarterly, 40,* 410–427.

Dreyer, L. G. (1984). Readability and responsibility. *Journal of Reading, 27,* 334–338.

Fawson, P. C., & Reutzel, D. R. (2000). But I only have a basal: Implementing guided reading in the early grades. *The Reading Teacher, 54,* 84–97.

Flesch, R. (1948). A new readability yardstick. *Journal of Applied Psychology, 32,* 221–233.

Fountas, I., & Pinnell, G. S. (1996). *Guided reading: Good first teaching for all children.* Portsmouth, NH: Heinemann.

Fountas, I., & Pinnell. G. S. (2009). Leveled Books: K-8 [curriculum materials]. Available from http://www . fountasandpinnellleveledbooks.com/default.aspx

Fry, E. G. (1989). Reading formulas—maligned but valid. *Journal of Reading, 32,* 292–297.

Gallaudet Research Institute. (2005). Stan*ford Achievement Test 10th edition, norming.* Retrieved from http://gri.gallaudet.edu/~catraxle/sat10-faq.html

Gallaudet University, Laurent Clerc National Deaf Education Center. (2009). *Guided reading and writing with deaf and hard of hearing children.* Retrieved from http://clerccenter.gallaudet.edu/Clerc_Center/Information_and_Resources/Info_to_Go/Hearing_and_Communication_Technology/Literacy-It_All_Connects/Guided_Reading_and_Writing.html

Gambrell, L. B., Malloy, J. A., & Mazzoni, S. A. (2007). Evidence-based practices for comprehensive literacy instruction. In L. B. Gambrell, L. M. Morrow, & M. Pressley (Eds.), *Best practices in literacy instruction* (pp. 11–29). New York, NY: Guilford.

Holt, J. (1993). Stanford Achievement Test—8th edition: Reading comprehension subgroup results. *American Annals of the Deaf. 138,* 172–175.

Irwin, J. W., & Davis, C. A. (1980). Assessing readability: The checklist approach. *Journal of Reading, 24,* 124–130.

Kincaid, J. P., Fishburne, R. P., Jr., Rogers, R. L., & Chisson, B. S. (1975). Derivation of new readability formulas (Automated Readability Index, Fog Count and Flesch Reading Ease Formula) for Navy enlisted personnel. *Research Branch Report 8–75.* Millington, TN: Naval Technical Training.

Kotula, A. W. (2003). Matching readers to instructional materials: The use of classic readability measures for students with language learning disabilities and dyslexia. *Topics in Language Disorders, 23,* 190–203.

McGraw-Hill School Education Group. (2010). SRA Direct Instruction [software and training materials]. Available from https://www.sraonline.com/di_home.html??PHPSESSID=7498a856b0aa6e40ec9df2027e498b6b

National Reading Panel. (2000). *Report of the National Reading Panel: Teaching children to read: An evidence-based assessment of the scientific research literature on reading and its implications for reading instruction.* Washington, DC: U.S. Department of Health and Human Services.

Newell, W., Caccamise, F., Boardman, K., & Holcomb, B. R. (1983). Adaptation of the Language Proficiency Interview (LPI) for assessing sign communicative competence. *Sign Language Studies, 41, 311–352.*

Rush, R. T. (1985). Assessing readability: Formulas and alternatives. *The Reading Teacher, 39,* 274–283.

Schirmer, B. R„ & McGough, S. M. (2005). Teaching reading to children who are deaf: Do the conclusions of the National Reading Panel apply? *Review of Educational Research, 75,* 83–117.

Schirmer, B. R., & Schaffer, L. (in press). Implementation of the guided reading approach with elementary deaf students. *American Annals of the Deaf.*

Slavin, R. E., & Madden, N. A. (2000). *One million children: Success for all.* Thousand Oaks, CA: Corwin.

Spache, G. (1953). A new readability formula for primary-grade reading materials. *The Elementary School Journal, 53,* 410–413. doi: 10.1086/458513

Success for All Foundation. (2010). Success for all [curriculum materials]. Available from http://www.successforall.net/

Vygotsky, L. S. (1978). *Mind in society: The development of higher psychological processes.* Cambridge, MA: Harvard University.

Wolk, S., & Allen, T. E. (1984). A 5-year follow-up of reading comprehension achievement of hearing-impaired students in special education programs. *The Journal of Special Education, 18,* 161–176.

Zakaluk, B. L., & Samuels, S. J. (Eds.). (1988). *Readability: Its past, present, and future.* Newark, DE: International Reading Association.

Barbara R. Schirmer *(CEC MI Federation), Professor of Education, University of Detroit, Michigan.*
Laura Schaffer *(CEC MI Federation), Special Education Teacher, Michigan School for the Deaf, Flint.*

Address correspondence to Barbara R. Schirmer, P.O. Box 700350, Plymouth, MI 48170 (e-mail: Barbara.schirmer@udmercy.edu).

TEACHING Exceptional Children, *Vol. 42, No. 5, pp. 52–58.*

POST-READING ACTIVITIES

1 On a separate document, complete this table using your own words.

THE GUIDED READING PROCESS	DESCRIPTION
Step 1	
Step 2	
Step 3	
Step 4	

2 What are the four main criteria in the leveling text process?

3 Why do you think guided reading is an effective instructional approach for DHH students who present learning challenges?

CHAPTER 7

READING 7.2 OVERVIEW

According to the Hearing Loss Association of America (2018), almost 15 percent of the student population (ages six through nineteen) in inclusive general education classes have been diagnosed with a degree of hearing loss. Mild or moderate hearing loss (MMHL) is an exceptionality because it is a communication disability. It can affect language development, as well as academic and social achievement. Based on self-determination theory and identity research, MMHL subjects who were interviewed divulge a reluctance to seek help from educators or peers. The author offers strategies that may help facilitate the inclusion of students with MMHL.

REFERENCE

Hearing Loss Association of America. 2018. *Basic Facts about Hearing Loss*. Retrieved from http://hearingloss.org/content/basic-facts-about-hearing-loss

PRE-READING ACTIVITIES

1 Reflect on the academic challenges associated with being a student with MMHL.

1 What do you think self-determination theory might be?

2 What strategies would you implement when working in a general education setting that includes MMHL students?

LESSONS FOR INCLUSION

CLASSROOM EXPERIENCES OF STUDENTS WITH MILD AND MODERATE HEARING LOSS

READING 7.2

BY CJ DALTON

ABSTRACT: *Up to 15% of the student population in integrated classrooms has mild or moderate hearing loss (MMHL) (Niskar et al., 2001), a communication disability that can impact language development, academic performance, and social-emotional quality of life. Due to the mostly intelligible speech of these students, teachers may easily overlook their challenges in gaining full inclusion in their classrooms. Framed by Self-determination Theory and disability identity research, data from interviewed participants reveal a reluctance to seek support from educators or peers, even when communication breaks down. Participants also offered practical classroom strategies for facilitating the inclusion of students with MMHL.*

Keywords: Inclusion, hearing loss, social-emotional, disability, identity.

C.J. Dalton, "Lessons for Inclusion: Classroom Experiences of Students with Mild and Moderate Hearing Loss," *Canadian Journal of Education*, vol. 36, no. 1, pp. 125-152.

INTRODUCTION

Mild or moderate hearing loss (MMHL) is a communication disability impacting academic performance, fatigue, and social and emotional quality of life for up to 15% of students (Niskar et al., 2001; Shargorodsky, Curhan, Curhan, & Eavey, 2010). Due to the mostly intelligible speech of these students, teachers may easily overlook their difficulties in classrooms and subsequently give little attention to their inclusion or mitigating the effects of their hearing loss (Antia, Jones, Reed, & Kreimeyer, 2009; Moeller, 2007). While research addressing social inclusion of more severely hard of hearing, deaf or culturally Deaf students is considerable (e.g., Eriks-Brophy et al., 2006; Rose, 2002), educational and psychological databases and major handbook chapters on special education and exceptional learners include little on the status, inclusion, or environmental contexts of students with MMHL (Andrews, Shaw, & Lomas, 2011; Reynolds & Fletcher-Janzen, 2007). Relatively few qualitative studies report the perceptions of this population in great detail and although informative, quantitatively designed studies provide limited opportunity for expression of what can be a complex lived experience (Kitchin, 2000; Marschark, & Albertini, 2004).

The purpose of this research is to investigate the experiences of students with MMHL to gain insight into how they conceptualized and managed their hearing loss during their school career and to develop recommendations for researchers and educators towards enhancing their full participation. Self-determination Theory (Deci & Ryan, 1985), a social cognitive theory examining motivation, development, and performance based on the fulfillment of three psychological needs—relatedness, competence, and autonomy—provide an analytical framework for investigating social interaction and intrinsic well-being (Roeser, Eccles & Sameroff, 2000). Ryan and Deci (2000) argue that adults can support students' psychological needs when they have a realistic understanding of the design of social environments and Best (1999) asserts that educators need to be sensitive to the impact that social construction of disability, social context, and student interactions have on students. Thus, in addition to Self-determination Theory, disability identity development research (e.g., Gill, 1997; Hindhede, 2011) provide analytical tools to expand the latent meanings of participants' lived experiences in integrated classrooms.

MILD AND MODERATE HEARING DISABILITY

THE MMHL POPULATION

MMHL can be defined as ranging from pure tone air-conduction thresholds of 15–30 decibels (dB) to 30–70 dB (Mehra, Eavey, Keamy, 2009). These terms however are audiological threshold categories which do not necessarily reflect student functionality in integrated school environments. For this report, MMHL encompasses a range of students who, compared to those with profound hearing loss or deafness, do not usually receive intensive educational interventions and "who generally have residual hearing sufficient to enable successful processing of linguistic information through audition" (Fischgrund, 1995, p. 231). Students with MMHL may have bilateral or unilateral, mild, moderate, moderately-severe hearing loss or progressive, fluctuating or temporary hearing loss during critical periods of academic and social development.

PREVALENCE

Research on prevalence is complicated by varying definitions and use of wide uncategorized ranges of hearing loss (Canadian Working Group on Childhood Hearing, 2005). In large population studies Bess, Dodd-Murphy and Parker (1998), Niskar et al. (2001) and Wake et al. (2006) have found that 11%, 12.5% and 13% respectively of school-aged children had hearing loss. Increasing numbers of deaf children have received cochlear implants over the past 20 years, and with a less severe functional status similar to MMHL, many are being educated orally in regular classrooms (Blamey et al., 2001; Francis & Niparko, 2003). White and Munoz (2008) have suggested that overall prevalence of this exceptionality is likely 25 times infant screening data of 1.1 to 3.61 per 1000 (Mehra et al., 2009). With all forms considered, 15% of the student population likely have MMHL. Educators may not be taking notice of this increasing population of learners or considering the challenges these students face in gaining full inclusion in their classrooms.

CLASSROOM CHALLENGES FOR INCLUSION

Any degree of hearing loss can interrupt normal development of communication, social-emotional well-being, and academic performance (National Workshop on Mild & Unilateral Hearing Loss, 2005). Most (2004) reported that participants with mild or unilateral hearing loss exhibited lower performance than those with more severe hearing loss, likely due to a lack of classroom supports usually afforded to the latter. Yet, Antia et al. (2009) found that although they may not be achieving their full potential, mainstreamed students with MMHL make adequate academic progress compared to typical hearing peers. Ross (1990) reminds us that academic achievement needs to be positioned alongside an understanding of psycho-social development. Thus discrepancy between "adequate performance" and achieving "full potential" likely lies in understanding the inclusion of students with hearing loss.

Basic communication needs of students with hearing loss, necessary for meaningful inclusion and satisfaction of psychological needs are compromised in integrated classrooms. Warick (1994) reported students' difficulties understanding their instructors and classmates; especially when attempting to speech-read new or substitute teachers (i.e., a skill consisting of watching the lips, face, and body language with residual hearing and contextual cues to understand speech). Johnson, Stein, Broadway, & Markwalter (1997) and Oyler and McKay (2008) have highlighted the substantial challenges that these students face in comprehending speech in classrooms with poor acoustics. Recommended classroom noise thresholds are set at 40–45 dB, yet many produce 60–75 dB or higher (Schick, Klatte, & Meis, 2000) which can contribute to increased stress and an inability to concentrate, while inhibiting motivation and performance outcomes (Norlander, Moas, & Archer, 2005). Tharpe (2008) concluded that students with relatively mild hearing loss may exert more cognitive energy than their typically-hearing peers, "leaving them with less energy and capacity for processing what they hear, taking notes, and other activities" (p. 12). Such classroom realities can adversely affect the sense of competence that these students experience at school.

Fatigue can also manifest in behaviour issues (e.g., distraction, inattentiveness, or disinterest) and be easily misinterpreted by teachers (Oyler & McKay, 2008). In a survey of teachers, 56% who reported professional experience with students with hearing loss, McCormick Richburg and Goldberg (2005) found it "disturbing" that over 35% agreed that preferential seating alone was "all that was needed" for these students while another 33% had no opinion on the matter. Overall this study revealed how unaware teachers can be about the challenges of this disability.

SOCIAL-EMOTIONAL STATUS

Health related quality of life investigators report that even mild or unilateral hearing loss (UHL) can pose significant threats to children's well-being (e.g., Bess et al, 1998; Umansky, Jeffe, & Lieu, 2011;Wake, Hughes, Collins, and Poulakis, 2004). Yet, few of these studies discuss specific educational variables impacting quality of life of students (e.g., itinerant, speech-language or teacher interventions, integrated or segregated classrooms) or implications to inform inclusive classroom teachers.

Over the past decades investigations of social-emotional status of students with MMHL have returned contradictory findings depending on methodological approaches. Evidence from multiple measures in a seminal mixed method study by Davis, Elfenbein, Schum, and Bentler (1986) indicated only some delays in vocabulary and difficulty getting along with classmates in the hard of hearing sample. During in-depth interviews however, participants expressed considerable concern about social acceptance and being teased or embarrassed in classrooms. In assessing personality, self-concept, and locus of control, Loeb and Sarigiani (1986) found that hard of hearing youth believed themselves to be unimportant, a disappointment to their families, and trouble makers at school compared to other children. Such a compromised sense of belonging at school is especially distressing considering that students' overall intellectual and academic performance scores were similar to typical hearing peers in both these studies. Punch and Hyde (2005) also reported no statistical differences between participants with hearing loss and typical hearing peers on social participation and loneliness scales. Yet, during interview, participants reported an aversion to attracting unwanted attention due to their hearing loss, a sense of isolation and vulnerability at school, and an intense need for "normalcy." Such incongruent reporting illuminates the complexities associated with social-emotional experiences at school that can impact the sense of inclusion experienced by this population; nuances not often revealed in scale responses.

The concept of "identity" implies an awareness of the self and refers to how one is labelled in a social context (Markus & Wurf, 1987) and given conflicting socio-cultural forces positive self-identity development for youth with a disability can be a complex undertaking (Weinberg & Sterritt, 1986). In designing inclusive classrooms, educators can benefit from an awareness of these complexities especially for students with invisible or less severe disabilities such as MMHL. Resistance to identifying as hard of hearing is evident in Kent (2003), a study which revealed few academic differences in surveyed youth with hearing loss, other than higher scores on loneliness. However, over half of the participants—who used hearing aids—did not self-identify as having a hearing disability when asked. Of the students who did self-identify, more were found to be at-risk physically and psychologically due to teasing and bullying, compared with those who did not.

In a second study, Kent (2006) interviewed adolescent hearing aid users who reported a resistance to using their "stigmatizing" assistive devices at school or self-identifying as someone whom they viewed as "less than normal. Evident is the irony of foregoing the benefits of assistive listening devices, prescribed to improve communication and independence, because of impaired sense of belonging and social anxiety. Hard of hearing students in a mixed method study stated during interviews that "we have to be normal ... talk and act like hearing students ... because you're just afraid what other people will think or do to you" (Israelite et al., 2002, p. 141). Such statements hint at students' efforts to manage the social environment of their classrooms, efforts which likely preclude academic learning.

These findings reveal consequences of negative social constructions about disability and identity development in those with mild or invisible disability. Youth can internalize society's devaluation of disability, regardless of severity, and expend enormous effort in "passing as normal" and proving "their validity at the cost of burn out, fear of failure and, ultimately, the lack of a comfortable identity" (Gill, 1997, p. 45). Hindhede (2011) argued that hearing loss in adults often threatens the stability of social interactions and can be damaging to both the self and to ones' social identity. Similar consequences are likely for youth with MMHL. Reviewed literature has highlighted the challenges that students with MMHL can face in gaining inclusion at school and the contentious relationships between disability identity, self-concept, and their sense of relatedness, competency, and autonomy.

METHOD

A key to unlocking inclusive education practice in Canada is through the investigation of students' voices (Gordon, 2010). This study examines the perspectives of students and reports their voices in an effort to better understand how MMHL impacted their experience of peer interactions, teacher relationships, communication, learning, and ultimately their sense of inclusion in classrooms.

PARTICIPANTS

Three self-selected students, aged 18 to 21 years diagnosed with bilateral MMHL for a minimum of two years were invited to describe educational experiences from their earliest memories to their current situations, and to use this forum to speak directly to educators on issues important to them. Angelina, a 20-year-old university student has had mild bilateral hearing loss since birth yet it was not diagnosed until age 16, after struggling to understand teachers facing the board during lessons. Angelina now uses two in-the-ear hearing aids and a notetaker in most of her university classes. Nicholai, a 21-year-old university student was deafened at eighteen months after a childhood illness and underwent cochlear implant (CI) surgery in one ear, at age three. Brooke, an 18-year-old high school student with bilateral moderate to severe hearing loss was diagnosed at age three and has always used two behind-the-ear hearing aids. Up to Grade 9 Brooke also used an FM system in her classes.

PROCEDURES

Ninety minute interviews were conducted across the province of Ontario, in environments conducive to effective communication (e.g., use of hearing aids, quiet room, adequate lighting, close proximity, and direct view of the researcher's face at all times), audio recorded, and transcribed verbatim. The researcher was uniquely positioned to conduct this study having had professional experience as both a counsellor and educator of individuals with hearing loss, in addition to lived experience with hearing loss since birth. Disclosure took place early during interviews and garnered immediate statements of appreciation from each participant for being given the opportunity to finally speak to someone who "gets it," and "who understands."

Following open coding, data labels were categorized to reflect participants' interests and concerns arising from emic perspectives. Data were then considered using etic terms organized to assess the motivational themes of sense of relatedness, competence, and autonomy identified in Self-determination Theory (Deci & Ryan, 1985), and to honour the complexity of disability identity development (e.g., Gill, 1997; Hindhede, 2011; Weinberg & Sterritt, 1986).

RESULTS

While reflecting on their school careers, participants revealed how they conceptualized and managed their hearing loss. Although she experienced difficulty at school "since Grade 2," Angelina didn't think that anything was wrong with her hearing: "I thought maybe I was just slower or it took me longer. But at the same time I always I understood everything, once I taught myself." To keep up in class, Angelina said she relied on copying notes and persistence: "I never ate lunch in high school. I was always in one teacher's office or another ... I was never afraid to ask for help" but quickly adds: "except for one science teacher ... he was intimidating. I didn't ask him for help." Angelina wishes teachers had noticed her hearing loss earlier admonishing that "school was tough ... basically I fooled everyone for 16 years."

When asked why he chose to be interviewed in a study aimed at students with MMHL, Nicholai explains that even though he is deaf, he functions as moderately hard of hearing with his CI: "I wanted other people with hearing loss to learn from this experience and to not be ashamed of who they are." Through much of his school career, Nicholai used an FM system and was supported academically by educational assistants. Overall, he feels that both interfered with his social inclusion and reports that teachers "were constantly fussing over my devices and basically I had everything taken care of for me by helpers ... I wasn't allowed to go off by myself to try to hang out with my friends ... it was hard to feel independent." Nicholai admits that he never had "the heart to tell teachers [he] didn't appreciate these modifications and accommodations."

Brooke has found that understanding lessons is problematic, especially when teachers walk around classrooms. Yet, she has never felt that she could tell her educators "to just stand in one spot!" Even with being assigned preferential seating, Brooke explains that most classes are "really difficult cause I can't hear it all ... after a while I am like, 'just forget it.' It takes too much energy." Brooke has also refused to use an FM system at high school, feeling that it has attracted negative attention from peers. Although she is often exhausted, Brooke also believes that these challenges to her inclusion have ultimately shaped her for the better "because I know what it is like to work hard, all that studying on my own."

Multiple case study analysis revealed three patterns in the data identifying a coherent message that highlighted the importance that educators (a) *understand* the lived experience of students with MMHL, (b) *recognize the inherent contradictions* that can accompany this disability, and (c) *attend to needs;* that is to communication, learning, and social-emotional needs. These messages also disclosed participants' need for a sense of relatedness with their teachers and peers, a sense of social competency in their classroom environment, and a sense of autonomy for self-determined learning often unwittingly undermined by adverse classroom contexts.

Understanding hearing loss. The first pattern highlighted issues and concerns unique to being a student with MMHL and revealed three themes *Explaining Hearing Loss, Frustrations,* and *Assistive Devices.* Overall, participants reported that they did not connect to teachers and peers when their experiences are not understood. Students also spoke of their efforts to describe the reality of MMHL at school as "a constant struggle" (Nicholai) and that "people don't know how to treat us ... It always feels like I am the one who has to educate everyone" (Brooke). Students wished that teachers recognized that they needed "to be able to hear what's going on, to be able to see what's going on, to know what context you're in, to know where you are, and what the conversation is about" (Angelina).

Frustration, annoyance, and compromised inclusion were evident in descriptions of being "left out" of classroom lessons due to background noise and teachers who "talk to the board" or teach in the dark, and of having to repeatedly remind teachers about communication needs. These participants recognized the inevitability of communication breakdown but noted that they usually do the work for quality communication, not their teachers or classmates: "I am constantly having to ask someone what was said ... it is really annoying ... I am in high school, I just want to fade into the background" (Brooke). Because asking for help requires additional effort and risk these students explained how they "decide what is important to pay attention to during class"

(Angelina). Nicholai admitted that speaking with peers often puts him "on edge" and Angelina who claimed to be normally very outgoing with close friends admitted that "in groups of two or three, I'm very quiet. I just sit back." Participants revealed that they opt-out, or avoid activities and places at school such as cafeterias, gymnasiums, and participation in groups, due to their hearing loss.

Students also wanted educators to understand that assistive devices like hearing aids, CIs or FM systems are not "a cure" for hearing loss: "you are always going to miss something that hearing people have naturally" (Brooke). Due to background noise, students felt that sometimes they were better off getting a break from devices; "often it is just easier to turn them off and lipread" (Angelina). Nicholai pointed to the irony of relying on assistive devices for independence in inclusive settings: "For most of my extracurricular school activities I had to take my cochlear implant off." Overall, participants' message to educators was: understand my lived experience with MMHL, the complications and limitations of assistive devices, and why I sometimes feel vulnerable and isolated in school and with my teachers and peers.

Identity and disability. The second pattern revealed how participants conceptualized their experiences with MMHL and touched on issues likely shared by many youth with disabilities. Themes in this pattern included *Self-identity, Stereotypes and Attitudes,* and *Difference and Shame* and highlighted compromised sense of belonging and competency in classrooms and confusion and discord with personal and social attitudes associated with disability. Angelina with mild and Brooke with moderate to severe hearing loss both identified as hard of hearing, while Nicholai who used a CI identified as deaf *and* moderately hard of hearing. Yet ambiguity about the concept of identity and with *whom* these students identified was evident. Students mentioned "others," "they," and "hearing people" implying self-concepts separate from the general populace which complicated their sense of inclusion. Even though their hearing loss is not profound and for the most part invisible, each participant admitted to not belonging in the "hearing world" of their classrooms because they do not hear "good enough." Each was convinced that he or she was the only student with hearing loss at their respective high schools and expressed feeling isolated as a consequence.

Students appeared motivated to distance themselves from both social and personal stereotypes associated with disability. Nicholai pointed to the portrayal of disabled people in the media: "it's maddening ... you always feel sorry for the disabled person. Or the disabled person has to triumph over obstacles." When asked if she feels disabled, Angelina exclaims: "No, no, I don't feel that way. Other people think that's how it is" and then explained how she waited weeks before advising educators and peers at university about her hearing loss: "I had to tell them because it wasn't working out. I wasn't catching on all the time." Brooke tells all her high school teachers, "I have a disability" but she is uncomfortable when other people say it about her: "I think of disability as not really being able to live your life. Like having someone help you live it. I am in a mainstream school. I can take care of myself. I am fine. But I can relate to them [disabled people]." Nicholai believed "classmates were probably nervous around me" and when people first notice her hearing aids, Angelina exclaimed, "they're like 'what the hell is in your ear?' ... then they'll treat me differently!" She added, "I take it as a compliment when no one notices my hearing loss."

Each participant acknowledged feeling different and having a sense of "shame" about hearing loss and spoke to difficulties "keeping up" with or feeling embarrassed in front of peers. Yet students also articulated an unrelenting determination to resist feeling this way insisting that others with MMHL not be afraid to say, "'I didn't hear it.' Put your hand up, if kids judge you based on that well then ... they are not good enough to be your friends" (Brooke). Participants said they can "compete on the same level" as their peers and "make the grade" but that at times, they also "just can't do it" and that they often "give up" trying. Their sense of exclusion and the challenges to their competence may have motivated these students to be exceptionally autonomous in their classrooms. Interestingly, reluctance to ask for help was expressed as not wanting to *bother* others: "I would always feel bad if I had to ask for a special accommodation" (Nicholai). Brooke said "I always feel bad for having to say, 'What did you say? I can't hear you' ... probably [teachers] think it is just another way for me get attention."

Participants indicated that they were motivated toward achieving academic goals but also towards that elusive and primary goal of passing as normal. The message to educators is recognize the inherent contradictions that come with having MMHL and its impact on inclusion.

Advice for educators. The final pattern included both pragmatic and conceptual recommendations for educators. Two themes, *Practical Considerations* and *Empathy*, emphasized how teachers can meet the three psychological needs of students with MMHL and enhance their inclusion in classrooms. To negotiate communication challenges at school, participants expressed the necessity that lesson content and classroom instructions be visible and clearly communicated. Students felt excluded when they were expected to do two or more learning tasks at once: "I know how to put in the effort ... but I can't look down and write and hear at the same time" (Brooke) and when speakers' faces are not visible due to talking to the board or turning out lights: "I'm only getting half of what is going on ... sort of like 'fill in the blanks.' Only everyone else got the blank and I didn't" (Angelina). Participants suggested that teachers should discreetly get their attention before speaking to the class to avoid being caught unaware in front of peers: "tap me on the shoulder or call out my name ... or give a hand signal, just little things" (Nicholai). Brooke wished teachers would come to her "personally, quietly, and say, "'how is everything going?'"

Students wanted teachers to know that fatigue and falling asleep plays a role in their exclusion and contributes to "zoning out." Angelina said, "I had headaches and fell asleep in almost all my classes … It was fine. I got the grades you know, but I hated it." Nicholai explained how "when you're tired you don't feel like standing up for yourself. You're just like, 'Go on with it, let's get this damn thing over with.'" Students explained that others with MMHL are "not going to catch everything you say … maybe it works for people with perfect hearing. I don't know it has never worked for me" (Angelina). Brooke concedes that she cannot really blame teachers because they have hundreds of students, "but I've been living through this for years and I am at a point now where I'm just like 'OK I can't do it,' blah!" She added that she does tell teachers "I'm hard of hearing" and "teach so I can see your face" but explains, "I don't want to have to keep repeating myself. Like, if I asked for subtitles to be on once, you need to do it again."

A belief was expressed that educators viewed students' hearing loss as an "extra problem" and that they were seen as "some kind of a technical difficulty that needs to be fixed" (Nicholai). Yet, the data indicates that participants craved understanding, respect, and someone with whom they could feel safe; all elements of inclusive classrooms. For effective inclusion, "knowing what that child is going through would make a whole lot difference" (Brooke). Angelina added, "Have some empathy, for the most part we are OK with it, but there are going to be times when it just sucks … I can only imagine how hard it is for teachers to try to relate us." Nicholai asked that teachers be "open and encouraging" with students with MMHL, so that "they are not ashamed for not understanding something" and Brooke implored educators to "be patient with them emotionally." Angelina advised, "If they keep asking questions … Don't get agitated … take a step back and try to think about what they're going through."

Participants also described incidents at school when they felt accommodated and fully included in their classrooms. Students felt empowered and were motivated to focus on learning in classrooms where educators understood them, were empathic to their needs, and practiced common communication courtesies. Participants' stories reflected instances of feeling connected to teachers who understood their challenges. Although not wanting to be singled out in class, Angelina felt close enough to a few teachers to go to them "every lunch hour for extra help." Nicholai gave an account of teachers who checked in with him: "not like other teachers who were a bit impatient with you" and described one who "would make sure to have the lights on before he'd start to talk, and he'd ask me if I could understand him … like a head nod or something … he did it effortlessly." Feeling forgotten or intimidated by teachers was described as a common experience by Brooke, but she lights up describing others "who were really, really great about it!" She gave an account of a teacher who consistently would say "'here is what I will be talking about' … she told me in advance. I didn't have to go to her. Like that was really nice of her."

The message to educators was please attend to the range of communication, learning, *and* social-emotional needs of students with MMHL. Students revealed that they want to learn and are working hard to understand lessons but that they need to be able to *hear* and *see* everyone in class and feel safe enough to disclose when help is needed.

DISCUSSION

Ryan and Deci (2000) stated that educators are in a position to positively influence learning environments to help students: (a) achieve a sense of relatedness with other adults and with peers, (b) increase their sense of competence during the academic and social components of learning, and (c) increase their feelings of autonomy, volition, and independence during educational endeavours. To support students with MMHL educators must also have an understanding of how the social environment contributes to their development, performance, and well-being. In considering participants lived experience and messages to teachers, their inclusion in classrooms has been challenging.

The data revealed that participants were motivated to relate to and be understood by people in their educational environment but were disinclined to communicate needs or build relationships with those with "perfect hearing," who did not understand or recognize their efforts and limitations. Of interest to all educators is that the data in this study have also revealed that participants responded positively, were more engaged in their learning, and better able to meet communication challenges when they felt that they, their efforts, and their disability were understood by their teachers and when they had a sense of belonging over feeling forgotten.

Maintaining a sense of competence at school was challenged by participants' difficulties "keeping up" with classroom content, discussions, and peers and to their admitted "bluffing," "opting out" and avoidance of activities and people, due to communication breakdown and embarrassment. Participants shared how they usually only seek assistance if their academic competency is questioned. Though they were motivated to "compete on the same level" students admitted that, at times, they "just can't do it" especially when fatigued. Participants described how assistive devices can be problematic in noisy environments and bring unwanted attention. Even with devices students said they still missed what others hear "naturally" and that at times, they are better off with a "break" from hearing. When students tune out, opt out or take off their assistive devices, clearly they have "given up" or are fatigued. Perhaps removing their devices are ways these students managed fatigue and took control over their learning environment.

It is evident that participants are acting autonomously when they tell teachers, "I'm hard of hearing; teach so I can see your face." Yet, in addition to expending effort to connect with teachers and peers and to meet academic expectations, students also described asking for basic communication courtesies multiple times. Students with MMHL are not reaching learning potential when with limited cognitive energy, they have to *choose* what is important to pay attention to in class, teach themselves ineffectively communicated lesson content, or "catch up" outside of class on a regular basis. In order to survive and manage in classrooms which have offered little support for competency and autonomy, these students have had to act with independence and resolve.

Self-identity and self-concept issues associated with hearing disability were interwoven throughout each participant's story. Collectively their message to other students with MMHL was to *not* be ashamed or embarrassed, evidently because they *have* felt these debilitating emotions at school. Participants take it as a "compliment" when nobody detects their MMHL. Even though they believe themselves to be as capable as hearing peers, participants expressed beliefs that some teachers viewed them as "slow" or an "extra problem." Consistent with literature (e.g., Gill, 1997; Israelite et al, 2002; Hindhede, 2011; Ross, 1990) conceptualizing one's self-concept with the realities of hearing disability remained un-reconciled for these participants. These students may have unwittingly sabotaged teachers' efforts to support self-determined learning by their ongoing analysis of the learning environment and their weighing the value of interrupting and asking for lessons to be communicated effectively or repeated, against standing out as different, being caught responding inappropriately, or to the possibility of being ridiculed by their peers.

This qualitative research benefitted from articulate and academically successful informants with MMHL, who are soon starting or completing university, yet even these capable learners expressed difficulty communicating their needs to educators. The reader is cautioned against assuming that these students are representative of all students with MMHL however, typical classroom scenarios were described in which participants were *disabled* by educators and peers who neglected their communication and social-emotional needs. When examining participants' inclusion, consideration must be given to the effort they reported expending to figure out speech when quality communication was lacking and to assess their social status; efforts they usually expended *prior* to the possibility of approaching their teachers for support.

Recent research on students with MMHL using survey tools has indicated that few academic differences are evident compared to typical hearing students (e.g., Antia et al., 2009; Davis et al., 1986; Kent, 2003; Punch & Hyde, 2005). Participants in this study were relatively successful *academically;* however, theoretical considerations and in-depth interviews have expanded our understanding of their lived experiences. These participants with MMHL revealed a multitude of coping strategies and efforts to distance themselves from the term *disabled*, energy that might otherwise have been channelled toward other productive learning endeavours and reaching their potential;

if not academically, perhaps in other areas of their educational experiences. With awareness of and pragmatic attention to students' psychological needs and their challenges related to disability identity, educators can contribute to sustained meaningful inclusion of these exceptional students.

RECOMMENDATIONS FOR EDUCATORS

Findings suggest that classroom teachers can proactively facilitate inclusion of students with MMHL by attending not only to academic and communication needs but to social-emotional needs also, and by being cognizant of the realities of disability identity development. Participants in this study worked hard to accommodate teachers and peers while getting the information they needed in class, in non-visible ways which left little energy for other pursuits. Meeting students' need for relatedness through empathic caring relationships may support positive participation, help-seeking behaviour, and facilitate their desire for normalcy and sense of community. Classroom teachers must also consider that students' sense of competence and autonomy are undermined by noise, cognitive fatigue, limitations of and compliance with assistive devices, and a need to exert some control over their communication and learning. The potential of this exceptional population could likely be realized with proactive design and enabling learning environments that encourage students with MMHL to set realistic goals, solve communication problems, and make positive and informed choices, all of which are autonomy enabling and consistent with the goals of inclusive practice.

IMPLICATIONS FOR FUTURE RESEARCH IN EDUCATION

With up to 15% of the student population experiencing MMHL, it is critical that researchers gain a better understanding of their experiences in schools and begin to investigate practices that support full participation. Apparent from this study is that qualitative inquiry, targeting key informant perspectives on the social-emotional factors impacting the entire educational experience of these exceptional students can enhance existing statistical knowledge and inform classroom teachers pursuing inclusive practice. Future educational research could target students' possible unique strengths, such as heightened attention to both verbal and non-verbal communication, intense discernment of how they are perceived by others, capacity for hard work, and early awareness of the need to be autonomous. Strength based research such as that found in the fields of developmental contextualism (Lerner et al, 1994; Trickett, Barone & Buchanan, 1996), and positive psychology (Gilman, Huebner & Furlong, 2009; Snyder & Lopez, 2009) may be effective in achieving this goal.

REFERENCES

Andrews, J., Shaw, P., & Lomas, G. (2011). Deaf and Hard of Hearing Students. In J. Kauffman & D. Hallahan (Eds.), *Handbook of special education* (pp. 233–246). New York, NY: Routledge.

Antia, S., Jones, P., Reed, S., & Kreimeyer, K. (2009). Academic status and progress of deaf and hard-of-hearing students in general education classrooms. *Journal of Deaf Studies and Deaf Education, 14*, 293–311.

Bess, F., Dodd-Murphy, J., & Parker, R. A. (1998). Children with minimal sensorineural hearing loss: Prevalence, educational performance, and functional status. *Ear and Hearing, 19*, 339–354.

Best, S. J. (1999). Psychosocial correlates of physical and health disabilities. In V.L. Schwean & D.H. Saklofske (Eds.), *Handbook of psychosocial characteristics of exceptional children* (pp. 336–343). New York: Kluwer Academic/Plenum Publishers.

Blamey, P., Sarant, J., Paatsch, L., Barry, J., Bow, C., Wales, R., Wright, M., Psarros, C., & Rattigan, K. (2001). Relationships among speech perception, production, language, hearing loss, and age in children with impaired hearing. *Journal of Speech, Language, and Hearing Research, 44*, 264–285.

Canadian Working Group on Childhood Hearing. (2005). *Early Hearing and Communication Development: Canadian Working Group on Childhood Hearing (CWGCH) Resource Document.* Ottawa: Minister of Public Works and Government Services Canada.

Davis, J., Elfenbein, J., Schum, R., & Bentler, R. (1986). Effects of mild and moderate hearing impairments on language, educational, and psychosocial behavior of children. *Journal of Speech & Hearing Disorders, 51*(1), 53–62.

Deci, E., & Ryan, R. (1985). *Intrinsic motivation and self-determination in human behavior.* New York: Plenum.

Eriks-Brophy, A., Durieux-Smith, A., Olds, J., Fitzpatrick, E., Duquette, C., & Whittingham, J. (2006). Facilitators and Barriers to the Inclusion of Orally Educated Children and Youth with Hearing Loss. *The Volta Review, 106*(1), 53–88.

Fischgrund, J. (1995). Learners who are deaf or hard of hearing. In M. C. Wang, M. C. Reynolds, & H. J. Walberg (Eds.), *Handbook of special and remedial education: Research and practice* (2nd ed., pp. 229–241). Oxford, UK: Pergamon.

Francis, H., & Niparko, J. (2003). Cochlear implantation update. *Pediatric Clinics of North America, 50*, 341–361.

Gordon, M. (2010). Student voice is key to unlocking inclusive education practices. *Canadian Journal for New Scholars, 3*(2), 1–11.

Gill, C. (1997). Four types of integration in disability identity development. *Journal of Vocational Rehabilitation, 9*, 39–46.

Gilman, R., Huebner, S., & Furlong, M. (Eds.). (2009). *Handbook of positive psychology in schools.* New York, NY: Routledge.

Hindhede, A.L. (2011). Negotiating hearing disability and hearing disabled identities *Health, 16*(2) 169–185. doi: 10.1177/1363459311403946.

Israelite, N., Ower, J., & Goldstein, G. (2002). Hard-of-hearing adolescents and identity construction: Influences of school experiences, peers, and teachers. *Journal of Deaf Studies and Deaf Education, 7*, 134–148.

Johnson, C., Stein, R., Broadway, A., & Markwalter, T. (1997). "Minimal" high-frequency hearing loss and school-age children: Speech recognition in a classroom. *Language, Speech, and Hearing Services in Schools, 28*, 77–85.

Kent, B. (2003). Identity issues for hard-of-hearing adolescents aged 11, 13 and 15 in mainstream settings. *Journal of Deaf Studies and Deaf Education, 8*, 315–324.

Kent, B. (2006). They only see it when the sun shines in my ears: Exploring perceptions of adolescent hearing aid users. *Journal of Deaf Studies and Deaf Education, 11*, 461–476.

Kitchin, R. (2000). The researched opinions on research: Disabled people and disability research. *Disability & Society, 15*, 25–47.

Lerner, R M., Miller, J. R., Knott, J. H., Corey, K. E., Bynum, T. S., Hoopfer, L. C, McKinney, M. H., Abrams, L. A., Hula, R. C, & Terry, P. A. (1994). Integrating scholarship and outreach in human development research, policy, and service: A developmental contextual perspective. In D. L. Featherman, R. M. Lerner, & M. Perlmutter (Eds.), *Life-span development and behavior* (Vol. 12, pp. 249–273). Hillsdale, NJ: Lawrence Erlbaum Associates, Inc.

Loeb, R., & Sarigiani, P. (1986). The impact of hearing impairment on self-perceptions of children. *The Volta Review, 88*(2), 89–100.

Markus, H., & Wurf, E. (1987). The dynamic self-concept: A social psychosocial perspective. *Annual Review of Psychology, 38*, 299–337.

Marschark, M., & Albertini J. (2004). Deafness and hearing loss. In W. E. Craighead & C. B. Nemeroff (Eds.), *The concise Corsini encyclopedia of psychology and behavioral science* (3rd ed., pp. 312–315). Hoboken, NJ: John Wiley & Sons.

McCormick Richburg, C., & Goldberg, L. R. (2005). Teachers' perceptions about minimal hearing loss: A role for educational audiologists. *Communication Disorders Quarterly, 27*, 4–19.

Mehra, S., Eavey, R., Keamy, D. (2009). The epidemiology of hearing impairment in the United States: Newborns, children, and adolescents. *Otolaryngology-Head and Neck Surgery, 140*, 461–472.

Moeller, M. (2007). Current state of knowledge: Psychosocial development in children with hearing impairment. *Ear & Hearing, 28*, 729–739.

Most, T. (2004). The effects of degree and type of hearing loss on children's performance in class. *Deafness and Education International, 6*, 154–166.

National Workshop on Mild and Unilateral Hearing Loss: Workshop Proceedings. (2005). Breckenridge, CO: Centers for Disease Control and Prevention. Niskar, A. S., Kieszak, Holmes, S., Esteban, E., Rubin, R., & Brody, D. (2001). Estimated prevalence of noise-induced hearing threshold shifts among children 6 to 19 years of age: The Third National Health and Nutrition Examination Survey, 1988–1994 (US). *Pediatrics, 108*(14), 40–43.

Norlander, T., Moas, L., & Archer, T. (2005). Noise and stress in primary and secondary school children: Noise reduction and increased concentration ability through a short but regular and relaxation program. *School Effectiveness and School Improvement, 16*(1) 91–99.

Oyler, R., & McKay, S. (2008). Unilateral hearing loss in children: Challenges and opportunities. *ASHA Leader, 13*, 12–15.

Punch, R., & Hyde, M. (2005). The social participation and career decision-making of hard-of-hearing adolescents in regular classes. *Deafness & Education International, 7*(3), 122–138.

Reynolds, C., & Fletcher-Janzen. E. (Eds.). (2007). *Encyclopedia of special education: A reference for the education of children, adolescents, and adults with disabilities and other exceptional individuals* (3rd ed.). Hoboken, NJ: Wiley.

Roeser, R., Eccles, J., & Sameroff, A. (2000). School as a context of early adolescents' academic and social-emotional development: A summary of research findings. *The Elementary School Journal, 100*, 443–471.

Rose, S. (2002). Inclusion of students with hearing loss in general education: Fact or Fiction? *The Teacher Educator, 37*(3), 216–229.

Ryan, R., & Deci, E. (2000). Self-determination theory and the facilitation of intrinsic motivation, social development, and well-being. *American Psychologist, 55*, 68–78.

Shargorodsky, J., Curhan, S., Curhan, G., & Eavey, R. (2010). Change in prevalence of hearing loss in US adolescents. *JAMA, 304*(7), 772–778. doi:10.1001

Schick, A., Klatte, M., & Meis, M. (2000), Noise and stress in classrooms. *Results of the 8th Oldenburg Symposium on Psychological Acoustics* (pp. 234–242). Oldenburg, Germany: University of Oldenburg.

Snyder, C., & Lopez, S. (Eds.). (2009). *Handbook of positive psychology.* New York, NY: Oxford University Press.

Tharpe, A. M. (2008). Unilateral and mild bilateral hearing loss in children: Past and current perspectives. *Trends in Amplification, 12*, 7–15.

Trickett, E. J., Barone, C., & Buchanan, R. (1996). Elaborating developmental contextualism in adolescent research and intervention: Paradigm contributions from community psychology. *Journal of Research on Adolescence 6*(3).

Umansky, A., Jeffe, D., & Lieu, J. (2011). The HEAR-QL: Quality of life questionnaire for children with hearing loss. *Journal of the American Academy of Audiology, 22*(10), 644–653.

Wake, M., Hughes, E., Collins, C., & Poulakis, Z. (2004). Parent-reported health-related quality of life in children with congenital hearing loss: A population study. *Ambulatory Pediatrics, 4*, 411–417.

Wake, M., Tobin, S., Cone-Wesson, B., Dahl, H., Gillam, L., McCormick, L., Poulakis, Z., Rickards, F., Saunders, K., Ukoumunne, O., & Williams, J. (2006). Slight/mild sensorineural hearing loss in children. *Pediatrics, 118*, 1842–1851.

Warick, R. (1994). A profile of Canadian hard-of-hearing youth. *Journal of Speech-Language Pathology and Audiology, 18*(4), 253–259.

Weinberg, N., & Sterritt, M. (1986). Disability and identity: A study of identity patterns in adolescents with hearing impairments. *Rehabilitation Psychology, 31*(2), 95–102.

White, K. & Muñoz, K. (2008). Screening. *Seminars in Hearing, 29*(2), 149–158.

Yoshinaga-Itano, C., DeConde Johnson, C., Carpenter, K., & Stredler Brown, A. (2008). Outcomes of children with mild bilateral hearing loss and unilateral hearing loss. *Seminars in Hearing, 29*, 196–211. *Review of Psychiatry, 13*(3), 194–200.

POST-READING ACTIVITIES

1. Create a list of challenges that a student with MMHL may encounter.
2. What is self-determination theory? Did your understanding of the term change after reading the selection?
3. What are three significant recommendations that teachers should follow when working with students with MMHL?

CHAPTER 8

LANGUAGE IMPAIRMENTS

INTRODUCTION

According to the IDEA, language impairments are categorized as an exceptionality. They are defined as "a communication disorder, such as stuttering, impaired articulation, language impairment, or a voice impairment, that adversely affects a child's educational performance." This section of the anthology explores how to implement reading and writing instructional strategies to foster the social and academic achievement of students with language impairments.

The first study was conducted to examine the level of engagement that language-impaired students exhibit in cooperative learning groups. Cooperative learning groups promote active engagement through student interaction. The researcher presents categories of student engagement, pragmatic language areas and skills, a checklist for assessing pragmatic language, sample front-loaded questions and answers, as well as educational implications.

The second study was performed to monitor language-impaired students' reading, writing, oral language, and handwriting over time. Students between the ages of eight and eleven were assessed to determine the effect of language impairment on literacy skills. The researchers present the procedures, data, and factors that relate to literacy development. Educational implications are reported.

According to the National Center for Educational Statistics, speech or language impairments are the second most common disability, superseded only by specific learning disabilities. That statistic will be significant to preservice or new teachers due to the strong possibility of having language-impaired students in their own classrooms. The instructional strategies provided will be beneficial for those who work with or will work with this group of diverse learners.

READING 8.1 OVERVIEW

A qualitative study was conducted to examine the extent of engagement that language-impaired students have in cooperative groups. The researcher conducted 20 hours of observation, collected 482 photographs, and determined five distinct categories of engagement. The categories include group exclusion, unengaged, passive, co-engaged, and engaged (Stockall 2018, 2). The researcher, who is also the author of the article, provides an assessment checklist, pragmatic goals, and strategies for engaging students who have been diagnosed with language impairments.

PRE-READING ACTIVITIES

1. What is the purpose of creating cooperative learning groups?
2. What do you think the term *pragmatic language* means?
3. Reflect on how you could facilitate group interaction for students who exhibit language impairments.

COOPERATIVE GROUPS

ENGAGING ELEMENTARY STUDENTS WITH PRAGMATIC LANGUAGE IMPAIRMENTS

READING 8.1

BY NANCY STOCKALL

Ms. Frost, a second-grade teacher, stops to talk to a group of students working on a cooperative group word-making lesson. She nods to Kevin, clearly the leader of the group, when he shows her how many cards they have matched. Ms. Frost turns her attention to another child in the group, James, who has been identified as having a learning disability. She asks James to show her how to do the first part of the task. James sits up in his seat, picks up an index card with the word out printed on it, taps the card softly on the desk, and looks at the other cards on the table. After about 4 seconds, Ms. Frost takes the card from his hand and places it next to an index card containing the word side. After this modeling, Ms. Frost pats James on the shoulder, smiles, and asks him to do another one. He complies and correctly matches the words base and ball. Ms. Frost congratulates him and walks over to another small group. As she steps away from James, he slouches down in his seat and starts rolling a pencil back and forth across his desk. He watches the other children as they encourage each other to find word matches.

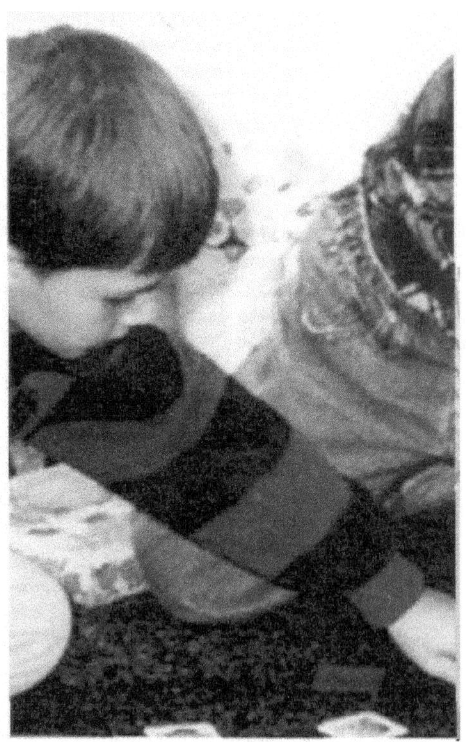

Peer-assisted learning continues to evolve and often takes a variety of shapes in today's elementary classroom. These strategies follow prescribed grouping of students, assigned roles, purposeful teacher facilitation, and related structured components. Although the methods are quite specific, the essence of student grouping is to further social interaction, provide opportunities for social/communication engagement, allow for multiple perspectives to be shared while completing a task, offer interactions where students listen and communicate with peers, and generally foster collaborative engagement. Kamps and her colleagues (2008) evaluated the effectiveness of classwide peer tutoring in the area of reading, and overall learning. Slavin and his colleagues (Slavin & Lake, 2008; Slavin, Lake, Chambers, Cheung, & Davis, 2009) highlighted the effectiveness of cooperative learning in enhancing academic achievement, attendance, appropriate behavior, intergroup relations, social cohesion, and more.

Although one of the critical features of student grouping is student level of engagement, little research has been conducted on the topic. *Engagement* means that students are actively contributing to the goals of the assigned task, within the structure of the group. Working in an elementary professional development school in which researchers and practitioners collaborated, I conducted a qualitative study to examine the level of engagement of students working in cooperative groups (Stockall, 2006). An analysis of 20 hours of observation, including 487 photographs of children working in groups, yielded five separate dimensions or categories of student engagement (see Table 8.1).

Table 8.1 **Categories of student engagement.**

CATEGORY	EXAMPLE
Group exclusion	Student is in the general education classroom but physically distanced from peers.
Unengaged	Student is physically grouped with peers but uninvolved and inattentive with the task or others.
Passive	Student is physically within a group but passively observing others.
Co-engaged	Student is physically grouped with peers but temporarily engaged in a one-to one interaction with the teacher.
Engaged	Student is visually and/or verbally attending to peer talk or a mutual task.

Although my earlier study (Stockall, 2006) focused on student levels of engagement, it raised other questions related to the quality of interaction taking place in the groups. Field notes revealed that some children identified as having language impairments seldom volunteered information, asked questions, or answered questions—and when

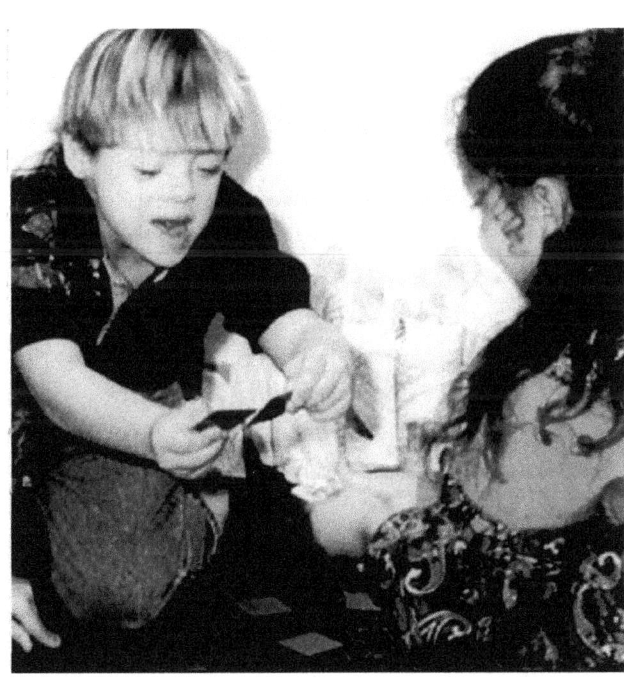

they did, others in the group tended to ignore their contributions. Using the levels of engagement as a quick screening assessment helped teachers pinpoint students who were excluded, unengaged, or passively involved within the group and make a decision to intervene or continue assessing the quality interaction. However, without knowing the cause of the breakdown in the cooperative learning group (Slavin, 1996, Stevens & Slavin, 1991), teachers either hesitated to act or responded to the breakdown in highly directed ways (e.g., "Let Tommie talk, too" or "Tommie, you need to participate"). Without knowing the exact nature of the breakdown, it can be difficult for teachers to determine appropriate intervention strategies.

COMMUNICATION BREAKDOWNS

For students with specific language disabilities, communication breakdowns can occur for a number of reasons (Yont, Hewitt, & Miccio, 2000). It may be that the speaker and listener do not share a common goal, or perhaps there is a lack of shared knowledge to ground the conversation.

Pragmatic language deals with the functional use of language and *includes* skills that are critical for communicating successfully with others in social situations (Levinson, 1983). Pragmatic skills involve not only knowing the rules of conversations such as staying on topic, taking turns in conversations, and asking and answering questions, but also the abstract linguistic regularities in functional language such as sharing a conversational goal (Clark, 1996; see Table 8.2). The research on cooperative learning identifies important elements of the cooperative process such as individual roles and accountability, a sense of group solidarity, rewards, and equal participation (Kagan, 1997; Margolis & Freund, 1991; McMaster & Fuchs, 2002); each of these elements is dependent upon the ability of the student to use language in appropriate ways.

When using true cooperative learning, students have a chance to use their language with support from the teacher, assistive technology, or their peers in the specific role they have been assigned. Students with specific language disabilities are less likely to initiate conversations or be acknowledged when they do offer a conversational bid (Hadley & Rice, 1991; Rice, Sell, & Hadley, 1991) and can be at a distinct disadvantage when participating in social tasks that are strongly dependent on language (Brinton, Fujiki, Spencer, & Robinson, 1997). To ensure that students have a chance to contribute, teachers may need to coach both the students with disabilities and their peer group. As noted by Kagan (1997), teaching social norms is a core value of effective cooperative learning.

Table 8.2 **Pragmatic language areas and skills.**

AREA	SKILL
Topic	Establishes a topic
	Stays on topic for an appropriate number of utterances (says so much and no more)
	Signals a change in topic
	Terminates a topic appropriately
Conversation	Initiates *and terminates a conversation*
	Begins and ends a sentence
	Asks and answers questions
	Acknowledges other speakers
	Volunteers to talk
	Listens to the speaker
	Responds to speaker
	Takes turns in conversation
Register	Uses language appropriate to the context and setting
	Uses language similar to others in group
	Uses intonation, pitch, and stress appropriately
Syntactic forms	Uses all modalities (i.e., declarative, imperative, negative, interrogative)
	Uses references appropriately
	Uses pronouns, articles, relative clauses, and adjectives to signal old and new information
	Sequences information or categorizes old and new information in sentences
	Uses grammar appropriate to context and setting
Nonverbal communication	Uses appropriate eye contact
	Understands verbal and nonverbal messages
	Uses personal space appropriate to culture, context, and setting
	Understands nonverbal signs of listener's attentiveness

LEARNING PRAGMATICS

Typically, children learn the pragmatic rules of communication implicitly. That is, they pick up these rules by watching others and interacting with the world—a kind of trial-and-error learning structure that provides most children the environmental feedback needed to communicate effectively. For children with pragmatic language problems, this trial-and-error learning is not sufficient to gain the knowledge required to engage effectively in groups (Fey, 1986).

Although speech and language therapists often can design instructional lessons and activities to explicitly teach pragmatic rules of communication, some students have difficulty generalizing these skills in naturalistic settings. Working in cooperative learning groups is a logical and reasonable context in which to learn and practice these rules. Teachers and speech/language therapists need to work together to create contexts in naturalistic environments to teach pragmatic rules to children (McCauley & Fey, 2006).

TYPES AND RULES OF PRAGMATICS

Each of the five areas of pragmatic language comprises specific skills (Ochs & Schieffelin, 1979). For example, to engage in a conversation, students must be able to initiate and terminate a conversation and to ask and answer questions. Teachers not only must be aware of the five ranges of pragmatic behaviors, they must also provide explicit and frequent feedback to students engaging in naturalistic settings. Children can become confused when working in a group because although their contributions may be accurate, the way in which they are delivered is inappropriate; any feedback they receive is often ambiguous. For example, let's revisit James's contributions to Ms. Frost's group word activity.

James sits on the carpet with three other second-graders as they play a matching card game. As he scans the words, he jumps onto his knees and grabs two cards that go together (*side* and *walk*). Oblivious to the turn-taking sequence the group has constructed, he announces, "I found a match!" A peer informs James that yes, they go together but it is not his turn and James has to return the cards to the floor. James complies, but rolls onto his back, crossing his arms, and ignores the other students.

Clearly, James is receiving different signals from his peer group. He is told that his answer is correct—but at the same time, unacceptable. Such ambiguity in the environmental feedback contributes to his confusion and inhibits his continued participation in the group. From examples like James, we can see that not only do teachers need to know the pragmatic rules and provide explicit instruction within social contexts, but also students must be able to identify the rules so they can provide specific feedback to each other in groups. What are some ways teachers can teach students the pragmatic rules for successful communication when working in groups?

Adults are quick to tell children, "Don't interrupt" when a child intrudes into an ongoing conversation. For children with pragmatic language problems, this statement is frequently interpreted as "don't talk," so it becomes easier and more conducive to stand idly beside others and remain silent. How do we know when it is okay to begin to talk during an ongoing conversation? Typically, in Western culture, we wait for a pause or break in the conversation before executing a comment or question. Children who have difficulty inhibiting their response find this rule to be particularly challenging. Teachers can help by telling students that in conversations, we take turns: When someone is talking it's your turn to listen; when they stop, it's your turn to talk (Ervin-Tripp, 1979).

TEACHING PRAGMATIC LANGUAGE SKILLS IN CONTEXT

Although it is critical to explicitly teach children with pragmatic language problems the rules of pragmatics, it is equally important for them to learn these concepts within the naturalistic setting. These skills should be incorporated into classroom rules for working in collaborative groups, posted in the classroom, and referred to frequently during routine times of the day. Such reminders help children generalize and transfer learning to a wider variety of communicative situations. A common model (Warren et al., 2006) for conducting pragmatic language in the classroom includes observational preassessment, identifying pragmatic goals, direct instruction with modeling, ongoing or postassessment, and revising instructional goals.

> *Children can become confused when working in a group because although their contributions may be accurate, the way in which they are delivered is inappropriate.*

OBSERVATIONAL PREASSESSMENT

Teachers need to be keen observers of children throughout the day and document both areas of strength and of weakness in the use of pragmatic language. Using a simple checklist (see Figure 8.1), teachers can document pragmatic language during different situations. Some of these situations may seem inconsequential but are in fact quite rich in opportunities. For example, children sometimes congregate around the teacher as they enter the classroom, sharing stories from home or the ride to school. Take note of any particular children who interrupt the conversation, who seem to stand ready to talk but never seem to get a word into the conversation, or who tend to use physical means such as tugging on another's clothing to signal their turn.

Other opportunities to observe and document pragmatic language skills arise while students are waiting. Waiting for the bus or for the school doors to open during the morning are often great times to listen to children's conversations. During lunchtime, you can easily note those children that use more physical means of gaining attention to enter a conversation. For instance, the seating arrangements in a cafeteria often require students to turn towards the speaker on their left, which means turning their back to the person on the right side. When the child on the right wants to talk, he or she may resort to hitting the listener on the back to gain attention. Tapping someone on the shoulder is considered appropriate but hitting is not. Taking note of the quality of physical prompts to initiate conversations is also important documentation.

Student name:____________________	Dates of observation From ________ to________		
DOES THE STUDENT ...	**ALWAYS**	**SOMETIMES**	**NEVER**
Listen to other speakers?			
Take a turn at appropriate times in conversation?			
Ask and answer questions?			
Acknowledge other participants/the interaction?			
Open and close conversations?			
Respond when asked a question?			
Volunteer to speak?			
Gain attention appropriately when wanting to speak (e.g., touching someone on the shoulder rather than pushing or hitting)?			
Stay on topic when participating in a conversation?			
Use transitions during conversations?			
Appropriately signal a change in topic?			

Figure 8.1 Checklist for assessing pragmatic language skills.

Conversations that occur during group work are critical to the level of productivity and final outcomes of a group. Teachers need to closely monitor and observe the types of pragmatic skills and their quality of interaction within the group. Observing helps to assess the specific quantity and quality of the conversations that occur. Does the child talk just enough and no more? Can the child "read" the body language of others to signal that the speaker has gone on too long? Does the child stay on topic? Can he or she use transitions to help the listeners follow his or her line of thinking? Although noting and documenting the *final subject content* of the group work is important, noting the way in which communication is used is key to building the abstract notions of accountability, role taking, sharing ideas, and negotiating consensus in a group.

IDENTIFYING PRAGMATIC GOALS

Identifying students' areas of strengths and difficulties with pragmatic skills permits teachers to address these areas as children work in groups. Teachers can set pragmatic language goals for students along with the content objectives for the group work; students without language disabilities can benefit from these instructional goals as well as those with language problems. For the student who has particular problems with topicalization, goals may include establishing a topic and making comments, staying on topic, and signaling a change of topic. For students who need training in the area of general conversation, the goals may include initiating and terminating a conversation, volunteering to talk at appropriate times, taking a turn at appropriate times in the conversation, asking and answering questions, and responding when called upon. The ability to maximize the power of pragmatics allows students to gain expertise in social skills and take on leadership roles.

Moving into and out of working groups helps teachers minimize their intrusiveness (Beilinson & Olswang, 2003). Doing so both helps to keep the group engaged in their line of thought and helps them to return to the topic of conversation quickly and smoothly.

When Ms. Frost observes James's interruption and the resulting feedback, she can move close to James and reinforce his correct selection of the cards; at the same time, she can prompt him to notice if someone is talking before he takes his turn (Beilinson & Olswang, 2003). This is also Ms. Frost's opportunity to remind all the team members that it is important to encourage everyone to take a turn. To guide students into becoming more autonomous in groups, teachers can encourage group facilitators to be specific in their feedback to others in the group. Using key phrases like, "Good turn taking" or "We are staying on topic today" makes the tacit understanding of pragmatics explicit.

DIRECT INSTRUCTION WITH MODELING

Providing Feedback. Presenting feedback to students with pragmatic language problems is also a concern because too little or too much feedback can disempower learners by calling attention to inappropriate behaviors. Rather than stopping student conversation, teachers should model ways to acknowledge individual contributions and provide positive instructive feedback. For example, Jeff, a third-grader with autism spectrum disorder, participates in a conversation on climate changes in the United States by stating that El Niño was responsible for the heavy rains during the preceding month. Other students offer input about the differences in rainfall from one season to another, and then Jeff shifts the conversation to a personal and persistent interest: "Lobsters like lots of water and they have large claws." The teacher turns to Jeff and says, "That's interesting, Jeff, but now we are talking about the weather. Do you have something else to say about the rainfall or El Niño?" Jeff replies, "Well, El Niño only comes about one time in 5 years." The teacher provides Jeff with positive feedback by saying, "Yes, Jeff, that is something to think about as we consider changes in daily weather." She goes on to address the group: "What might we predict about the rainfall this summer?"

In this example, the teacher not only redirects Jeff but also provides him with explicit reinforcement for staying on topic and extends the conversation using a question related to Jeff's initial comment. Such positive and thoughtful reinforcement provides Jeff with recognition for his contribution to the conversation and empowers him by giving his voice a valued place in the group. Similarly, when students talk out of turn, teachers might prompt them by saying, "It is my turn to talk and your turn to listen"; as the conversation switches, the teacher can state, "Now it is your turn to talk and my turn to listen." When teachers remember to note whose role is next and assume the role of conversationalist themselves, they allow children to experience equity in conversations.

Addressing Grammar Challenges. Grammar is often an area of difficulty for younger students with language impairments, and teachers tend to respond to children's errors more as blunders than as logical responses to our perplexing English language system. Children who use words such as *sheeps* rather than *sheep* or *foots* rather than *feet* are actually demonstrating their understanding of the rule of plurals: In general, we add an *s* to form the plural in English. Thus, some errors in grammar are really an indication that the child has not yet learned the exception to the general rule. Explaining the exception helps children make sense of the structure of our language. After learning that there are exceptions to the plural rule; students may still make errors because of habit. In this case, the teacher can ask "Did you say *foots* or *feetl*" Allowing the child to hear the correct form provides a safe context in which to recognize and repeat the correct word (Fey, Long, & Finestack, 2003), which reduces teacher intrusiveness while sustaining a supportive environment.

Students who tend to use nonstandard English can also be encouraged to *code switch* (Bernstein, 1966, Knestrict & Schoensteadt, 2005; Palmer, 2009; Wheeler & Swords, 2006). *Code switching* is the ability to shift from one register, language, or dialect to another given a particular context or situation. For example, a child who uses the phrase, "I don't got none here" can be reminded to use standard English

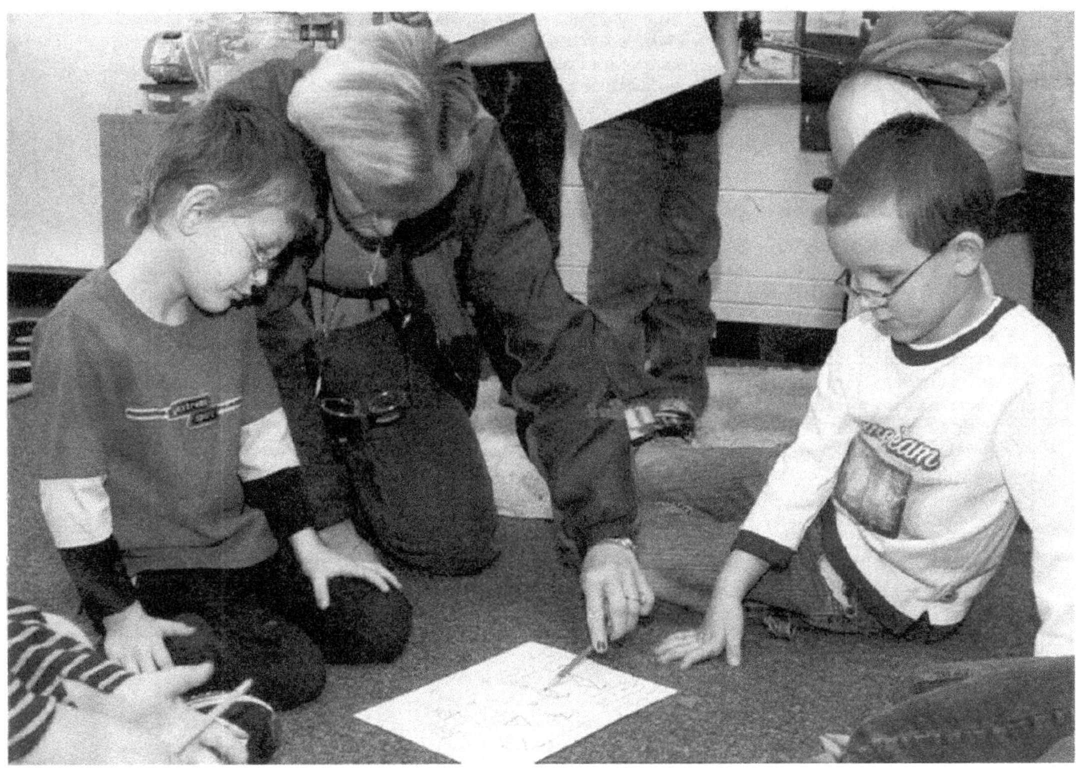

when working in collaborative groups. Group members can assist by modeling ("I don't have any here, either") rather than criticizing the student's language expression. Of course how the teacher responds to nonstandard English often depends upon his or her sense of social justice.

> *It is important for teachers to allow students opportunities to select topics of conversation as well as contribute as listeners.*

Teaching children to code switch sends a message of empowerment to students by valuing multiple forms of expression. Teachers can also draw student attention to the times when they use more informal language in conversation and when it is appropriate to use more formal language. Code switching empowers students to gain entrance and hold a position of status in multiple settings and contexts.

ONGOING ASSESSMENT AND REVISING INSTRUCTIONAL GOALS

It is important to assess student progress in pragmatics throughout the year. Some children will naturally respond quicker than others; the key to generalization is for the teacher to take advantage of multiple and natural opportunities to initiate and sustain conversations with and among children. Class discussions can be a great opportunity if the teacher instructs students to first share information with a partner about the topic. As each partner shares, the teacher can observe and note difficulties that may arise in the sharing process. When everyone has shared with each other, the teacher selects three volunteers to share their story with the group. Using this structure allows all children to interact with each other. It also allows the teacher to select speakers with varying levels of skills to respond to the whole group, minimizing wait time.

Front loading is another strategy for helping children with language impairments practice the forms of language. In this approach, the teacher first coaches the student by modeling the form for a question and answer (e.g., "What idea do you have, John?" and "I think we should describe the [character, scene, figure, etc.]"). Asking the question again and allowing the student to respond is a rehearsal strategy that allows the student to practice the skill in cooperative learning groups until he is able to respond to the question from other peers. Then, when working in collaborative groups, peers begin to use front-loaded questions to prompt the appropriate response (see Table 8.3).

Table 8.3 **Sample front-loaded questions and answers.**

QUESTION	ANSWER
What is the main idea of the poster?	This main idea is ...
What do you think we need now?	I think we need ...
How can we show ... ?	1 can show ... by ...
What is your idea?	My idea is ...
What do we do next?	Next, we can ...

Other opportunities for posing situation-specific questions and responses include lunchtime, recess, and during transitions. It is important for teachers to allow students opportunities to select topics of conversation as well as contribute as listeners. Collecting data during these informal conversations is essential to monitoring the growth of individual students with language problems.

However, documenting these skills in conversation can sometimes be overwhelming. Some teachers have come up with interesting ways to collect the data, including using a small rope or ribbon tied to a belt loop. When a child interrupts, the teacher simply ties a knot in the ribbon. Later she can return to her desk and record the frequency of errors. Another strategy is to place a piece of masking tape on your pant leg or sleeve and use a pen to mark each instance of the behavior. There are also a number of software programs for collecting and analyzing data, for smartphones and computers (e.g., eCOVE Observation Software). Collaborative group members can also collectively record their use of appropriate social language at the end of group work; student self-assessments can be compared against the teacher's observations. This can help identify specific skills as priorities for the next group activity.

Teachers need to conduct postassessments after several instructional but naturalistic episodes to determine the need for continued focus on certain goals or to revise the goals. This process assists the teacher in identifying areas of strength and weakness and also allows for the alignment of skills with curriculum standards. Specific pragmatic skills can be paired with standards in the areas of oral language for primary-age students, and speech and communication for the older student. It's important to remember that pragmatic language is the foundation for more complex and abstract thinking. Skills such as turn taking, staying on topic, asking questions, responding to the speaker, and using appropriate register are all fundamental to creating and sharing information, posing an argument, conveying information, promoting a cause, or revising one's own thinking.

FINAL THOUGHTS

Continued research is needed related to students with specific learning disabilities and pragmatic language issues and how they contribute in groups. Currently, there is limited empirical research on the precise nature of the communication that occurs in classroom-based groups. For children with language impairments, full engagement depends upon the degree to which they can use social language to gain entrance into a group and sustain the ongoing interaction. Without explicit instruction in pragmatic language skills, children with language impairments will have difficulty moving from being unengaged to full engagement. Teachers and therapists can work together to integrate pragmatic skills into existing structures of cooperative group learning. Only then will students with language impairments gain an equitable chance to benefit from the complex and rich communication of classroom-based groups.

REFERENCES

Beilinson, J., & Olswang, L. (2003). Facilitating peer-group entry in kindergartners with impairments in social communication. *Language, Speech, and Hearing Services* in *Schoob, 34,* 154–166. doi:10 . 1044/0161-1461 (2003/013)

Bernstein, B. (1966). Elaborated and retricted codes: An outline. *Sociological Inquiry, 36,* 254–261. doi:10.1111/j. 1475-682X .1966.tb00628.x

Brinton, B. F., Fujiki, M., Spencer, J. C., & Robinson, L. A. (1997). The ability of children with specific language impairment to access and participate in an ongoing interaction. *Journal of Speech, Language, and Hearing Research, 40,* 1011–1025.

Clark, H. H. (1996). *Using language.* New York, NY: Cambridge University Press.

Ervin-TYipp, S. (1979). Children's verbal turn taking. In E, Ochs and B. Schieffelin (Eds.), *Devebpmenlal pragmatics* (pp. 391–414). New York, NY: Academic Press.

eCove Observation Software [Computer software]. *Pacific City,* OR: *eCOVE Software* LLC.

Fey, M. (1986). *Language intervention with young children.* Boston, MA: Allyn & Bacon.

Fey, M. L., Long, S. H., & Finestack, L. H. (2003). Ten principles of grammar facilitation for children with specific language impairments. *American Journal of Speech Language Pathobgy, 12,* 3–15. doi:10 . 1044/1058-0360(2003/048)

Hadley, P., & Rice. M. L. (1991). Conversational responsiveness of speech-and language-impaired preschoolers. *Journal of Speech and Hearing Research, 34,* 1308–1317.

Kagan, S. (1997). *Cooperative learning.* San Clemente, CA: Kagan.

Kamps, D., Abbott, M., Greenwood, C., Wills, H., Veerkamp, M., & Kaufman, J. (2008). Effects of small-group reading instruction and curriculum differences for students most at risk in kindergarten two-year results for secondary- and tertiary-level interventions. *Journal of Learning Disabilities, 41,* 101–114. doi:10.1177/0022219407313412

Knestrict. T., & Schoensteadt, L. (2005). Teaching social register and code switching in the classroom. *Journal of Children & Poverty, 11,* 177–185. doi:10.1080 /10796120500195774.

Levinson, S. C. (1983). *Pragmatics.* England: Cambridge University Press.

Margolis, H., & Freund, L. A. (1991). Implementing cooperative learning with mildly handicapped students in regular classrooms. *International Journal of Disability Devebpment and Education, 38,* 117–133. doi: 10.1080/0156655910380203

McCauley, R. J. & Fey, M. E. (2006). *Treatment of Language Disorders in Children.* Baltimore: Paul H. Brookes.

McMaster, K. N., & Fuchs, D. (2002). Effects of cooperative learning on the academic achievement of students with learning disabilities: An update of Tateyama-Sniezek's review. *Learning Disabilities Research Practice, 17,*107–117. doi: 10 .1111/1540-5826.00037

Ochs, E., & Schieffelin, B. (Eds.) (1979). *Developmental pragmatics.* New York, NY: Academic Press.

Palmer, D. K. (2009). Code-switching and symbolic power in a second-grade two-way classroom: A teacher's motivation system gone awry. *Bilingual Research Journal,* 32(1), 42–59. doi:10/1080 /15235880902965854.

Rice, M. L., Sell, M. A., & Hadley, P. A. (1991). Social interactions of speech- and language-impaired children. *Journal of Speech and Language Research, 34,* 1299–1307.

Schwartz, I. (2000). Supporting young children's IEP goals in inclusive settings through embedded learning opportunities. *Topics in Early Childhood Special Education, 20, 208–223. doi: 10.1177* /027112140002000402

Slavin, R., & Lake, C. (2008). Effective programs in elementary mathematics: A best-evidence synthesis. *Review of Educational Research, 78,* 427–515. doi: 10.3102 /0034654308317473

Slavin, R., Lake, C., Chambers, B., Cheung, A., & Davis, S. (2009). Effective reading programs for the elementary grades: A best-evidence synthesis. *Review of Educational Research,* 79(4), 1391–1466. doi: 10.3102/0034654309341374.

Slavin, R. E. (1996). Research on cooperative learning and achievement: What we know, what we need to know. *Contemporary Educational Psychobgy, 21,* 43–69. doi: 10.1006/ceps. 1996.0004
Stevens, R., & Slavin, R. E. (1991). When cooperative learning improves the achievement of students with mild disabilities: *A response to Tateyama*-Sniezek. *Exceptional Children, 57,* 276–280.
Stockall, N. (2006, April). *Picture perfect: What does inclusion really look like?* Paper presented at the 2006 Council for Exceptional Children Annual Convention & Expo, Salt Lake City, Utah.
Warren, S., Bredin-Oja, S., Fairchild, M., *Finestack,* L., *Fey, M.* & *Brady,* N. *(2006).* In R. McCauley & M. Fey (Eds.), *Treatment of language disorders in children* (pp. 47–75). Baltimore, MD: Paul H. Brookes.
Wheeler, R., & Swords, R. (2006). *Codeswitching: Teaching standard English in an urban classroom.* Urbana, IL: National Council of Teachers of English.
Yont, K. M., Hewitt, L., & *Miccio, A. (2000).* A coding system for detecting the source of conversational breakdowns in preschool children. *American Journal of Speech Language Pathobgy, 9,* 300–309.

Nancy Stockall (Texas CEC), Associate Professor, Department of Language, Literacy, and Special Populations, Sam Houston State University, Huntsville, Texas.

Address correspondence concerning this article to Nancy Stockall, Language, Literacy, and Special Populations, Eleanor & Charles Garrett Teacher Education Center, Box 2119, 1908 Bobby K. Marks Drive, Suite 100, Huntsville, TX 77341 (e-mail: nxs016@shsu.edu).

The author would like to thank F. Lee Bruegger and Rachel Erin Smith for their insights and suggestions for this article.

TEACHING Exceptional Children, Vol. 44, No. 2, pp. 18–25.

POST-READING ACTIVITIES

1. Why do students with language impairments experience communication breakdowns?
2. What is *pragmatic language*? Did your understanding of the term change after reading?
3. Create a list of strategies you could implement to help students with language impairments practice the forms of language.

CHAPTER 8

READING 8.2 OVERVIEW

A longitudinal and concurrent study was conducted to examine the writing performance of students with specific language impairments. The students were evaluated at the ages of 8, 11, 12, 14, and 16. The purpose of the study was to determine if there was a long-term correspondence between literacy performance, oral language, and handwriting proficiency. The authors present the results of the study and discuss the educational implications that must be considered by those who educate this diverse population.

PRE-READING ACTIVITIES

1. How might language impairment affect writing performance? Write down your thoughts to refer to after reading the study.
2. How might language impairment affect handwriting? Write down your thoughts to refer to after reading the study.
3. Reflect on strategies you could implement to facilitate the writing proficiency of students who have been diagnosed with a language impairment.

THE IMPACT OF SPECIFIC LANGUAGE IMPAIRMENT ON ADOLESCENTS' WRITTEN TEXT

READING 8.2

BY JULIE E. DOCKRELL, GEOFF LINDSAY, AND VINCENT CONNELLY

ABSTRACT: *This study examined the writing performance of 58 students with a history of specific language impairment, assessing them at ages 8, 11, 12, 14, and 16 to evaluate longitudinal trajectories of writing performance and relationships with oral language, reading, and handwriting fluency. At age 16, participants continued to experience problems with oral language and literacy: Their writing evidenced short texts, poor sentence structure, and difficulties with ideas and organization. Concurrent measures of vocabulary and spelling were significant factors in explaining writing performance. Handwriting fluency remained a particular difficulty for the current cohort and directly affected writing performance. Path analysis indicated that previous levels of literacy mediated the impact of oral language skills.*

Creating written text is a major challenge for children who experience difficulties with the cognitive processes that underpin writing (Dockrell,

Julie E. Dockrell, Geoff Lindsay and Vincent Connelly, "The Impact of Specific Language Impairment on Adolescents' Written Text," *Exceptional Children*, vol. 75, no. 4, pp. 427-446.

2009); their texts are shorter, more error prone, and poorly organized compared to those of typically developing peers of the same age (Hooper, Swartz, Wakely, de Kruif, & Montgomery, 2002; McArthur & Graham, 1987). These difficulties often continue to challenge young people through their school career and beyond (Connelly, Campbell, MacLean, & Barnes, 2006; Riddick, Farmer, & Sterling, 1997). Establishing the ways in which barriers and mediators interact over time to influence the production of written text for specific profiles of learning difficulties is a prerequisite to the development of theory and evidence-based interventions. Using a longitudinal data set, we examined the relationships of language, literacy, and nonverbal ability with the written text production of a cohort of young people with a history of specific language impairment (SLI) at the end of compulsory education in the United Kingdom (age 16). Practitioners, policy makers, and researchers use a range of different terms to describe this population (see Dockrell, Lindsay, Letchford, & Mackie 2006; see also Tomblin et al., 2003, for *primary language disorder*). Moreover, different terms are used in Europe (*dysphagia*) and North America (SLI in the United States, dysphagia in parts of Canada). The population is heterogeneous, with the specific nature of their problems residing with one or more subcomponents of the language system. We use the term *specific language impairment* to reflect the most common usage in the literature.

Children with SLI experience problems with the acquisition and processing of oral language skills. The most commonly used core criterion to identify children with SLI is that their language problems cannot be explained in terms of other cognitive, neurological, or perceptual deficits (Leonard, 1998). Language problems are evident by a protracted rate of language development as well as difficulties with subcomponents of the language system (Leonard). Measurements that tap into children's proficiencies with phonological processing, sentence recall, nonword repetition, and tense marking have all demonstrated high levels of specificity and sensitivity in differentiating children with SLI from their typically developing peers (Conti-Ramsden, Botting, & Faragher, 2001; Ellis Weismer et al., 2000). Although conventionally identified by discrepancy criteria, children with SLI are heterogeneous in their profile of language impairments and in terms of nonverbal ability (Botting, Faragher, Simkin, Knox, & Conti-Ramsden, 2001). Patterns of performance also vary over time (Botting, 2005; Conti-Ramsden & Botting, 1999). For many young people with SLI, difficulties with spoken communication skills persist into adolescence (Beitchman, Wilson, Brownlie, Walters, & Lancee, 1996; Botting et al.; Stothard, Snowling, Bishop, Chipchase, & Kaplan, 1998) and adulthood (Clegg, Hollis, Mawhood, & Rutter, 2005; Johnson et al., 1999). Older students continue to experience difficulties with reduced vocabulary levels (Johnson et al.); accurate use of verb morphology (Clahsen, Bartke, & Göllner, 1997); and some syntactic structures (Norbury, Bishop, & Briscoe, 2001).

These linguistic deficits have marked effects on the processing of written text (Bishop & Snowling, 2004), resulting in difficulties in both word reading and comprehension (Catts, Fey, Tomblin, & Zhang, 2002; Stothard et al., 1998).

As with linguistic performance there is considerable variability within the population on these measures, only some of which is explained by language competence and cognitive skills (Young et al., 2002). Variations in phonological and nonphonological language skills relate to different patterns of reading behavior (Bishop & Snowling). Phonological processing skills are closely related to reading decoding (Castles & Coltheart, 2004) and spelling (Caravolas, Hulme, & Snowling, 2001), whereas measures of receptive language have been associated with poor reading comprehension (Nation, Clarke, Marshall, & Durand, 2004). Both receptive and expressive vocabulary are related to reading performance (Ouellette, 2006; Tannenbaum, Torgesen, & Wagner, 2006; Wise, Sevcik, Morris, Lovett, & Wolf, 2007).

Specific relationships between oral language competence and the production of written text have been reported both for children with continuing and those with resolved language problems, leading to the hypothesis that written language can be conceptualized as a window into residual language problems (Bishop & Clarkson, 2003; Fey, Catts, Proctor-Williams, Tomblin, & Zhang, 2004). Phonological processes directly impact childrens spelling, a prerequisite to extended text generation (Berninger, Abbott, Whitaker, Sylvester, & Nolen, 1995). Wider oral language comprehension skills have been implicated as important factors in the children's text production (Bishop & Clarkson; Cragg & Nation, 2006; Dockrell, Lindsay, Connelly, & Mackie, 2007). Vocabulary appears to provide a building block for written language (see Green et al., 2003). A range of lexical items provides children with the ability to build a text and provide the basic infrastructure of text meaning (see Berninger et al., 1997).

A recent comparative study of adolescents with dyslexia, those with language impairment, and typically developing matched adolescents demonstrated the ways in which different profiles of language skills can impact writing performance (Puranik, Lombardino, & Altman, 2007). Participants with SLI (but not dyslexia) produced fewer words and numbers of ideas than typically developing peers. In contrast, both students with dyslexia and students with language impairment produced more spelling and grammatical errors than their matched peers. Puranik and colleagues argued that the difference between the performance of these two groups was due to the difficulties experienced by the students with language impairment in the nonphonological dimensions of text production.

Difficulties with literacy compromise the developmental trajectories of children with SLI. The combined effect of language and literacy difficulties typically results in reduced educational attainments (Dockrell, Lindsay, Palikara, & Cullen, 2007). However, the ways in which language and literacy interact to support writing require further clarification if theoretical models are to address the nature and extent of the childrens difficulties and appropriately targeted interventions are to be developed.

Compared to studies examining the reading profiles of children with SLI (Kelso, Fletcher, Lee, & Kelso, 2007; McArthur, Hogben, Edwards, Heath, & Mengler, 2000), investigations into their difficulties with writing are relatively recent. The few published studies that have examined the written texts of children with SLI provide a mixed picture of the factors that limit the production of written text. Between the ages of 7 and 11, children with SLI produce a high number of spelling errors (Bishop & Clarkson, 2003)—particularly phonological errors (Mackie & Dockrell, 2004)— and error patterns deviate from those of chronological age but not language-age-matched peers (Mackie & Dockrell). Children with SLI also show an increased level of grammatical errors in the written form (Gillam & Johnston, 1992; Scott & Windsor, 2000; Windsor, Scott, & Street, 2000). However, the most common associated problems are not grammatical difficulties but problems with spelling and punctuation, as well as poorer semantic content (Bishop & Clarkson).

To date, studies of individuals with language impairment point to a delay in patterns of writing development, where the factors that constrain text production are similar to those experienced by younger typically developing children. Over time, for typically developing children, idea generation and the translation of those ideas into written text production become more automatic, allowing time for the cognitively demanding processes of planning and revision. In addition, the relationships between reading and writing change. Studies of the writing skills of students with SLI have failed to examine developmental changes. Important gaps remain in our understanding of the writing profiles of children with SLI and the factors that underpin difficulties in text production. Specifically, evidence examining the writing performance of adolescents with a history of SLI is missing and the ways in which earlier language and literacy skills contribute to the development of text production over time is unexplored. A further major omission, given the motor incoordination difficulties experienced by many children with SLI (Hill, 2004), is the lack of measures of handwriting fluency. Transcription skills uniquely predict compositional fluency throughout the elementary grades (Graham, Berninger, Abbott, Abbott, & Whitaker, 1997) and motor incoordination can impact handwriting fluency (Graham, Struck, Richardson, & Berninger, 2006); students with a history of SLI may be disadvantaged in written text production by transcription skills, their semantic competence, and their literacy levels.

Students with a history of SLI may be disadvantaged in written text production by transcription skills, their semantic competence, and their literacy levels.

PURPOSE

The current study aimed to address the ways in which measures of language, literacy, and processing limitations are related to writing, by studying a sample of adolescents with a history of SLI. No longitudinal data about the writing skills of students with SLI at this phase of education have previously been published. We predicted that, similar to other groups of children with learning disabilities, students with a history of SLI would continue to exhibit difficulties in producing written text in late adolescence. Given the processing demands of producing written text, performance would be differentially impaired in relation to oral language and reading. We expected their texts to be short and marred by both spelling and grammatical errors. Some relative growth in writing skills might be possible, given that previous studies have found a relative improvement in the production of written story composition towards the end of elementary school (Fey et al., 2004). This slow growth may continue into the secondary school years. However, we predicted that performance would be influenced both by previous levels of written language and by concurrent language abilities, as well as limitations in transcription skills. In addition, the relationships between oral language and reading (Wise et al., 2007) led us to predict that over time students' writing performance would be mediated by their levels of reading.

To test these predictions, a cohort of adolescents that had been identified with SLI at 8 years 3 months (and followed for the subsequent 8 years) completed a battery of language and literacy tests, cognitive measures, and a handwriting fluency measure at age 16. We assessed writing skill through the analytic scoring scale for the writing measure of the Wechsler Objective Language Dimensions (WOLD; Wechsler, 1996; Rust, 1996) and computed measures of text length given the relationships between text length and quality for elementary school students (Gansle, Noell, VanDerHeyden, Naquin, & Slider, 2002; Graham et al., 1997). We predicted that limited expressive language would reduce text length and thereby reduce the performance of older students with a history of SLI. We used hierarchical regression and path analysis to examine the pattern of relationships among language, literacy, and writing measures both concurrently and over time to produce a model of the factors supporting text production.

METHOD

PARTICIPANTS

Following a survey of educational provision in two local education authorities (LEAs) in the United Kingdom, our research team asked professionals (speech and language therapists, educational psychologists, and special educational needs coordinators) to identify children at age 8 who had a discrepancy between their level of functioning in the area of speech and language and that which would be expected given the child's functioning in other areas, and who were also experiencing significant language-based learning needs. This process identified a total of 133 children (Dockrell & Lindsay, 2000), from which we derived a subsample from each LEA (*N* = 59). We excluded children with any additional complicating factors that might preclude the diagnosis of SLI, and included children in two regional special schools for children with SLI in the study (*N* = 10).

The resulting participants (*N* = 69, 17 girls and 52 boys) had been identified as having SLI at a mean age of 8 years 3 months (*SD* = 4 months). All participants had English as their only language and were of white English background. Eleven percent of the total sample was eligible for free school meals, a measure of disadvantage in England (Strand & Lindsay, in press), comparable to the national school average of 14.3%. All participants required special education support to access the curriculum, and 54% had a statement of special educational needs (SEN) under the Education Act for England 1996. The SEN, similar to an individualized education program in the United States, specifies the provision that must by law be made to meet the child's unique educational needs. This status is applied to about 3% of students in the United Kingdom, over half of whom attend mainstream schools.

Participants were assessed an additional four times as part of a wider longitudinal government-funded study charting the educational and social needs of children with SLI (Dockrell, Lindsay, Palikara, et al., 2007; see Table 8.4 for mean age at assessment and skills assessed). The longitudinal study also examined the students' production of written text at age 11 (Dockrell, Lindsay, Connelly, et al., 2007), 14, and 16—data reported here.

Table 8.4 **Assessment points and skills assessed.**

TIME	MEAN AGE (SD IN MONTHS)	EDUCATIONAL PHASE UK	EQUIVALENT PHASE U.S.	SKILLS ASSESSED
1	8 years 3 months (4)	Year 3 (Key Stage 2)	Elementary school	Language, literacy, nonverbal ability
2	10 years 8 months (4)	Year 6 (Key Stage 2) Last year primary school	Elementary school	Language, literacy, writing, nonverbal ability
3	12 years 1 month (4)	Year 7 (Key Stage 3) Entry to secondary school	Junior high/ middle school	Literacy, writing
4	13 years 11 months (5)	Year 9 (Key Stage 3)	Middle school/ high school	Language, literacy, writing, nonverbal ability
5	15 years 10 months (4)	Year 11 (Key Stage 4) Final year compulsory education	High school	Language, literacy, writing

Note. A Key Stage is one of the set stages of the national curriculum in the United Kingdom.

As Table 8.5 shows, at the end of formal education the students continued to experience difficulties with oral language and literacy. The continued specificity of their difficulty is evident from the statistically significant differences with nonverbal ability.

Table 8.5 **Mean Z scores and standard deviations for language and literacy measures at ages 14 and 16.**

COMPETENCY ASSESSED	STUDENT AGE	MEAN	SD	DIFFERENCE WITH NONVERBAL ABILITY
Nonverbal ability (BAS *z* score)	14	−.81	.6	
Receptive vocabulary (BPVS *z* score)	16	−1.23	1.12	$F(1, 56) = 9.03$, $p = .004$, $\eta p^2 = .14$;
Formulated sentences (CELF *z* score)	14	−2.4	.35	$F(1, 56) = 174.48$, $p<.0005$, $\eta p^2 = .76$
Listening comprehension (CELF *z* score)	16	−1.14	.66	$F(1, 56) = 5.90$, $p = .018$, $\eta p^2 = .10$;
Single word reading (BAS *z* score)	16	−1.79	.99	$F(1, 55) = 60.49$, $p < .0005$, $\eta p^2 = .53$;
Reading comprehension (WORD *z* score)	16	−1.59	.73	$F(1, 56) = 60.85$, $p < .0005$, $\eta p^2 = .71$
Spelling (BAS *z* score)	16	−1.69	1.07	$F(1, 53) = 43.70$, $p <.0001$, $\eta p^2 = .45$

Note. BAS = British Ability Scales II (Elliott, Murray, & Pearson, 1997). BPVS = British Picture Vocabulary Scale (Dunn, Dunn, Whetton, & Burley, 1997). CELF = Clinical Evaluation of Language Fundamentals (Peers, Lloyd, & Foster, 1999). WORD = Wechsler Objective Reading Dimensions (Wechsler, 1993).

We attempted to contact all participants in their final year of compulsory education (age 16). Sixty-two students out of the original 69 agreed to complete formal assessments; 58 agreed to complete the writing task (15 girls and 43 boys).

Of the students who refused to write, 3 completed reading and language measures. Refusers typically achieved lower scores on language and literacy measures, but there were no statistically significant differences between the two groups.

The children who completed writing assessments were being educated in a variety of ways: 35 in mainstream classes, 8 in special units within mainstream schools, and 15 in special schools including residential schools for children with SLI. Over the previous 8 years, a significant proportion of the participants had moved between different types of provision. As was the case at previous points in the study (Dockrell & Lindsay, 2008) there were few differences between participants in different settings on the psychometric measures. Students in specialist settings scored significantly lower on measures of reading comprehension, $F(1, 57) = 6.112$, $p = .02$, $\eta p^2 = .10$, formulated sentences, $F(1, 57) = 4.498$, $p = .04$, $\eta p^2 = .08$, and nonverbal ability, $F(1, 57) = 4.995$, $p = .03$, $\eta p^2 = .08$, but not on any other language (vocabulary, receptive grammar, listening to paragraphs) or literacy (single word reading, fluency or spelling) measures.

MATERIALS

We identified measures to tap oral language skills, literacy, nonverbal ability, and written language, and selected tests that were age and culturally appropriate and standardized with measures of reliability and validity. All measures are commonly used for the identification and assessment of children with SLI in the United Kingdom. Measures of reliability and validity are reported for each scale on first mention, and unless otherwise stated information was gained from technical manuals and refers to the overall reliability and validity.

NONVERBAL ABILITY

The British Ability Scales II (BAS II) Matrices subtest (Elliott, Murray, & Pearson, 1997), presents children with a set of patterns where one pattern is incomplete. There is a choice of six responses and children are required to point to the missing piece: reliability, .85; validity with the Wechsler Intelligence Scale for Children (WISC-III; Wechsler, 1991) performance scale, .47.

RECEPTIVE VOCABULARY

In the British Picture Vocabulary Scale (BPVS; Dunn, Dunn, Whetton, & Burley, 1997), children are shown four line drawings and asked to point to the one that best illustrates a word spoken by the investigator: reliability, .89; validity with the Expressive One-word Vocabulary test (Gardner, 1990), .72.

GRAMMAR

In the Test of Reception of Grammar (TROG; Bishop, 1983), children are shown four pictures and the investigator reads a sentence. The child selects a picture that matches the sentence structure: reliability, .88; validity with the Clinical Evaluation of Language Fundamentals: Revised UK Edition (CELF-R^{UK}; Peers, Lloyd, & Foster, 1999), .53.

The CELF-R^{UK} (Peers et al., 1999) Formulated Sentences subtest requires a child to produce a sentence in response to an orally presented single word or two-word combination: reliability, .82; validity with other CELF-R^{UK} expressive subscales, .43-.49. The Listening to Paragraphs subtest requires the child to attend to a short paragraph and answer specific questions related to the content: reliability, .74; validity with other receptive scales, .30-.43

READING DECODING

The BAS II Word Reading scale (Elliott et al., 1997) assesses recognition and oral reading of single words: reliability, .93; validity with Wechsler Objective Reading Dimensions reading scale, .71 (WORD; Wechsler, 1993). The Test of Word Reading Efficiency (TOWRE; Torgesen, Wagner, & Rashotte, 1999) contains two subtests. The Sight Word Efficiency (SWE) subtest assesses the number of real printed words that can be accurately read within 45 sec, and the Phonetic Decoding Efficiency (PDE) subtest measures the number of pronounceable printed nonwords that can be accurately decoded within 45 sec: interscorer reliability, .99; test-retest reliability, .90 and above; validity, .92–.94 SWE and .89–.91 PWE (Woodcock Reading Mastery Scales-Revised, Woodcock, 1987).

READING COMPREHENSION

The WORD Reading Comprehension scale (Wechsler, 1993) measures the students understanding of short written passages of text. With this test, the child reads a passage out loud or silently and then answers comprehension questions posed orally by the examiner. The measure has a split-half reliability for children age 15 to 16 of .82

SPELLING

The BAS II Spelling scale (Elliott et al., 1997) provides a number of phonetically regular and irregular words to assess the child's ability to produce correct spellings. Each item is first presented in isolation, then within the context of a sentence, and then again in isolation. The child has to respond by writing the word: reliability, .91; validity with WORD Spelling (Wechsler, 1993), .63.

WRITTEN LANGUAGE

The WOLD Writing Expression test (Wechsler, 1996; Rust, 1996) requires children to write a letter describing their ideal house. Children are allowed 15 min to complete the task. The written output can be scored either holistically or analytically: reliability, .89, correlation with Woodcock-Johnson Psycho-Educational Battery-Revised (Mather & Jaffe, 1996) Dictation = 0.72. The analytic scale comprises six dimensions, each rated on a 4-point scale, which are scored independently of each other: ideas and development; organization, unity and coherence; vocabulary; sentence structure and variety; grammar and usage; and capitalization and punctuation.

WRITING FLUENCY

Our handwriting fluency task (based on Berninger, Mizokawa, & Bragg, 1991) requires students to write out the letters of the alphabet, in lower case, in order, as quickly as possible in 1 min. Letters are only counted towards a total number of letters per minute if the letters are in the correct order and legible. The task has an interrater reliability of $r = 0.97$ (Berninger et al, 1997). It has been incorporated into the Process Assessment of the Learner™ (PAL™) Test Battery (Berninger, 2001), where it has been shown to conform fully with psychometric standards of reliability and validity.

PROCEDURE

Schools, parents, and participants provided informed consent prior to any testing. A qualified educational psychologist assessed each student individually in a quiet room at school over 3 days. The first session involved a familiarization with the assessor and a discussion about the longitudinal study. Participants were allowed to terminate the session or opt out of a test if they wished. All tests were administered using the standard procedures in the manuals. Participants received a certificate of merit for participation in the study.

For the writing measure (WOLD; Wechsler, 1996), assessors noted the time taken to produce the written text in seconds and participants were asked to read back their written texts to prevent penalizing children who were poor spellers; Unclear words were noted on a separate sheet. Two research assistants performed reliability checks for the six dimensions of the analytical scoring of the WOLD. In the case of an interrater disagreement, the scores were further discussed with the research team and informed the final scoring of the texts. Mean interrater reliability for a randomly selected 36 ratings was 80% with a Kappa score of .66. The research assistants counted spelling errors and the total number of words produced, excluding numerals. There was 100% agreement between raters for these measures.

RESULTS

We report data only for children completing the writing measure at age 16 (N = 58). To normalize performance on the test we transformed each standard score, the centile or T score, to a z score to provide a common metric for analysis. In this section, we first examine student performance in written text production, both on the total analytic score of the WOLD (Wechsler, 1996) and in terms of words written and errors produced. We then describe the relationships between language and literacy and the total analytic score on the WOLD. To consider further the different relationships between the variables, we present two path analysis models to examine the magnitude and significance of the relationships between literacy, language, and written text production concurrently and over time.

STUDENT PERFORMANCE IN WRITTEN LANGUAGE AT 16

As a group, the participants performed poorly on the total analytic scale of the WOLD (Wechsler, 1996) with a mean z score of −2.20 (SD = 1.14); this pattern of performance did not vary by gender (girls M = −2.34, SD = .89; boys M = −2.15, SD = 1.21; t = 0.58, df = 56, ns) or special and mainstream settings (mainstream M = −2.00, SD = 1.21; special M = −2.50, SD = .98; t = 1.6, df = 56, ns). As such, all further analyses treat the participants as one group.

Performance on the written language measure was significantly poorer than the students' nonverbal ability scores (t = 9.12, df = 56, p < .0005, Cohen's d = 1.31).

We examined the extent to which performance in writing was commensurate with language and literacy assessments through a series of repeated measures ANOVAs. Performance on the written language measure was poorer than performance on the oral language measures, $F(3, 168) = 51.89$, $p < .0005$, $\eta p^2 = .48$. Post hoc comparisons, adjusting for multiple comparisons, indicated that performance on the written language measure was significantly poorer than both vocabulary and listening to paragraphs ($p < .0005$), but did not differ significantly from the expressive language measure, recalling sentences. We also considered the literacy measures of spelling, reading decoding, and reading comprehension in relation to writing. There was a significant effect of literacy measure, $F(3, 159) = 8.336$, $p < .0005$, $\eta p^2 = .14$. Post hoc comparisons adjusting for multiple comparisons indicated that performance on the written language measure was significantly poorer than spelling ($p = .001$), reading decoding ($p = .005$), and reading comprehension ($p < .0005$). Participants thus experienced significant difficulties in the production of written text; the degree of impairment for writing, as measured by norm-referenced tests, was significantly greater than their difficulties with receptive oral language and other aspects of literacy.

We examined written texts in terms of text length, writing time, and spelling errors. Participants produced short texts; the mean length of texts produced was 86 words (range 12–182). Of the 15 min allocated for the task, participants wrote for an average of 10 min (range 2–15). There were high and statistically significant relationships between text length and writing time ($r = .55$, $p < .0005$) and between text length and the WOLD (Wechsler, 1996) *z* score ($r = .66$, $p < .0005$). On average, participants produced 9 words per minute ($SD = 4.5$). Spelling errors in the text were frequent ($M = 5.5$, $SD = 4.2$; range 0–17) but there were no significant correlations between the numbers of spelling errors and the numbers of words written ($r = -.10$, *ns*) or WOLD total score ($r = .04$, *ns*).

Participants produced a mean rate of 53.75 ($SD = 27.61$) letters per minute for the handwriting fluency measure. The mean number of letters per minute produced was equivalent to that of children between 8 and 9 years old (Grade 3 $M = 47.3$; Grade 4 $M = 63.26$; Graham, Berninger, Weintraub, & Schafer, 1998). Handwriting fluency at 16 years was significantly and positively correlated ($r = .54$, $p = .002$) concurrently with the WOLD reading and spelling *z* scores, and at 14 with the reading, spelling, and nonverbal ability *z* scores. Writing fluency was significantly correlated with both the numbers of words written ($r = .54$, $p < .0005$) and WOLD *z* score ($r = .42$, $p < .0005$), but there was no relationship with the numbers of spelling errors produced ($r = .18$, *ns*).

ANALYTIC SCORES

To identify specific patterns of difficulties, we examined the analytic scores of WOLD (Wechsler, 1996) subtests. The best performances were on measures of grammar

(*M* = 1.71, *SD* = .88) and capitalization (*M* = 1.67, *SD* = .85), although both means were still at the lower end of the scale. The poorest performance was on the measure of sentence structure (*M* = 1.45, *SD* = .73), a score indicative of poor sentence structure containing many errors that inhibit clarity or fluency (Rust, 1996). Measures of ideas and development (*M* =1.5, *SD* = .73), vocabulary (*M* = 1.47, *SD* = .73), and organization and coherence (*M* = 1.57, *SD* = .79) were also in the low range. A Freidman's Analysis indicated that the scores differed statistically significantly across the subtests ($X^2 = 25.86$, $df = 5$, $p < .0005$). Measures of grammar and capitalization did not differ from each other ($z = .564$, *ns*). There were significant differences between grammar compared with organization and coherence ($z = -2.138$, $p = .03$), ideas and development ($z = -2.558$, $p = .01$), vocabulary ($z = -3.500$, $p < .0005$), and sentence structure ($z = -3.638$, $p < .0005$). Scores for capitalization were significantly better than vocabulary ($z = -2.683$, $p = .007$) and sentence structure ($z = -3.153$, $p = .002$), but did not differ statistically from the measures of ideas and development ($z = -1.908$, *ns*) or organization and coherence ($z = -1.414$, *ns*). The measure of organization and coherence was significantly better than vocabulary ($z = -2.121$, $p = .03$) but did not differ from ideas and development ($z = -1.00$, *ns*) or sentence structure ($z = -1.748$, *ns*). Ideas and development, vocabulary, and sentence structure did not differ significantly from each other ($z = -.577$, *ns*; $z = -.832$, *ns*; $z = -.302$ *ns*).

We computed a factor analysis to investigate further the pattern of subtest relationships. The factor analysis met all the necessary statistical assumptions; we considered only those factors with eigenvalues greater than 1.0. The analysis generated a single factor solution accounting for 83% of the variance. There were large and significant loadings (.87) for all of the WOLD (Wechsler, 1996) subtests.

WRITING TRAJECTORIES OVER TIME

Data for the total analytic score of the WOLD (Wechsler, 1996) were available for 51 participants at four time points (ages 11, 12, 14, and 16). Four participants had refused to write at 11, and data were missing for 1 student at age 12 and 2 participants at age 14. There was no significant difference between writing scores at age 16 for participants with missing data ($M = -2.66$) and those with data for all four time points ($M = -2.14$, $t = 1.159$, $df = 56$, *ns*). As Figure 8.2 shows, there was a significant decrease in relative performance as measured by *z* scores, $F(3, 150) = 23.888$, $p < .0005$, $\eta p^2 = .32$. Post hoc comparisons of *z* scores adjusting for multiple comparisons indicated that the participants' writing performance at age 11 was significantly better than their performance at age 12 ($p = .002$), 14 ($p = .002$), and 16 ($p < .0005$). Performance at age 12 and age 14 did not differ whereas there was a significant decline in performance again at age 16 ($p < .0005$ for both ages 12 and 14).

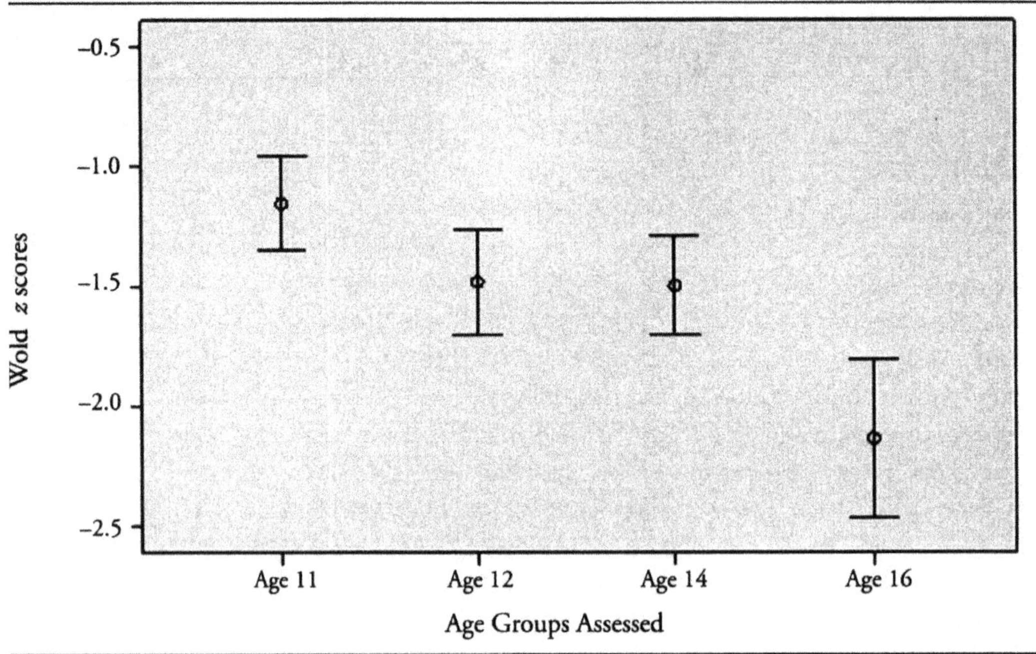

Figure 8.2 WOLD z scores over the four age groups.

Note. WOLD = Wechsler Objective Language Dimensions (Wechsler, 1996).

Although the mean drop between ages 11 and 16 was one *SD* (*M* = 1.0), patterns of change varied across participants. A change score was computed where the *z* score at age 11 was subtracted from the *z* score at age 16, thereby providing a pattern of change across 5 years, where positive scores would indicate a relative increase in writing performance. Table 8.6 presents the relationships between literacy, language, and nonverbal abilities and change scores. Using a Bonferroni correction of .004 for multiple correlations there were significant relationships between WOLD change score handwriting fluency ($r = .54$, $p < .0005$; Wechsler, 1996) and spelling ($r = .38$, $p = .006$). There were no significant relationships with nonverbal ability, vocabulary, reading decoding, and reading comprehension. We examined this pattern of relationships using multiple regression. In all cases residuals were normally distributed. The extent of the relationship between gain score and handwriting fluency was confirmed with a multiple regression controlling for nonverbal ability which revealed a significant model, $F(2, 49) = 9.689$, $p < .0005$) accounting for 29% of the variance. Fluency was the only significant predictor in the model ($\beta = .479$); the less fluent students were in producing the alphabet the more likely were their writing scores to decrease (in relation to their peers) over time.

Table 8.6 **Correlations Between WOLD Change Score, Language, Literacy, Cognitive Measures, and Writing at Time 4 and Time 5.**

VARIABLE	1	2	3	4	5	6	7	8	9	10	11
WOLD change score											
WOLD *z* score (T5)	.81*										
Nonverbal *z* score (T4)	.23	.42*									
Formulated sentences *z* score (T4)	.23	.37*	.31*								
BPVS *z* score (T5)	.25	.55*	.52*	.54*							
Listening to paragraphs z score (T5)	.36	.47*	.25	.40*	.47*						
TROG *z* score (T5)	.20	.31	.26	.31	.41*	.14					
BAS word reading *z* score (T5)	.34	.59*	.51*	.38*	.51*	.19	.34				
TOWRE—word reading efficiency *z* score	.35	.57*	.44*	.41*	.50*	.28	.29	.55*			
Word comprehension *z* score (T5)	.23	.45*	.63*	.43*	.56*	.27	.29	.54*	.62*		
Spelling *z* score (T5)	.38*	.65*	.46*	.18	.30	.08	.32	.75*	.58*	.41*	
Writing fluency *z* score	.54*	.54*	.47*	.40*	.43*	.23	.32	.41*	.57*	.51*	.41*

Note. WOLD = Wechsler Objective Language Dimensions (Wechsler, 1996). BPVS = British Picture Vocabulary Scale (Dunn, Dunn, Whetton, & Burley, 1997). TROG = Test of Reception of Grammar (Bishop, 1983).
BAS = British Ability Scales II (Elliott, Murray, & Pearson, 1997). TOWRE = Test of Word Reading Efficiency (Torgesen, Wagner, & Rashotte, 1999).
*p = .004 with Bonferonni correction.

RELATIONSHIPS BETWEEN LANGUAGE, LITERACY, AND THE WOLD

There were statistically significant correlations for the WOLD *z* score (Wechsler, 1996) at age 16 and all the predictor variables apart from the TROG (Bishop, 1983). As expected, the literacy measures of spelling, reading decoding, and reading comprehension were significantly related to writing. In addition, the language measures of vocabulary (BPVS; Dunn et al. 1997) and formulated sentences were statistically significantly related and each correlated with reading decoding and comprehension.

We predicted that the most significant influence on students' writing would be previous levels of writing, but that vocabulary and reading levels would account for additional variance (Dockrell, Lindsay, Connelly, et al., 2007). Three sequential multiple regression analyses examined prediction of WOLD writing (Wechsler, 1996) at age 16. In the first analysis, we entered writing at age 14 into the model as the first step to control for previous written language performance. On the second step, we entered vocabulary, resulting in a significant increase in R^2 (significant *F* Change, $p = .001$); on the third step, single word reading again resulted in a significant increase in R^2 (significant *F* Change, $p = .005$). The full model R^2 is shown in Table 8.7 and was significant, $F(3, 57) = 20.624$, $p < .0005$, adj $R^2 = .53$.

Table 8.7 **Predicting WOLD writing at age 16: the role of word reading accuracy.**

PREDICTOR	R^2 CHANGE	β	P
WOLD z score at age 14	.326	.353	.001
Vocabulary z score at age 16	.134	.266	.018
Single word reading z score at age 16	.074	.322	.005

Note. WOLD = Wechsler Objective Language Dimensions (Wechsler, 1996).

The second sequential multiple regression used word reading efficiency (TOWRE; Torgesen et al., 1999) as the predicting literacy variable. We reasoned that for later literacy, fluency in word reading and phonological decoding were likely to have greater impacts on the production of written text than untimed measures of single word reading. There was no statistically significant difference between the participants' performance on single word reading efficiency and phonemic decoding efficiency (reading efficiency $M = 69$, $SD = 27$; phonemic decoding efficiency $M = 71$, $SD = 30$, $t = -1.871$, $df = 58$, ns). As in the previous analysis, writing at age 14 was entered into the model to control for previous written language performance, followed by vocabulary. In this case, entering the TOWRE as the third step resulted in a significant increase in R^2 (significant F Change, $p = .003$). The full model R^2 is shown in Table 8.8 and was significant, $F(3, 57) = 21.624$, $p < .0005$, adj $R^2 = .52$, with all variables having significant effects. Thus, the impact on writing of both reading fluency and single word decoding reading measures was similar.

Table 8.8 **Predicting WOLD writing at age 16: the role of word reading efficiency.**

PREDICTOR	R^2 CHANGE	β	P
WOLD z score at age 14	.326	.381	.001
Vocabulary z score at age 16	.134	.243	.031
Word reading efficiency z score at age 16	.081	.333	.003

Note. WOLD = Wechsler Objective Language Dimensions (Wechsler, 1996).

Both the differential correlations between spelling and the other variables and analyses highlighting the importance of writing fluency indicated that their relative roles in writing performance should be considered. Thus, we employed a third sequential multiple regression analysis to examine the impact of these variables. As in the previous models, WOLD writing (Wechsler, 1996) at age 14 was entered into the model followed by vocabulary and reading. On the fourth step, we added writing fluency but this did not significantly change the model R^2 (F Change, p = .24). On the fifth and final step, we entered spelling, which resulted in significant increase in R^2 (significant F Change, p = .001). The full model R^2 was significant, $F(5, 58) = 18.891$, $p < .0005$, adj $R^2 = .61$. As Table 8.9 shows, reading efficiency and writing fluency did not have a significant partial effect in the full model, but previous WOLD score, vocabulary, and spelling did have significant partial effects.

Table 8.9 **Predicting WOLD writing at age 16: the role of reading, writing, and spelling.**

PREDICTOR	R^2 CHANGE	β	P
WOLD z score at age 14	.335	.264	.01
Vocabulary z score at age 16	.114	.232	.03
Word reading efficiency z score at age 16	.075	.041	.746
Writing fluency	.024	.154	.167
Spelling z score at age 16	.093	.395	.001

Note. WOLD = Wechsler Objective Language Dimensions (Wechsler, 1996).

PATH ANALYSES

The regression analyses clarified the relationships between language, literacy, and writing. We tested two path analysis models in order to examine the relative importance of oral language and literacy on the participants' writing scores. The regression analyses had indicated that large effect sizes were to be predicted and that, with appropriate parameter estimates and tests of alternative models, the small sample could be used to build an exploratory path model using maximum likelihood estimation (Ullman, 1996). The stronger the correlations, the more power there is to detect an incorrect model, and this would reduce Type 1 errors in the models.

We used Amos 7.0 to test the models. Model 1 examined concurrently the relative contribution of language, literacy, and writing speed at age 16. Model 2 examined the longitudinal effects of language and literacy from age 8 to age 16. A variety of fit indices are available with Amos. The overall fit of the final model was assessed by X^2 and by root mean square error of approximation (RMSEA). Following Hu and Bender (1999), who recommend joint criteria to retain a model, we only considered models a good fit if the X^2 was not significant, RMSEA < .06 and CFI > .96 (RMSEA and CFI being a more sensitive fit index with small sample sizes; Fan, Thompson, & Wang, 1999).

For the concurrent model we predicted that spelling, vocabulary, and speed of writing would have direct effects on writing at age 16, with reading revealing an indirect effect at this point through spelling. We also predicted that both vocabulary and reading would be associated. As predicted, the path analysis in Figure 8.3 indicates a direct relationship between vocabulary and writing (β = .32), speed of writing (β = .21) and spelling (β = .47). Reading fluency revealed an indirect effect on writing through both spelling (β = .58) and speed of writing (β = .57). The goodness of fit measures indicated a good fit: $X^2(4) = 3.602$, $p = .46$, RMSEA = .00, $CFI = 1.000$. We also tested models, including nonverbal ability and reading comprehension, to eliminate potentially relevant factors. These models failed to provide a fit with the data.

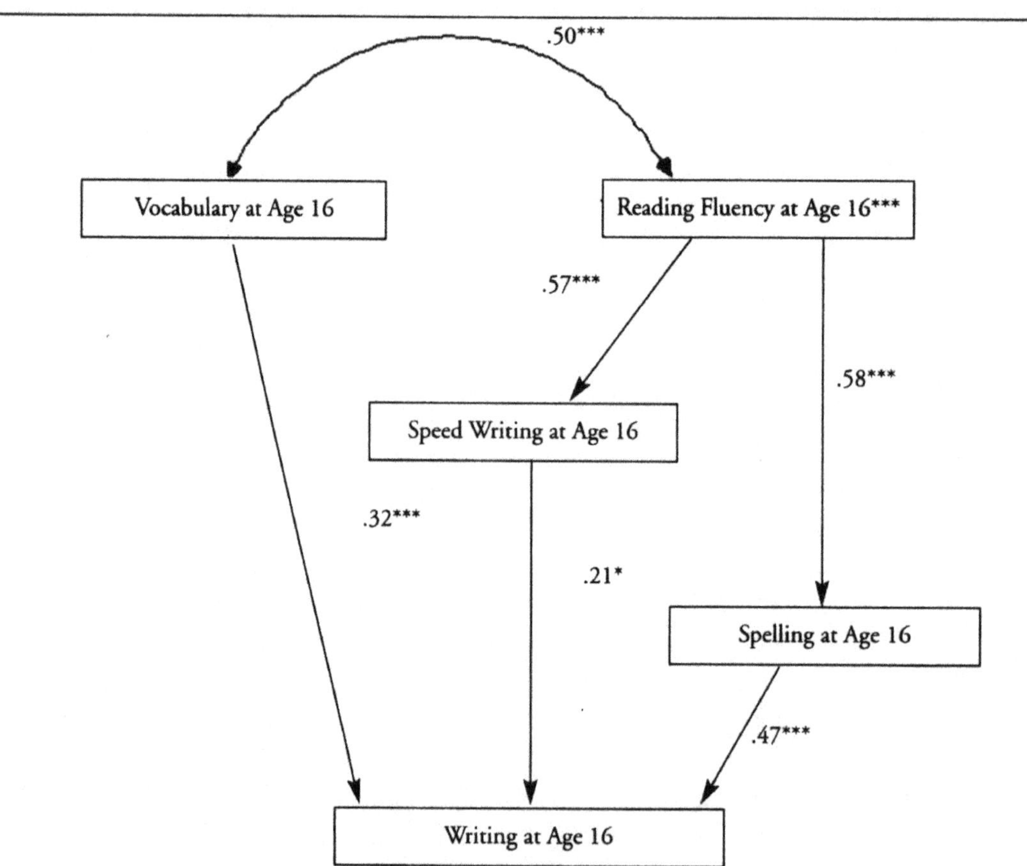

Figure 8.3 Path analysis examining concurrent contributions of literacy and language to writing at age 16.

***p < .001, **p <. 01, *p <.05.

For the exploratory predictive path analysis, we considered measures assessed at ages 8, 11, and 14 and writing at age 16. We predicted that vocabulary and reading at age 8 would be significant factors in supporting writing at age 11 and that from age 11 writing, itself, would show the strongest relationships with subsequent writing performance. No model including reading at age 8 or reading at age 11 fit the data; however, a longitudinal model including vocabulary at age 8 having an indirect effect on writing provided a good fit. The path analysis in Figure 8.4 indicates direct effects of reading (β = .27), spelling (β = .34), and writing (β = .32) at age 14 with writing at age 16. Oral language skills had an indirect effect through reading at age 14 (β = .34) and writing at age 14 (β = .25). Vocabulary at age 8 revealed indirect effects on writing through vocabulary at age 11 (β = .75). Moreover, vocabulary at age 11 revealed indirect effects on writing at age 16 through oral language at age 14 (β = .51). More important, the indirect effect of writing at age 11 was evident through spelling at age 14 (β = .55) but not, as predicted,

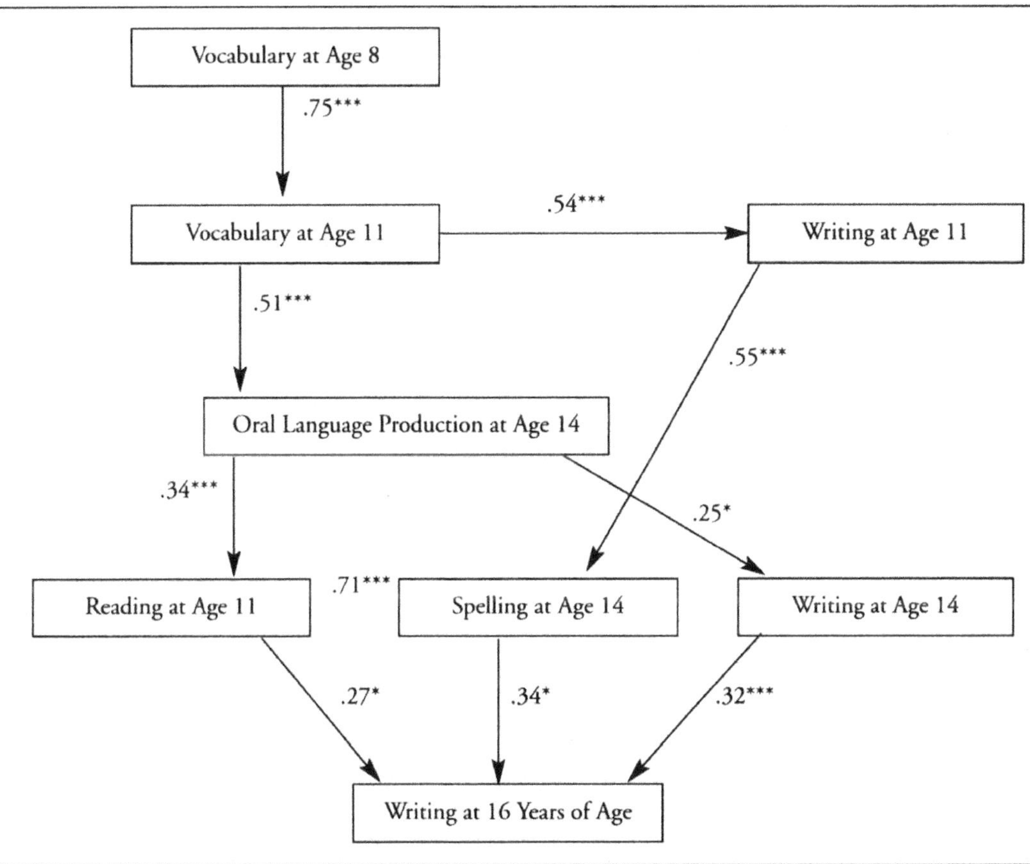

Figure 8.4 Path analysis examining predictions of literacy and language to writing at age 16.

***p < .001, **p <. 01, *p <.05.

writing at age 14 (β = .16). The goodness of fit measures indicated a good fit: X^2 (16) = 11.350, p = .79, RMSEA = .00, *CF1* = 1.000. We also tested models examining alternative directions of effect and models including nonverbal ability and reading comprehension to explore a better fit. These alternative models did not provide a fit with the data.

DISCUSSION

We examined longitudinally the writing skills of a cohort of students with a history of SLI to age 16. We examined measures of language and literacy assessed both longitudinally and concurrently to establish their relative contribution to written text production. The students in this study continued to experience specific difficulties with language and literacy. Production of written text continued to be an area of marked vulnerability, with writing scores being the lowest standardized score of the receptive language and literacy measures. Moreover, during their teenage years the students' writing skills decreased relative to standardized norms. Thus, the current data contrast with data in the elementary years for children with SLI where a relative improvement in the production of written story composition has been noted (Fey et al., 2004). These differences are important to address. The decreases in student performance on written measures may reflect specific language difficulties. For typically developing children, increasing language and literacy skills support later development of writing; for those with continued difficulties these resources are not available. In conjunction it is important to consider the specific support provided to children when developing their written language skills. This decrease in writing skills occurred at the time (age 11) when, in the United Kingdom, it is expected that students have mastered the basic skills in reading and writing, have moved towards the analysis of genres, are writing with technical accuracy, and able to organize text into planned and coherent sequences (Department for Children, Schools and Families, n.d.)—a major challenge for the students in this study.

WOLD (Wechsler, 1996) provided the tool for comparing performance on writing dimensions over time. Results on the WOLD subscales at age 16 were consistent with assessments at previous points in development (Dockrell, Lindsay, Connelly, et al., 2007; Mackie, 2007): Performance was reduced across all subscales, but the poorest performance was evident in measures of sentence structure, ideas and development, and vocabulary. The factor analysis of the WOLD subscales provided evidence that at this point in development, the students' written work could be captured by a single dimension. This differs from the patterns at age 11 (Dockrell, Lindsay, Connelly, et al., 2007) and age 14 (Dockrell & Connelly, 2007), where two different dimensions underpinned performance on the WOLD: semantics and rules. This single factor for the WOLD is, however, consistent with data for younger (age 11) typically developing children (Connelly & Dockrell, 2008) and suggests that for students with a history of SLI the coordination of idea generation and sentence production and grammar is an extended developmental process.

> *For typically developing children, increasing language and literacy skills support later development of writing; for those with continued difficulties these resources are not available.*

Despite the apparent coordination of the two dimensions, difficulties in relation to form (spelling and handwriting), and content generation still posed major difficulties for the students in our study. Texts produced were short with frequent spelling errors. Previous research has failed to consider writing fluency for students with SLI, and current data indicate that shorter texts are associated with reduced levels of handwriting fluency. Indeed, the cohorts handwriting fluency was equivalent to the average obtained for students some 7 years younger (Graham et al., 1998). This is consistent with slow production of text, as evidenced by words produced per minute. The less fluent students were also more likely to show decreases in their writing standard scores over time.

Regression analyses revealed that at age 16 the significant concurrent predictors of text production were spelling and vocabulary. The importance of vocabulary as a key predictor of text production at this age extends work with younger students which has identified limitations in text generation and reduced levels of word use and lexical diversity (Fey et al., 2004; Scott & Windsor, 2000) and semantic content (Bishop & Clarkson, 2003) as critical limiting factors for children with SLI. The continuity of the importance of vocabulary as a determinant of text quality for this cohort of children (Dockrell, Lindsay, Palikara, et al., 2007) adds further weight to the view that vocabulary provides a building block for written language.

The poor spelling skills of the participants were evident both in their written text productions and when assessing their single word spellings. At age 11, the participants' writing levels were mediated by their reading levels. The point of fracture has moved, and on the surface appears similar to difficulties exhibited by young adults with dyslexia (Connelly et al., 2006), where writing was constrained by transcription skills (in the form of poor spelling and slow handwriting). However, the Connelly et al. population was different from the current cohort in that they could produce compositions that were age appropriate in terms of ideas and development, sentence structure and organization, unity, and coherence scales of the WOLD (Wechsler, 1996)—all areas of weakness for the students described here. As shown by Puranik et al. (2007, with a younger cohort), problems with spelling and transcription combined with wider problems with language led to very poor performance in writing.

Given the relationships between the different variables and the predictions derived from previous studies, we used path analysis to provide estimates of the magnitude and significance of hypothesized causal connections between sets of variables. Our first model explored the potential interactions between concurrent measures. The best-fit model included direct effects of vocabulary, spelling, and writing fluency, with reading fluency (a timed measure of reading decoding) having an indirect effect through spelling and writing fluency. The concurrent model confirms both the effects of semantic factors (as measured by vocabulary) and phonological factors (as measured by spelling), and suggests an independent contribution of writing fluency.

There has been a longstanding concern about the information processing constraints experienced by children with SLI (Ellis Weismer & Hesketh, 1996; Montgomery, 2000), and their reduced performance on tasks requiring quick and accurate performance (Leonard et al., 2007). Measures of speed of writing and reading fluency are both significantly related—either directly or indirectly—to text production. These deficits may reflect reduced performance in both verbal working memory (reading fluency) and processing speed (speed of writing; see Leonard et al.). Yet the highly significant relationship in the current study between the two (.57) suggests that the underlying factor may be the ability to coordinate and efficiently manage different information, and this limits children's text production. This interpretation would also be consistent with the difficulties experienced by children with language impairment in monitoring and editing their written productions (Scott, 1999). As long as translating continues to place heavy cognitive demands on writing, management of planning will be impaired.

In our second model we explored the longitudinal predictors for the participants' writing performance at age 16. This model identified direct effects of reading, spelling, and writing at age 14 on writing at age 16. These data demonstrate the ways in which both phonological and morphological literacy measures come to the fore in the writing performance for these students. As in the regression models, nonphonological factors were also evident and, unlike the literacy measures, their impact was traced back to age 8. Vocabulary appears to provide an indication of the semantic knowledge which supports both writing at age 11 and sentence formulation at age 14. Over time, both reading and writing skills mediate the impact of oral language.

The concurrent and the longitudinal models both provide evidence to support specific student-based factors that impinge on the production of written text, and offer scope for targeted and strategic interventions (Troia, 2006) and interventions which could compensate for text production difficulties (MacArthur, in press). It is unlikely that these factors alone explain the relative decline in writing performance. As the change scores demonstrate, only writing fluency predicted change—and this factor accounted for 29% of the variance. An important question remains about the support in writing that is provided once students enter secondary school, both to maintain current levels of text production and to enhance their capacity to produce texts closer to expected targets. Support for those who struggle at this phase of education in England is "uneven" (Office for Standards in Education, Ofsted, 2007, 5¶75, page 31), and differentiation of the curriculum often involves simplifying activities (Dockrell & Lindsay, 2007). Government initiatives to improve skills at this stage have not been successful, with less able children being left behind and catch-up classes for those who struggled in primary school failing to bring students up to the expected standard (Ofsted). Typically these interventions focus on word reading and are provided for most students aged 12 to 14. Thus, given evidence from both the school reports for these students (Dockrell, Lindsay, Palikara, et al., 2007) and the current educational context, it is unlikely that students with SLI are receiving the support they require to develop their writing skills. A lack of appropriate interventions and support resources further disadvantages these struggling writers. This lack of support has been highlighted in other educational systems (see Moni et al., 2007; Troia & Maddox, 2004).

STUDY LIMITATIONS

Investigations of written language are complex and subject to a number of limitations. The current study is limited by the small sample, the use of a single writing measure, and the lack of information on the children's wider information processing skills. Given the purported importance of vocabulary a more detailed examination of the students' competence in this area is needed. It is not clear the extent to which the vocabulary measure is tapping the breadth of the children's knowledge, the depth of their semantic representations, or the efficiency of lexical retrieval. There is increasing evidence that measures of depth and breadth of vocabulary may have differential effects on reading, and we expect similar patterns to be evident in writing (see, e.g., Ouellette, 2006; Tannenbaum et al., 2006). Future work should pay specific attention to the nature of the evidence for interventions provided to support writing, including the skills that underpin performance in writing and the strategies provided for coordination of these skills.

Care also needs to be taken in generalizing performance on our writing task. The decline in writing scores could be explained by a lack of emphasis on this kind of writing in secondary school. Studies of more complex writing tasks demanded by the secondary school system might lead to fewer problems. However, the very poor level of the participants' performance on English exams suggests that this is unlikely to be the case (Dockrell, Lindsay, Palikara, et al., 2007). Although the data suggest widespread failure with writing tasks in relation to peers, the importance of examining writing profiles and predictors of writing performance across genres remains an important avenue of further research.

EDUCATIONAL IMPLICATIONS

The current study highlights the importance of phonological and nonphonological dimensions of oral language as important factors in supporting (or limiting) the production of written text. In addition, we identified writing fluency as a particular problem for these students. Further automating the processes involved in transcription is an important consideration; a recent UK-based intervention to improve the spelling of subject-specific words by students with dyslexia (Sterling, Ertubey, Brownfield, O'Reilly, & Noyce, 2004) seems a step in the right direction. Other schemes that have been used successfully with other children—those that do not advocate lower-level writing instruction at the expense of higher-level writing skills—could also be potentially adapted for use with students with SLI (see Berninger et al., 1997). We have shown that the writing produced by these students is directly related to literacy level; schemes to improve literacy levels, particularly spelling, should also have a long-term benefit provided they are embedded within interventions that support the coordination of text production and meaning generation.

In addition, there is a need to consider the vocabulary that these students possess to support idea generation. Previously we have argued that the development of semantic skills may be seen as a compensatory mechanism to support the writing instruction for students with SLI (Dockrell, Lindsay, Connelly, et al., 2007). The data presented here confirm that this is a continuing issue as children become older. Students with poor vocabulary skills will need explicit support with vocabulary to generate ideas; this dimension is particularly important because we identified no changes in the participants' relative vocabulary across their education (Dockrell, Lindsay, Connelly, et al., 2007).

Finally, an important consideration for students who have experienced such a history of failure to write will be motivation. Interventions will need to be developed which both address the major limitations with basic skills and motivate the young people within an empowering educational environment. This remains a major challenge.

REFERENCES

Beitchman, J. H., Wilson, B., Brownlie, E. B., Walters, H., & Lancee, W. (1996). Long-term consistency in speech/language profiles: I. Developmental and academic outcomes. *Journal of the American Academy of Child and Adolescent Psychiatry, 35*, 804–824.

Berninger, V. (2001). *Process assessment of the learner™ (PAL™) test battery far reading and writing.* San Antonio, TX: The Psychological Corporation.

Berninger, V., Abbott, R., Whitaker, D., Sylvester, L., & Nolen, S. (1995). Integrating low-level skills and high-level skills in treatment protocol for writing disabilities. *Learning Disability Quarterly, 18*, 293–309.

Berninger, V. W., Mizokawa, D., & Bragg, R. (1991). Theory-based diagnosis and remediation of writing disabilities. *Journal of School Psychology, 29*, 57–79.

Berninger, V. W., Vaughn, K., Abbott, R., Abbott, S., Rogan, L., Brooks, A., et al. (1997). Treatment of handwriting problems in beginning writers: Transfer from handwriting to composition. *Journal of Educational Psychology, 89*, 652–666.

Bishop, D. V. M. (1983). *Test of reception of grammar.* Manchester, England: Author and University of Manchester Age and Cognitive Performance Research Centre.

Bishop, D. V. M., & Clarkson, B. (2003). Written language as a window into residual language deficits: a study of children with persistent and residual speech and language impairments. *Cortex, 39*, 215–237.

Bishop, D. V. M., & Snowling, M. (2004). Developmental dyslexia and specific language impairment: Same or different? *Psychological Bulletin, 130*, 858–886.

Botting, N. (2005). Non-verbal cognitive development and language impairment. *Journal of Child Psychology and Psychiatry, 46*, 317–326.

Botting, N., Faragher, B., Simkin, Z., Knox, E., & Conti-Ramsden G. (2001). Predicting pathways of specific language impairment: What differentiates good and poor outcome? *Journal of Child Psychology and Psychiatry and Allied Disciplines, 42*, 1013–1020.

Caravolas, M., Hulme, C., & Snowling, M. (2001). The foundations of spelling ability: Evidence from a three-year longitudinal study. *Journal of Memory and Language, 45*, 751–774.

Castles, A., & Coltheart, M. (2004). Is there a causal link from phonological awareness to success in learning to read? *Cognition, 91*, 77111.

Catts, H. W., Fey, M. E., Tomblin, J.B., & Zhang, X. (2002). A longitudinal investigation of reading outcomes in children with language impairments. *Journal of Speech, Language, and Hearing Research, 45*, 1142–1157.

Clahsen, H., Bartke, S., & Göllner, S. (1997). Formal features in impaired grammars: A comparison of English and German children. *Journal of Neurolinguistics, 10*, 151–171.

Clegg, J., Hollis, C., Mawhood, L., & Rutter, M. (2005). Developmental language disorders: A follow-up in later adult life. Cognitive, language and psychosocial outcomes. *Journal of Child Psychology and Psychiatry and Allied Disciplines, 46*, 128–149.

Connelly, V., Campbell, S., MacLean, M., & Barnes, J. (2006). Contribution of lower order skills to the written composition of college students with and without dyslexia. *Developmental Neuropsychology, 29*, 175–196.

Connelly, V., & Dockrell, J. E. (2008) *The role of vocabulary in the production of written text: development and delay.* Manuscript in preparation.

Conti-Ramsden, G., & Botting, N. (1999). Classification of children with specific language impairment: Longitudinal considerations. *Journal of Speech, Language, and Hearing Research, 42*, 1195–1204.

Conti-Ramsden, G., Botting, N., & Faragher, B. (2001). Psycholinguistic markers for specific language impairment (SLI). *Journal of Child Psychology and Psychiatry and Allied Disciplines, 42*, 741–748.

Cragg, L., & Nation, K. (2006). Exploring written narrative in children with poor reading comprehension. *Educational Psychology, 26*, 55–72.

Department for Children, Schools and Families, (n.d.). *English curriculum standards.* Retrieved September 10, 2007, from www.standards.dfes.gov.uk/keystage3/

Dockrell, J. E. (2009). Causes of delays and difficulties in writing development. In R. Beard, D. Myhill, M. Nystrand, & J. Riley (Eds.), *Sage Handbook of Writing Development* (pp. 489–505). London: Sage.

Dockrell, J. E., & Connelly, V. (2007, June). *SLI, language skills and writing.* Paper presented at British Journal of Educational Psychology Current Trends Conference: Learning & Teaching Writing, Oxford, England.

Dockrell, J. E., Lindsay, G., Palikara, O., & Cullen, M. A. (2007). *Raising the achievements of children and young people with specific speech and language difficulties and communication needs and other special educational needs through school, to work and college.* Nottingham, England: Department for Education and Skills.

Dockrell, J. E., & Lindsay, G. A. (2000). Meeting the needs of children with specific speech and language difficulties. *European Journal of Special Needs Education*, 75, 24–41.

Dockrell, J. E., & Lindsay, G. A. (2007). Identifying the educational and social needs of children with specific speech and language difficulties on entry to secondary school. *Educational and Child Psychology, 24,* 100–114.

Dockrell, J. E., & Lindsay, G. A. (2008). Inclusion versus specialist provision: Ideology versus evidence-based practice for children with language and communication difficulties. In C. Norbury, B. Tomblin, & D. V. M. Bishop (Eds.), *Understanding developmental language disorders,* (pp. 131–147). London: Psychology Press.

Dockrell, J. E., Lindsay, G. A., Connelly, V., & Mackie, C. (2007). Constraints in the production of written text in children with specific language impairments. *Exceptional Children, 73,* 147–164.

Dockrell, J. E, Lindsay, G., Letchford, B., & Mackie, C. (2006). Educational provision for children with specific speech and language difficulties: Perspectives of speech and language therapist managers. *International Journal of Language and Communication Disorders, 41,* 423–440.

Dunn, L. M., Dunn, L. M., Whetton, C., & Burley, J. (1997). *British picture vocabulary scale* (Rev. ed.). Windsor, England: NFER-Nelson.

Elliott, C. D., Murray, D. J., & Pearson, L. S. (1997). *British ability scales II: Matrices.* Windsor, England: NFER-Nelson.

Ellis Weismer, S., & Hesketh, L. (1996). Lexical learning by children with specific language impairment: Effects of linguistic input presented at varying speaking rates. *Journal of Speech, Language, and Hearing Research, 39,* 177–190.

Ellis Weismer, S., Tomblin, J. B., Zhang, X., Buckwalter, P., Gaura Chynoweth, J., & Jones, M. (2000). Nonword repetition performance in school-age children with and without language impairment. *Journal of Speech, Language, and Hearing Research, 43,* 865–878.

Fan, X., Thompson, B., & Wang, L. (1999). The effects of sample size, estimation methods, and model specification on SEM fit indices. *Structural Equation Modeling: A Multidisciplinary Journal, 6,* 56–83.

Fey, M. E., Catts, H. W., Proctor-Williams, K., Tomblin, J., & Zhang, X. Y. (2004). Oral and written story composition skills of children with language impairment. *Journal of Speech, Language, and Hearing Research, 47,* 1301–1318.

Gansle, K., Noell, G., VanDerHeyden, A., Naquin, G., & Slider, N. (2002). Moving beyond total words written: The reliability, criterion validity, and time cost of alternative measures for curriculum-based measurement in writing. *School Psychology Review, 31, 477–497.*

Gardner, M. F. (1990). *Expressive one-word picture vocabulary test-revised* (Eowpvt-R). Novato, CA: Academic Therapy.

Gillam, R., & Johnston, J. (1992). Spoken and written language relationships in language/learning-impaired and normally achieving school-age children. *Journal of Speech and Hearing Research, 35,* 1303–1315.

Graham, S., Berninger, V., Abbott, R., Abbott, S., & Whitaker, D. (1997). The role of mechanics in composing of elementary school students: A new methodological approach. *Journal of Educational Psychology, 89,* 170–182.

Graham, S., Berninger, V. W., Weintraub, N., & Schafer, W. (1998). Development of handwriting speed and legibility in grades 1–9. *Journal of Educational Research, 92,* 42–56.

Graham, S., Struck, M., Richardson, J., & Berninger, V. (2006). Dimensions of good and poor handwriting legibility in first and second graders: Motor programs, visual-spatial arrangement, and letter formation parameter setting. *Developmental Neuropsychology, 29*, 43–60.

Green, L., McCutchen, D., Schwiebert, C., Quinlan, T., Eva-Wood, A., & Juelis, J. (2003). Morphological development in childrens writing. *Journal of Educational Psychology, 95*, 752–761.

Hill, E. (2004). Non-specific nature of specific language impairment: A review of the literature with regard to concomitant motor impairments. *International Journal of Language & Communication Disorders, 36*, 149–171.

Hooper, S., Swartz, C., Wakely W., de Kruif, R., & Montgomery, J. (2002). Executive functions in elementary school children with and without problems in written expression. *Journal of Learning Disabilities, 35*, 57–68.

Hu, L., & Bentler, P. M. (1999). Cutoff criteria for fit indexes in covariance structure analysis: Conventional criteria versus new alternatives. *Structural Equation Modeling, 6*, 1–55.

Johnson, C., Beitchman, J., Young, A, Escobar, M., Atkinson, L., Wilson, B., et al. (1999). Fourteen-year follow-up of children with and without speech/ language impairments: Speech/language stability and outcomes. *Journal of Speech, Language, and Hearing Research, 42*, 744–760.

Kelso, K, Fletcher, J., Lee, P., & Kelso, A. (2007). Reading comprehension in children with specific language impairment: An examination of two subgroups. *International Journal of Language & Communication Disorders, 42*, 39–57.

Leonard, L. B. (1998). *Children with SLI.* Cambridge, MA: MIT Press.

Leonard, L. B., Ellis Weismer, S., Miller, C., Francis, D., Tomblin, B., & Kail, R. (2007). Speed of processing, working memory and language impairment. *Journal of Speech, Language, and Hearing Research, 50*, 408–428.

Mackie, C. (2007). *The written language of children with specific speech and language difficulties.* Unpublished doctoral dissertation, University of Warwick, Coventry, England.

Mackie, C., & Dockrell, J. E. (2004). The writing skills of children with SLI. *Journal of Speech, Language, and Hearing Research, 47*, 1469–1483.

Mather, N., & Jaffe, L. (1996). *Woodcock-Johnson psycho-educational battery-revised.* Oxford, England: John Wiley and Sons.

McArthur, C. A., & Graham, S. (1987). Learning disabled students' composing with three methods: Handwriting, dictation and word processing. *The Journal of Special Education, 21*, 22–42.

McArthur, G. M., Hogben, J. H., Edwards, V. T., Heath, S. M., & Mengler, E. D. (2000). On the "specifics" of specific reading disability and specific language impairment. *Journal of Child Psychology and Psychiatry, 41*, 869–874.

Moni, K., Jobling, A., van Kraayenoord, C., Elkins, J., Miller, R., & Koppenhaven, D. (2007). Teachers' knowledge attitudes and the implementation of practices around the teaching of writing in inclusive middle years' classrooms: No quick fix. *Educational and Child Psychology, 24*, 18–35.

Montgomery, J. (2000). Verbal working memory and sentence comprehension in children with specific language impairment. The role of phonological working memory. *Journal of Speech, Language, and Hearing Research, 43*, 293–308.

Nation, K, Clarke, P., Marshall, C. M., & Durand, M. (2003). Hidden language impairments in children: Parallels between poor reading comprehension and specific language impairment. *Journal of Speech, Language, and Hearing Research, 47*, 199–211.

Norbury, C. F., Bishop, D. V. M., & Briscoe, J. (2001). Production of English finite verb morphology: A comparison of mild-moderate hearing impairment and specific language impairment. *Journal of Speech, Language, and Hearing Research, 44*, 165–178.

Office for Standards in Education. (2007). *The annual report of Her Majesty's chief inspector of education, childrens services and skills 2006/07.* London: The Stationery Office.

Ouellette, G. (2006). What's meaning got to do with it: The role of vocabulary in word reading and reading comprehension. *Journal of Educational Psychology, 98*, 554–566.

Peers, I. S., Lloyd, P., & Foster, C. (1999). *British standardisation of the CELF.* The Psychological Corporation's Speech and Language Assessment. Available from Pearson's Assessments Web site, http://www.tpcweb.com

Puranik, C., Lombardino, L., & Altman, L. (2007). Writing through retellings: An exploratory study of language impaired and dyslexic populations. *Reading and Writing, 20,* 251–272.

Riddick, B., Farmer, M., & Sterling, C. (1997). *Students and dyslexia: Growing up with a specific learning difficulty.* London: Whurr.

Rust, J. (1996). *The manual of the Wechsler objective language dimensions (WOLD): UK Edition.* London: The Psychological Corporation.

Scott, C. M. (1999). Learning to write. In H. W. Catts & A. G. Kahmi (Eds.), *Language and reading disabilities* (pp. 224–259). Boston: Allyn & Bacon.

Scott, C. M., & Windsor, J. (2000). General language performance measures in spoken and written narrative and expository discourse of school-age children with language learning disabilities. *Journal of Speech, Language, and Hearing Research, 43,* 324–339.

Sterling, C., Ertubey, C., Brownfield, K., O'Reilly, S., & Noyce, S. (2004). *Helping students with dyslexia learn to read and spell specialist terminology.* London South Bank University: Dyslexicon. Retrieved June 7, 2008, from http://www.lsbu.ac.uk/psycho/dyslexicon/

Stothard, S. E., Snowling, M., Bishop, D. V. M., Chipchase, B. B., & Kaplan, C. A. (1998). Language-impaired preschoolers: A follow-up into adolescence. *Journal of Speech, Language, and Hearing Research, 41,* 407–418.

Strand, S., & Lindsay, G. (in press). Ethnic disproportionality in special education. Evidence from an English population study. *The Journal of Special Education.*

Tannenbaum, K, Torgesen, J., & Wagner, R. (2006). Relationships between word knowledge and reading comprehension in third-grade children. *Scientific Studies of Reading, 10,* 381–398.

Tomblin, J. B., Zhang, X., Buckwalter, P., & O'Brien, M. (2003). The stability of primary language disorder: four years after kindergarten diagnosis. *Journal of Speech, Language, and Hearing Research, 46,* 1283–1296.

Torgesen, J. K., Wagner, R. K., & Rashotte, C. A. (1999). *Test of word reading efficiency (TOWRE).* Austin, TX: Pro-Ed.

Troia, G. A. (2006). Writing instruction for students with learning disabilities. In C. A. MacArthur, S. Graham, & J. Fitzgerald (Eds.), *Handbook of Writing Research* (pp. 324–336). New York: Guilford Press.

Troia, G. A., & Maddox, M. E. (2004). Writing instruction in middle schools: Special and general education teachers share their views and voice their concerns. *Exceptionality, 12,* 19–37.

Ullman, J. (1996). Structural equation modeling. In B. Tabachnick & L. Fidell (Eds.), *Using multivariate statistics* (4th ed., pp. 653–771). Needham Heights, MA: Allyn & Bacon.

Wechsler, D. (1991). *Wechsler intelligence scale for children* (3rd ed.). San Antonio, TX: The Psychological Corporation.

Wechsler, D. (1993). *Wechsler objective reading dimensions (WORD).* Sidcup, UK: The Psychological Corporation.

Wechsler, D. (1996). *Wechsler objective language dimensions (WOLD).* Sidcup, UK: The Psychological Corporation.

Windsor, J., Scott, C. M., & Street, C. K. (2000). Verb and noun morphology in the spoken and written language of children with language learning disabilities. *Journal of Speech, Language, and Hearing Research, 43,* 1322–1336.

Wise, J., Sevcik, R., Morris, R., Lovett, M., & Wolf, M. (2007). The relationship among receptive and expressive vocabulary, listening comprehension, pre-reading skills, word identification skills, and reading comprehension by children with reading disabilities. *Journal of Speech, Language, and Hearing Research, 50,* 1093–1109.

Woodcock, R. W. (1987). *Woodcock reading mastery tests-Revised.* Circle Pines, MN: American Guidance Service.

Young, A., Beitchman, Y., Johnson, C., Douglas, L., Atkinson, L., Escobar, M., et al. (2002). Young adult academic outcomes in a longitudinal sample of early identified language impaired and control children. *Journal of Child Psychology and Psychiatry, 43*,635-645.

ABOUT THE AUTHORS

JULIE E. DOCKRELL, Professor, Institute of Education, University of London, England. **GEOFF LINDSAY,** Professor and Director, Centre for Educational Development, Appraisal and Research, University of Warwick, Coventry, England. **VINCENT CONNELLY,** Senior Lecturer, Department of Psychology, Oxford Brookes University, England.

Address correspondence to Julie E. Dockrell, Institute of Education, University of London, 20 Bedford Way, London WC1H OAL, United Kingdom (e-mail: j.dockrell@ioe.ac.uk).

The authors would like to thank all the students, parents, teachers, and support staff who gave willingly of their time; the Department for Children, Schools, and Families who funded the final phase of the project; and all the research assistants who contributed to different phases of the study: Becky Clark, Clare Hall, Rebecca Jeanes, and Clare Mackie. Measures collected at age 14 for part of the sample contributed to the doctoral dissertation completed by Clare Mackie (2006).

Manuscript received November 2007; accepted June 2008.

POST-READING ACTIVITIES

1. How might language impairment affect writing performance? Did your understanding of the implications change after reading?
2. How might language impairment affect handwriting? Did your understanding of the implications change after reading?
3. Reflect on the interventions that need to be developed to address motivation and basic writing skills.

CHAPTER 9

INTELLECTUAL DISABILITIES

INTRODUCTION

Mild (MD) and moderate intellectual disabilities (MoID) are exceptionalities classified under IDEA. The terms were formerly referred to as mental retardation. MD and MoID are cognitive impairments that can affect academic and social abilities, adaptive life skills, speech development, memory, and attention span.

MILD INTELLECTUAL DISABILITY (MD)	MODERATE INTELLECTUAL DISABILITY (MOID)
IQ 50 to 70	IQ 35 to 49
Slower than typical in all developmental areas	Noticeable developmental delays (i.e., speech, motor skills)
No unusual physical characteristics	May have physical signs of impairment (i.e., thick tongue)
Able to learn practical life skills	Can communicate in basic, simple ways
Attains reading and math skills up to grade levels 3 to 6	Able to learn basic health and safety skills
Able to blend in socially	Can complete self-care activities
Functions in daily life	Can travel alone to nearby, familiar places

(Gluck 2013, paras. 3, 4).

The first study was conducted to determine how to shift from basic phonics instruction to more complex word-analysis skills when working with students who have MoID. Elementary and middle school students were explicitly taught initial phonics and functional phonics with a prescribed instructional sequence. The methods, results, and discussion of the study are presented.

The second reading includes research-based literacy methods for working with students who have moderate to severe intellectual disabilities. The approaches include adapting and augmenting grade-level text, as well as teaching text-comprehension strategies. The authors present a thorough description of each method along with examples.

The Individuals with Disability Act (IDEA) requires that students with disabilities must be placed in the least restrictive environment (LRE). This provides students with mild, moderate, and severe intellectual disabilities access to the same curriculum as their nondisabled peers. The articles in this section were chosen to provide preservice and new teachers with research-based strategies that can be implemented in a general education classroom when working with this specific population. The methods are meaningful, relevant, and can also be used with general education students who are struggling or are nonreaders.

REFERENCE

Gluck, Samantha. 2013. *Mild, Moderate, Severe Intellectual Disability Differences.* Retrieved from https://www.healthyplace.com/neurodevelopmental-disorders/intellectual-disability/mild-moderate-severe-intellectual-disability-differences/

CHAPTER 9

READING 9.1 OVERVIEW

Moderate intellectual disabilities (MoID), formerly known as mental retardation, is a cognitive exceptionality classified under IDEA. "Depending on the educational jurisdiction, criteria for MID will often state that the child is functioning approximately 2–4 years behind or 2–3 standard deviations below the norm or have an IQ under 70–75" (Watson 2018, para. 3). It has been common practice to limit reading instruction to sight-word recognition to this population. In the study presented, the researchers developed an instructional sequence, based on direct instruction, to use word-analysis skills to identify environmental print. Methods and results are presented.

REFERENCE

Watson, Sue. 2018. *How Mild Intellectual Disability Is Defined.* Last updated April 19, 2018. Retrieved from https://www.thoughtco.com/mild-intellectual-disability-3110889

PRE-READING ACTIVITIES

1. What is your current understanding of MoID? Write down your initial thoughts.
2. How would you describe environmental print?
3. What are word-analysis skills? List any categories you know.

FROM INITIAL PHONICS TO FUNCTIONAL PHONICS

TEACHING WORD-ANALYSIS SKILLS TO STUDENTS WITH MODERATE INTELLECTUAL DISABILITY

BY LAURA D. FREDRICK, DAWN H. DAVIS, PAUL A. ALBERTO, AND REBECCA E. WAUGH

ABSTRACT: *Reading instruction for students with MoID is typically limited to sight-word instruction. We developed a 2-part, phonetic instructional sequence based upon Direct Instruction teaching methodology to teach students with MoID word-analysis skills that generalize to untaught words encountered in their environment. Elementary and middle-school students with MoID learned word-analysis skills using simultaneous prompting procedures to explicitly teach verbal imitation of sounds, letter-sound correspondences, retrieval of learned letter-sounds to a predetermined rate of automaticity, and blending with telescoping. After demonstrating mastery of the word-analysis skills the students generalized taught blending skills to untaught CVC words; functional, community*

Laura D. Fredrick, et al., "From Initial Phonics to Functional Phonics: Teaching Word-Analysis Skills to Students with Moderate Intellectual Disability," *Education and Training in Autism and Developmental Disabilities*, vol. 48, no. 1, pp. 49-66.

words; and environmental, connected-text phrases. A changing-criterion design embedded within a multiple baseline across sound and word sets was implemented for 3 elementary and 2 middle-school students diagnosed with MoID. Students reached mastery criterion for each phase of Initial Phonics and Functional Phonics, and a functional relation was demonstrated between the instructional sequence and students' acquisition of word-analysis skills.

Students with moderate intellectual disability (MoID) who receive phonics instruction are provided the opportunity to learn generalizable word-analysis skills that increase the probability of decoding a novel, untaught word encountered in their environment. Word-analysis skills are considered an academic form of literacy and include phonological awareness, letter-sound correspondences, blending—saying each sound in a word slowly without stopping between sounds, and telescoping—saying the sounds quickly to read the word (Carnine, Silbert, Kame'ennui, & Tarver, 2004; Foorman, Francis, Shaywitz, Shaywitz, & Fletcher, 1997). For students with MoID, these generalizable word-analysis skills also can be considered a functional form of literacy because mastery of word-analysis skills allows greater access to community resources thereby increasing functional independence.

Until recently, however, phonics instruction seldom was provided for students with MoID. Joseph and Seery (2004) reviewed all forms of literacy instruction for students with all levels of intellectual disability and only found seven studies in which phonics instruction was provided, and of those studies, only one participant was diagnosed with MoID. Browder, Wakeman, Spooner, Ahlgrim-Delzell, and Algozzine (2006) reported that almost 90% of published research studies examining reading instruction for students with moderate to severe disabilities (MSD) focused on acquisition of functional sight words. Sight-word instruction has been and remains the dominant form of literacy instruction to increase the functional independence of students with MoID.

The reason that educators rely on sight-word instruction for students with MoID is possibly because of the difficulty these students have with phonological coding hindering their acquisition of phonetic reading (Conners, Atwell, Rosenquist, & Sligh, 2001). However, students with severe reading disabilities who were thought to be unable to learn phonetic skills have been shown to benefit from systematic instruction in phonemic awareness and decoding (Torgesen et al., 2001). Similarly, students with intellectual disability may have difficulty in these areas due to lack of instruction in phonetic skills (Stanovich, 1985). A small body of research over the last 3 decades suggests that with effective instruction, students with MoID can learn generalizable word-analysis skills (Allor, Mathes, Roberts, Jones, & Champlin, 2010; Bracey, Maggs,

& Morath, 1975; Browder, Ahlgrim-Delzell, Courtade, Gibbs, & Flowers, 2008; Cossu, Rossini, & Marshall, 1993; Davis, Fredrick, Alberto, & Gagné, 2010; Davis et al., 2013; Hoogeveen, Smeets, & Lancioni, 1989; Katims, 1996; Nietupski, Williams, & York, 1979; Waugh, Fredrick, & Alberto, 2009).

Bracey et al. (1975) demonstrated long ago that children with MoID can learn phonetic decoding skills. Through the use of a Direct Instruction (DI) program, *Distar Reading* (Engelmann & Bruner, 1969), students learned letter-sound correspondences, blended sounds into words, and spelled words using their sounds. Results in another early study by Nietupski et al. (1979), revealed that students with MoID could learn letter-sound correspondences through explicit instruction although not specifically a DI program.

These early findings are supported in more recent research. Working with middle-school students, Bradford, Shippen, Alberto, Houchins, and Flores (2006) demonstrated that students with MoID are capable of learning word-analysis skills including (a) letter-sound correspondences, (b) sounding out words, (c) blending sounds, (d) decoding irregularly spelled words, and (e) reading sentences and short passages at approximately a second-grade level. In only 6 months, these middle-school students learned phonetic decoding skills through the use of the DI *Corrective Reading Program* (Engelmann, Becker, Hanner, & Johnson, 1980), substantiating findings by Conners (1992) and Katims (2000).

Working with elementary-school students with MoID, Flores, Shippen, Alberto, and Crowe (2004) used systematic and explicit instruction to teach phonetic decoding by incorporating modified sequences and formats of the DI program, *Corrective Reading: Word-Attack Basics, Decoding A* (Engelmann, Carnine, & Johnson, 1988). All five of the students learned letter-sound correspondences, blending, and sounding out. All but one student mastered the four sounds taught and were able to blend the sounds slowly on both instructional and generalization words; however, they struggled with telescoping. Only one student was able to telescope novel consonant-vowel-consonant (CVC) words.

More recently, researchers demonstrated the effectiveness of time delay and simultaneous prompting procedures (Cohen, Heller, Alberto, & Fredrick, 2008; Waugh et al., 2009) for students with intellectual disability. Cohen et al. used time delay procedures with five participants–three with IQs in the mild-delayed range and two with IQs in the moderate range. All five students learned decoding skills with one of the student's whose IQ was in the moderate range acquiring mastery the fastest. Through the use of simultaneous prompting procedures Waugh et al. found that three students with MoID learned letter-sound correspondences and applied blending skills to previously-learned sight words; although, not without difficulty in some areas. One student was unable to generalize the blending skill to novel, untaught words, while two students generalized blending to one untaught word but could not telescope.

Students with MoID can learn word-analysis skills when teachers use time delay (Cohen et al., 2008) and simultaneous prompting procedures (Waugh et al., 2009) based on Direct Instruction teaching strategies. However, some students have demonstrated difficulty in the areas of blending, telescoping, and generalization (Flores et al., 2004; Waugh et al., 2009). Difficulty with blending and telescoping could result from a lack of automatic retrieval of learned letter-sound correspondences. Automaticity with letter sounds is necessary for word reading to occur (LaBerge & Samuels, 1974), and consistent practice is necessary for automaticity to develop (Shiffron & Schneider, 1977). Shiffron and Schneider found that automaticity did not develop when tasks were inconsistent; moreover, the degree of automaticity depended upon the amount of consistency. Cohen, Dunbar, and McClelland (1990) found that the most important mechanism underlying automaticity is the strengthening of connections between stimuli and responses. Practice makes these connections stronger and performances are subsequently faster and less effortful. Taken together, these findings strongly support incorporating formal, systematic development of automaticity within reading instruction. Additionally, it is likely that once blending and telescoping skills are acquired students will need extensive practice before these skills generalize.

We designed an instructional sequence to provide many opportunities for students to learn verbal imitation of sounds, master letter-sound correspondences, become automatic with letter-sound correspondences to maximize phonological information processing efficiency, practice blending and telescoping, and then generalize these skills to novel, untaught words. The instructional sequence is based on DI teaching strategies such that it teaches components of word-analysis skills to mastery/automaticity (Carnine et al., 2004). To address automatic retrieval of letter sounds, we included a component not found in DI programs. That is, students practiced naming learned letter sounds to an individual mastery criterion that was determined by each student's rate of naming speed demonstrated on the Rapid Object Naming (RON) subtest of the Comprehensive Test of Phonological Processing (CTOPP; Wagner, Torgesen, & Rashotte, 1999). Blending and telescoping sounds into words was not attempted until each student reached his or her individualized automaticity rate for taught letter-sound correspondences.

This study was part of a larger Institute of Educational Sciences (IES) research project to develop a comprehensive and integrated literacy curriculum (ILC) for students with moderate to severe disabilities (Alberto & Fredrick, 2007). The ILC includes three components. The Visual-Literacy Component provides instruction in picture and logo reading while the Sight-Word Component provides instruction in reading and demonstrating comprehension of individual sight words and connected text (Alberto, Waugh, & Fredrick, 2010). The research reported here is based on the Phonics Component of the ILC which was conducted to determine the effectiveness of the Phonics Component in teaching word-analysis skills to individuals with MoID.

The Phonics Component includes *Initial Phonics* and *Functional Phonics*. While both parts of the curriculum were designed to answer the research question through the use of the same instructional sequence, each part differed in some important aspects. *Initial Phonics* was introduced first to provide ample opportunities to develop initial emergent-literacy and phonological-awareness skills, to develop initial learning of instructional procedures, to teach a selection of individual letter-sound correspondences to be blended and telescoped into CVC words, and to provide many opportunities to generalize blending and telescoping skills to untaught, CVC words. That is, *Initial Phonics* was an opportunity for students to learn how to learn phonics. The second part of the Phonics Component, *Functional Phonics*, was introduced to students after they mastered all phases of *Initial Phonics*. The purpose of *Functional Phonics* was to build upon *Initial Phonics* by emphasizing instruction of common, functional community words and phrases. During *Functional Phonics* students continued to receive instruction in prerequisite skills such as phonological awareness; they were taught a much larger selection of individual letter-sound correspondences and letter-sound combinations; and they were taught to generalize blending and telescoping skills to more complex, functional words and to functional, environmental-connected text.

METHOD

PARTICIPANTS

Participants included five students with MoID and their classroom teachers. All students were between 7 and 14 years old with IQs in the 40–55 range. Students were identified by their classroom teachers based on the teacher's report that the students communicated verbally, performed successfully in their current Edmark (Austin & Boekman, 1990) sight-word reading program, and did not have any behaviors that would interfere with 15 minutes of continuous instruction. Parents or guardians provided permission for all students. The students were served in two different self-contained special education classrooms for students with MoID, in two different schools (one elementary and one middle), across two school districts. Two students were boys and three were girls; three students were African-American and two were Hispanic.

The students' classroom teachers provided all of the instruction and conducted all of the data probes. The elementary students received 1:1 teaching sessions during *Initial Phonics* and the first two sound sets of *Functional Phonics,* and small-group instruction for the remaining sound and word sets of *Functional Phonics.* The two middle-school students received group instruction during both *Initial* and *Functional Phonics.*

TEACHER TRAINING

Teachers were trained prior to beginning instruction with students. Doctoral students who were part of the research project presented the overall program to teachers and modeled instructional steps for them. Teachers practiced implementing the instructional procedures by role playing with the researchers until they followed program steps with 100% accuracy based on the procedural fidelity instrument developed for the Phonics Component of the ILC. Researchers provided ongoing feedback and answered teacher questions for a minimum of one instructional sequence per week.

INDEPENDENT AND DEPENDENT VARIABLES

The independent variable (IV) was the Phonics Component of the ILC implemented with simultaneous prompting procedures. The dependent variables (DV) were the word-analysis skills that were taught in the Phonics Component—verbal imitation of sounds, letter-sound correspondences, automaticity, blending with telescoping, and generalization. Within the Phonics Component of the ILC the Blending Phase included both blending and telescoping such that students practiced saying the sounds in a word slowly without stopping between sounds and then saying the sounds quickly to read the word.

For *Initial Phonics*, a total of eight sounds were taught for the Sounds, Letter-Sound Correspondences, and Automaticity Phases, along with 14 blending words and 10 generalization words. For ease of learning, letter sounds were selected that had distinct auditory and visual characteristics. Words for Blending and Generalization Phases were common CVC words made up of previously-mastered letter sounds.

For *Functional Phonics*, a total of 16 sounds (four of which were previously-mastered sounds from *Initial Phonics* per the cumulative design) and four sound combinations were presented for the Sounds, Letter-Sound Correspondences, and Automaticity Phases along with 48 blending words, 15 functional generalization words, and 20 functional phrases. To select sounds and blending words for Sound Sets 1 through 4, we identified functional, community words such as "open" and "stairs." The sounds from the functional words were taught in the Sounds, Letter-Sound Correspondences, and Automaticity Phases, and we chose words for Blending Phases that were comprised of those letter sounds. We used the originally-selected functional words as the untaught words to be blended within the Generalization Phases providing students the opportunity to generalize the skill of blending to novel, untaught words made up of previously-mastered letter sounds. For Word Sets 5 and 6 we selected two- and three-word environmental, connected-text phrases from lists of the most commonly-used functional, community phrases. For Word Set 5, we selected phrases that contained previously-mastered letter sounds and one previous generalization word from Sound Sets 1 through 4. Environmental, connected-text phrases for Word Set 6 were selected that were comprised of previously-mastered letter sounds from Sound Sets 1 through 4, yet all words within these phrases were novel words that the students had never been taught.

ASSESSMENT

Before instruction began, the RON subtest of the CTOPP (Wagner et al., 1999) was administered as a measure of naming speed. Naming speed is typically measured by asking students to name, as quickly and accurately as possible, an array of stimuli such as objects, colors, letters, or digits that are pictured on a page. Many students with MoID do not know the names of letters, digits, or colors, so the RON subtest was selected for use because it utilizes pictures of everyday common objects such as ball, star, and chair.

Prior to the onset of instruction, in private testing areas of students' schools, the RON subtest was administered individually by doctoral students. Raw scores were used because no standardized assessments have been developed to measure processing speed for this population.

DESIGN

A multiple-baseline design across sound and word sets with an embedded changing criterion was used to determine the effectiveness of the Phonics Component. *Initial Phonics* stimuli were divided into three sound sets for a 3-tier, multiple-baseline design across sound sets. *Functional Phonics* stimuli were divided into four sound sets and two word sets for a 6-tier, multiple-baseline design across sound and word sets.

The embedded changing criterion occurred as the number of sounds and words accumulated across tiers of corresponding Sound, Letter-Sound, Blending, and Generalization Phases of the multiple baseline design. As the number of sounds and words increased across tiers, each set included at least 20% of the previously-mastered stimuli. For example, Sound Set 1 of *Initial Phonics* contained /a/ /m/ /t/ /s/ and Sound Set 2 contained the same sounds plus the new sounds /i/ and /f/. Therefore Sound Set 2 contained all previously-mastered sounds and new sounds to be learned making the entire set of sounds /a/ /m/ /t/ /s/ /i/ /f/. In the same manner, Sound Set 3 contained all previous sounds from Sound Sets 1 and 2, plus two additional sounds. Another example can be seen in Sound Set 1 of *Initial Phonics* in which the blending words were /mat/ /sam/ /at/ and /am/. Sound Set 2 blending words included the previously-mastered words from Sound Set 1 plus the words /fit/ /tim/ and /it/ thereby forming cumulative groups of blending words across sound sets (tiers). The exception was for the Automaticity Phase in which all sounds were cumulative across all sound and word sets. The total number of sounds and words increased across sound and word sets.

Each tier of *Initial Phonics* and *Functional Phonics* included six consecutive phases: a Baseline Phase and the five skill phases (verbal imitation of sounds, letter-sound correspondences, automaticity of letter sounds, blending, and generalization). After establishing stability within the Baseline Phase of each tier, each student reached mastery for a phase before beginning a subsequent phase. The mastery criterion for each Sound, Letter-Sound Correspondence, Blending, and Generalization Phase was 80% correct for two out of three consecutive sessions for group instruction and 100% correct for two consecutive sessions for individual instruction. The individualized mastery criterion for all automaticity phases was 100% of each student's RON pretest rate for two consecutive sessions. Phase sequences across *Initial Phonics* and *Functional Phonics* are presented in Table 9.1.

Table 9.1 **Instructional Sequence for the Phonics Component**

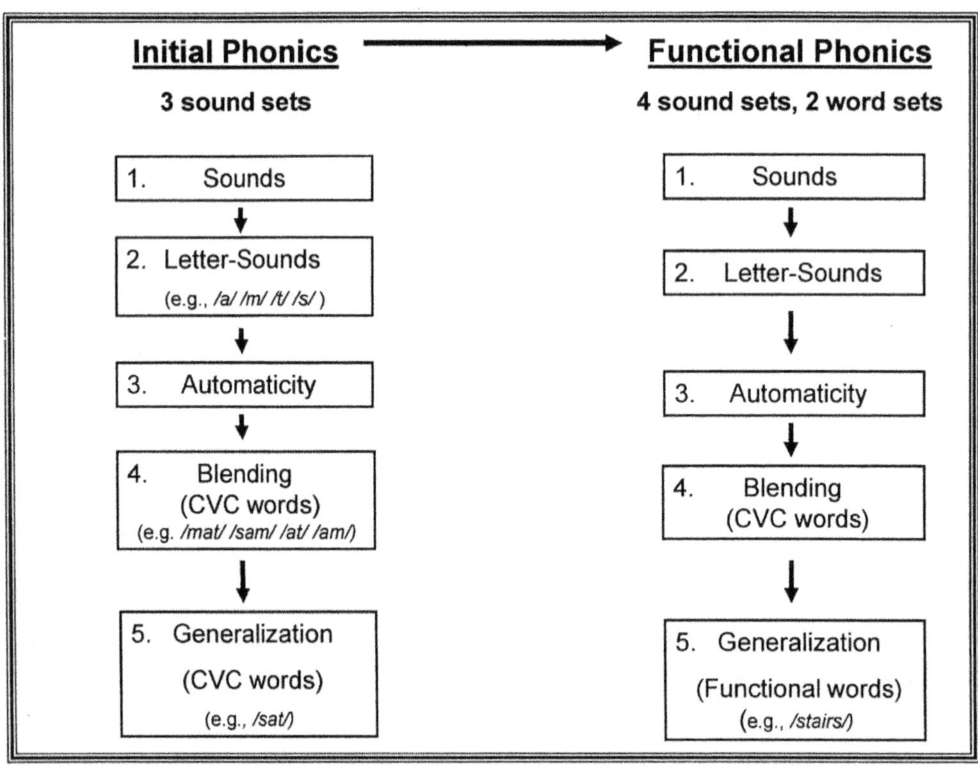

Note. Phases were mastered sequentially for each of 3 sound sets in *Initial Phonics* and for each of 4 sound sets and 2 word sets in *Functional Phonics*.

Baseline data were collected for each student individually. All sounds and words to be taught were presented to each student prior to the onset of the study. Additional baseline probes were conducted for all sounds and words to be taught immediately prior to the onset of the respective sound or word set. All sounds and words were printed in 150 Comic Sans MS font on white 5 × 7 index cards. During the initial Baseline Phase and baseline probes, the teacher presented a sound or word card and asked the student to touch the card as a joint-attention prompt. Then the teacher said "What sound/word?" Correct and incorrect responses were recorded, but no feedback was provided.

DAILY SEQUENCE FOR INITIAL AND FUNCTIONAL PHONICS

Simultaneous prompting procedures were used to teach verbal imitation of sounds, letter-sound correspondences, and blending skills within the Phonics Component of the ILC. The daily sequence of activities consisted of priming activities, probes, and a teaching session. Learning was measured before each teaching session through the use of probes, described below. The stimuli for probes and teaching sessions consisted of the sounds or words of the particular phase in which students were working towards mastery.

PRIMING ACTIVITIES

The researchers wrote storybooks that included a controlled vocabulary (blending and generalization words) for respective sound sets, creating six storybooks for elementary students and two for middle-school students. Researchers made sock puppets for some of the characters and provided objects from the stories so students could interact with the storybooks thereby increasing student interest, attention, and comprehension. The overall purpose of the storybooks was to develop emergent-literacy skills, phonological awareness, and comprehension of blending and generalization words; and to ensure that the words students were expected to blend existed in the students' receptive vocabulary. Teachers developed these skills through shared-storybook reading (Whitehurst & Lonigan, 1998) and language-expansion activities that included: modeling and having students track lines and words on pages, stressing a reading vocabulary, asking comprehension questions, and asking students to predict and retell stories. Magnetic letters also were used to promote phonological awareness through unstructured word-play activities. Teachers guided students in physical manipulation of magnetic letters to demonstrate combining sounds into words and breaking words into sounds. Priming activities also included practice naming previously-mastered letter sounds. No data were collected on priming activities.

PROBE SESSIONS

Teachers conducted one probe session in a 1:1 format for each participant prior to each instructional session using the same sound and word cards used in baseline and during instructional sessions. The data from these probe sessions are the data used to determine the effectiveness of the Phonics Component. Teachers recorded the number of correct and incorrect responses of each student on researcher-prepared, data-collection sheets. As in baseline, a joint-attention prompt was provided in all phases (e.g., touch the card). Unlike the Baseline Phase, if students made an incorrect response, the teacher provided the correct response, and if students made a correct response the teacher praised the student and repeated the correct response. During the Sounds Phase the teacher asked the student to repeat sounds she modeled (e.g., *Say /s/*). During the Letter-Sound Correspondence Phase the teacher presented a letter-sound card, asked the student to touch the card and then asked *what sound?* During the Automaticity Phase, the teacher presented a sound sheet with six rows each containing seven previously-learned letters and asked students to *say the sounds as quickly as you can.* The teacher recorded the number of correct sounds students provided in 1 minute. During the Blending Phase, the teacher presented a word card, asked the student to touch the card, say each sound in the word while pointing to the sounds, and then say the word fast. Probes during the Generalization Phase were conducted the same way as probes during the Blending Phase, except no corrective feedback was provided during the Generalization Phase. Probes were always conducted prior to teaching sessions in order to assess what students retained from previous teaching sessions; all correct responses counted toward mastery for that particular phase.

TEACHING SESSIONS

After probe sessions, teachers conducted a teaching session using simultaneous prompting procedures, that we adapted by adding a lead step for phonics students, in either a 1:1 or small-group format. The elementary-school students received 1:1 instruction for *Initial Phonics* and the first two sound sets of *Functional Phonics,* and small-group instruction for the remaining sound and word sets of *Functional Phonics.* The middle-school students received small-group instruction for both *Initial* and *Functional Phonics.* No data were collected during these teaching sessions because the controlling prompt was always provided before the students were asked to respond.

During all teaching sessions simultaneous prompting procedures that included a model, lead, test sequence were repeated until students responded correctly and independently. The teacher provided the controlling prompt simultaneously with the instructional cue and then modeled for the students by providing the correct response. Next, the teacher provided the controlling prompt simultaneously with the instructional cue and asked the students to respond with her as a lead step. Finally, the teacher provided the controlling prompt simultaneously with the instructional cue and asked individual students to respond.

During the Sounds Phase, verbal imitation of sounds was taught for the respective group of sounds within each sound set. The teacher modeled continuous sounds (e.g., /m/, /s/) by saying them for 2 seconds and stop sounds (e.g., /t/, /b/) by saying them quickly without adding uh (e.g., tuh, buh). Students imitated each sound. During the Letter-Sound Correspondence Phase, letter-sound correspondences were taught for the respective group of letter sounds within each sound set. The teacher held up a letter-sound card (the same ones used in baseline) and said *Touch the card. This sound is ___ , what sound?* following simultaneous prompting procedures of model, lead, test until the student responded correctly and independently.

During the Automaticity Phase automatic retrieval of learned letter-sound correspondences was taught for the respective group of letter sounds within each sound set. The authors created automaticity charts consisting of previously-mastered letter sounds in random order and in the same format as objects on RON charts. Students practiced naming the sounds as fast as they could for 1 minute until their naming rate, measured as correct sounds per minute (CSPM), matched their individual RON pretest rate. Only after students reached this level of automaticity was the skill of blending introduced.

During the Blending Phase for each sound and word set, students were taught to blend and telescope the previously-mastered letter sounds into words. Blending was operationally defined as holding each continuous sound (e.g., /s/, /m/) in the blending word for 2 seconds without stopping between sounds. This is called "saying the word slowly" and is a DI technique (Engelmann et al., 1988) used as an indicator that the student actually manipulated and blended sounds rather than having memorized the word as a sight word after seeing it in many teaching sessions. After blending the sounds, the student was asked to telescope, or to "say the word fast" in order to practice the correct pronunciation of the word. Teachers used simultaneous prompting procedures that included a model, lead, test sequence for students to practice saying the words slowly and saying the words fast until they responded correctly and independently. After each correct blending and telescoping response students selected the corresponding object from an array of objects displayed on the table. This motor demonstration of comprehension ensured that the students understood the meaning of the words they read.

During the Generalization Phase of *Initial Phonics*, students were presented with untaught consonant-vowel-consonant (CVC) words made up of previously-mastered sounds to test for generalization of blending and telescoping. During the Generalization Phase of *Functional Phonics* students were presented with untaught, functional words made of previously-mastered sounds to test for generalization. There was no instruction during the Generalization Phase.

PROCEDURAL FIDELITY

To measure procedural fidelity each week, teachers and the researchers used video cameras to record 20% of instructional sequences. The investigator viewed the tapes while comparing procedures to a behavior checklist. The total number of teacher behaviors observed during the session was divided by the total number of teacher behaviors on the behavior checklist and multiplied by 100%. Procedural fidelity for teacher implementation ranged from 91% to 100% with a mean of 96%.

INTEROBSERVER AGREEMENT

The researcher observed probe sessions on video while simultaneously recording correct and incorrect student responses. Data were compared to data collected by the primary data collector, the teacher. Interobserver agreement was calculated using point-by-point agreement. The total number of agreements was divided by the total number of agreements plus disagreements and converted to a percent. Interobserver agreement was calculated for 20% of probe sessions and ranged from 93% to 100% with a mean of 95%.

SOCIAL VALIDITY

Teachers were provided with a social validity rating scale to complete at the end of the study. They were asked to answer questions pertaining to the usefulness of the study in determining appropriate instruction for their students, ease of implementation, and relevance to curriculum development for students with MoID. They also were asked how important they felt phonics instruction was for their students, and how likely they would be to continue to develop word-analysis skills and automaticity with their students. Teachers rated their responses on a 1 to 5 Likert-type scale with 1 indicating strongly disagree and 5 indicating strongly agree for a maximum positive score of 25. Teachers' scores ranged from 20 to 25 with a mean of 23.

RESULTS

Visual analysis was conducted for all five participants revealing a functional relation between the Phonics Component of the ILC and mastery of word-analysis skills as evidenced by a pattern of increase in correct responding during intervention phases replicated across sound and word sets. Due to space limitations graphic presentation of data is provided for a sample of one elementary student who received individual and group instruction, and for the middle-school group of two participants who received group instruction. The data for each sample are displayed in a 3-tier (*Initial Phonics*) and a 6-tier (*Functional Phonics*) multiple baseline design across sound and word sets with an embedded changing criterion, depicting the number of correct responses on the left y-axis and the number of correct sounds per minute on the right y-axis. Dashed lines across each phase indicate the criterion for that phase and the numbers in parentheses indicate the actual number of correct responses needed for mastery. Also, we have provided a table that includes the mastery criterion for all Blending and Generalization Phases as well as the number of sessions required to reach mastery for the elementary student and for the middle-school group of students, highlighting the change in rate of learning across sound and word sets.

Taniesha represents the elementary students who received individual instruction during *Initial Phonics* (see Figure 9.1). Taniesha demonstrated mastery of all phases of *Initial Phonics* except the Generalization Phase of Sound Set 1 (Tier 1). Her learning was replicated across subsequent tiers representing Sound Sets 2 and 3. Baseline data points of zero indicate that Taniesha did not know any sounds or blending words before instruction began and an increase in word-analysis skills did not occur until treatment was introduced in each phase. Baseline probes were conducted immediately prior to the onset of each sound set to measure her most current knowledge of verbal imitation of sounds, letter-sound correspondences, and words for each respective tier. The baseline probes just prior to instruction in each tier show that Taniesha retained previously-mastered sounds and words that were included in subsequent sound sets. As seen in Table 9.2, during Sound Set 1 Taniesha reached the mastery criterion of 12 correctly blended words in 14 sessions. In Sound Set 2 she reached the mastery criterion of 21 correctly blended words in 17 sessions, and in Sound Set 3 she reached the mastery criterion of 24 correctly blended words in 10 sessions. During generalization Taniesha read zero novel words in Tier 1, 12 in Tier 2, and 18 in Tier 3.

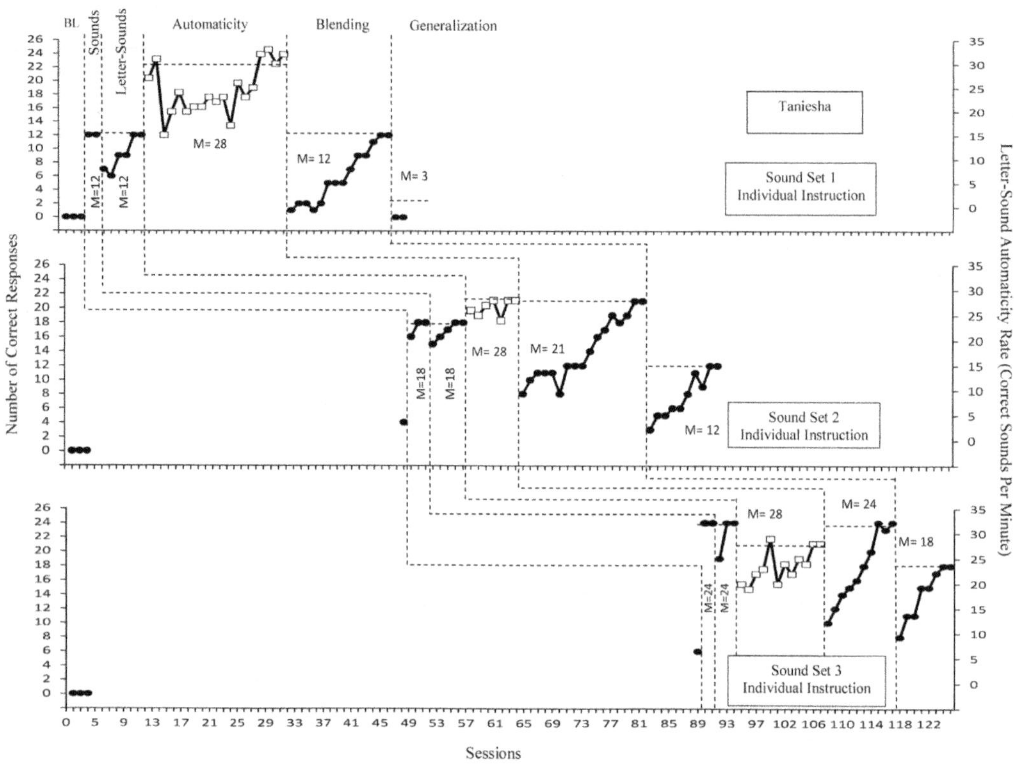

Figure 9.1 A multiple baseline design across sound sets with an embedded changing criterion design depicting the number of correct responses produced by one elementary student during initial phonics. Open square data points depict automaticity rates and correspond with the secondary Y-axis.

Taniesha also represents the elementary-school students who received instruction in *Functional Phonics.* They received individual instruction for Sound Sets 1 and 2, during which mastery for each phase was 100% correct responses for two consecutive sessions (Figure 9.2, Tiers 1 and 2). Students received group instruction for Sound Set 3 and 4 and for Word Sets 5 and 6, during which mastery was a group average of 80% correct responses for two out of three consecutive sessions. Taniesha mastered all word-analysis skills in Sound Set 1 only after instruction was introduced for each phase. This is replicated across Sound Sets 2–4 and Word Sets 5 and 6. Baseline data for Sound Sets 1 through 4 show that Taniesha knew a range of two to three items and indicate that she retained the previously-mastered sounds and words from *Initial Phonics.* Baseline probes immediately prior to the onset of Sound Sets 2 through 4 also show that she retained previously-mastered items from previous *Functional Phonics* sound sets. Baseline data show that Taniesha did not know any of the functional, connected-text phrases prior to beginning Word Sets 5 and 6. Table 9.2 shows that during

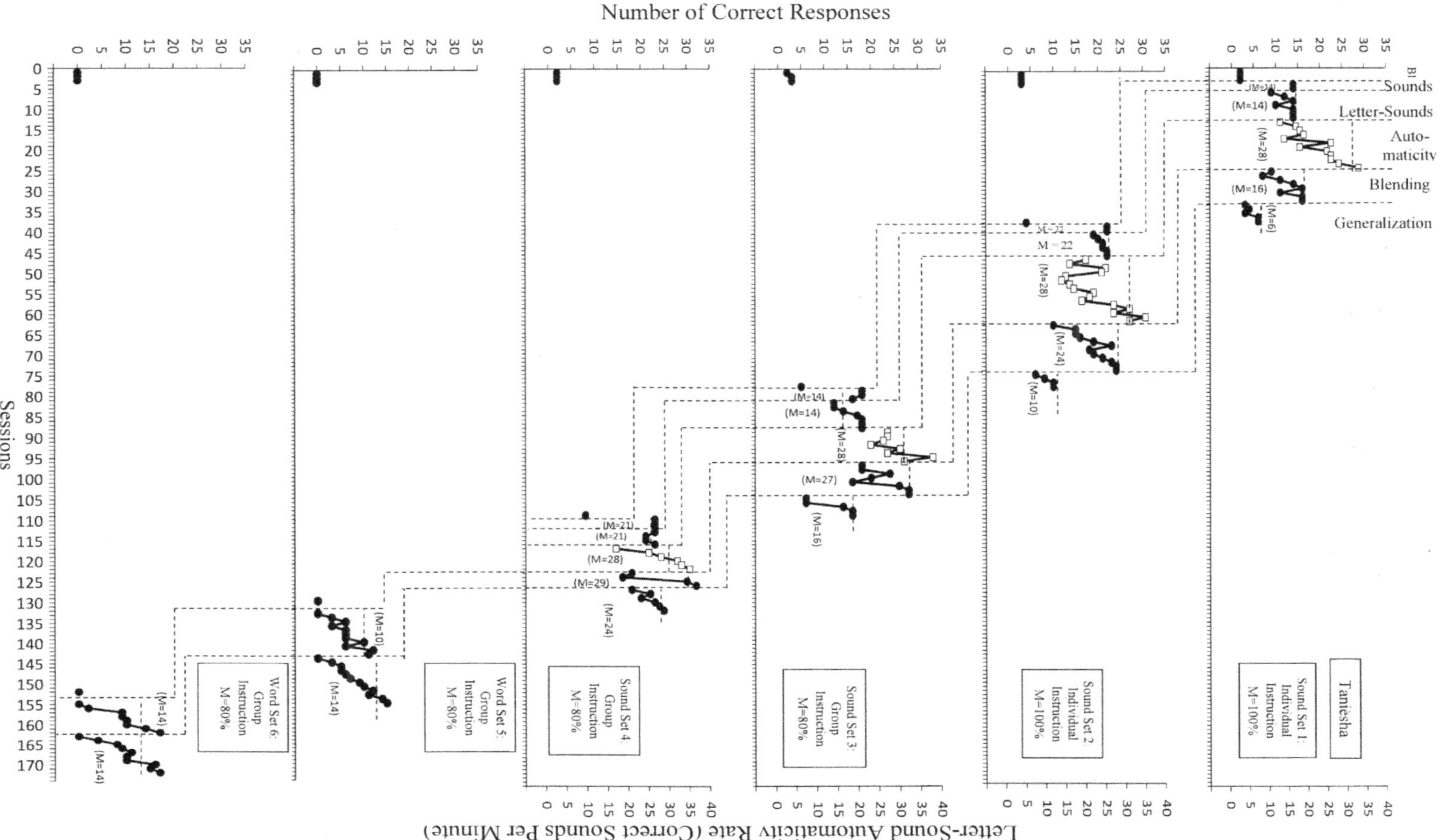

Figure 9.2 A multiple baseline design across sound sets with an embedded changing criterion design depicting the number of correct responses produced by one elementary student during functional phonics. Open square data points depict automaticity rates and correspond with the secondary Y-axis.

Sound Sets 1 through 4 Taniesha demonstrated mastery of 16, 24, 27, and 29 blending words in 8, 12, 8, and 4 sessions respectively. She correctly generalized the skills of blending and telescoping to 6, 10, 16, and 24 novel, functional words in 5, 4, 5, and 6 sessions respectively.

During Word Set 5 of *Functional Phonics,* Taniesha mastered 10 functional, connected-text phrases (in which one word was a previously-mastered generalization word) in 10 sessions, and during Word Set 6 she mastered 14 functional, connected-text phrases (in which all words were novel, untaught words) in eight sessions. During Word Set 5 Taniesha successfully generalized blending and telescoping skills to 14 functional, connected-text phrases (all novel, functional words) in 12 sessions. During Word Set 6, she successfully generalized these skills to 14 functional, connected-text phrases in 9 sessions (See Table 9.2).

Table 9.2 **Initial and Functional Phonics Blending Phases mastery criteria (number of words) along with number of sessions required to reach blending mastery, and Generalization Phases mastery criteria (number of functional words and environmental connected-text phrases) along with number of sessions required to reach generalization mastery for one elementary-age student.**

INITIAL PHONICS-ELEMENTARY STUDENT				FUNCTIONAL PHONICS-ELEMENTARY STUDENT						
	SOUND SET 1	SOUND SET 2	SOUND SET 3		SOUND SET 1	SOUND SET 2	SOUND SET 3	SOUND SET 4	WORD SET 5	WORD SET 6
Blending Phases				**Blending Phases**						
Mastery Criterion	12	21	24	Mastery Criterion	16	24	27	29	10	14
# of Sessions Required for Mastery	14	17	10	# of Sessions Required for Mastery	8	12	8	4	10	8
Generalization Phases				**Generalization Phases**						
Mastery Criterion	3	12	18	Mastery Criterion	6	10	16	24	14	14
# of Sessions Required for Mastery	N/A	10	8	# of Sessions Required for Mastery	5	4	5	6	12	9

Figure 9.3 displays average learning performance during *Initial Phonics* for a middle-school group of two students. For group instruction, mastery criterion was 80% correct for two out of three consecutive sessions for each phase. The group demonstrated mastery of all phases of *Initial Phonics,* and learning was replicated across subsequent tiers representing Sound Sets 2 and 3. Students knew a range of two to four items before instruction began for Sound Set 1. Increases in verbal imitation of

sounds, letter-sound correspondences, automaticity of letter-sounds, blending, and generalization did not occur until treatment was introduced within each phase. Baseline probes were conducted immediately prior to the onset of each sound set and show that the students retained previously-mastered sounds and words that were included in previous *Initial Phonics* sound sets per the cumulative design. As seen in Table 9.3, during Sound Sets 1 through 3 the students reached the mastery criteria of 6, 11, and 13 correctly blended words in 5, 3, and 8 sessions respectively. During Generalization Phases of Sound Sets 1 through 3, the students successfully generalized the skills of blending and telescoping to 2, 6, and 10 novel words in 2 to 3 sessions.

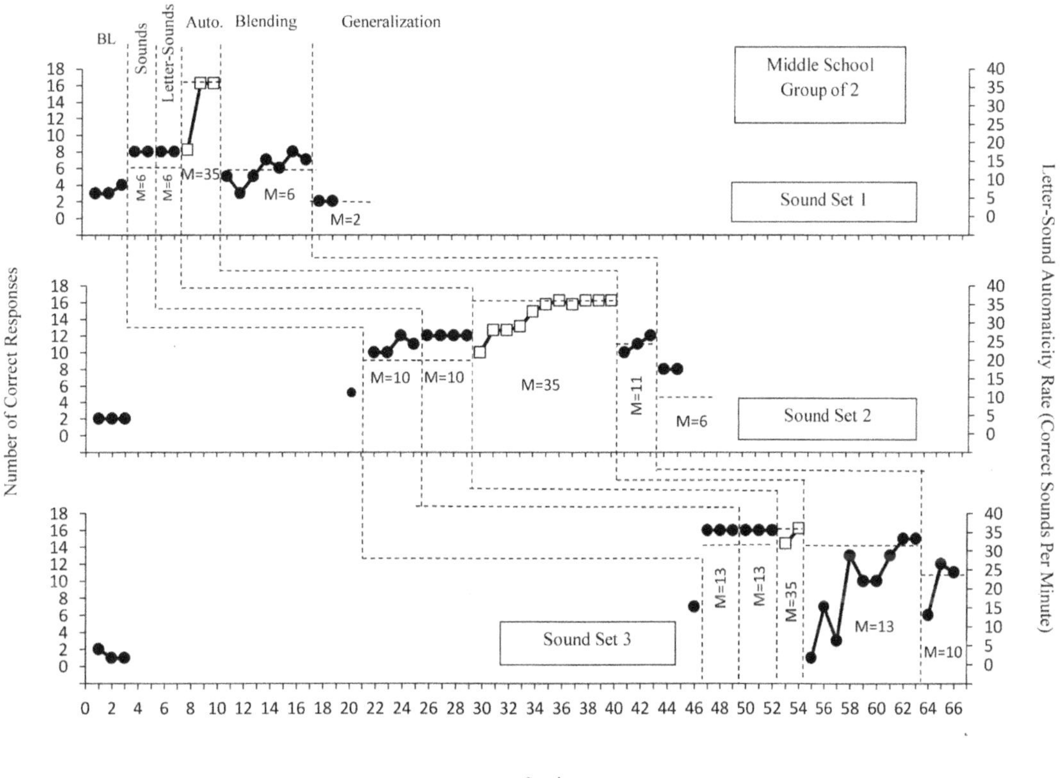

Figure 9.3 A multiple baseline design across sound sets with an embedded changing criterion design depicting the number of correct responses produced by one middle school group of two students during initial phonics. Open square data points depict automaticity rates and correspond with the secondary Y-axis.

Figure 9.4 depicts the learning performance during *Functional Phonics* for the middle-school group of two students, whose mastery criterion was a group average of 80% correct responses across two out of three consecutive sessions. The students mastered all phases of Tier 1, and mastery of all phases was replicated across each tier representing Sound Sets 2, 3, and 4 and Word Sets 5 and 6. Initial baseline data for Sound Sets 1 through 4 show that the students knew a range of two to four items and indicate that students retained the previously-mastered sounds and words from *Initial Phonics*. Baseline probes immediately prior to the onset of Sound Sets 2 through 4 show also that students retained previously-mastered items from previous *Functional Phonics* sound sets. Students did not know any of the functional, connected-text phrases prior to beginning Word Sets 5 and 6. During Sound Sets 1 through 4 students mastered blending and telescoping of 13, 19, 27, and 29 words in 3, 5, 3, and 5 sessions, respectively. The students generalized these skills to 5, 8, 16, and 24 novel, functional words in 2 to 3 sessions (see Table 9.3).

During Word Set 5 of *Functional Phonics,* the middle-school group mastered 10 functional, connected-text phrases (in which one word was a previously-mastered generalization word) in three sessions, and during Word Set 6 they mastered 14 functional, connected-text phrases (in which all words were novel, untaught words) in four sessions. During Word Set 5 they generalized blending and telescoping skills to 14 functional, connected-text phrases (all novel, functional words) in three sessions. During Word Set 6, the students generalized these skills to 14 functional, connected-text phrases in five sessions (See Table 9.3).

Table 9.3 **Initial and Functional Phonics Blending Phases mastery criteria (number of words) along with number of sessions required to reach blending mastery, and Generalization Phases mastery criteria (number of functional words and environmental connected-text phrases) along with number of sessions required to reach generalization mastery for a group of two middle school students.**

INITIAL PHONICS-MIDDLE SCHOOL GROUP				FUNCTIONAL PHONICS-MIDDLE SCHOOL GROUP						
	SOUND SET 1	SOUND SET 2	SOUND SET 3		SOUND SET 1	SOUND SET 2	SOUND SET 3	SOUND SET 4	WORD SET 5	WORD SET 6
Blending Phases				**Blending Phases**						
Mastery Criterion	6	11	13	Mastery Criterion	13	19	27	29	10	14
# of Sessions Required for Mastery	5	3	8	# of Sessions Required for Mastery	3	5	3	5	3	4
Generalization Phases				**Generalization Phases**						
Mastery Criterion	2	6	10	Mastery Criterion	5	8	16	24	14	14
# of Sessions Required for Mastery	2	2	3	# of Sessions Required for Mastery	2	2	2	3	3	5

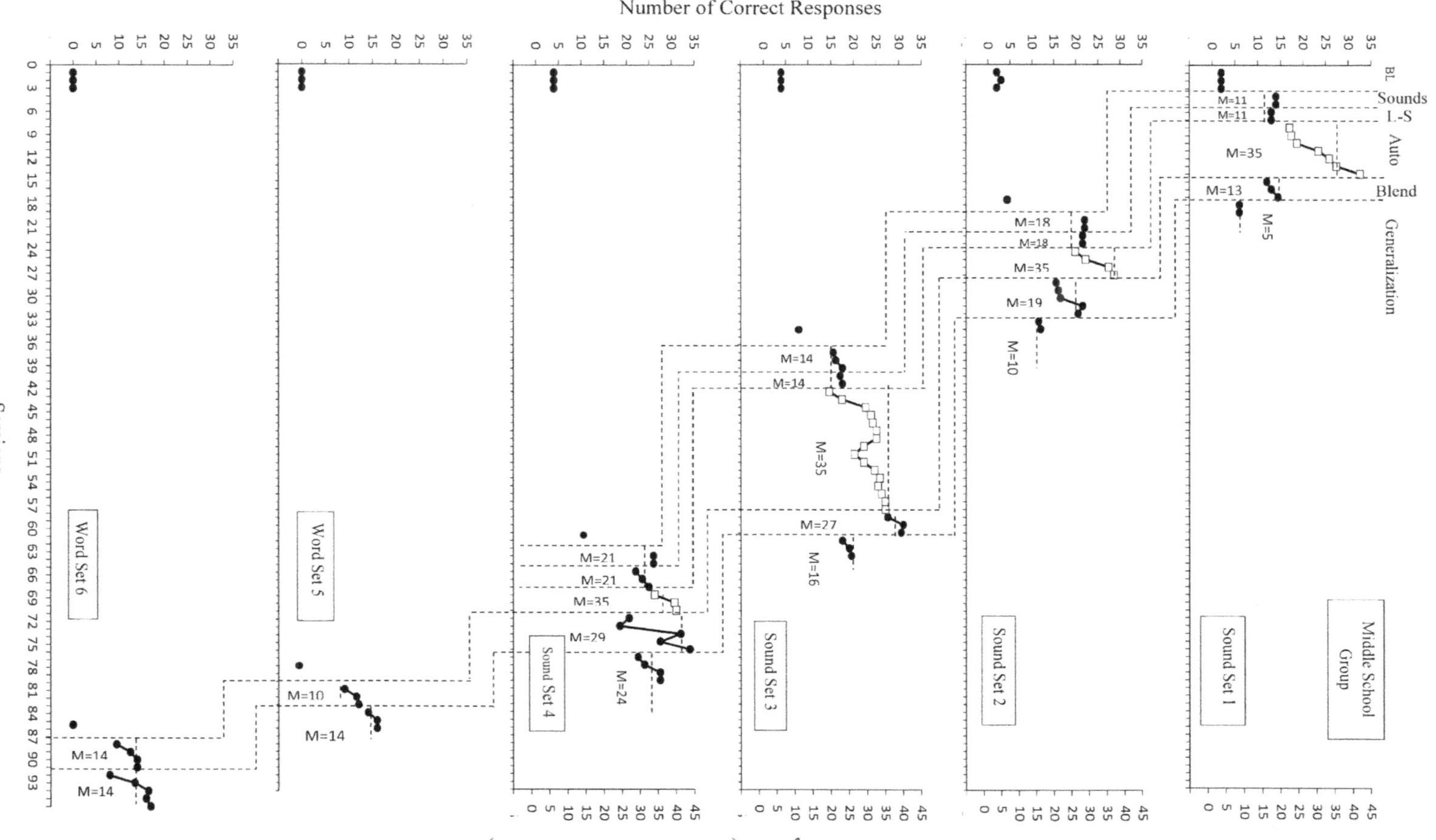

Figure 9.4 A multiple baseline design across sound sets with an embedded changing criterion design depicting the average number of correct responses produced by one middle school group of two students during functional phonics. Open square data points depict automaticity rates and correspond with the secondary Y-axis.

DISCUSSION

This study supports and extends previous demonstrations of the effectiveness of simultaneous prompting procedures in teaching word-analysis skills to students with MoID (Waugh et al., 2009). All five students acquired word-analysis skills that included verbal imitation of sounds, letter-sound correspondences, retrieval of letter-sound correspondences to a level of automaticity, blending of the learned letter sounds to words by holding each sound for 2 seconds without stopping ("saying it slowly") and producing each sound quickly without stopping (telescoping), and generalizing the skill of blending to untaught words and connected-text phrases. A clear rise to mastery is shown for all phases, as compared to baseline phases, for all students except Taniesha's first opportunity to generalize the skill of blending to a novel word during Sound Set 1 of *Initial Phonics*. We anticipated that students with MoID needed many more opportunities to generalize phonetic skills to untaught words than have been provided in the past (Bracey et al., 1975; Bradford et al., 2006; Flores et al., 2004). Our cumulative data within the changing-criterion across tiers buoyed this important aspect of the Phonics Component. Per the design, Taniesha was provided additional opportunities to practice and master precursor word-analysis skills before attempting to generalize the skills to untaught words. The next set of generalization words included the original generalization word (*sat*) plus three additional, untaught words (*mat, at, am*), and she was able to read all of them. In addition to identifying and addressing blending and generalization as specific areas of difficulty, we have shown that repetition of systematically presented stimuli is an effective approach to successful learning of phonetic skills for students with MoID. Historically, teachers may have "given up" before students received sufficient systematic repetition to facilitate learning, leading to the generally accepted assumption that students with MoID cannot learn phonics.

The use of cumulative stimuli within the design revealed another important finding. As the students progressed through sound sets of *Initial Phonics* and *Functional Phonics* the number of sessions required to reach mastery often decreased even though the mastery criterion increased. Students began mastering more items in progressively fewer sessions. As seen in Table 9.2, during *Initial Phonics* Taniesha reached the mastery criteria of 12, 21, and 24 correctly blended words in 14, 17, and 10 sessions, respectively. During Generalization Phases Taniesha did not read any novel words in Tier 1, but read12 in Tier 2, and 18 in Tier 3.

In Sound Set 1 of *Functional Phonics* Taniesha demonstrated mastery of 16 words in eight blending sessions and generalized blending and telescoping to six novel, functional words in five sessions. In Sound Set 4, she correctly read 29 words in half as many sessions as she read 16 words in Sound Set 1, and she generalized blending and telescoping to 24 novel, functional words. During Word Set 5 of *Functional Phonics,* Taniesha mastered 10 connected-text phrases (in which one word was a previously-mastered generalization word) in 10 sessions, and during Word Set 6 she increased her mastery of connected-text phrases to 14 while decreasing the number of sessions required for mastery. During Word Set 5 Taniesha generalized blending and telescoping to 14 connected-text phrases (all words within phrases were novel functional words) in 12 sessions. During Word Set 6, she generalized to 14 connected-text phrases and decreased the number of sessions to nine.

As can be seen on Table 9.3, during Sound Set 1of *Initial Phonics* the middle-school group reached a mastery criterion of six correctly blended words in only five sessions. By Sound Set 3 they reached a mastery criterion of 13 correctly blended words in eight sessions. For Generalization Phases, during Sound Set 1 the students reached a mastery criterion of two correctly-blended words in two sessions, and by Sound Set 3 generalized to 10 untaught words in only three sessions. Although, the data do not show the same decrease in number of sessions to mastery as for Taniesha, students mastered progressively more items in approximately the same number of sessions. Also, they began mastering skills in fewer sessions than Taniesha (e.g., 14 vs. 5 sessions for mastery of the Blending Phase during Sound Set 1 of *Initial Phonics*). The older students might have learned more quickly because they had better-developed attention skills, more prior practice with in-seat behavior, and more opportunities to interact with reading stimuli because of additional years in school.

As the students acquired basic word-analysis skills, and then applied them to words and phrases that increased in number and complexity, they demonstrated that word-analysis skills are strategy-based skills that once learned can be applied to many, unanticipated words in an individual's environment. This use of a strategy-based skill remains in contrast to sight-word reading that requires the same amount of memory load for every word memorized, and does not prepare an individual to read untaught words that have a functional use in the individual's environment.

In addition to the word-analysis skills targeted in this study, students developed prerequisite-reading skills for which we did not collect data. These prerequisite-reading skills developed during Automaticity Phases and storybook-priming activities. When presented with an automaticity chart consisting of 42 previously-mastered letter sounds, and asked to name the sounds as quickly as they could for one minute, most of the students could not attend to individual stimuli on a page nor track left to right and from one line to the next. To address this we alternated between red and black font for each line, and used hand over hand guidance until the students learned to attend to each stimulus on the page and to track independently. Not only were students increasing their ability to retrieve letter sounds quickly and accurately, they learned the emergent-literacy skill of tracking and improved their attention skills.

The shared-storybook activities facilitated their learning of prerequisite-reading skills including, phonological awareness, emergent literacy, comprehension, language expansion, and vocabulary. The age-appropriate storybooks corresponded with the curriculum and as the students participated in the interactive reading we observed these skills begin to emerge. As the study progressed, students began to make predictions about events in the stories, identify sentences and words on pages, provide a motor demonstration of comprehension of reading vocabulary, read individual sounds in CVC words, and practice saying CVC words slowly and quickly.

Phonological awareness and emergent literacy are prerequisite skills for phonetic-reading acquisition (Ehri, 2004; Share, Jorm, MacLean, & Matthews, 1984). Prior to participating in this study, our students had not been systematically taught these prerequisite skills because phonics instruction is seldom provided for children with MoID (Browder et al., 2006). Because sight-word instruction is the most common method of reading instruction for students with MoID, these prerequisite-reading skills are often not acquired, with the exception of some emergent-literacy skills.

When word-analysis skills have been taught (Bracey et al., 1975; Bradford et al., 2006; Flores et al., 2004) they have not included an automaticity requirement. Automaticity training was one of the most unique aspects of the Phonics Component. Due to limited working-memory capacity, we speculated that the students needed to learn to retrieve letter-sound correspondences to some level of automaticity before attempting to blend them into words. For the Automaticity Phase mastery criterion we selected each student's rate on the RON subtest as the best reflection of the individual student's phonological processing rate. All students blended successfully after first reaching mastery in Automaticity Phases suggesting that automaticity practice facilitated the skill of blending. However, we do not know if the criterion for automaticity that we selected is a necessary threshold for successful blending, or if the automaticity practice is sufficient with a less stringent criterion.

The Phonics Component included academic-literacy and functional-literacy goals. Historically, the definition of literacy instruction has been binary. Academic literacy has been viewed as the approach for typically-developing students and has involved phonetic-decoding skills while functional literacy has been viewed as the approach for individuals with developmental delays and has included sight-word instruction (Cegelka & Cegelka, 1970). We have shown that the two types of goals can be combined. With this alignment of goals, students with MoID can be taught phonetic-decoding skills to promote optimal participation in their community. Typically-developing students are taught phonics as a method of obtaining information from connected-narrative text which includes sentences and passages. Students with MoID should be provided the same opportunity even if their full potential may be connected-environmental text which consists of functional words and short phrases.

LIMITATIONS AND FUTURE RECOMMENDATIONS

One limitation of this study is a change that we made to the changing-criterion requirement. The elementary students began phonics instruction before the middle-school students. As originally designed the elementary students had three trials in each session. Because of the increase in the number of sounds and blending words in *Functional Phonics*, the number of trials was reduced from three to two trials per session and we applied this new criterion to all future participants. By the time the middle-school students began *Initial Phonics* the criterion had changed to two trials per session. The mastery criterion for 1:1 instruction was 100% correct for two consecutive sessions and the criterion for group instruction was a group average of 80% correct across two out of three consecutive sessions. The elementary-school students received 1:1 instruction throughout *Initial Phonics* and the first two sound sets of *Functional Phonics*, and the middle-school students received group instruction throughout the study.

Considering our participants were from multiple schools in multiple districts, and at multiple age levels, we were not able to control for their previous literacy experiences beyond the Edmark program that all of the participants received prior to this research. Further, all students with MoID may not be equally successful. There were only three elementary-school students and two middle-school students who completed the Phonics Component limiting the external validity.

We have not found the floor effect of cognitive ability for students who can learn to read phonetically. Future research should include different students with MoID with varied previous literacy instruction and cognitive abilities. It will be important to examine cognitive and language skills such as vocabulary level, processing speed, and working memory as possible predictors of phonetic reading ability to better understand what skills need to be developed to be successful in this program. Close inspection of underlying cognitive processing skills for reading can facilitate identification of students who are prepared to learn to read phonetically.

Future research also should include a close examination of automaticity requirements for blending acquisition. In this study all students mastered Blending and Generalization Phases after mastering individual automaticity requirements. However, it is possible that students could have mastered Blending and Generalization Phases with lower levels of automaticity than what were required in this study.

Finally, it would be helpful to collect data on the development of phonological-awareness skills. Anecdotally, we observed important phonological-awareness skill acquisition, but without systematic measurement and careful inclusion of this in the design of our study, it is impossible to know the extent to which the shared-storybook activities impacted the development of phonological-awareness skills.

REFERENCES

Alberto, P. A., & Fredrick, L. D. (2007). Integrated literacy for students with moderate to severe disabilities. Washington, DC: U.S. Department of Education, Institute of Educational Sciences (IES Grant #R324A070144).

Alberto, P. A., Waugh, R. E., & Fredrick, L. D. (2010). Teaching the reading of connected text through sight-word instruction to students with moderate intellectual disabilities. *Research in Developmental Disabilities, 31*, 1467–1474.

Allor, J. H., Mathes, P. G., Roberts, J. K., Jones, F. G., & Champlin, T. M. (2010). Teaching students with moderate intellectual disabilities to read: An experimental examination of a comprehensive reading intervention. *Education and Training in Autism and Developmental Disabilities, 45*, 3–22.

Austin, P., & Boekman, K. (1990). *Edmark functional word series.* Redmond, WA: PCI Educational Publishing.

Bracey, S., Maggs, A., & Morath, P. (1975). The effects of a direct phonic approach in teaching reading with six moderately retarded children: Acquisition and mastery learning stages. *Exceptional Child, 22*, 83–90.

Bradford, S., Shippen, M. E., Alberto, P. A., Houchins, D. E., & Flores, M. (2006). Using systematic instruction to teach decoding skills to middle school students with moderate intellectual disabilities. *Education and Training in Developmental Disabilities, 41*, 333–343.

Browder, D., Ahlgrim-Delzell, L., Courtade, G., Gibbs, S. L., & Flowers, C. (2008). Evaluation of the effectiveness of an Early Literacy Program for students with significant developmental disabilities. *Exceptional Children, 75*, 33–52.

Browder, D., Wakeman, S., Spooner, F., Ahlgrim-Delzell, L., & Algozzine, B. (2006). Research on reading instruction for individuals with significant cognitive disabilities. *Exceptional Children, 72*, 392–408.

Carnine, D. W., Silbert, J., Kame'ennui, E. J., & Tarver, S. G. (2004). *Direct Instruction reading (4th ed.).* Upper Saddle River, NJ: Pearson Education, Inc.

Cegelka, P., & Cegelka, W. (1970). A review of research: Reading and the educable mentally handicapped. *Exceptional Children, 37*, 187–200.

Cohen, J. D., Dunbar, K., & McClelland, J. L. (1990). On the control of automatic processes: A parallel distributed processing account of the Stroop effect. *Psychological Review, 97*, 332–361.

Cohen, E. T., Heller, K. W., Alberto, P., & Fredrick, L. D. (2008). Using a three-step decoding strategy with constant time delay to teach word reading to students with mild and moderate mental retardation. *Focus on Autism and Other Developmental Disabilities, 23*(2), 67–78.

Conners, F. A. (1992). Reading instruction for students with moderate mental retardation: Review and analysis of research. *American Journal on Mental Retardation, 96*, 577–597.

Conners, F. A., Atwell, J. A., Rosenquist, C. J., & Sligh, A. C. (2001). Abilities underlying decoding differences in children with intellectual disability. *Journal of Intellectual Disability Research, 45*, 292–299.

Cossu, G., Rossini, F., & Marshall, J. C. (1993). When reading is acquired but phonemic awareness is not: A study of literacy in Down's syndrome. *Cognition, 46*, 129–138.

Davis, D. H., Fredrick, L. D., Alberto, P. A., & Gagné, P. (2010). *Naming speed, letter-sound automaticity, and acquiring blending skills among students with moderate intellectual disabilities.* (Unpublished doctoral dissertation). Georgia State University, Atlanta, Ga.

Davis, D. H., Gagné, P., Fredrick, L. D., Alberto, P. A., Waugh, R. E., & Haardörfer, R. (2013). Augmenting visual analysis in single-case research with hierarchical linear modeling. *Behavior Modification, 37*, 62–89.

Ehri, L. C. (2004). Teaching phonemic awareness and phonics: An explanation of the National Reading Panel meta-analysis. In P. McCardle & V. Chhabra (Eds.), *The voice of evidence in reading research* (pp. 153–186). Baltimore, MD: Paul H. Brookes.

Engelmann, S., Becker, W., Hanner, S., & Johnson, G. (1980). *Corrective reading program.* Chicago, Il: Science Research Associates.

Engelmann, S., & Bruner, E. C. (1969). *Distar reading: An instructional system.* Chicago, IL: Science Research Associates.

Engelmann, S., Carnine, L., & Johnson, G. (1988). *Corrective reading: Word-attack basics, Decoding A.* Columbus, OH: MacMillian/MacGraw-Hill.

Flores, M. M., Shippen, M. E., Alberto, P., & Crowe, L. (2004). Teaching letter-sound correspondence to students with moderate intellectual disabilities. *Journal of Direct Instruction, 4,* 173–188.

Foorman, B., Francis, D., Shaywitz, S., Shaywitz, B., & Fletcher, J. (1997). The case for early reading intervention. In B. Blachman (Ed.), *Foundations of reading acquisition* (pp. 243–264). Hillsdale, NJ: Erlbaum.

Hoogeveen, F. R., Smeets, P. M., & Lancioni, G. E. (1989). Teaching moderately mentally retarded children basic reading skills. *Research in Developmental Disabilities, 10,* 1–18.

Joseph, L., & Seery, M. E. (2004). Where is the phonics? A review of the literature on the use of phonetic analysis with students with mental retardation. *Remedial and Special Education, 25,* 88–94.

Katims, D. S. (1996). The emergence of literacy in elementary students with mild mental retardation. *Focus on Autism and Other Developmental Disabilities, 11,* 147–157.

Katims, D. S. (2000). Literacy instruction for people with mental retardation: Historical highlights and contemporary analysis. *Education & Training in Mental Retardation & Developmental Disabilities, 35,* 3–15.

LaBerge, D., & Samuels, S. J. (1974). Toward a theory of automatic information processing in reading. *Cognitive Psychology, 6,* 293–323.

Nietupski, J., Williams, W., & York, R. (1979). Teaching selected phonic word analysis reading skills to TMR labeled students. *Teaching Exceptional Children, 11*(4), 140–143.

Share, D., Jorm, A., MacLean, R., & Matthews, R. (1984). Sources of individual differences in reading achievement. *Journal of Educational Psychology, 76,* 1309–1324.

Shiffrin, R. M., & Schneider, W. (1977). Controlled and automatic human information processing: II. Perceptual learning, automatic attending, and a general theory. *Psychological Review, 84,* 127–190.

Stanovich, K. E. (1985). Cognitive determinants of reading in mentally retarded individuals. In N. R. Ellis & N. W. Bray (Eds.), *International review of research in mental retardation, Vol. 13* (pp. 181–214). San Diego, CA: Academic Press.

Torgesen, J. K., Alexander, A. W., Wagner, R. K., Rashotte, C. A., Voeller, K. K., & Conway, T. (2001). Intensive remedial instruction for children with severe reading disabilities: Immediate and long-term outcomes from two instructional approaches. *Journal of Learning Disabilities, 34,* 33–58.

Wagner, R. K., Torgesen, J., & Rashotte, C. A. (1999). *CTOPP: Comprehensive Test of Phonological Processing.* Austin, TX: PRO-ED.

Waugh, R. E., Fredrick, L. D., & Alberto, P. A. (2009). Using simultaneous prompting to teach sounds and blending skills to students with moderate intellectual disabilities. *Research in Developmental Disabilities, 30,* 1435–1447.

Whitehurst, G., & Lonigan, C. (1998). Child development and emergent literacy. *Child Development, 69,* 848–872.

POST-READING ACTIVITIES

1. Has your understanding of MoID changed? If so, how?
2. Reflect on how you could implement the procedures presented in this study with your own students.
3. List five categories of word-analysis skills.

CHAPTER 9

READING 9.2 OVERVIEW

In this article, preservice and new teachers will learn about research-based strategies that can be used to help students with intellectual disabilities who are nonreaders or early readers. The authors present practical methods for adapting grade-level text. Students will have access to grade-level content in ways that are comprehensible. Thorough descriptions and examples of each strategy are provided. The methods are effective for students identified with intellectual disabilities and for all struggling readers.

PRE-READING ACTIVITIES

1. Create a list of strategies for adapting text for students with intellectual disabilities or struggling readers.
2. How would you increase text complexity while still ensuring the student comprehends the reading?
3. "Some books will not require any changes to the text itself, but may need augmentations to increase accessibility" (Hudson, Browder, and Wakeman 2013, 3). What does that statement mean to you?

HELPING STUDENTS WITH MODERATE AND SEVERE INTELLECTUAL DISABILITY ACCESS GRADE-LEVEL TEXT

BY MELISSA E. HUDSON, DIANE BROWDER, AND SHAWNEE WAKEMAN

Teaching students with moderate and severe intellectual disability who are early readers or nonreaders to engage with grade-level text is challenging. How can teachers promote text accessibility and teach text comprehension? This article describes research-based strategies educators can use to adapt grade-level text and teach text comprehension for students with moderate and severe intellectual disability who are early readers or nonreaders. These approaches can support teachers in developing materials and instruction to promote student interaction with grade-level text.

One of the challenges in teaching language arts to students who are just beginning to read or who are nonreaders is creating access to grade-level text. Even when text is read aloud with the assistance of technology or a reading partner, the text may be too complex for the student's level of receptive communication. To help address this challenge, Erickson and Koppenhaver (1995) suggested making literacy an interactive process by reading a book aloud with frequent opportunities for the student to interact with the text (i.e., shared story reading). In a recent comprehensive review of experimental research, Hudson and Test (2011) found shared story reading—when a partner reads the text aloud and provides opportunities

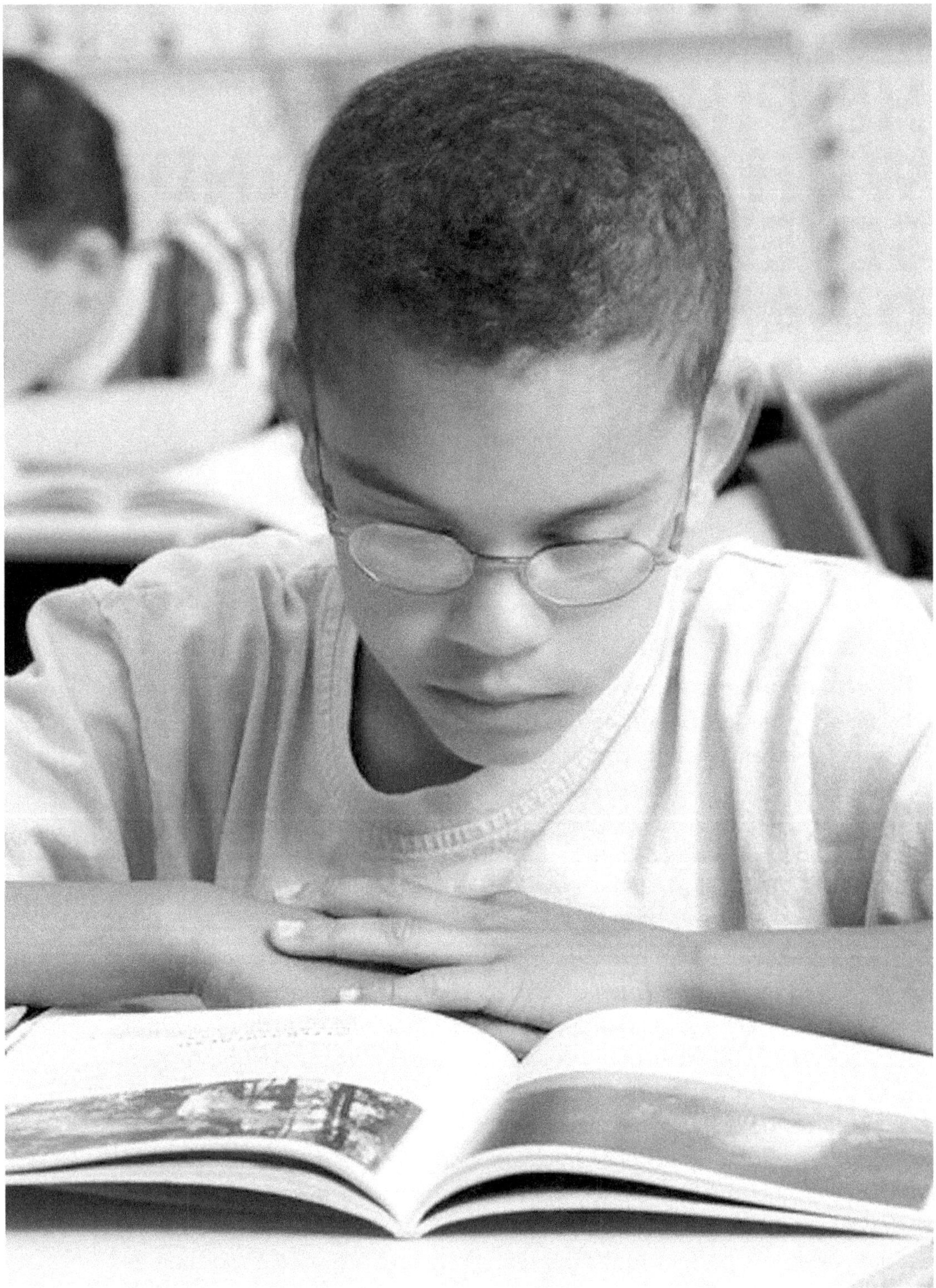

for the listener to interact with the text and demonstrate comprehension—to be an effective way to make text accessible.

There is also research evidence for using text adapted from the grade level for these interactive read-alouds. Browder, Trela, and Jimenez (2007) adapted literature from the upper grades as part of a treatment package in which teachers followed a task analysis to conduct an age-appropriate read-aloud. Adaptations included summarizing novels in brief passages, pairing keywords with picture symbols, and adding a repeated story line that emphasized the main idea of the story. Students increased both their engagement with the text and comprehension responses. Mims, Hudson, and Browder (2012) also found that middle school students with moderate intellectual disability learned to answer comprehension questions about biographies adapted from grade-level literature (i.e., summary of original text and some picture symbol support). The intervention also incorporated a prompt hierarchy to help students locate the correct answer, beginning with re-reading smaller portions of the text that contained the answer. Mims, Browder, Baker, Lee, and Spooner (2008) demonstrated how students with severe intellectual disability who were legally blind could learn to answer comprehension questions by using objects affixed to each page of the book. Their intervention also used a system of least intrusive prompting to help students locate the correct object to answer literal recall questions. Hudson, Browder, and Jimenez (in press) continued to build on this adapted text methodology by having typically developing peers read text summaries and use the system of least intrusive prompting in a general education class. All of the participants with moderate intellectual disability increased their comprehension responses.

All of these studies (a) used adapted versions of the text (e.g., shortened, augmented with pictures and repeated story lines), (b) gave students response options (i.e., pictures or objects), and (c) used a system of least intrusive prompting that included re-reading key portions of the text. Teachers can apply these findings to support their own adaptation of grade-level text, increasing access to the curriculum for students with moderate and severe intellectual disability.

STRATEGIES FOR ADAPTING THE TEXT

SHORTEN THE TEXT

The simplest adaptation is to shorten the text and divide it into segments for oral reading. In selecting a shorter passage, consider the student's attention span for a read-aloud which may be as short as a few minutes or as long as most of a class period. For some printed material, abbreviating the content is the only adaptation needed. For instance, a long narrative poem (e.g., Longfellow's *Paul Revere's Ride*) might be taught using selected stanzas, or a children's picture book might be shortened by omitting pages or paragraphs. When deciding what text to omit, teachers should consult with a content expert (e.g., literacy consultant).

AUGMENT THE TEXT

Some books will not require any changes to the text itself, but may need augmentations to increase accessibility. Text augmentations can include adding pictures, repetitions of the main idea (e.g., repeated story lines), and including objects to build comprehension. Pictures can be used to augment text by adding simple illustrations at the beginning of chapter summaries or by adding picture symbols paired with keywords in the text. Be cautious when adding pictures or picture symbols to text for students learning to read independently, however, as they may focus on the pictures instead of the words. For students relying on a partner to read the text aloud, pictures or picture symbols added to the text may help students track the text and build comprehension.

Adding a repeated story line is another way to augment text. Repeated story lines are often used in preschool picture books to help young students build understanding. The same method can be made age-appropriate by using the main idea of the story or chapter as the repeated story line. For example, in the first chapter of *Charlotte's Web* (White, 1952), the repeated line might be "Wilbur was special." Reading this line at the end of each page can help students build understanding. See Figure 9.5 for another example.

Another augmentation that can benefit some students who are just learning to interact with text or students with visual impairments is to affix actual objects to the pages of the book. For example, in a story about a baseball team, a small ball might be affixed to the page where the topic is first introduced. When the story describes getting to first base, a small sandbag base might be used. Augmentations may also include adding other sensory experiences to prime or support understanding—such as an attention getter at the beginning of the story (e.g., touching sand for a story about the beach) or a surprise during the read-aloud (e.g., the lights go off in the classroom when it gets dark in the story).

Some books will not require any changes to the text itself, but may need augmentations to increase accessibility.

REWRITE THE TEXT AS A SUMMARY

Text can also be adapted by rewriting the original text as a summary.

Writing text summaries involves three steps.

1. *Reduce the number of words in the text* by prioritizing information. This can be done in collaboration with the general education teacher or other content expert (e.g., curriculum specialist) so that the text summary contains the most important information to be learned and that the information is accurate.

2. *Add definitions and explanations* for important unfamiliar words. As text grows more complex across the grade bands (e.g., increased use of dialect, dialogue, technical words), more words in the text may be unfamiliar to students. Adding definitions and explanations helps students make meaning of the most important unfamiliar words. For example, in adapting the novel *A Wrinkle in Time* (L'Engle, 1962), a description of an ant crawling across a wrinkle on a skirt was added to explain *tessering*, an unfamiliar but important word in the story.

3. *Write summaries at a reduced Lexile level.* A Lexile measure indicates a text's complexity and includes sentence length and word frequency. Summaries can vary in complexity depending on the grade band, original text, and purpose of the text (e.g., read-aloud or independent reading; see Figures 9.6, 9.7, and 9.8). Browder et al., 2007 used a Lexile level between 400L and 600L (which span Grades 2–4; see http://lexile.com) for read-alouds. In contrast, when adapting text for independent readers, a lower Lexile level may be needed (e.g., 200L–300L). The Lexile Framework for Reading web site (http://lexile.com) has a free tool to help teachers determine the Lexile measure of adapted text.

USE PREDICTABLE STRUCTURE

Using predictable structure in adapted text helps students find the information they need to answer questions about the text. At early grades, this may include placing the author and illustrator's names in the same location on the front page and the repeated story line in the same place in the text (e.g., at the bottom of the page). For older students, predictable text structure can include stating the main idea in the first sentence of the first paragraph and adding signal words (e.g., first, next, last) to help students complete a graphic organizer about the main facts or story elements (see Figures 9.7 and 9.8 for examples).

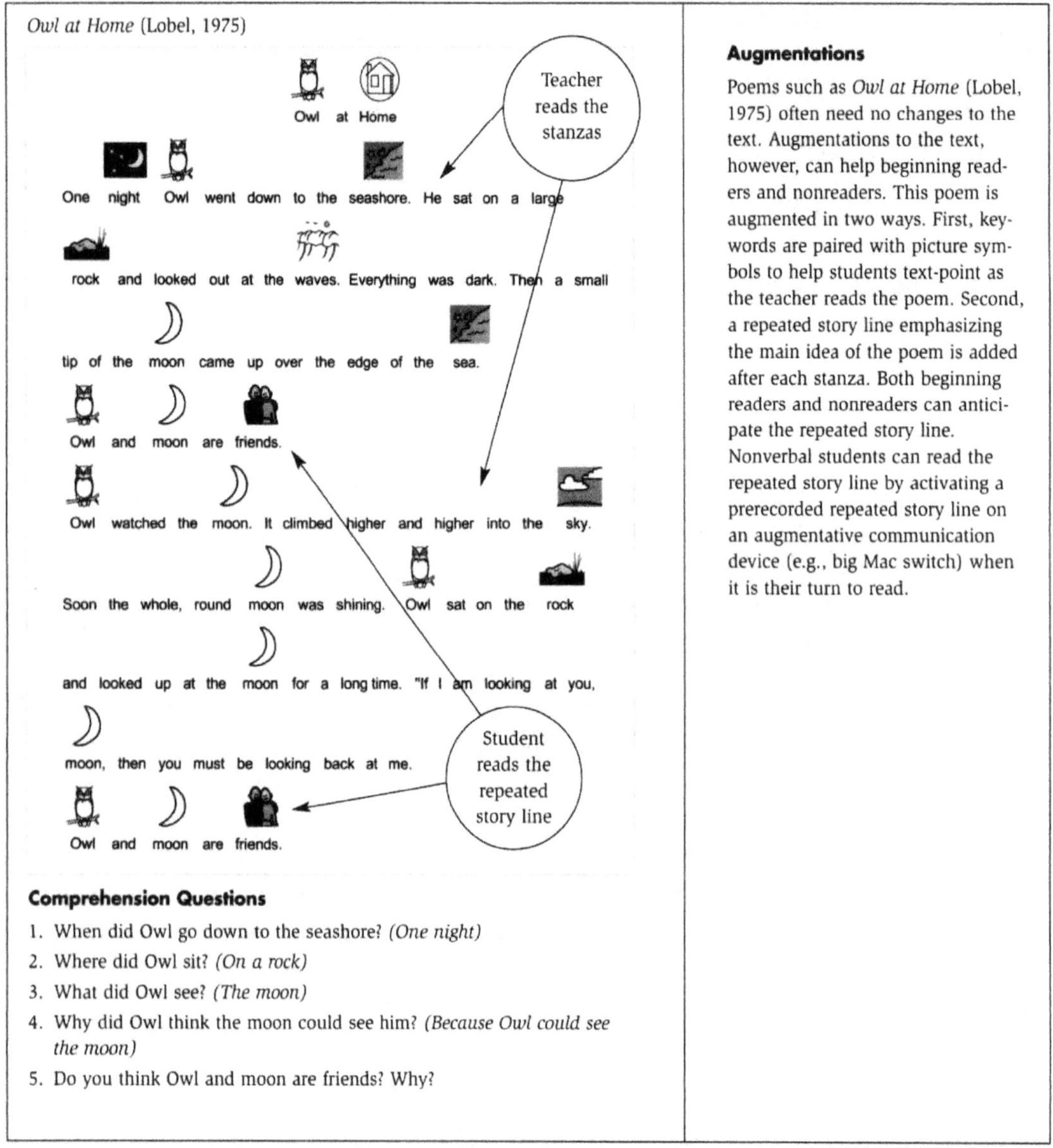

Owl at Home (Lobel, 1975)
Owl at Home
Teacher reads the stanzas
One night Owl went down to the seashore. He sat on a large
rock and looked out at the waves. Everything was dark. Then a small
tip of the moon came up over the edge of the sea.
Owl and moon are friends.
Owl watched the moon. It climbed higher and higher into the sky.
Soon the whole, round moon was shining. Owl sat on the rock
and looked up at the moon for a long time. "If I am looking at you,
moon, then you must be looking back at me.
Student reads the repeated story line
Owl and moon are friends.
Comprehension Questions
1. When did Owl go down to the seashore? *(One night)*
2. Where did Owl sit? *(On a rock)*
3. What did Owl see? *(The moon)*
4. Why did Owl think the moon could see him? *(Because Owl could see the moon)*
5. Do you think Owl and moon are friends? Why?
Augmentations
Poems such as *Owl at Home* (Lobel, 1975) often need no changes to the text. Augmentations to the text, however, can help beginning readers and nonreaders. This poem is augmented in two ways. First, keywords are paired with picture symbols to help students text-point as the teacher reads the poem. Second, a repeated story line emphasizing the main idea of the poem is added after each stanza. Both beginning readers and nonreaders can anticipate the repeated story line. Nonverbal students can read the repeated story line by activating a prerecorded repeated story line on an augmentative communication device (e.g., big Mac switch) when it is their turn to read.

Figure 9.5 Grades K to 1 example.

The amount of text presented on a page can also be changed to promote accessibility. For example, when adapting text for Grades K to 2, limit print to one or two sentences on a page. In contrast, for Grades 3 to 5 (see Figure 9.7), text may be limited to one or two paragraphs on a page. This can be expanded to two or more paragraphs on a page for students in middle grades and high school.

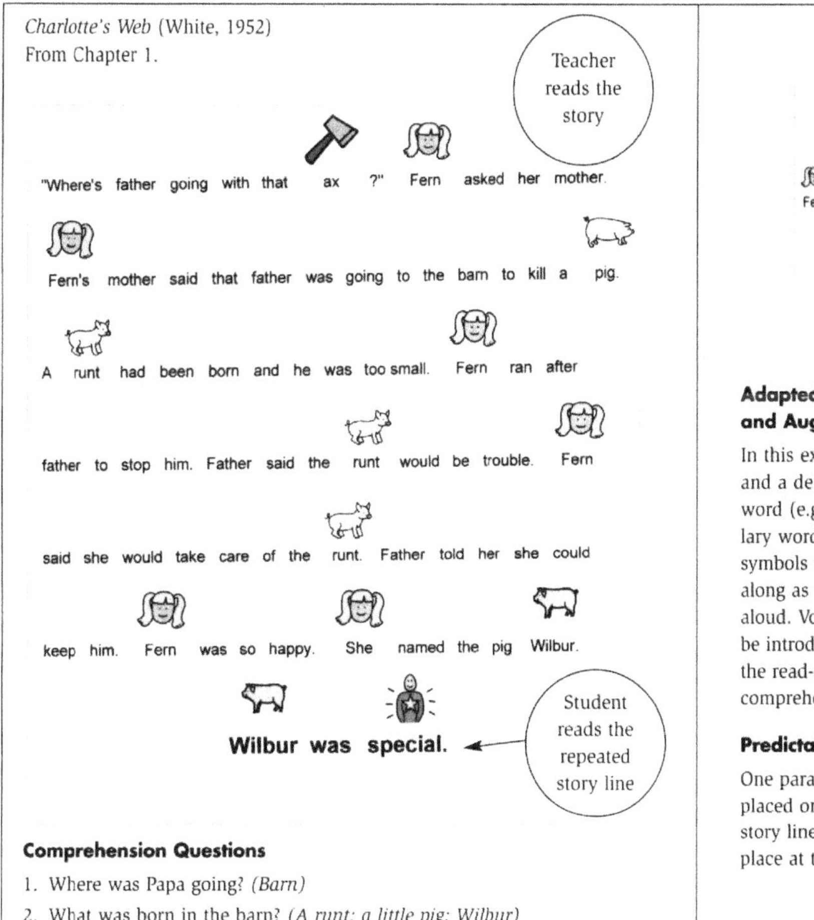

Charlotte's Web (White, 1952)
From Chapter 1.
Teacher reads the story
"Where's father going with that ax ?" Fern asked her mother.
Fern's mother said that father was going to the barn to kill a pig.
A runt had been born and he was too small. Fern ran after
father to stop him. Father said the runt would be trouble. Fern
said she would take care of the runt. Father told her she could
keep him. Fern was so happy. She named the pig Wilbur.
Wilbur was special.
Student reads the repeated story line

Comprehension Questions

1. Where was Papa going? *(Barn)*
2. What was born in the barn? *(A runt; a little pig; Wilbur)*
3. Why was Fern happy? *(Got to keep the pig; pig lived; papa didn't kill the pig)*
4. Why was Papa going to kill the pig? *(It was small; it was trouble)*
5. How did Fern feel about saving the pig? *(Happy)*

Chapter 1

Vocabulary

Fern special ax Wilbur runt

Adapted Text and Augmentations

In this example, text is summarized and a definition for an unfamiliar word (e.g., *runt*) is added. Vocabulary words are paired with picture symbols to help students follow along as the teacher reads the story aloud. Vocabulary words can also be introduced at the beginning of the read-aloud to help build comprehension.

Predictable structure

One paragraph of adapted text is placed on a page and a repeated story line is added in a predictable place at the end of the page.

Figure 9.6 Grades 2 to 3 example (narrative).

Tuck Everlasting (Babbitt, 1975)
From Chapter 12

Page 1 - It is getting dark. A toad croaks. Tuck and Winnie slide the rowboat into the water. Tuck stops in the middle of the lake.

Tuck says that life is all around them. Life is always moving and changing like the water. Water comes in one side of the lake. It goes out the other. It does not stop until it gets to the ocean.

Winnie has a secret.

Page 2 - The sun dries up the water. Clouds carry the water back. Rain falls from the clouds into the stream. The stream takes the water back to the lake. It is like a big wheel.

Everything changes - toads, bugs, fish, and people. They grow and change. That is the way it is.

Winnie has a secret.

Comprehension Questions

1. When does the story happen? *(Dusk or night)* How do you know? *(It is getting dark)*
2. Where do Winnie and Tuck go? *(Into the rowboat; on the lake)*
3. What is all around them? *(Life; water)*
4. Why is it important that things change? *(Without change, things die; get stuck)*
5. What happens after rain falls from clouds? *(A stream carries the water back to the lake)*

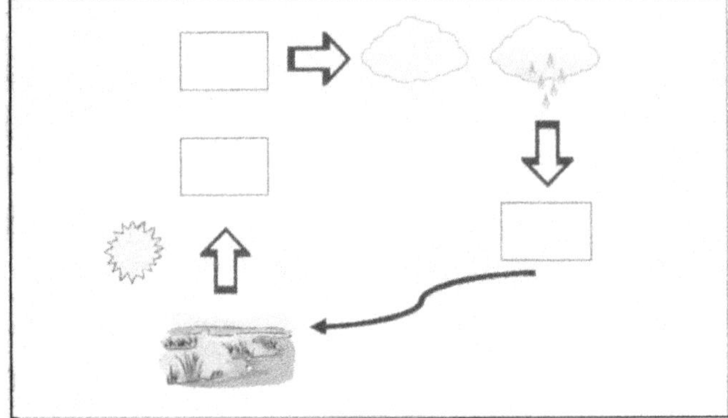

Adapted Text and Augmentations

The original text is summarized at a 280 Lexile level for independent reading. A repeated story line at the bottom of the page emphasizes the main idea of the chapter. Key words can be paired with picture symbols or the text can be read aloud as needed.

Predictable Structure

Two paragraphs appear on each page and a repeated story line is placed at the bottom of the page.

Graphic Organizer

A graphic organizer can help both beginning readers and nonreaders organize information from the story. Pictures or words paired with picture symbols can be used to complete the graphic organizer when students do not write independently. The author's use of the water cycle to describe change is a good opportunity to incorporate a water cycle graphic organizer from science to illustrate the idea.

Figure 9.7 Grades 4 to 5 example (narrative).

PROVIDE OPTIONS FOR STUDENTS TO DEMONSTRATE COMPREHENSION

Response options can be individualized to meet the student's understanding of symbols. For example, response options for students just beginning to understand symbols may be objects from the story. For students who have some understanding of symbols, response options may be pictures of objects or picture symbols paired with words. For students who have a good understanding of symbols, response options may be printed words. For students with intellectual disability who use some form of augmentative communication system, teachers may want to develop response options for these students that can be used with their augmentative and alternative communication (AAC) devices (e.g., Co-Talk 9).

The number of response options presented to students can be individualized, too. For students who are just beginning to answer comprehension questions, perhaps first provide two response options for the student to select from—one correct option and one not plausible—and build from there. As students gain skills in answering comprehension questions, add more response options. In addition to increasing the number of response options for students to select from, another way to increase complexity is to include response options that are plausible but not correct. For example, if teaching *The Watsons Go to Birmingham—1963* (Curtis, 1995), two response options for the question "What did Byron kiss?" are *the mirror* and *his mother.* Both are plausible and could be correct, but only one is correct according to the text (i.e., mirror). This example also highlights the importance of creating comprehension questions that are textually dependent. Text-dependent questions require the student to read or hear the text read to be able to select the correct response.

> *Another way to increase complexity is to include response options that are plausible but not correct.*

Before creating response options, consider the types of comprehension questions to be asked. Questions might focus on specific standards in the Common Core State Standards (http://www.corestandards.org); students may identify story elements, use supporting details in answering questions, or identify theme or author's purpose.

A question template can be useful for generating comprehension questions:

- Who [verbed] the noun?
- Where do/did [main character] [verb]?

- When do/did [event] take place?
- What did [character] [verb]?
- Why did [action from the story]?

USE A PROMPT HIERARCHY TO TEACH COMPREHENSION

SYSTEM OF LEAST PROMPTS

The system of least prompts is a response-prompting procedure commonly used to teach students with disabilities (see Wolery, Ault, & Doyle, 1991). Rather than relying on a single prompt, the system uses a hierarchy of prompts that differ in the amount of support or information provided to the learner and gives the interventionist the opportunity to use each prompt of the hierarchy during each instructional trial. Typically the system of least prompts has been used to provide increasing levels of assistance for a student to make a motor response (e.g., completing the steps for making a sandwich, selecting the correct response card from an array); however, it is also useful for teaching comprehension during read-alouds. Prompts can include opportunities to hear selected text again (Mims et al., 2009) and rules for answering *wh-* word questions (Mims et al., 2012).

THINK-ALOUDS

Think-alouds can be used in the system of least prompts to help students answer inferential questions. In a study using read-alouds of adapted science chapters, Hudson et al. (in press) included think-alouds as the prompt hierarchy. Students were first asked to relate to their personal experience (e.g., "How do you feel when [event] happens to you?"), then, when more help was needed, a model of the inference was provided (e.g., "I feel_____ when that happens to me.").

Harcourt Horizons North Carolina
(Henson & Berson, 2003)
"From a Colony to a State" (Chapter 3)

Page 1 - Important battles were fought in North Carolina. One was the battle at Moores Creek Bridge. The battle was between the Patriots and the British. (Who fought at Moores Creek Bridge? *Patriots and British*)

Page 2 - The Patriots were smart. Before the battle, they took some wooden boards out of the bridge. Then they greased it with soap and animal fat. When the British crossed the bridge, they fell into the water. (Why did soldiers fall off the bridge? *The bridge was slippery*)

Page 3 - After the war, they built a new capital. They named the new capital Raleigh for Sir Walter Raleigh. Sir Walter Raleigh was the founder of the first colony on Roanoke Island. (Where was the new capital built? *Raleigh*)

Page 4 - North Carolina grew slowly. Farmers only grew the crops they needed to live. Few farmers raised crops to sell for cash. Selling crops was dangerous and expensive because the roads were bad. (What happened after the war? *North Carolina grew slowly*)

Page 5 - Two things helped North Carolina grow. One was new roads. The state built plank roads out of wood because wood was cheap. To travel on the roads, people had to pay money, called a toll. (What kind of roads were built? *plank, toll*)

Page 6 - The railroad also helped North Carolina grow. The railroad connected the towns of Charlotte, Salisbury, and Greensboro with Raleigh and Goldsboro. The railroad made traveling easier. Many people moved to these towns. The towns grew into big cities. (Why was the railroad important? *Made traveling easier; helped cities grow*)

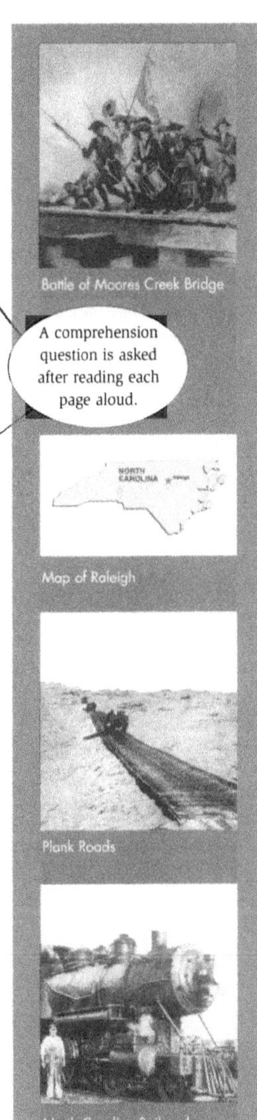

A comprehension question is asked after reading each page aloud.

Battle of Moores Creek Bridge

Map of Raleigh

Plank Roads

North Carolina Railroad

Adaptations and Augmentations

This chapter from a Grade 4 social studies text is shortened to 196 words and rewritten at a 550 Lexile level. Captions added to pictures, illustrations, and maps support comprehension of text.

Graphic Organizers

Graphic organizers can help students organize information from the text. Students can fill in the information during reading or after reading.

Who	
When	
Where	
What	
Why	
How	

Figure 9.8 Grade 4 example (nonfiction text).

The Watsons Go to Birmingham - 1963 (Curtis, 1995)
Chapter 1 - And You Wonder Why They Call Us the Weird Watsons

This story is about Kenny and his family. He has an older brother named Byron and a younger sister named Joetta. They call her Joey for short. Kenny and his family live in Michigan with their momma and Dad. People call them the weird Watsons because strange things happen to them.

It is winter in Michigan. Your spit freezes before it hits the ground. Momma did not like the cold. She grew up in Alabama. It is warm in Alabama, even in the winter.

Inferential Questions

Teachers may use think-alouds to help students take the information they already know and the information found in the text to infer a correct response. For example, to help students answer the question *Why does spit freeze?*, students think about what they know about why things freeze (i.e., *water freezes because it is cold*) and about winter in Michigan (e.g., *it is cold in Michigan in the winter*). Spit is a liquid like water so it freezes *because it is cold*.

Adapted Text and Augmentations

The original text is summarized and definitions and explanations for unfamiliar words are added. Text summaries are written at a 500-600 Lexile level. Each chapter is six pages long. The original text is shortened from 210 pages to 90 pages.

Predictable Structure

The structure of the original book is maintained (e.g., chapters) as well as the original chapter titles. Two paragraphs appear on each page. One picture appears at the beginning of each chapter that illustrates the theme of the chapter.

***Wh-* Word Question Rules**

Teaching rules for answering *wh-* word questions (e.g., When you hear *who*, listen for a person's *name*) can improve comprehension of text.

Figure 9.9 Grade 5 example (literature).

Pictures, illustrations, and captions in the text also can be used to answer inferential questions. For example, after reading the adapted text from *The Grapes of Wrath* (Steinbeck, 1939; Figure 9.10), perhaps ask a question about why the boys are dirty. The answer is not directly stated in the text; however, the picture at the beginning of the chapter provides students important information. Teachers could ask students what they see in the picture (e.g., boys working in the field) and how this information might help explain why the boys were dirty (e.g., you get dirty working in the field; the boys have no place to get clean clothes or wash). Figures 9.9 and 9.10 present examples of think-alouds to assist students in answering inferential questions; also see box, "Adapting Text for Jacob and Carol."

The Grapes of Wrath (Steinbeck, 1939)

The picture provides students information helpful for answering the inferential question *Why are the boys dirty?*

The man stood at the door. "Can we buy some bread?"

Mae said, "We sell sandwiches, not bread."

The man said, "We are hungry and only have money for bread."

Al yelled, "Give them the bread."

Mae did not want to but she opened the door.

The man and two boys came in. The boys looked alike. They were dirty. Their clothes were thin.

Mae got a loaf of bread. "This is 15 cents."

"Can you cut off 10-cents' worth?" said the man. "We have to make our money last to California."

Al yelled again, "Give them the bread."

Mae gave the bread to the man.

The man saw the boys staring at the peppermint candy. "Is them penny candy?" he asked.

Mae said, "No. Them's two for a penny."

The man laid the money on the counter. Mae gave each boy a candy stick.

Comprehension Questions

1. What did the man want to buy? *(Bread)*
2. Why was this a problem for Mae? *(She sold sandwiches; they might run out of bread)*
3. Why did the man only want to buy 10 cents worth of bread? *(They were poor)*
4. What were the boys looking at? *(Peppermint candy)*
5. Why did the man buy the candy? *(Loved the boys; to surprise them; to make them happy)*
6. Why are the boys dirty? *(Worked in the field; traveling; no place to wash)*

Adapted Text and Augmentations

The original text is summarized at a 290 Lexile level for independent readers. The text summary maintains some of the dialogue and dialect of the original because they are important literary elements for the story.

Predictable Structure

One picture is placed at the beginning of the text summary and is used to answer an inferential comprehension question (see Question 6).

Graphic Organizers

Character motives are important in this passage. A graphic organizer can help students organize information about each character (e.g., name, problems/challenges, motivation) as they read or hear the text. They can use the graphic organizer to identify the motives behind characters' actions.

The Grapes of Wrath Character Graphic Organizer

1. Name of each character
2. Description of the character (physical appearance)
3. Character's role
4. Character's problems/challenges
5. Strengths/weaknesses
6. Motivation

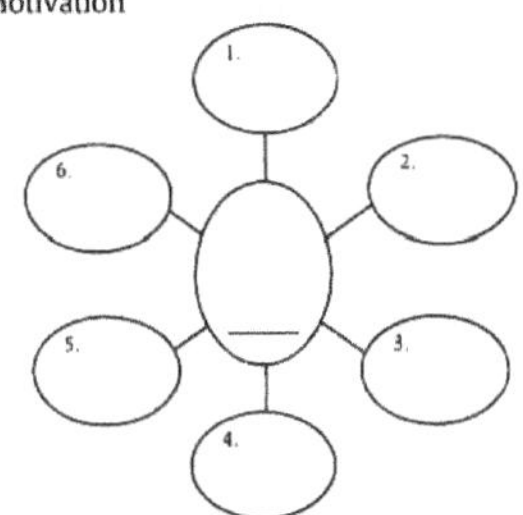

Figure 9.10 High school example (literature).

ADAPTING TEXT FOR JACOB AND CAROL

Mr. Bryce, a fifth-grade general education teacher, is planning to teach the novel *The Watsons Go to Birmingham—1963* (Curtis, 1995). Mrs. Leigh, the special education teacher, noted that the book was 15 chapters long, written at a 5.5 grade reading level, and had a 1000 Lexile level. One of her students, Jacob, was a nonreader but could participate in read-alouds for about 10 minutes; for him, she created chapter summaries that were an average of 240 words long and between 500L and 600L (see Figure 5). She used a question template to create comprehension questions for each chapter. To support Jacob's receptive responding, she created response option cards pairing words or phrases with a picture symbol. She decided to give him three response cards to select from when answering comprehension questions. In the array, one response would be correct, one plausible but incorrect, and one not plausible. She also implemented the system of least intrusive prompts: (a) stating a rule for answering *wh-* word questions (e.g., When you hear *who*, listen for a person) and reading the text again, (b) reading the sentence with the correct answer again, (c) telling the correct answer, and (d) telling and showing the correct answer. After the first week, she planned to teach a peer in Jacob's fifth-grade class to do the read-aloud and follow the prompts to help him answer the comprehension questions.

Another student of Mrs. Leigh's, Carol, had severe intellectual disability and was legally blind. Carol could participate in a 5-minute read-aloud if given objects as referents. For Carol, Mrs. Leigh split the adapted chapters in half and added everyday objects that went with the story and could be used to answer comprehension questions about the story. For example, when reading aloud about Kenny's brother Byron getting his lips stuck on the car mirror when he kissed it, a mirror was the object. When asking Carol what Byron kissed, she would give Carol two objects to select from: the mirror and a glove (a distractor object). She also planned to use least intrusive prompts for Carol, and when reading the text again, she would help Carol read with her by touching the objects being used as referents for the story.

FINAL THOUGHTS

Students with moderate and severe intellectual disability who are early readers or nonreaders need to have access to grade-level text. When necessary, text augmentations (e.g., adding a repeated story line for the main idea) and adaptations (e.g., text summaries) can help students gain meaning from the text they read independently or hear read aloud. The examples provided here are intended to assist teachers in applying current research through a practical approach. Adapting grade-level text, creating response options to match the text, and using the system of least prompts to teach comprehension of text during read-alouds can support students with intellectual disability in learning to read and comprehending text.

REFERENCES

Babbitt, N. (1975). *Tuck everlasting.* New York, NY: Farrar, Straus and Giroux.

Browder, D. M., Trela, K., & Jimenez, B. (2007). "Training teachers to follow a task analysis to engage middle school students with moderate and severe developmental disabilities in grade-appropriate literature. *Focus on Autism and Other Developmental Disabilities, 22,* 206–219. http://dx.doi.org/10.1177/10883576070220040301

Curtis, C. P. (1995). *The Watsons go to Birmingham—1963.* New York, NY: Bantam Doubleday Dell.

Erickson, K. A., & Koppenhaver, D. A. (1995). Developing a literacy program for children with severe disabilities. *The Reading Teacher, 48,* 676–685.

Henson, T. S., & Berson, M. J. (Ed.). (2003). *Harcourt horizons North Carolina 2003.* Orlando, FL: Harcourt School.

Hudson, M. E., Browder, D. M., & Jimenez, B. (in press). Effects of a peer-delivered system of least prompts with adapted text read-alouds on listening comprehension for students with moderate intellectual disability. *Education and Training in Autism and Developmental Disabilities.*

Hudson, M. E., & Test, D. W. (2011). Evaluating the evidence base for using shared story reading to promote literacy for students with extensive support needs. *Research and Practice for Persons with Severe Disabilities, 36,* 34–45. http://dx.doi.org/10.2511/rpsd.36.l-2.34

L'Engle, M. (1962). *A wrinkle in time.* New York, NY: Farrar, Straus and Giroux.

Lobel, A. (1975). *Owl at home.* New York, NY: HarperCollins.

Mims, P., Browder, D., Baker, J., Lee, A., & Spooner, F. (2009). Increasing comprehension of students with significant intellectual disabilities and visual impairments during shared stories. *Education and Treatment in Developmental Disabilities, 44,* 409–420. http://dx.doi.org/10.1177/1088357612446859

Mims, P. J., Hudson, M. E., & Browder, D. M. (2012). Using read-alouds of grade-level biographies and systematic prompting to promote comprehension for students with moderate and severe developmental disabilities. *Focus on Autism and Other Developmental Disabilities, 27,* 65–78.

Steinbeck, J. (1939). *The grapes of wrath.* New York, NY: Viking.

White, E. B. (1952). *Charlotte's web.* New York, NY: HarperCollins.

Wolery, M., Ault, M. J., & Doyle, P. M. (1992). *Teaching students with moderate and severe disabilities: Use of response prompting strategies.* White Plains, NY: Longman.

Melissa E. Hudson *(District of Columbia CEC), Alternate Assessment Specialist, American Institutes for Research, Washington, DC.* **Diane Browder** *(North Carolina CEC), Professor of Special Education; and* **Shawnee Wakeman** *(North Carolina CEC), Clinical Assistant Professor of Special Education, University of North Carolina at Charlotte.*

Address correspondence concerning this article to Melissa Hudson, Office 5280, American Institutes for Research, 1000 Thomas Jefferson Street, NW, Washington, DC 20007 (e-mail: mhudson@air.org*).*

TEACHING Exceptional Children, *Vol. 45, No. 3, pp. 14–23.*

POST-READING ACTIVITIES

1. List at least five ways to adapt text for students with intellectual disabilities or struggling readers.
2. What is the system of least prompts?
3. Reflect on how you could implement the strategies with your own students.

CHAPTER 10

GIFTED AND ADVANCED LEARNERS

INTRODUCTION

According to the US Department of Education, the definition for gifted or talented students is described as "children and youth with outstanding talent who perform or show the potential for performing at remarkably high levels of accomplishment when compared with others of their age, experience, or environment" (US Department of Education 1993). This section includes two articles that explore the past and present of gifted and advanced learners.

The first article, "Research on Giftedness and Gifted Education: Status of the Field and Considerations for the Future" (Plucker and Callahan 2014), includes the foundational underpinnings of the history of gifted education, dating back to the early 1900s. The authors then look at the current condition of education for advanced learners. They present an analysis of the empirical strengths and weaknesses associated with existing research. They also focus on advances in current theories and provide suggestions for improving the quality of gifted education.

The second article is "The Common Core State Standards: Where Do Gifted and Advanced Learners Fit?" (Johnsen 2013). After providing a brief but thorough overview of the

Common Core State Standards (CCSS), the author provides suggestions for educators and parents to ensure that the needs of this exceptional population are being appropriately met. She also includes a series of "mostly true" and mostly false" statements (also included in the pre-reading and post-reading activities) regarding the education of advanced learners.

These articles were specifically chosen to provide preservice and new teachers with a comprehensive overview of advanced education. The readings are seamlessly linked, with the first article examining the history of gifted instruction and the second article examining current practice. The chosen articles will benefit readers because they focus on gifted and advanced learners, a population they will likely work with in the future.

REFERENCE

US Department of Education. (1993). *National Excellence: A Case for Developing America's Talent*. Washington, DC: Office of Educational Research and Improvement.

CHAPTER 10

READING 10.1 OVERVIEW

The authors of this article provide a clear description of the history of gifted education. Included in the description is a presentation of conflicting research. This allows the reader to consider opposing opinions and reflect on the implications for their own students. In this special feature article, advances in theory and current research are shared. Proposals for additional research and suggestions for improving the quality of gifted education are provided.

PRE-READING ACTIVITIES

1. What is your current understanding of the term *giftedness*?
2. Do you think giftedness can be attributed to nature, nurture, or a combination of both? Explain your thinking.
3. Do you think there is ethnic disparity and socioeconomic disproportionality among the population of identified gifted students? Explain your thinking.

RESEARCH ON GIFTEDNESS AND GIFTED EDUCATION

STATUS OF THE FIELD AND CONSIDERATIONS FOR THE FUTURE

READING 10.1

BY JONATHAN A. PLUCKER, AND CAROLYN M. CALLAHAN

ABSTRACT: *Gifted education has a rich history and a solid if uneven research base. As policy makers and educators increasingly turn their attention to advanced students and educational excellence, the time is ripe for a dispassionate analysis of the field's conceptual and empirical strengths and weaknesses. The purpose of this special feature article is to highlight advances in theories and research related to giftedness and gifted education, note the promising areas for additional research, and propose next steps for improving the quality and utility of empirical work in this important area.*

The field of gifted education has a long history in the United States, dating back over 100 years to the establishment of schools for bright students, but education for a society's most intellectually talented students has existed,

Jonathan A. Pluker and Carolyn M. Callahan, "Research on Giftedness and Gifted Education: Status of the Field and Considerations for the Future," *Exceptional Children*, vol. 80, no. 4, pp. 390-406.

in various forms, for hundreds if not thousands of years (Missett & McCormick, 2014; Tannenbaum, 1958). The scientific study of giftedness has a more limited history, with Galton's (1869) *Hereditary Genius*, often credited as the first scientific study of high ability and achievement. Other early, seminal efforts included Hollingworths (1926) studies of high IQ students in New York City and Terman's (1926) longitudinal study of high IQ students in California.

Funding for research on giftedness has ebbed and flowed over the decades. The federal government has funded significant work in this area, most notably during the Cold War in the 1960s and through support of the Javits Gifted and Talented Students Education Act, which included funding for a National Research Center on the Gifted and Talented (NRC/GT) beginning in the early 1990s. Research programs on gifted education developed at several major research universities around the country, and the field is presently represented by long-standing journals and professional organizations devoted to research and advocacy for gifted students and their education. The purpose of this article is to critically review the state of theory and research in the field, identify and prioritize areas in need of further empirical development, and share thoughts about the future of gifted education research.

The purpose of this article is to critically review the state of theory and research in the field, identify and prioritize areas in need of further empirical development, and share thoughts about the future of gifted education research

CURRENT STATUS OF THEORY

Conceptions of giftedness mirror theoretical progress with related constructs, such as intelligence and creativity (Plucker & Esping, 2014). For example, many early intelligence theories, whether unitary (Cattell, 1987; Spearman, 1904) or more multifaceted (Guilford, 1967; Thurstone, 1938), emphasized the importance of the individual as the unit of interest and were largely psychometrically derived. Creativity theories from that era had similar characteristics (e.g., Guilford, 1950; MacKinnon, 1965). Early approaches to giftedness followed a similar trajectory, focusing largely on psychometric, unitary conceptions, such as that of Terman (1926) and Hollingworth (1942). Many successful programs for gifted youth, such as the Talent Search programs, were initially based by Julian Stanley and his colleagues on these psychometric conceptions (Olszewski-Kubilius & Thomson, 2014; Stanley, 1973).

During the 1970s, just as theories of intelligence and creativity began to emphasize multidimensional constructs and the role of environmental influences, definitions and theories of giftedness began to change. One of the most significant developments was the first definition offered by the federal government that proposed that giftedness was manifested in six distinct areas—general intellectual ability, specific academic aptitude, creative or productive thinking, leadership ability, visual and performing arts, and psychomotor ability (Marland, 1971)—and was directly related to a need for specialized programming in schools. Callahan et al. (1995) found that nearly 50% of surveyed school districts based their gifted education identification procedures on this definition, making it the most popular definition at the time. However, that definition still focused largely on the capacity of the individual student and devoted little attention to potential environmental influences.

Soon after the federal definition appeared, broadened theories of giftedness emerged. A hallmark of these conceptions was that intelligence, largely synonymous with giftedness in earlier theories, was seen as a necessary but not sufficient condition for high achievement. For example, Renzullis (1978) three-ring conception of giftedness, perhaps the most well-known model in the field, focuses on the interaction among above average ability, creativity, and task commitment. Renzulli and his colleagues have conducted a number of studies of the validity of the three-ring conception (e.g., Delisle & Renzulli, 1982; Gubbins, 1982; Renzulli, 1984, 1988), including studies of the effectiveness of interventions based on the model. Although Renzulli s approach is not without its critics (e.g., Johnsen, 1999; Olsze-wski-Kubilius, 1999), the model is often portrayed in its original form, when in actuality Renzulli and colleagues have continually refined and improved the model (see Renzulli, 2005; Renzulli & D'Souza, 2014; Renzulli & Sytsma, 2008). Perhaps the major contribution of the three-ring conception of giftedness is that it was among the first efforts to make creative productivity a goal of gifted education.

Concurrent with Renzulli s strong influence on the field of gifted education, Gardner (1983) published the Theory of Multiple Intelligences (MI Theory), and Sternberg's (1988, 1996) Triarchic Theory of Successful Intelligence emerged. Like Renzullis three-ring conception, MI Theory and Triarchic Theory appealed to educators who wished to expand notions about how students are considered to be gifted and talented. Despite MI Theory's popularity, empirical support has been mixed (Castejon, Perez, & Gilar, 2010; Jensen, 1998; Visser, Ashton, & Vernon, 2006), and assessment has been difficult, limiting its impact on gifted education (e.g., see Gardner, 1995; Plucker, 2000; Plucker, Callahan, & Tomchin, 1996; Pyryt, 2000). Research on the Triarchic Theory has provided more empirical support in the areas of assessment and effective educational interventions (Sternberg, 2011; Sternberg, Castejón, Prieto, Hautamäki, & Grigorenko, 2001). Renzulli, Gardner, and Sternbergs work clearly broadened educators' conceptions of what talent and giftedness can be and where it can be found. Furthermore, all three theoretical approaches also emphasize the role of sociocultural context in defining, identifying, and fostering giftedness.

Another theoretical milestone was Gagnés (1995, 2000) development of the Differentiated Model of Giftedness and Talent (DMGT). In the DMGT, *gifts* are defined as innate abilities in at least one domain area (i.e., intellectual, creative, socioaffective, sensorimotor) that place the individual in the top 10% of age peers. Talent is the demonstrated mastery of the gift as evidenced by skills in academics, arts, business, leisure, social action, sports, or technology that place the individual in the top 10% of age peers. By proposing the gifts-talents distinction, Gagné differentiates between potential and real-world outcomes, with underachievement occurring when gifts do not translate into talents. Perhaps not coincidentally, some state definitions now differentiate between potential and actual achievement. Gagné also recognized intrapersonal and environmental catalysts, which can either support or hinder the development of talent. The acknowledgment of variables that can both hurt and help foster talents is a unique theoretical addition that mirrors earlier work by Tannenbaum (1983) and later changes to the three-ring conception (i.e., Operation Hound-stooth; Renzulli, 2002, 2012).

Around the turn of the 21st century, a wave of new philosophical perspectives began to influence views of learning and talent. Many educators had grown weary of conceptualizations that described constructs, including giftedness, as being either largely cognitive or environmental. Barab and Plucker (2002) reviewed theory and research within five such perspectives (i.e., ecological psychology, situated cognition, distributed cognition, activity theory, legitimate peripheral participation) and concluded that "the separation of mind and context at the heart of traditional conceptions of talent development polarizes learner and context, either implicitly or explicitly stating that, in the case of talent and giftedness, the individual impacts or influences the environment" (Plucker & Barab, 2005, p. 204; see Corno et al., 2002; Snow, 1992, for related analyses).

Around, the turn of the 21st century, a wave of new philosophical perspectives began to influence views of learning and talent. Many educators had grown weary of conceptualizations that described constructs, including giftedness; as being either largely cognitive or environmental.

Barab and Plucker (2002) proposed an integrated model of giftedness in which talents, broadly defined, are developed through the interaction of the individual, environment, and sociocultural content. From their perspective, talent development is an ever-spiraling process, as continued interactions build on themselves over time and lead to greater opportunities to develop talent—and greater success as a result. The primary implications are that solving real-world problems, within realistic contexts and with considerable support, should be the focus of talent development programs, and that unless advanced learners have their talents fostered and remain challenged in K-12 schools, they will never develop their full potential as creative, real-world problem solvers. The situated view is more popular outside of the field than within, which is not surprising given that many gifted education programs continue to use an "identify the bright student" intervention model, against which the situated approach explicitly argues.

The latest major theoretical development is the model proposed by Subotnik, Olszewski-Kubilius, and Worrell (2011, 2012; Worrell, Olszewski-Kubilius, & Subotnik, 2012), who define giftedness as:

> performance that is clearly at the upper end of the distribution in a specific talent domain even relative to other high-functioning individuals in that domain. Further, giftedness can be viewed as developmental in that in the beginning stages, potential is the key variable; in later stages, achievement is the measure of giftedness; and in fully developed talents, eminence is the basis on which this label is granted. (Subotnik et al., 2012, p. 176)

This approach deals with the potential versus outcomes issue differently than other theories, and it explicitly states how the construct changes as people develop. Subotnik et al. also emphasize that giftedness results from a combination of cognitive and psychosocial variables, keeping with the theme of broad-based influences on giftedness that we see across many recent conceptions. Furthermore, they endorse views that intelligence is malleable and that beliefs about intelligence matter (Dweck, 1998). The practical implications of their model run parallel to their definition:

> Although we recognize that the generation of creative performances or ideas requires person, process, and product, it is also the case that the relative emphasis on these factors shifts over time. For example, it is important that young children develop a creative approach and attitude (person), that older children acquire skills (process), and that the acquisition of these mindsets and process skills are then coupled with deep multidisciplinary content knowledge and are applied to the creation of intellectual, aesthetic, or practical products or performances (product). (Subotnik et al., 2011, p. 33)

This approach to interventions extends the situated view of Barab and Plucker (2002) by noting that the relative contributions of the parts of the person–environment–sociocultural interaction may vary over time and across different contexts. Collectively, the past several decades of theory, including the highly cited efforts in recent years, provide evidence that thinking about the nature and development of giftedness and talent continues to develop.

CURRENT STATUS OF RESEARCH

The literature in gifted education, as in most fields, involves theory and model generative essays, research studies, and applied/advice pieces. Within the research category, the bulk of the research in gifted education has been descriptive and correlational (Dai, Swanson, & Cheng, 2011; VanTassel-Baska, 2006). Unfortunately, whether because of the dearth of funding that would support experimental research or the difficulty in implementation of randomized, controlled studies in a field with small sample sizes, the lack of causal research leaves the field with considerable ambiguity about effective practices. A further confounding factor in interpreting even the descriptive and correlational research is the widely varying definitions of giftedness applied in research studies and the accompanying diversity in identification of subjects across studies. The small number of intervention studies in combination with inconsistency and lack of specificity when defining giftedness has made much statistical modeling difficult within gifted education.

Regardless of these methodological limitations—and perhaps as a result of them—research on giftedness and gifted education has some well-understood aspects and well-supported interventions, other areas where advocacy tends to outstrip efficacy evidence, and yet other aspects common in the field but unsupported by research or in need of a great deal more investigation. In the following sections, we review the state of research in the field.

AREAS WHERE RESULTS CAN GUIDE POLICY AND PRACTICE

As noted above, the field does not have a large number of areas that have been comprehensively studied, but a few topics have been studied extensively, and the results can guide policy and practice related to gifted students. For example, a major concern of advocates is that the regular classroom environment, in the absence of interventions for advanced students, provides little challenge for students who already mastered the content and skill or can learn the material at an above-average pace. Prior to funding of the NRC/GT in 1991, many advocates were concerned that a of lack attention to curricular and instructional differentiation provided insufficient challenge for gifted students in general education classrooms. The first research studies produced by the NRC/GT (Archambault et al., 1993; Moon, Callahan, Tomlinson, & Miller, 2002; Westberg, Archambault, Dobyns, & Salvin, 1993; Westberg & Daoust, 2004) provided evidence across subject areas in elementary and middle schools that these concerns were warranted.

A later study by Brighton, Hertberg, Moon, Tomlinson, and Callahan (2005) extended this research and found that when teachers do differentiate their focus is on students who are struggling to learn, holding to a belief that gifted students do not need differentiation. Reis et al. (2004) further documented the dearth of opportunities for advanced readers (those reading above grade level) to be challenged by the school curriculum. Policies based on the assumption that differentiation in the general education classroom meets gifted students' academic needs are likely to create situations in which modifications in curriculum and instruction for the gifted learner are absent. Yet differentiation within the regular classroom is one of the most common forms of programming for advanced students (National Association for Gifted Children, 2011).

Another area with a rich research base is acceleration. Schools around the world tend to be age-based, with students of similar ages progressing through their education at a fixed pace (see Mullis et al., 2011). This is based on the assumption that individuals of a similar age have had roughly equivalent opportunities to learn and educational experiences, thereby leaving them with similar content yet to be mastered. Because this assumption is tenuous at best, a range of academic acceleration strategies have been developed to address the atypical intellectual development often seen in bright students. These strategies are often placed into two categories: subject-or content-based acceleration and grade-based acceleration. In subject-based acceleration such as studying one discipline with students in a more advanced grade, curriculum compacting, allowing students to take a single college course or distance learning course, and participation in Talent Search programs, students remain with same-aged peers for other instruction. Grade-based acceleration strategies, in which students do not remain with same-aged peers, include early entrance (to kindergarten or college), grade skipping, multi-age classrooms, and early graduation from high school and college. Authors of meta-analyses (Kulik, 2004; Rogers, 2010; Steenbergen-Hu & Moon, 2011) and traditional reviews (e.g., Colangelo, Assouline, & Gross, 2004; Lubinski, 2004) reach largely positive conclusions about the academic efficacy of almost all forms of acceleration. For example, Kulik's meta-analysis estimated an average effect of nearly a year's additional academic growth for accelerated students, an effect that, as Assouline, Marron, and Colangelo (2014) noted, compares very favorably to the effects of the most effective and popular school reform models. The research also provides evidence of social and emotional benefits for most forms of acceleration (Assouline et al., 2014; Colangelo et al., 2004), although others note that these effects can be less pronounced (Steenbergen-Hu & Moon, 2011).

Ironically, the one type of acceleration with mixed evidence of effectiveness includes the very popular Advanced Placement and International Baccalaureate programs, whose widespread use is probably due to the fact that they fit conveniently into the grade-level structure of most high schools and do not require significant organizational accommodations. Research on the benefits of such programs provides evidence that enthusiasm for the exclusiveness of this option may not be warranted, both in general (Plucker, Chien, & Zaman, 2006; Sadler, 2010) and for gifted students (Foust, Hertberg-Davis, & Callahan, 2008; Hertberg-Davis & Callahan, 2008, 2014; Kyburg, Hertberg-Davis, & Callahan, 2007). Policy based on the evidence of effectiveness of some acceleration practices and the issues that surround other practices (i.e., Advanced Placement) would provide a more appropriate range of options for gifted learners as well as comply with recommendations that gifted students be provided services that can be matched to their learning needs.

Ironically, the one type of acceleration with mixed evidence of effectiveness includes the very popular Advanced Placement and International Baccalaureate programs, whose widespread use is probably due to the fact that they fit conveniently into the grade-level structure of most high schools and do not require significant organizational accommodations.

A third area with a significant depth of research is curriculum design. Gifted education is rife with advice for developing curriculum and instructional interventions to be used with gifted students. These models can be characterized as descriptive framework for implementation of curriculum (in which teachers use a model as a guide in developing daily lessons) or as prescriptive (in which teachers follow a predeveloped unit based on a framework or model's guiding principles). Descriptive curriculum authors may provide examples based on their model, but predeveloped units are not a part of a descriptive framework; prescriptive curriculum always provides predeveloped units for instruction.

Studies of descriptive curricular model implementation with gifted students provide limited evidence of effectiveness. Although researchers have described student growth during curricular implementation (e.g., Reis & Boeve, 2009), studies of descriptive curriculum efficacy using randomized control designs or even quasi-experimental studies are rare. One experimental study did not support the effectiveness of a model of differentiated instruction in bringing about deep change in teacher behavior or instruction or differences in student achievement (Brighton et al., 2005). In contrast, data from several quasi-experimental studies support the use of prescriptive units (Feng, VanTassel-Baska, Quek, Bai, & O'Neil, 2004; Gavin, Casa, Adelson, Carroll, & Sheffield, 2009; Tieso, 2005). The relative effectiveness of prescriptive curriculum (teachers teaching according to specific unit frameworks with lesson plans and resources specified) has been supported in randomized control studies of the implementation of language arts units based on the Challenge Leading to Engagement, Achievement and Results (CLEAR) Curriculum framework (Callahan, Azano, Oh, & Hailey, 2012), units based on the Triarchic Theory of Intelligence (Sternberg, Grigorenko, & Zhang, 2008), and mathematics units (Gavin et al., 2009). Overall, the empirical support for prescriptive unit success (units often based on the descriptive frameworks) far outweighs the support for the implementation of a descriptive framework, suggesting that programs based on prescriptive models of curriculum and instruction are more likely to produce improvements in student growth. These examples show that researchers within the field have made tremendous strides in determining the types of programming that can aid educators in planning effective interventions for advanced students.

AREAS WHERE SOLID EMPIRICAL FOUNDATIONS ARE EVOLVING

The knowledge base in several important areas is increasing, with significant developments in research regarding areas such as identification, talent development, and creativity. The deepening of the empirical foundation in these areas is also leading to better designed interventions that hold promise for advancing the field.

Perhaps the most discussed and most controversial area of concern within the field is the process of screening and identification of gifted students, in large part because traditional approaches are widely perceived to be highly biased in favor of students from some demographic groups and against those in other groups. Numerous recommendations for improving identification practice abound (see Callahan, Renzulli, Delcourt, & Hertberg-Davis, 2013), and current publications and policy development have focused a great deal of attention on the identification of historically underrepresented populations of students (African-American, Hispanic/Latino, American Indian, and students from low-income families). Indeed, several projects funded under the Javits Act were proposed to improve identification of talented students independent of their demographic characteristics. Recent identification work has focused on the assumption that "multiple measures" are more effective with respect to identifying greater numbers of identified students from minority and low-income families (Worrell, 2009). However, in a compelling study by McBee, Peters, and Waterman (2014), the authors showed that common multiple measure identification policies may not have the predicted outcome of improved identification of talent among all student groups. Simply using more measures is not as important as how those measures are actually used.

However, research on identification policies and practices has been limited, and evidence of the success of efforts to improve such practices is not overwhelming (Borland, 2014). Several lines of promising research are emerging, giving hope that identification can be turned from being one of the field's weaknesses to one of its strengths. This research is occurring at several different levels. For example, Peters and Gentry (2010, 2012a) have gathered promising criterion-related validity evidence for a teacher rating scale as well as its use in a multicriteria identification system (Peters & Gentry, 2012b), and McBee (2006, 2010a) has conducted state-level identification policy studies that provide insight into how current and proposed state-level policies impact practice. Peters, Matthews, McCoach, and McBee (2014) have also presented an argument for the de-emphasis of identification as a barrier to most gifted programming, instead arguing that identification should be used as a means of inclusion (locating more students) as opposed to exclusion (keeping students out) and that most programs be made much more open to those who would like to challenge themselves. In combination with the new conceptions of giftedness mentioned above (e.g., Barab & Plucker, 2002; Subotnik et al., 2011), there is reason for optimism about improvements in identification practices.

Another area with impressive recent gains is the field of creativity and innovation. These constructs have become hot topics across a number of fields, including business, economics, and social entrepreneurship, to name but a few (e.g., Pellegrino & Hilton, 2012). However, much of this attention has a "we don't know enough" flavor, when in fact the research base on identifying, fostering, and evaluating creativity has significantly deepened over the past 20 years. For example, progress has been made on defining and conceptualizing creativity (Li & Kaufman, 2014; Plucker, Beghetto, & Dow, 2004), correcting a widely acknowledged, long-standing weakness in the lack of clear, common definitions and conceptualizations of the construct. After years of debate, a consensus is emerging that creativity has both content-general and content-specific characteristics, and that efforts to foster creativity should be designed accordingly (Beghetto & Plucker, 2006; Plucker et al., 2004). Research on assessment has diversified, with serious lines of research regarding a range of measurement strategies (Kaufman, Plucker, & Baer, 2008; Plucker & Makel, 2010). And researchers have considerable knowledge about how creativity develops and can be fostered (Beghetto, 2014; Beghetto & Kaufman, 2010; Sawyer, 2011, 2012). Beghetto (2014) noted several areas in need of additional research, including linking creativity to specific academic content areas and determining the most effective ways to help prospective teachers learn to teach for creativity, but in general the knowledge base regarding creativity in education is more advanced than most researchers and educators realize and continues to grow rapidly.

Identification and creativity are examples of areas within the field that have traditionally been criticized for poor conceptualization, thin empirical bases, mixed evidence of effectiveness, but have a number of researchers doing promising work. These lines of research provide reason for optimism that many of gifted educations traditional weaknesses are being successfully addressed.

AREAS IN NEED OF RESEARCH

Still other areas are in need of significant further research. Researchers in gifted education, like those in many applied fields, deal with a constant tension between research and advocacy. This is not surprising: Why would someone devote a career to studying gifted students without a strong belief that addressing the needs of those students was a good and necessary activity? This tension, of and by itself, is not necessarily a bad thing, as long as researchers draw conclusions from their data and not their advocacy beliefs. However, as outside observers have noted (e.g., Richie, 2013), some of the widely held tenets in gifted education are not well supported empirically, or the evidence is quite mixed. Our sense of the field is that these issues emerge from a desire to advocate on topics with thin research bases, and that strengthening these areas of relative empirical weakness would improve the efficacy of advocacy efforts.

One example is the role of social and emotional issues in the lives of gifted children, with the range of studied phenomena being vast and varied. Conclusions in the research range from claims that gifted students have unique social and emotional needs to assurances that the social development and emotional adjustment of gifted students are equal to or superior to that of the general population. Other researchers believe that gifted students do not possess unique social and emotional characteristics, but rather that family, school, and cultural contexts influence the manifestations of traits in unique ways (see Neihart, Reis, Robinson, & Moon, 2002; Reis & Renzulli, 2004). This large body of research is strong in some areas, especially descriptive research on the prevalence and manifestation of certain constructs within gifted populations, but weaker in others, such as the efficacy of specific interventions to help high-potential students deal with specific social and emotional issues.

For example, in a recent review, Wiley and Hébert (2014) concluded asynchrony (the degree to which the gifted child may exhibit a mismatch between intellectual, emotional, and psychomotor capabilities) has not been documented as a cause of depression; that gifted students do not require treatment to fight off the effects of low-self-concept in any domain, except perhaps the physical; and that the incidence of unhealthy perfectionism and depression in gifted students is no greater than the incidence in the general population. They also concluded that the appearance of multipotentiality (equal aptitude and achievement across multiple, diverse domains) may actually be a consequence of using assessments with low ceilings, and that even if multipotentiality does exist, gifted students who exhibit this trait do not appear to manifest less life or job satisfaction. Many of these conclusions fly in the face of practice or recommendations, such as those offered by the NAGC (2011) that educators participate in professional development to support the social and emotional needs of students with gifts and talents. Wiley and Hébert (2014) contended that this research–practice misalignment stems from a lack of systematic study of the phenomena that fall under the social-emotional umbrella, with the result that psychologists and clinicians have formulated a "collective wisdom" based on their experiences.

A similar research–practice mismatch exists regarding efforts to reduce racial and ethnic disparities in gifted program participation and improve outcomes for gifted minority students. The history of race and equity in gifted education is not particularly pleasant, although as Ford (2012) has noted, the entire, broader field of special education has historical and contemporary problems with racial and socioeconomic disproportionality as well. Despite several decades of concerted effort to address underrepresentation and narrow achievement gaps among subgroups of bright students, considerable evidence exists that underrepresentation remains a problem—and that "excellence gaps" in many cases have grown over the past generation (Plucker, Burroughs, & Song, 2010; Plucker, Hardesty, & Burroughs, 2013). Worrell (2014), after a comprehensive review of research on racially and ethnically diverse gifted children, observed that the research base in this area is neither broad nor deep, with many unsubstantiated claims about causes of and solutions for underrepresentation, too few replications of the research that does exist, and insufficient attention to the interaction of race and socioeconomic status. However, Worrell also acknowledged that given all the literature on race and poverty in gifted education, the fields progress in this area is disappointing.

As a case in point, one of the frequently recommended and adopted policies for addressing concerns about underrepresentation is the use of nonverbal assessments. However, current examination of the underlying validity and bias issues (Lohman & Gambrell, 2012; Worrell, 2014) and recent data on proportions of minority students identified by use of nonverbal instruments have raised questions about their effectiveness in locating more minority students (Giessman, Gambrell, & Stebbins, 2013). These findings have led to a somewhat fierce debate about whether nonverbal intelligence tests find smaller group differences than verbal tests (e.g., Lohman, 2005; Naglieri & Ford, 2003, 2005). What is not often appreciated is just how different students are in terms of academic readiness when they enter a given grade level. Because of sometimes massive differences in educational opportunity (differences that are partially due to economic inequality, which itself is not randomly distributed across racial groups), individuals from certain subgroups show lower average observed test scores. The question remains whether or not these observed differences are due to bias or do to actual differences in academic readiness. Additional research is needed to determine whether nonverbal assessments are having their desired effect on reducing underrepresentation—or possibly exacerbating the problem.

Another example of an area in need of additional research is that of ability grouping. A commonly espoused belief among gifted education scholars and advocates is that the available research clearly demonstrates the efficacy of homogeneous ability grouping over heterogeneous grouping, with demonstrated benefits regarding student achievement and self-concept across ability levels. In recent years, a number of proreform think tanks have adopted this talking point, calling for increased use of ability grouping in schools. On the other side of the argument, critics claim that homogeneous grouping leads to a wide range of academic and social ills, including lower student achievement and self-concept, poor and underresourced education for students in lower ability groups, and even *de facto* segregation for poor and minority students (e.g., Slavin & Braddock, 1993). A major, teacher union–funded think tank even went so far as to conclude that "the vast majority of research into so-called tracking or ability grouping of students has reached a definite conclusion: it's harmful. Students placed in low-track classes fall further behind" (Great Lakes Center for Education Research and Practice, 2013).

It is difficult to imagine a wider range of conclusions on an issue.

It is difficult to imagine a wider range of conclusions on an issue. However, interpretations of the research are clouded by a number of issues and limitations. For example, advocates on both sides of the debate tend to use "tracking" and "ability grouping" interchangeably (e.g., Loveless, 2009; Oakes, 2005), a rhetorical issue with which most gifted education researchers take issue. Tracking involves placing students over the long term in ability groups that are difficult to leave; such tracking was used for decades to justify segregation of students by race and socioeconomic status, and as such, the use of the term to refer to contemporary ability grouping is not only incorrect but also emotionally charged. Ability grouping is a term used to represent a variety of different organizational strategies, such as between-or within-class groupings, with flexibility that allows for changes in instructional placement over time. The research bases on tracking and ability grouping are not identical, making any synonymous usage very problematic (Loveless, 1998).

That said, considerable research has been done on ability grouping, with meta-analytic studies by Slavin (1987, 1990) and Kulik and Kulik (1982, 1992) being the most cited. Contrary to most interpretations, these studies generally find small or negligible effects for ability grouping of students at all levels of ability without curricular or instructional modification. Slavin (1990), echoing observations by Kulik and Kulik, went so far as to conclude:

> The lesson to be drawn from research on ability grouping may be that unless teaching methods are systematically changed, school organization has little impact on student achievement ... if teachers continue to use some form of lecture/discussion/seatwork/quiz, then it may matter very little in the aggregate which ... students the teachers are facing, (pp. 491–492)

This is an important finding, not least because it applies to gifted students participating in other organizational reforms (e.g., Plucker, Makel, Hansen, & Muller, 2008; Plucker, Makel, & Rapp, 2007). In other words, for ability grouping to work for *any* students, appropriate instructional and curricular differentiation must occur across the ability levels. For this reason, the research suggests that decisions to implement ability grouping may be negative or positive for high-ability students, depending on how the grouping is implemented. Given that, according to some sources, the implementation of ability grouping is on the rise in American K-12 schools, the "grouping always helps the gifted" and "grouping always hurts low-performing students" fallacies should be more assertively questioned.

Slavin (1990) also raised a limitation to ability grouping research that, in the two decades since his study was published, appears to be highly relevant: A great deal of research that has been included in the major meta-analyses is decades old at this point. With an emphasis on differentiation in teacher training and professional development in recent years, instruction within homogeneous and heterogeneous ability groups may look different today than they did from the 1960s to the 1990s, when much of the cited research was conducted. Although a handful of more recent studies have been conducted with roughly similar results (e.g., Collins & Gan, 2013; Nomi, 2010), the results are not consistent relative to the benefits or deficits caused by ability grouping for all levels of student ability.

These are but three examples of areas within gifted education that need a stronger research base, yet we see these three areas as having among the best payoffs in terms of investments in research. In other words, learning more about social and emotional development of gifted students, the ways that specific interventions can help underrepresented populations, and better knowledge of how and under what conditions ability grouping does or does not promote positive student outcomes at various ability levels would result in huge gains in the education of gifted students and the development of talent.

FUTURE POLICY AND PRACTICE

The development of policy and practice for the future will be complex in the absence of support mechanisms to support further research. The demise of Javits Act funding, including the lack of funding support for a national research center, will hamper the development of our understandings of gifted students and effective services. However, as noted above, some policies can be justified based on the evidence at hand, including acceleration and the use of prescriptive curriculum models, and other policies can be avoided, such as focusing on differentiation in the general education classroom to the exclusion of other interventions. In this final section, we offer some thoughts about how research on giftedness and gifted education can be strengthened.

NEED FOR EXPERIMENTAL RESEARCH ON INTERVENTIONS

Although several researchers have ventured into assessing impacts of interventions, the field still lacks a body of research that allows for causal inferences (Matthews, Peters, & Housand, 2012). As a result, policy makers are often left with the option of relying on collective "wisdom" or limited experimental evidence—limited in both quantity and generalizability of findings. Intervention research is costly, and current support for such research by federal and state agencies or foundations is absent. Hence, the probability that such research will be executed in the future is low.

NEED FOR ASSESSMENT THAT ALIGNS WITH OUTCOMES

One lingering issue with the studies of curricular impact is the lack of appropriate standardized instruments to measure the outcomes of the instructional units and curriculum offered to gifted students; as a result, most intervention studies are dependent on—and criticized for—the use of experimenter-constructed instruments (e.g., Callahan et al., 2012; Feng et al., 2004; Gavin, Casa, Firmender, & Carroll, 2013; Tieso, 2005; VanTassel-Baska, Zuo, Avery, & Little, 2002). Existing standardized instruments suffer from two serious limitations for use in experimental studies: insufficient validity for this purpose because of the mismatch between the level and complexity (and sometimes topical content) of curriculum offered to gifted students and ceiling effects

(Callahan, 2009; McBee, 2010b). Lack of common consensus on appropriate goals impedes the development of these measures. Some advocate for creative productivity as a goal, whereas others look for differentiation of common core standards within content domains, and others look to process goals such as critical and creative thinking. Yet others look to acceleration of content knowledge attainment as the goal for gifted students. Gifted education, quite frankly, continues to struggle with its goals, which is a major barrier for an applied field.

USE OF NEW DESIGNS AND STATISTICAL ANALYSES

The rigor of research on giftedness has increased over the past generation, with many calls to apply more sophisticated quantitative and qualitative models and techniques, especially those that provide insight into causality (e.g., Coleman, Guo, & Dabbs, 2007; Dai et al., 2011; Simonsen & Little, 2011; VanTassel-Baska, 2006). However, the most rigorous methods will not mediate design flaws, making sophistication of design a critical area for research development. For example, very few replications occur within the field, yet replicating research is a critical component of a robust, reliable research base (Makel, in press; Makel, Plucker, & Hegarty, 2012). Mirroring developments in other areas of education and the social sciences, many scholars entering the field have strong empirical skills, suggesting that the increasing rigor of research on giftedness and gifted education will continue to improve.

INVOLVEMENT OF GOVERNMENT REGARDING DATA COLLECTION

Federal and state governments expend considerable resources in the collection of achievement and developmental data on children. Collection of data on the subpopulation of students who are identified as gifted is very limited, and what is collected is rarely reported. For example, Plucker et al. (2010) noted that press releases about the results of state and national assessments almost never address advanced performance or the scores of high-ability students. Although researchers have been able to tap into these data for limited research, more systematic efforts to structure data collection that makes analysis for this subpopulation possible would provide the field with a richer research base for documenting effects of school interventions. This need is especially acute (and would be especially helpful if addressed) due to the small sample sizes often encountered by researchers of giftedness. By definition, the student populations being studied are small, and if a particular subgroup is studied (e.g., poor, minority students of high ability), the numbers get even smaller. Access to large-scale, representative federal education data sets with appropriate variables would be a great help to researchers, assuming the data address issues related to ceiling effects and other empirical issues associated with the study of giftedness.

A VISION FOR THE FUTURE

Although advocacy by researchers is understandable, research in the field must avoid the bias of promotion. The formulation of questions and data collection strategies should reflect open consideration of possible outcomes. Furthermore, a significant portion of research on identification, processes, and models is often conducted by the developers of the models and instruments under consideration, with few third-party studies and almost no replications. Although keeping advocacy and research separate is admittedly easier said than done, it is not impossible. To best serve the field, researchers need to address issues as research questions to be examined and assessed, not as platforms for advocating a point of view or to show that their particular instrument or curriculum is effective.

If gifted education is to advance, a second issue that cannot be avoided is diversity. Many in the field talk about the need to address issues of inequity as the country becomes more diverse, but this tenet needs to be directly challenged: The country is already diverse, and has been for some time. In order for gifted education to survive and thrive, the field needs to take several bold steps to shrink excellence gaps—and to do so by raising the achievement levels of underachieving groups, not by allowing already high-performing groups to slip.

Such bold steps in this context could include being outspoken when policies are proposed or implemented that research tells us will make programs inequitable. A recent case in point involves the gifted and talented programs in New York City. In the spring of 2013, the media was full of stories of outrage over the revelations that a testing company incorrectly scored thousands of tests that were used to qualify students for the city's gifted education programs. Yet in none of the stories about the scandal did anyone question why one of the most diverse districts in the country is using identification procedures that research tells us are almost guaranteed to produce underrepresentation of students of poverty in its gifted programs. Many in the field may be staying silent because they view having any gifted program in New York as better than having no program, or perhaps the lack of sound research on alternatives puts researchers in a position where they are reluctant to offer poorly supported options. Regardless, it is difficult to look at that situation and not feel that the field has failed many bright students in that district.

Examining new paradigms for definition, talent development, and identification in conjunction with proposed curricular and service interventions would provide policy makers with clear pathways in decision making. The values held by individuals and school district communities will always play a part in decisions about whom they believe to be gifted and what the goals of education might be, but the research recommended above has the potential to inject valuable information into education, increasing the probability that quality services will be delivered to students equitably and that resources will be more effectively and efficiently expended.

REFERENCES

Archambault, F. X., Jr., Westberg, K. L., Brown, S., Hallmark, B. W., Emmons, C., & Zhang, W. (1993). *Regular classroom practices with gifted students: Results of a national survey of classroom teachers* (Research Monograph No. 93102). Storrs: The National Research Center on the Gifted and Talented, University of Connecticut.

Assouline, S. G., Marron, M., & Colangelo, N. (2014). Acceleration. In J. A. Plucker & C. M. Callahan (Eds.), *Critical issues and practices in gifted education: What the research says* (2nd ed., pp. 15–28). Waco, TX: Prufrock Press.

Barab, S. A., & Plucker, J. A. (2002). Smart people or smart contexts? Talent development in an age of situated approaches to learning and thinking. *Educational Psychologist, 37*, 165–182. doi: 10.1207/S15326985EP3703_3

Beghetto, R. A, (2014), Creativity: Development and enhancement. In J. A. Plucker & C. M. Callahan (Eds.), *Critical issues and practices in gifted education: What the research says* (2nd ed., pp. 183–196). Waco, TX: Prufrock Press.

Beghetto, R. A., & Kaufman, J. C. (Eds.). (2010). *Nurturing creativity in the classroom*. New York, NY: Cambridge University Press.

Beghetto, R. A., & Plucker, J. (2006). The relationship among schooling, learning, and creativity: "All roads lead to creativity" or "You can't get there from here"? In J. C. Kaufman & J. Baer (Eds.), *Creativity and reason in cognitive development* (pp. 316–332), New York, NY: Cambridge University Press.

Borland, J. H. (2014). Identification of gifted students. In J. A. Plucker & C. M. Callahan (Eds.), *Critical issues and practices in gifted education: What the research says* (2nd ed., pp. 323–342). Waco, TX: Prufrock Press.

Brighton, C. M., Hertberg, H. L., Moon, T. R., Tomlinson, C. A., & Callahan, C.M. (2005). *The feasibility of high-end learning in a diverse middle school* (RM 05210) (ED505377). Storrs University of Connecticut, National Research Center on the Gifted and Talented.

Callahan, C. M. (2009). Making the grade or achieving the goal: Evaluating learner and program outcomes in gifted education. In F. A. Karnes & S. M. Bean (Eds.), *Method and materials for teaching the gifted* (3rd ed., pp. 221–258). Waco, TX: Prufrock Press.

Callahan, C. M., Azano, A., Oh, S., & Hailey, E. (2012, April). *What works in gifted education: Integrated language arts curricular models for gifted students*. Paper presented at the American Educational Research Association Annual Meeting, Vancouver, British Columbia, Canada.

Callahan, C. M., Hunsaker, S. L., Adams, C. M., Moore, S. D., & Bland, L. C. (1995). Instruments used in the identification ofgifted and talented students (Report No. RM-95130). *Charlottesville, VA: National Research Center on the Gifted and Talented.*

Callahan, C. M., Renzulli, J. S., Delcourt, M. A. B., & Hertberg-Davis, H. L. (2013). Considerations for identification of gifted and talented students. In C. M. Callahan & H. L. Hertberg-Davis (Eds.), *Fundamentals of gifted education: Considering multiple perspectives* (pp. 83–91). New York, NY: Routledge.

Castejon, J. L., Perez, A. M., & Gilar, R. (2010). Confirmatory factor analysis of Project Spectrum activities: A second-order g factor or multiple intelligences? *Intelligence, 38,* 481–496. doi: 10.1016/j.intell.2010.07.002

Cattell, R. B. (1987). *Intelligence: Its structure, growth, and action.* New York, NY: Elsevier.

Colangelo, N., Assouline, S., & Gross, M. U. M. (2004). *A nation deceived: How schools hold back America's brightest students* (Vol. 1). Iowa City: The University of Iowa, The Connie Belin & Jacqueline N. Blank International Center for Gifted Education and Talent Development.

Coleman, L. J., Guo, A., & Dabbs, C. S. (2007). The state of qualitative research in gifted education as published in American journals: An analysis and critique. *Gifted Child Quarterly, 51,* 51–63. doi: 10.1177/0016986206296656

Collins, C. A., & Gan, L, (2013). *Does sorting students improve scores? An analysis of class composition* (National Bureau of Economic Research Working Paper 18848). Cambridge, MA: National Bureau of Economic Research.

Corno, L., Cronbach, L. J., Kupermintz, H., Lohman, D. F., Mandinach, E. B., Porteus, A. W., & Talbert, J. E. (2002), *Remaking the concept of aptitude: Extending the legacy of Richard E. Snow.* Mahwah, NJ: Erlbaum.

Dai, D. Y., Swanson, J. A., & Cheng, H. (2011). State of research on giftedness and gifted education: A survey of empirical studies published during 1998–2010. *Gifted Child Quarterly,* 55, 126–138. doi: 10.1177/0016986210397831

Delisle, J. R., & Renzulli, J. S. (1982). The Revolving Door Identification and Programming Model: Correlates of creative production. *Gifted Child Quarterly, 26,* 89–95.

Dweck, C. S. (1999). *Self-theories: Their role in motivation, personality and development.* Philadelphia, PA: The Psychology Press.

Feng, A. X., VanTassel-Baska, J., Quek, C., Bai, W., & O'Neil, B. (2004). A longitudinal assessment of gifted students' learning using the integrated curriculum model (ICM): Impacts and perceptions of the William and Mary language arts and science curriculum. *Roeper Review, 27,* 78–83. doi: 10.1080/02783190509554294

Ford, D. Y. (2012). Culturally different students in special education: Looking backward to move forward. *Exceptional Children, 78,* 391–405.

Foust, R. C., Hertberg-Davis, H. M., & Callahan, C. M. (2008). "Having it all" at sleep's expense: The forced choice of participants in Advanced Placement courses and International Baccalaureate programs. *Roeper Review, 30,* 121–129. doi: 10.1080/02783190801955293

Gagné, F. (1995). From giftedness to talent: A developmental model and its impact on the language of the field. *Roeper Review, 18,* 103–111. doi: 10.1080/02783190801955293

Gagné, F. (2000). Understanding the complex choreography of talent development through DMGT-based analysis. In K. A. Hell, F. J. Monks, R. J. Sternberg, & R. Subotnik (Eds.), *International handbook for research on giftedness and talent* (2nd ed., pp. 67–79). Oxford, UK: Pergamon Press.

Galton, F. (1869). *Hereditary genius: An inquiry into its laws and consequences.* London: Macmillan.

Gardner, H. (1983). *Frames of mind: The theory of multiple intelligences.* New York, NY: Basic Books.

Gardner, H. (1995). Reflections on multiple intelligences: Myths and messages. *Phi Delta Kappan, 77,* 200–209.

Gavin, M. K., Casa, T. M., Adelson, J. L., Carroll, S. R., & Sheffield, L. J. (2009). The impact of advanced curriculum on the achievement of mathematically promising elementary students. *Gifted Child Quarterly, 53,* 188–202. doi: 10.1177/001698209334964

Gavin, M. K, Casa, T. M., Firmender, J. M., & Carroll, S. (2013). The impact of advanced geometry and mathematics curriculum units on the mathematics achievement of first grade students. *Gifted Child Quarterly, 57,* 71–84. doi: 10.1177/0016986213479564

Giessman, J. A., Gambrell, J. L., & Stebbins, M. S. (2013). Minority performance on the Naglieri Nonverbal Ability Test, Second Edition, versus the Cognitive Abilities Test, Form 6: One gifted program's experience. *Gifted Child Quarterly, 57,* 101–1009.

Great Lakes Center for Education Research and Practice. (2013). *Tracking students continues to be an unproven strategy.* Retrieved May 10, 2013 from http://greatlakescenter.org/docs/Think_Twice/TT_Burris_Tracking.htm

Gubbins, E. J. (1982). *Revolving door identification model: Characteristics of gifted students.* Unpublished doctoral dissertation, The University of Connecticut, Storrs.

Guilford, J. P. (1950). Creativity. *American Psychologist, 5,* 444–454.

Guilford, J. P. (1967). *The nature of human intelligence.* New York, NY: McGraw-Hill.

Hertberg-Davis, H. L., & Callahan, C. M. (2008). A narrow escape: Gifted students' perceptions of Advanced Placement and International Baccalaureate programs. *Gifted Child Quarterly, 52,* 199–216.

Hertberg-Davis, H. L., & Callahan, C. M. (2014). Advanced Placement and International Baccalaureate programs. In J. A. Plucker & C. M. Callahan (Eds.), *Critical issues in gifted education* (2nd ed., pp. 47–64). Waco, TX: Prufrock Press.

Hollingworth, L. S. (1926). *Gifted children: Their nature and nurture.* Oxford, United Kingdom: Macmillan.

Hollingworth, L. S. (1942). *Children above 180 IQ.* New York, NY: World Book.

Jensen, A. R. (1998). *The g factor: The science of mental ability.* Westport, CT: Praeger.

Johnsen, S. K. (1999). Renzulli's model: Needed research. *Journal for the Education of the Gifted, 23,* 102–116.

Kaufman, J. C., Plucker, J. A., & Baer, J. (2008). *Essentials of creativity assessment.* New York, NY: Wiley.

Kulik, J. A, (2004). Meta-analytic studies of acceleration. In N. Colangelo, S. Assouline, & M. U. M. Gross (Eds.), *A nation deceived: How school hold back America's brightest students* (Vol. 2, pp. 13–22). Iowa City: The University of Iowa, The Connie Belin &: Jacqueline N. Blank International Center for Gifted Education and Talent Development.

Kulik, C. L. C„ & Kulik, J. A. (1982). Effects of ability grouping on secondary school students: A meta-analysis of evaluation findings. *American Educational Research Journal, 19,* 415–428.

Kulik, J. A., & Kulik, C. L. C. (1992). Meta-analytic findings on grouping programs. *Gifted Child Quarterly, 36,* 73–77.

Kyburg, R. M., Hertberg-Davis, H. M., &: Callahan, C. M. (2007). Advanced Placement and International Baccalaureate programs: Optimal learning environments for talented minorities? *Journal of Advanced Academics, 18,* 172–215.

Li, Q., & Kaufman, J. C. (2014). Creativity: Definitions and conceptualizations. In J. A. Plucker & C. M. Callahan (Eds.), *Critical issues and practices in gifted education: What the research says* (2nd ed., pp. 173–182). Waco, TX: Prufrock Press.

Lohman, D. F. (2005). Review of Naglieri and Ford (2003): Does the Naglieri Nonverbal Ability Test identify equal proportions of high-scoring White, Black, and Hispanic students? *Gifted Child Quarterly, 49,* 19–28.

Lohman, D. F., & Gambrell, J. L. (2012). Using nonverbal tests to help identify academically talented children. *Journal of Psychoeducational Assessment, 30,* 25–44.

Loveless, T. (1998). *Making sense of the tracking and ability grouping debate.* Washington, DC: Fordham Foundation.

Loveless, T. (2009). *Tracking and detracking: High achievers in Massachusetts middle schools.* Washington, DC: Fordham Foundation.

Lubinski, D. (2004). Long-term effects of educational acceleration. In N. Colangelo, S. Assouline, & M. U. M. Gross (Eds.), *A nation deceived: How schools hold back America's brightest students* (Vol. 2, pp. 23–38). Iowa City: The University of Iowa, The Connie Belin & Jacqueline N. Blank International Center for Gifted Education and Talent Development.

MacKinnon, D. W. (1965). Personality and the realization of creative potential. *The American Psychologist, 20,* 273.

Makel, M. C. (in press). The empirical march: Making science better at self-correction. *Psychology of Aesthetics, Creativity, and the Arts.*

Makel, M. C., Plucker, J. A., & Hegarty, B. (2012). Replications in psychology research: How often do they really occur? *Perspectives on Psychological Science,* 7, 537–542.

Marland, S. P., Jr. (1971, August). *Education of the gifted and talented-volume 1: Report to the Congress of the United States by the U.S. Commissioner of Education.* Washington, DC: Department of Education, Department of Health, Education, and Welfare. (ERIC Document Reproduction Service No. ED 056 243)

Matthews, M. S., Peters, S. J., & Housand, A. (2012). Regression discontinuity design in gifted and talented education research. *Gifted Child Quarterly, 56,* 105–112.

McBee, M. T. (2006). A descriptive analysis of referral sources for gifted identification screening by race and socioeconomic status. *Journal of Advanced Academics, 17,* 103–111.

McBee, M. (2010a). Examining the probability of identification for gifted programs for students in Georgia elementary schools: A multilevel path analysis study. *Gifted Child Quarterly, 54,* 283–297.

McBee, M. T. (2010b). Modeling outcomes with floor or ceiling effects: A brief introduction to the Tobit model. *Gifted Child Quarterly, 54,* 314–320.

McBee, M. T., Peters, S. J., & Waterman, C. (2014). Combining scores in multiple-criteria assessment systems: The impact of combination rules. *Gifted Child Quarterly, 58,* 69–89.

Missett, T. C., & McCormick, K. M. (2014). Conceptions of giftedness. In J. A. Plucker &: C. M. Callahan (Eds.), *Critical issues in gifted education* (2nd ed., pp. 143–158). Waco, TX: Prufrock Press.

Moon, T. R., Callahan, C. M., Tomlinson, C. A., & Miller, E. M. (2002). *Middle school classrooms: Teachers' reported practices and student perceptions* (Research Monograph 02164). Storrs: The National Research Center on the Gifted and Talented, University of Connecticut.

Mullis, I. V. S., Martin, M. O., Minnich, C. A., Stanco, G. M., Victoria, A. A., Centurino, *A. S.,* & Castle, C. E. (Eds.). (2011). *TIMSS 2011 encyclopedia: Education policy and curriculum in mathematics and science. Volume 2: L-Z and benchmarking participants.* Boston, MA: TIMSS and PIRLS International Study Center, Boston College.

Naglieri, J. A., & Ford, D. Y. (2003). Addressing underrepresentation of gifted minority children using the Naglieri Nonverbal Ability Test (NNAT). *Gifted Child Quarterly, 47,* 155–160.

Naglieri, J, A., & Ford, D. Y. (2005). Increasing minority children's participation in gifted classes using the NNAT: A response to Lohman. *Gifted Child Quarterly, 49,* 29–36.

National Association for Gifted Children. (2011). *State of the states in gifted education: 2010–2011.* Washington, DC: Author,

Neihart, M., Reis, S. M., Robinson, N. M., & Moon, S.M. (Eds.). (2002). *The social and emotional development of gifted children.* Waco, TX: Prufrock Press.

Nomi, T. (2010). The effects of within-class ability grouping on academic achievement in early elementary years. *Journal of Research on Educational Effectiveness, 3,* 56–92.

Oakes, J. (2005). *Keeping track: How schools structure inequality* (2nd ed.). New Haven, CT: Yale University Press.

Olszewski-Kubilius, P. (1999). A critique of Renzulli's theory into practice models for gifted learners. *Journal for the Education of the Gifted, 23,* 55–66.

Olszewski-Kubilius, P., & Thomson, D. (2014). Talent search. In J. A. Plucker & C. M. Callahan (Eds.), *Critical issues and practices in gifted education* (pp. 633–643). Waco, TX: Prufrock Press.

Pellegrino, J. W., & Hilton, M. L. (Eds.). (2012). *Education for life and work: Developing transferable knowledge and skills in the 21st century.* Washington, DC: National Research Council.

Peters, S. J., & Gentry, M. (2010). Multi-group construct validity evidence of the *HOPE Scale*-Instrumentation to identify low-income elementary students for gifted programs. *Gifted Child Quarterly, 54,* 298–313.

Peters, S. J., & Gentry, M. (2012a). Additional validity evidence and across-group equivalence of the HOPE teacher rating scale. *Gifted Child Quarterly, 57,* 85–100.

Peters, S. J., & Gentry, M. (2012b). Group-specific norms and teacher rating scales: Implications for underrepresentation. *Journal of Advanced Academics, 23,* 125–144.

Peters, S. J., Matthews, M., McCoach, D. B., & McBee, M. (2014). *Beyond gifted education: Designing and implementing advanced academic programs.* Waco, TX: Prufrock Press.

Plucker, J. A. (2000). Flip sides of the same coin or inarching to the beat of different drummers? A response to Pyryt. *Gifted Child Quarterly, 44,* 193–195.

Plucker, J. A., & Barab, S. A. (2005). The importance of contexts in theories of giftedness: Learning to embrace the messy joys of subjectivity. In R. J. Sternberg & J. A. Davidson (Eds.), *Conceptions of giftedness* (2nd ed., pp. 201–216). New York, NY: Cambridge University Press.

Plucker, J. A., Beghetto, R. A., & Dow, G. T. (2004). Why isn't creativity more important to educational psychologists? Potentials, pitfalls, and future directions in creativity research. *Educational Psychologist, 39,* 83–96.

Plucker, J. A., Burroughs, N., & Song, R. (2010). *Mind the (other) gap! The growing excellence gap in K–12 education.* Bloomington: Indiana University, Center for Education and Evaluation Policy.

Plucker, J. A., Callahan, C. M., & Tomchin, E. M. (1996). Wherefore art thou, multiple intelligences? Alternative assessments for identifying talent in ethnically diverse and economically disadvantaged students. *Gifted Child Quarterly, 40,* 81–92.

Plucker, J. A., Chien, R.} & Zaman, K. (2006). *Enriching the high school curriculum through postsecondary credit-based transition programs* [Education Policy Brief, 4(2)]. Bloomington: Indiana University Center for Evaluation and Education Policy.

Plucker, J. A., & Esping, A. (2014). *Intelligence 101.* New York, NY: Springer.

Plucker, J. A., Hardesty, J., & Burroughs, N. (2013). *Talent on the sidelines: Excellence gaps and America's persistent talent underclass.* Storrs: Center for Education Policy Analysis, University of Connecticut. Retrieved from http://cepa.uconn.edu/mindthegap.

Plucker, J. A., & Makel, M. C. (2010). Assessment of creativity. In J. C. Kaufman & R. J. Sternberg (Eds.), *Handbook of creativity* (pp. 48–73). New York, NY: Cambridge University Press.

Plucker, J. A., Makel, M. C., Hansen, J. A., & Muller, P. A. (2008). Achievement effects of the Cleveland voucher program on high ability elementary school students. *Journal of School Choice,* (4), 77–88. doi: 10.1300/15582150802098746

Plucker, J. A., Makel, M. C., & Rapp, K. E. (2008). The impact of charter schools on promoting high levels of mathematics achievement. *Journal of School Choice, 1(4),* 63–76. doi; 10.1300/15582150802098738

Pyryt, M. C. (2000). Finding "g": Easy viewing through higher order factor analysis. *Gifted Child Quarterly, 44,* 190–192. doi: 10.1177/001698620004400305

Reis, S. M., & Boeve, H. (2009). How academically gifted elementary, urban student respond to challenge in an enriched, differentiated reading program. *Journal for the Education of the Gifted, 33,* 203–240.

Reis, S. M., Gubbins, E. J., Briggs, C., Schreiber, F, J., Richards, S., Jacobs, J. K. ... Renzulli, J. S. (2004). Reading instruction for talented readers: Case studies documenting few opportunities for continuous progress. *Gifted Child Quarterly, 48,* 315–338. doi: 10.1177/001698620404800406

Reis, S. M., & Renzulli, J. S. (2004). Current research on the social and emotional development of gifted and talented students: Good news and future possibilities. *Psychology in the Schools, 41,* 119–130. doi: 10.1002/pits. 10144

Renzulli, J. S. (1978). What makes giftedness? Reexamining a definition. *Phi Delta Kappan, 60,* 180–184, 261.

Renzulli, J. S. (Ed.). (1984), *Technical report of research studies related to the Revolving Door Identification Model* (2nd ed.). Storrs: Bureau of Educational Research and Service, The University of Connecticut.

Renzulli, J. S. (Ed.). (1988). *Technical report of research studies related to the Revolving Door Identification Model* (2nd ed., *Vol. II).* Storrs: Bureau of Educational Research and Service, The University of Connecticut.

Renzulli, J. S. (2002). Emerging conceptions of giftedness: Building a bridge to the new century. *Exceptionality, 10(2),* 67–75. doi: 10.1207/S 15327035EX1002_2

Renzulli, J. S. (2005). The three-ring definition of giftedness: A developmental model for promoting creative productivity. In R. J. Sternberg & J. E. Davidson (Eds.), *Conceptions of giftedness* (2nd ed., pp. 246–280). New York, NY: Cambridge University Press.

Renzulli, J. S. (2012). Reexamining the role of gifted education and talent development for the 21st century: A four-part theoretical approach. *Gifted Child Quarterly, 56,* 150–159. doi: 10.1177/0016986212444901

Renzulli, J. S., & D'Souza, S. (2014). Intelligences outside the normal curve: Co-cognitive factors that contribute to the creation of social capital and leadership skills in young people. In J. A. Plucker & C. M. Callahan (Eds.), *Critical issues and practices in gifted education: What the research says* (2nd ed., pp. 343–362). Waco, TX: Prufrock Press.

Renzulli, J. S., & Sytsma, R. E. (2008). Intelligences outside the normal curve: Co-cognitive traits that contribute to giftedness. In J. A. Plucker & C. M. Callahan (Eds.), *Critical issues and practices in gifted education: What the research says* (pp. 57–84). Waco, TX: Prufrock Press.

Ritchie, S. J. (2013). Review of *Giftedness 101. Intelligence,* 41, 275–276.

Rogers, K. B. (2010). Academic acceleration and giftedness: The research from 1990 to 2008. A best-evidence synthesis. In N. Colangelo, S. Assouline, D. Lohman, & M. A. Marron (Eds.), *Proceedings of the 2008 Wallace Symposium poster session on academic acceleration* (pp. 1–6). Iowa City: The University of Iowa.

Sadler, P. M. (2010). Advanced placement in a changing educational landscape. In P. M. Sadler, G. Sonnert, R. H. Tai, & K. Klopfenstein (Eds.), *AP: A critical examination of the Advanced Placement program* (pp. 3–15). Cambridge, MA: Harvard University Press.

Sawyer, R. K. (Ed.). (2011). *Structure and improvisation in creative teaching.* New York, NY: Cambridge University Press.

Sawyer, R. K. (2012). *Explaining creativity: The science of human innovation.* New York, NY: Oxford University Press.

Simonsen, B., & Little, C. A. (2011). Single-subject research in gifted education. *Gifted Child Quarterly*, 55, 158–162. doi: 10.1177/0016986211398331

Slavin, R. E. (1987). Ability grouping and student achievement in elementary schools: A best-evidence synthesis. *Review of Educational Research, 57,* 293–336. doi: 10.3102/00346543057003293

Slavin, R. E. (1990). Achievement effects of ability grouping in secondary schools: A best-evidence synthesis. *Review of Educational Research, 60,* 471–499. doi: 10.3102/00346543060003471

Slavin, R. E., & Braddock, J. H., III. (1993). Ability grouping: on the wrong crack. *College Hoard Review, 168,* 11–17.

Snow, R. E. (1992). Aptitude theory: Yesterday, today, and tomorrow. *Educational Psychologist, 27,* 5–32. doi: 10.1207/s 15326985ep2701_3

Spearman, C. (1904). "General intelligence," objectively determined and measured. *American Journal of Psychology, 15,* 201–293. doi: 10.2307/1412107

Stanley, J. C. (1973). Accelerating the educational progress of intellectually giftedyouths. *Educational Psychologist, 10,* 133–146. doi: 10.1080/00461527309529108

Steenbergen-Hu, S., & Moon, S. M. (2011). The effects of acceleration on high-ability learners: A meta-analysis. *Gifted Child Quarterly,* 55(1), 39–53.

Sternberg, R. J. (1988). *The triarchic mind: A new theory of human intelligence.* New York, NY: Viking.

Sternberg, R. J. (1996). *Successful intelligence: How practical and creative intelligence determine success in life.* New York, NY: Simon & Schuster.

Sternberg, R. J. (2011). The theory of successful intelligence. In R. J. Sternberg & S. B. Kaufman (Eds.), *The Cambridge handbook of intelligence* (pp. 504–527). New York, NY: Cambridge University Press.

Sternberg, R. J., Castejon, J. L., Prieto, M. D., Hautamäki, J., & Grigorenko, E. L. (2001). Confirmatory factor analysis of the Sternberg Triarchic Abilities Test in three international samples. *European Journal of Psychological Assessment, 17,* 1–16. doi: 10.1027//1015-5759.17.1.1

Sternberg, R. J., Grigorenko, E. L., & Zhang, L. F. (2008), Styles of learning and thinking matter in instruction and assessment. *Perspectives on Psychological Science, 3,* 486–506. doi: 10.111 l/j. 1745-6924.2008.00095.x

Subotnik, R. F., Olszewski-Kubilius, P., & Worrell, F. C. (2011). Rethinking giftedness and gifted education: A proposed direction forward based on psychological science. *Psychological Science in the Public Interest, 12,* 3–54. doi: 10.1177/1529100611418056

Subotnik, R. F., Olszewski-Kubilius, P., & Worrell, F. C. (2012), A proposed direction forward for gifted education based on psychological science. *Gifted Child Quarterly, 56,* 176–188. doi: 10.1177/0016986212456079

Tannenbaum, A. J. (1958). History of interest in the gifted. In N. B. Henry (Ed.), *Education for the gifted: The 57th yearbook for the National Society for the Study of Education, Part 2* (pp. 21–38). Chicago, IL: University of Chicago Press, doi: 10.1037/13174-002

Tannenbaum, A. J. (1983)-*Gifted children: Psychological and educational perspctives.* New York, NY: Wiley.

Term an, L. M. (1926). *Mental and physical traits of a thousand gifted children. Vol. 1. Genetic studies of genius* (2nd ed.). Stanford, CA: Stanford University Press.

Thurstone, L. L. (1938). *Primary mental abilities.* Chicago, IL: University of Chicago Press.

Tieso, C. (2005). The effects of grouping practices and curricular adjustments on achievement. *Journal for the Education of the Gifted, 29,* 60–89.

VanTassel-Baska, J. (2006). *NAGC symposium: A report card on the state of research in the field of gifted education. Gifted Child Quarterly, 50,* 339–341. doi: 10.1177/001698620605000406

VanTassel-Baska, J., Bracken, B., Feng, A., & Brown, A. (2009). A longitudinal study of enhancing critical thinking and reading comprehension in Title I classrooms. *Journal for the Education of the Gifted, 33,* 7–37.

VanTassel-Baska, J., Zuo, L., Avery, L. D., & Little, A.A. (2002). A curriculum study of gifted-student learning in the language arts. *Gifted Child Quarterly, 46,* 30–44. doi: 10.1177/001698620204600104

Visser, B. A., Ashton, M. C., & Vernon, P. A. (2006). Beyond *g*. Putting multiple intelligences theory to the test. *Intelligence, 34,* 487–502. doi: 10.1016/ j.intell.2006.02,004

Westberg, K. L., Archambault, F. X., Jr., Dobyns, S. M., & Salvin, T. J. (1993). *An observational study of instructional and curricular practices used with gifted and talented students in regular classrooms* (Research Monograph 93104). Storrs: The National Research Center on the Gifted and Talented, University of Connecticut.

Westberg, K. L., & Daoust, M. E. (2004). *The results of the replication of the classroom practices survey replication in two states.* Storrs: National Research Center on the Gifted and Talented, University of Connecticut.

Wiley, K., & Hébert, T. P. (2014). Social and emotional traits of gifted youth. In J. A, Plucker & C. M, Callahan (Eds.), *Critical issues and practices in gifted education: What the research says* (2nd ed., pp. 593–608). Waco, TX: Prufrock Press.

Worrell, F. C. (2009). Myth 4: A single test score or indicator tells us all we need to know about giftedness. *Gifted Child Quarterly, 53,* 242–244. doi: 10.1177/ 0016986209346828

Worrell, F. C. (2014). Ethnically diverse students. In J. A. Plucker & C. M. Callahan (Eds.), *Critical issues and practices in gifted education: What the research says* (2nd ed., pp. 237–254). Waco, TX: Prufrock Press.

Worrell, F. C., Olszewski-Kubilius, P., & Subotnik, R. F. (2012). Important issues, some rhetoric, and a few straw men: A response to comments on "Rethinking giftedness and gifted education." *Gifted Child Quarterly, 56,* 224–231. doi: 10.1177/0016086212456080

ABOUT THE AUTHORS

JONATHAN A. PLUCKER, Neag School of Education, University of Connecticut; **CAROLYN M. CALLAHAN**, Curry School of Education, University of Virginia.

The authors appreciate the encouragement of Joseph Renzulli and the constructive feedback of the editors, reviewers, and Scott Peters during the writing of this article.

Address correspondence concerning this article to Jonathan A. Plucker, PhD, Raymond Neag Professor of Educational Leadership, Professor of Educational Psychology, Neag School of Education, University of Connecticut, 2131 Hillside Road, U-3007, Storrs, CT 06269-3007 (e-mail: Jonathan.plucker@uconn.edu).

Manuscript received May 2013; accepted January 2014.

POST-READING ACTIVITIES

1. In one or two paragraphs, describe the history of the field of gifted education.
2. In one or two paragraphs, describe the current status of the research.
3. In one or two paragraphs, describe the vision the authors present for the future of gifted education.

CHAPTER 10

READING 10.2 OVERVIEW

In this article, Johnsen provides a comprehensive overview of the CCSS. She describes how the CCSS can be differentiated to meet the needs of gifted and advanced students. In addition to providing instructional strategies for educators, the author shares advice for parents and guardians. She explains how they can ensure that their talented children are being served properly.

PRE-READING ACTIVITIES

1. Summarize the purpose of the CCSS. Write it down so you can refer to it after reading the article.
2. Write down your responses to the following:

STATEMENT	MOSTLY TRUE OR MOSTLY FALSE?	
1. Given that the CCSS focus on twenty-first-century skills, they are sufficiently rigorous for gifted and advanced learners.	Mostly True	Mostly False
2. Although gifted students may advance more rapidly, the CCSS scope and sequences need to be closely followed to ensure that gifted and advanced students do not miss any important knowledge and skills.	Mostly True	Mostly False
3. Curricular pathways for gifted and advanced students are similar to general education students.	Mostly True	Mostly False
4. Gifted students from poverty have different pathways from their more advantaged peers.	Mostly True	Mostly False
5. Schools must be flexible in the implementation of CCSS.	Mostly True	Mostly False
6. Advanced and rigorous curriculum should be used with all learners.	Mostly True	Mostly False
7. Teachers need to differentiate the CCSS.	Mostly True	Mostly False
8. The most important practice in differentiating the standards is providing students with choices.	Mostly True	Mostly False
9. All educators need professional development in implementing the CCSS with gifted and advanced learners.	Mostly True	Mostly False

(Johnsen, 2013, 6).

3. How would you teach the CCSS to gifted and advanced students? Write it down for reference after reading the article.

THE COMMON CORE STATE STANDARDS

WHERE DO GIFTED AND ADVANCED LEARNERS FIT?

READING 10.2

BY DR. SUSAN K. JOHNSEN

Over the past 20 years, standards have assumed a major accountability role in schools influencing curriculum, assessments, and the hiring of teachers and administrators. The No Child Left Behind Act of 2001

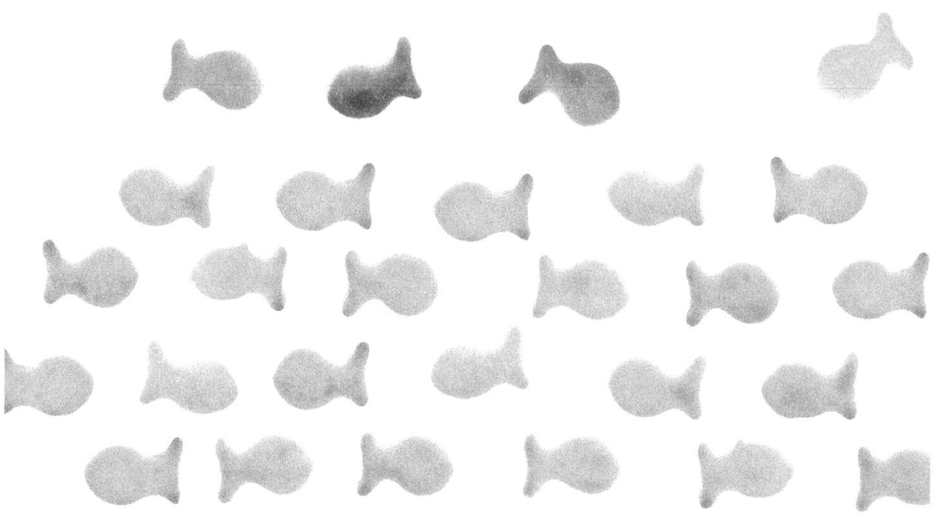

Susan K. Johnsen, "The Common Core State Standards: Where Do Gifted and Advanced Learners Fit?," *Parenting for High Potential*, vol. 3, no. 1, pp. 4-7.

required that states report results on standards-related accountability measures (U.S. Department of Education, 2008). Since that time, all states have adopted some form of a standards-based education system that includes assessment of student performance and reports on each school's annual progress in meeting the standards. This article will provide an introduction to the newly developed national Common Core State Standards for English Language Arts and Mathematics, how they might be used with gifted and talented students, and what parents and guardians might do to ensure that their children are served appropriately.

OVERVIEW OF THE COMMON CORE STATE STANDARDS

Stimulated by the inconsistencies across current state standards and the United States' lackluster performance on international assessments, the National Governors Association (NGA) and the Council of Chief State School Officers (CCSSO) initiated the development of new standards (NGA & CCSSO, 2010a, 2010b). The new standards are called the Common Core State Standards for English Language Arts and the Common Core State Standards for Mathematics (CCSS). Teachers, administrators, and content experts designed the CCSS, organizing them into key content domains, which were articulated across K–12 grade levels. The content of the standards were based on the National Assessment of Educational Progress (NAEP) frameworks (NAEP, 2011) and international studies (National Center for Education Statistics [NCES], 2007). To date, the CCSS have been adopted by 45 states, the District of Columbia, and four territories.

The CCSS provide a framework for curriculum development and emphasize knowledge and skills required for the 21st century such as creativity and innovation, critical thinking and problem solving, communication and collaboration, technology literacy, information media literacy, and social skills (Partnership for 21st Century Skills, n.d.). These skills are intended to help all students be successful in college and careers and to compete internationally.

The Common Core State Standards for English Language Arts identify literacy performance expectations in the strands of reading, writing, speaking, listening, and language, with grade-specific standards for monitoring progress. All of the literacy strands, while distinct, are closely connected within specific standards. The Common Core State Standards for Mathematics include two sets of standards: the Content Standards and Mathematical Practice Standards. The Content Standards are organized by grade and secondary levels, standards, clusters of related standards, and domains of larger groups of related standards. The eight standards for Mathematical Practice focus on specific thinking processes such as making sense of problems, reasoning abstractly, and constructing viable arguments that teachers need to incorporate in their learning experiences so that all students are actively engaged in these types of thinking.

Teachers are given great latitude in implementing the CCSS in mathematics and English language arts. For example, the math standards include this note on courses: "the Standards themselves do not dictate curriculum, pedagogy, or delivery of content" and "should be validated by subsequent performance of students in college and the workforce" (NGA & CCSSO, 2010b, p. 84). Similarly, the English language arts standards emphasize that "teachers are thus free to provide students with whatever tools and knowledge their professional judgment and experience identify as most helpful for meeting the goals set out in the Standards" (NGA & CCSSO, n.d., para. 4).

USE OF THE CCSS WITH GIFTED AND TALENTED STUDENTS

What do these new standards mean to the field of gifted education? How will these standards influence curriculum and the gifted educator's role in supporting gifted and high-potential learners in these core content areas? What can parents and guardians do to support their gifted and talented children? To address these questions, I have compiled a set of "mostly true" and "mostly false" statements gleaned from two recent National Association for Gifted Children (NAGC) publications on using the CCSS with gifted and advanced learners (Johnsen & Sheffield, 2013; VanTassel-Baska, 2013). Check yourself to see how your thinking aligns with these leaders in the field of gifted education (see page 6).

CONCLUSION

Now that you have some knowledge about the CCSS and how they might be used with gifted and talented students, what might you do to make sure that your gifted child is served appropriately? First, you will want to learn more about the standards and ways that they might be differentiated for gifted and advanced learners. I would suggest that you read the NAGC books related to this topic (see Johnsen & Sheffield, 2013, and VanTassel-Baska, 2013). Both of these books elaborate on the areas discussed in this article and provide additional resources for teachers and for parents. Next, identify how your child's school is providing for gifted and advanced students. Is the teacher using formative, above-level assessments to identify what your child knows? Is the teacher differentiating within the classroom? Is the school or school district allowing for acceleration? Is the school or school district individualizing the scope and sequence? Are their policies flexible so that individual student needs might be addressed? Third, once you are aware of what your school is doing, advocate for policies that will support a more differentiated curriculum for gifted and talented students. Attend school meetings and get to know the directors of programs. Look for ways that you can become a partner in developing favorable policies and services so that not only your child will benefit but also all students. Fourth, support your child within the school. Be aware of identification assessments, enrichment activities, advanced courses, program sequences that lead to careers that your child might want to pursue, and teachers who are interested in serving gifted and talented students. Collaborate with your child's teacher in identifying your child's interests. Finally, support your child outside of school. Find clubs, competitions, community opportunities, higher education courses, and other extracurricular activities that might stimulate and develop his or her interests. You clearly have an important role to play in selecting and promoting skills and activities that will develop your child's talents and in creating a positive attitude toward learning.

MOSTLY TRUE OR MOSTLY FALSE?

Mostly

True False 1. Given that the CCSS focus on 21st century skills, they are sufficiently rigorous for gifted and advanced learners.

True False 2. Although gifted students may advance more rapidly, the CCSS scope and sequence needs to be closely followed to ensure that gifted and advanced students do not miss any important knowledge and skills.

True False 3. Curricular pathways for gifted and advanced students are similar to general education students.

True False 4. Gifted students from poverty have different pathways than their more advantaged peers.

True False 5. Schools must be flexible in the implementation of CCSS.

True False 6. Advanced and rigorous curriculum should be used with all learners.

True False 7. Teachers need to differentiate the CCSS.

True False 8. The most important practice in differentiating the standards is providing students with choices.

True False 9. All educators need professional development in implementing the CCSS with gifted and advanced learners.

Answers on Page 426

REFERENCES

Colangelo, N., Assouline, S. G., & Gross, M. U. M. (Eds.). (2004). *A nation deceived: How schools hold back America's brightest students* (Vol. 2). Iowa City: The University of Iowa, The Connie Belin & Jacqueline N. Blank International Center for Gifted Education and Talent Development.

Johnsen, S. K., Ryser, G. R., & Assouline, S. G. (in press). *A teacher's guide to using the Common Core State Standards with mathematically gifted and advanced learners.* Waco TX: Prufrock Press.

Johnsen, S. K., & Sheffield, L. J. (Eds.). (2013). *Using the Common Core State Standards for Mathematics with gifted and advanced learners.* Waco, TX: Prufrock Press.

National Assessment of Educational Progress. (2011). *NAEP mathematics framework.* Retrieved from http://nces.ed.gov/nationsreportcard/mathematics/whatmeasure.asp

National Association for Gifted Children. (2010). *NAGC pre-K–grade 12 programming standards.* Retrieved from http://www.nagc.org/ProgrammingStandards.aspx

National Center for Education Statistics. (2007). *Trends in International Mathematics and Science Study.* Retrieved from http://nces.ed.gov/timss

National Governors Association Center for Best Practices, & Council of Chief State School Officers. (2010a). *Common Core State Standards for English Language Arts.* Retrieved from http://www.corestandards.org/the-standards

National Governors Association Center for Best Practices, & Council of Chief State School Officers. (2010b). *Common Core State Standards for Mathematics.* Retrieved from http://www.corestandards.org/assets/CCSSI_Mathematics_Appendix_A.pdf

National Governors Association Center for Best Practices, & Council of Chief State School Officers. (n.d.). *English language arts standards, introduction, key design considerations.* Retrieved from http://www.corestandards.org/ELA-Literacy/introduction/key-design-consideration

Partnership for 21st Century Skills. (n.d.). *Framework for 21st century learning.* Retrieved from http://www.p21.org/overview

U.S. Department of Education (2008). *A nation accountable: Twenty-five years after a nation at risk.* Washington, DC: U.S. Department of Education. Retrieved from http://www2.ed.gov/rschstat/research/pubs/accountable/accountable.pdf

VanTassel-Baska, J. (Ed.). (2013). *Using the Common Core State Standards for English Language Arts with gifted and advanced learners.* Waco, TX: Prufrock Press.

AUTHOR'S NOTE

Susan K. Johnsen, Ph.D., is professor in the Department of Educational Psychology at Baylor University where she directs the Ph.D. program and programs related to gifted and talented education. She is the author of tests used in identifying gifted students and more than 200 publications including *Implementing RtI With Gifted Students* and books related to the national teacher preparation standards in gifted education, identification of gifted students, and using the Common Core State Standards with gifted students. She is editor-in-chief of *Gifted Child Today*. Correspondence may be addressed to: Susan_Johnsen@baylor.edu.

ANSWERS TO MOSTLY TRUE AND MOSTLY FALSE

1. Mostly false. Although the standards are strong, they are not sufficiently rigorous or advanced to accommodate the needs of learners who are gifted in mathematics and/or English language arts. Some students may advance more rapidly through the standards, requiring acceleration and enrichment. Enrichment needs to include open-ended opportunities in meeting the standards; learning experiences that require complex, creative, and innovative thinking; and real-world problem-solving contexts. Gifted educators need to use deliberate strategies to ensure that these differentiated practices are used with gifted and advanced students.

2. Mostly false. Although scopes and sequences help teachers identify what is expected from students at a particular grade level, individual variations in experiences, abilities, and responsiveness to learning activities will alter the pace. For the most part, the learning progressions are based on state and international comparisons, not necessarily on research (NGA & CCSSO, 2010b, p. 4). Therefore, educators need to be diligent in observing how students respond to curriculum and instruction and pace the curriculum accordingly.

3. Mostly false. Although some of the CCSS address higher level skills and concepts, there are discrete skills that may be clustered across grade levels and compressed for more efficient mastery by gifted students. Teachers must use preassessments to determine which students need accelerated pacing. In addition, gifted students should be provided with multiple pathways that not only accelerate them in their areas of special talent but also advance them to their next level of interest, motivation, and capacity to perform in specific domain areas.

4. Mostly true. For gifted children from poverty, schools are the primary source for developing domain-specific potential. These students often lack the resources and support for extracurricular experiences such as tutors and special programs that frequently stimulate early interests and develop knowledge and skills within a domain. These students may even appear less able than their more advantaged peers. Schools therefore have a special obligation to differentiate the pathway to help students of promise develop their talents.

5. Mostly true. Schools need to be flexible in the implementation of policies related to acceleration, waivers, and course credit that may impact gifted and advanced learners. These students may advance more readily through the standards and require more accelerated options such as early admission, grade-skipping, mentoring, dual enrollment courses, telescoped curriculum, and credit by examination (Colangelo, Assouline, & Gross, 2004)

6. Mostly true. The CCSS provides benchmarks that are aligned to 21st century skills so that students might be successful when they graduate and competitive in the world of work or in higher education settings. Therefore, for future success, all learners should receive an advanced and rigorous curriculum.

7. Mostly true. The CCSS need to be differentiated for gifted and high-potential students. A more developmental, individual approach is essential for developing students with promise. Differentiated learning experiences provide pathways with appropriate pacing and acceleration; integrate greater complexity and depth in a more advanced curriculum base; incorporate creativity; include higher level questions; create authentic, interdisciplinary problem-solving opportunities; group students with similar interests and abilities; involve collaborators and mentors; and engage students in outside-of-school opportunities (Johnsen, Ryser, & Assouline, in press). In addition, standards in math and English language arts can be grouped together to create even richer learning opportunities.

8. Mostly false. The use of preassessments is the most important practice in differentiating the standards. As is true with all standards, assessments should drive the instructional practices. Assessments such as performances and products often require higher level learning outcomes and need to be used to identify what students need to learn, their progress, and what they have accomplished. Moreover, more traditional assessments should incorporate above-level content so that gifted students are able to show what they already know and can do.

9. Mostly true. Because gifted and talented students spend the majority of their time within general education classrooms, all educators—including administrators, teachers, counselors, and other instructional support staff—need to receive professional development in how to differentiate the CCSS and provide services that are flexible in meeting individual needs. Professional development may take many forms such as district-sponsored workshops, university courses, independent studies, professional conferences, and mentoring from gifted educators (NAGC, 2010). Moreover, parents and guardians need to learn about ways of differentiating the CCSS so that they might become partners in the education process and advocate for their children as they progress in school.

POST-READING ACTIVITIES

1 Revisit your summary of the CCSS. Is there anything you would revise? If so, what?

2 On a separate document, complete the following table using your own words.

STATEMENT	MOSTLY TRUE OR MOSTLY FALSE	EXPLANATION
1. Given that the CCSS focus on twenty-first-century skills, they are sufficiently rigorous for gifted and advanced learners.		
2. Although gifted students may advance more rapidly, the CCSS scope and sequences needs to be closely followed to ensure that gifted and advanced students do not miss any important knowledge and skills.		
3. Curricular pathways for gifted and advanced students are similar to general education students.		
4. Gifted students from poverty have different pathways from their more advantaged peers.		
5. Schools must be flexible in the implementation of CCSS.		
6. Advanced and rigorous curriculum should be used with all learners.		
7. Teachers need to differentiate the CCSS.		
8. The most important practice in differentiating the standards is providing students with choices.		
9. All educators need professional development in implementing the CCSS with gifted and advanced learners.		

(Johnsen 2013, 6)

3 Now that you have read the article, revisit your response to the third pre-reading activity question. Is there anything you would revise? If so, what?

REFERENCE

Johnsen, Susan K. 2013. "The Common Core State Standards: Where Do Gifted and Advanced Learners Fit?" *Parenting for High Potential* (3:1).

CONCLUSION

After reading *Teaching and Learning Language Arts from a Diverse Perspective: An Anthology*, you should feel confident that the pre-reading activities, informative articles and book chapters, and the post-reading activities have prepared you to teach diverse students using inclusive methods. Remember, the CCSS determine *what* we teach, not *how* we teach. It is our responsibility to differentiate instruction using research-based methods that build on students' strengths and accommodate their individual needs.

The ten chapters of the book included specifically chosen selections to broaden your understanding of theory and effective practice from a diverse perspective. You learned about culturally responsive teaching and developing culturally responsive practices. You were provided specific strategies for working with ELLs and high-ability ELLs. Ideas were offered for academic, social, and behavioral support to help students reach their full potential in urban, high-poverty schools. Detailed strategies and appropriate interventions for working with exceptional students, including autistic, ED, DHH, hearing impaired, language impaired, and intellectually disabled students, were described. Finally, you learned about working with gifted and advanced learners.

Why is this relevant to you? The idea that "one size fits all" has not been proven effective. In fact, quite the opposite is true. Your classroom will likely be filled with students from different backgrounds who come with different abilities, strengths, and challenges. "By teaching and designing inclusive educational programs, faculty and staff who value diversity and know how to work with diverse students will provide the necessary scaffolding for student success" (Hurtado and Ruiz Alvarado 2013, para. 12).

I will leave you with these final suggestions for teaching language arts from a diverse perspective:

- Promote a collaborative climate
- Encourage student input and dialogue regarding expectations and consequences

- Engage students in the purpose and process of learning
- Maintain high academic and social expectations for all
- Use culturally responsive teaching
- Address inequities to promote student understanding of equality
- Create classroom learning communities
- Connect content to student experiences
- Understand motivation from a sociocultural perspective
- Encourage social negotiation

To be the most effective educator, you need to be equipped with diverse strategies and methods for facilitating student learning. The purpose of this anthology is to provide you with foundational knowledge to prepare you to be an inclusive teacher. There is a paradigm shift occurring in education right now, and you have the wonderful opportunity to be part of it! As Malcom Forbes (n.d.) has notably stated, diversity is "the art of thinking independently together." Now, go out there and make a difference ...

REFERENCES

Hurtado, Sylvia, and Adrianna Ruiz Alvarado. 2013. *Diversity in Teaching and Learning: Affirming Students as Empowered Learners*. Retrieved from https://www.aacu.org/publications-research/periodicals/diversity-teaching-and-learning-affirming-students-empowered

Malcolm Forbes Quotes. BrainyQuote.com, Xplore Inc. 2018. Retrieved from https://www.brainyquote.com/quotes/malcolm_forbes_151513

CPSIA information can be obtained
at www.ICGtesting.com
Printed in the USA
LVHW101958040119
602803LV00001B/1/P

9 781516 538645